Policification of Early Childhood Education and Care

D1798484

The third volume in the Early Childhood Education in the 21st Century: International Teaching, Family and Policy Perspectives miniseries focuses on research highlights and policy aspects of early childhood education and care from 22 different countries around the world.

This volume provides a platform for authors to discuss and debate the implications of research findings on current practices that reflect policies of each country. The research presented spans from challenges in teacher training to case studies of family practices around early child development to problematise the key components of teacher education and family practices that impact young children's education and care. By problematising the key issues, chapter authors discuss the shifting paradigm of early childhood education and the importance of future research in informing these changes.

Offering key policy and practice insights across 19 different countries, this book is a must-read for early childhood educators, researchers, early childhood organisations, policy makers and those interested to know more about early childhood within an international perspective.

Susanne Garvis is Professor of Child and Youth Studies (Early Childhood) at the University of Gothenburg, Sweden. She is a guest professor at Stockholm University and the current leader of the Nordic Early Childhood Group (NECA). Her research interests include quality, policy and learning in early childhood education and care.

Sivanes Phillipson is Professor of Education and Associate Dean International at the Faculty of Health, Arts and Design, Swinburne University of Technology. She is also the Routledge Series Editor for Evolving Families. With 20 years in higher education sector, she is currently leading and consulting on a number of national and international projects on families and children education.

Evolving Families

Series Editor: Sivanes Phillipson

This series focuses on issues, challenges and empirical best practices surrounding evolving families that impact upon their survival, development and outcomes. The aim of this series is twofold: (1) to showcase the diversity of evolving families and the multiple factors that make up the function of families and their evolution across time, systems and cultures; (2) to build on preventative, interventionist, engagement and recovery methods for the promotion of healthy and successful evolving families across generations, social and political contexts and cultures.

Early Childhood Intervention
Working with Families of young Children with Special Needs
Edited by Hanan Sukkar, Carl J. Dunst and Jane Kirkby

Nordic Dialogues on Children and Families
Edited by Susanne Garvis and Elin Eriksen Ødegaard

International Perspectives on Early Childhood Education
Early Childhood Education in the 21st Century Volume I
Edited by Susanne Garvis, Sivanes Phillipson and Heidi Harju-Luukkainen

Teachers' and Families' Perspectives in Early Childhood Education and Care
Early Childhood Education in the 21st Century Volume II
Edited by Sivanes Phillipson and Susanne Garvis

Policification of Early Childhood Education and Care
Early Childhood Education in the 21st Century Volume III
Edited by Susanne Garvis and Sivanes Phillipson

For more information about this series, please visit: www.routledge.com/Evolving-Families/book-series/EF

Policification of Early Childhood Education and Care

Early Childhood Education in the 21st Century Volume III

Edited by Susanne Garvis and Sivanes Phillipson

Routledge
Taylor & Francis Group

LONDON AND NEW YORK

First published 2020
by Routledge
2 Park Square, Milton Park, Abingdon, Oxon OX14 4RN

and by Routledge
605 Third Avenue, New York, NY 10017

First issued in paperback 2021

Routledge is an imprint of the Taylor & Francis Group, an informa business

Publisher's Note
The publisher has gone to great lengths to ensure the quality of this reprint but points out that some imperfections in the original copies may be apparent.

British Library Cataloguing in Publication Data
A catalogue record for this book is available from the British Library

Library of Congress Cataloging in Publication Data
Names: Phillipson, Sivanes, editor. | Garvis, Susanne, editor.
Title: Early childhood education in the 21st century. Volume III,
Policification of early childhood education and Care / Edited Sivanes
Phillipson and Susanne Garvis.
Other titles: Policification of early childhood education
Description: Abingdon, Oxon ; New York : Routledge, 2020. | Series:
Evolving families | Includes bibliographical references and index.
Identifiers: LCCN 2019033681 (print) | LCCN 2019033682 (ebook) |
ISBN 9781138303959 (hardback) | ISBN 9780203730539 (ebook)
Subjects: LCSH: Early childhood education–Cross-cultural studies. |
Education and state–Cross-cultural studies. | Parent-teacher
relationships–Cross-cultural studies.
Classification: LCC LB1139.23 .I687 2020 (print) | LCC LB1139.23
(ebook) | DDC 372.21–dc23
LC record available at https://lccn.loc.gov/2019033681
LC ebook record available at https://lccn.loc.gov/2019033682

Typeset in Galliard
by Wearset Ltd, Boldon, Tyne and Wear

ISBN 13: 978-1-03-208683-5 (pbk)
ISBN 13: 978-1-138-30395-9 (hbk)

Printed in the United Kingdom
by Henry Ling Limited

Contents

Figures

Tables

Contributors

Marit Alvestad is Professor in Education at the Department of Early Childhood Education, University of Stavanger, Norway. She has a background as a preschool teacher. Her research interests are questions of curriculum, profession, learning and quality. She has a number of national and international publications, and is involved in several research projects, like the longitudinal research project the Norwegian BePro-study (www.goban.no)

Karyn Aspden is Lecturer at the Institute of Education, Massey University, New Zealand. She began her career as a teacher and leader in a range of early childhood services, before moving into initial teacher education. Her teaching and research interests include practicum, professional practice, effective teaching practice, early intervention and infant/toddler pedagogy.

Maria Birbili is Associate Professor in Early Childhood Education at Aristotle University of Thessaloniki, Greece. She has taught at different levels and in a variety of contexts in Greece and England. Her current research and teaching interests include children's interests and funds of knowledge, teacher and student questioning, assessment for learning in early childhood education and concept-based teaching.

Elisabeth Bjørnestad is Associate Professor in Pedagogy at the Department of Primary and Secondary Teacher Education, Oslo Metropolitan University. She has a background as a preschool teacher and here research interests are quality in ECEC, longitudinal studies, assessment and transition from Preschool to Primary school. She is currently leading the ongoing longitudinal ECEC project 'Better Provision for Norway's children in ECEC' (GoBaN) – www.goban.no.

Tijana Bogovac is Master Pedagogue from Serbia. She works in a preschool institution in Belgrade as an expert associate. She studied an International Masters programme in Early Childhood Education and Care. She is interested in the issues of teachers' professionalism, preschool education in international perspective and innovative practices.

Annu Brotherus has a PhD in Education and is a University Lecturer in the Faculty of Education, at the University of Helsinki. In her research, she has focused for decade on the curriculum and development of pre-primary and basic education. She has extensive experience of teaching and developing the teacher education programmes in Finland.

Rodrigo A. Cárcamo is Full Professor at the Department of Psychology at the University of Magallanes in Chile. He finished his PhD at Leiden University in the Netherlands. He has focused his research on the role of child care in attachment relationships as well as the quality of the child's environment.

Şenil Ünlü Çetin is Assistant Professor in the Department of Early Childhood Education at Kırıkkale University. Her research is broadly focused on parent involvement, and particularly father involvement, along with music in early years, outdoor education and infant–toddler education.

Sue Cherrington is Associate Professor in the School of Education at Victoria University of Wellington and has a PhD. Her research is particularly focused on early childhood teachers' professional and pedagogical practices, and on professional learning and development (PLD) in education.

Sharryn Clarke is Early Years Lecturer at Monash University and specialises in areas of professional partnerships, leadership and the impact of social media on wellbeing. Her current research explores local and global impacts on childhood, including policy, educational leadership, media and pop culture.

Elisabeth Duursma is Senior Lecturer in Education at the University of Wollongong, Australia. She received her doctorate in Education from Harvard University. Her research focuses on language and literacy in early childhood, in particular in low-income and vulnerable populations. She also conducts research in the area of father engagement and the impact on child development.

Kristín Dýrfjörð is Associate Professor at University of Akureyri, School of Humanities and Social Sciences, Faculty of Education. She has long-term experience as a preschool principal, working for the teacher's union and has taken part in the development of the national curriculum at the Ministry of Education. Her research interests are early childhood studies, democracy, policy studies and neoliberalism.

Stefan Faas is Professor in Social Pedagogy at the University of Education Schwäbisch Gmünd, Germany. His research is focused on early childhood education, family and parent education, transformation research as well as internationalisation of education and social support.

Alejandra García-Riquelme is Assistant Professor at the Department of Education at the University of Magallanes. She finished her Master's degree on Public Policies in Latin America at Leiden University in the Netherlands. Her research interest involves children's wellbeing at preschool centres and caregiver's sensitivity.

Susanne Garvis is Professor of Child and Youth Studies (Early Childhood) at the University of Gothenburg, Sweden. She is a guest professor at Stockholm University and the current leader of the Nordic Early Childhood Group (NECA). Her research interests include quality, policy and learning in early childhood education and care.

Liam Gearon is Associate Professor in the Department of Education, and Senior Research Fellow, Harris Manchester College, University of Oxford. Concurrently Conjoint Professor at the University of Newcastle, New South Wales, and Visiting Professor, Irish Institute for Catholic Studies, MIC, Limerick, Ireland, he was formerly Adjunct Professor at the Australian Catholic University and also previously Professor of Education at the University of Roehampton and Research Professor at the Faculty of Education, University of Plymouth.

Sine Penthin Grumløse is Associate Professor at the University College of Copenhagen. She holds a PhD in Danish family policy 1960–2010 and her research interests include policy, children's everyday life and teachers' professional development with special attention to the connection between policy and practice in family life as well as in schools.

Heidi Harju-Luukkainen is Professor of Education at Nord University (Norway) and holds a PhD in education, a special education teacher qualification and a qualification in leadership and management from Finland. She has published more than 100 international books, journal articles and reports and has worked on more than 25 projects globally. She has worked at top-ranked universities in the USA like UCLA and USC as well as in many Nordic research universities.

Jonna Kangas is a PhD of Education and University Lecturer and joint research member in Playful Learning Center, Faculty of Education Science, University of Helsinki. Her research focus is on play-based pedagogy. She seeks to understand children's learning processes through joy and participation and she uses her findings for designing innovative teacher training and mentoring programmes in Finland and developing countries.

Dagmar Kasüschke is Full Professor of Early Childhood Education at the University of Education in Schwäbisch Gmünd, Germany. Her research areas are cultural and gender studies, history, pedagogy and didactics in early childhood institutions.

Arniika Kuusisto is Professor in Child and Youth Studies, especially Early Childhood Education and Care, at Stockholm University, Sweden; Honorary Research Fellow at the Department of Education, University of Oxford, UK, and Research Director and Docent at the Faculty of Educational Sciences,

University of Helsinki, Finland. Her research interests include children's and young people's worldviews, value learning trajectories and identity negotiations in diverse growing up contexts.

Rachel Langford is Professor in the School of Early Childhood Studies at Ryerson University. Her research and scholarly work focuses on child care advocacy and policy development, workforce professionalisation, and conceptualisations of care and care work. She is a co-editor of a 2017 UBC Press edited volume, *Caring for Children: Social Movements and Public Policy in Canada*.

Yi-Hui Lin is Assistant Professor at the Center for Teacher Education & Department of Early Childhood Education and Care at Minghsin University of Science and Technology, Taiwan. She received her PhD degree from the Department of Human Development and Family Studies at National Taiwan Normal University. Her research interests include early childhood learning and early science education.

Claire McLachlan is Professor and Dean at the School of Education at Federation University, Australia. Her primary research interests are in curriculum, assessment and evaluation, with a particular focus on teachers' beliefs and practices in relation to languages, literacy and physical activity in the curriculum.

Tara McLaughlin, PhD, is a senior lecturer in the Institute of Education at Massey University. Her research interests focus on: teaching practices that support children's learning and social – emotional competence; professional learning and development; innovative data systems to inform teaching and learning; and assessment practices in early childhood care and education.

Elisabeth Mellgren is Senior Lecturer at the Department of Education, Communication and Learning/University of Gothenburg. She took part in the research group in Early Childhood Education (ECE) in the theme Policy, Quality and Children's Learning. She has a background as a preschool teacher and her research mainly deals with Early Literacy Learning, transition and quality issues in the context of preschool and preschool class.

Lidija Miškeljin is Assistant Professor at the University of Belgrade – Faculty of Philosophy, Department of Pedagogy and Andragogy and researcher at the Institute of Pedagogy and Andragogy. Her fields of interest are early childhood education, systems and programmes of preschool education, contemporary childhood studies and teacher professional development. Research topics include action research, diversity and diversification in early childhood education and childhood studies. She has participated in many research and applied projects for the Ministry of Education, UNICEF and IPA. She has published two books (one as the sole author) and several articles, mainly in the field of early childhood education, in relevant journals and scientific conference proceedings.

Hilary Monk is Lecturer in Early Childhood Education at Monash University, Australia. Her research investigates the ways in which young children's learning and development are shaped by family and societal practices over time, early childhood curriculum, teacher professionalism, cultural–historical theory and visual methodologies.

Tiia Õun is Associate Professor of Early Childhood Education at the School of Educational Sciences, Tallinn University, Estonia. She specialises in early childhood education and the main areas of her research are quality and leadership of early childhood education, curriculum development and different learning and teaching methods in early childhood.

Tiina Peterson is Chief Expert of General Education Department of Estonian Ministry of Education and Research. Her main professional tasks are management of preschool educational and early childhood intervention policy in Estonia and advising heads and teachers of preschools institutions. Currently she is a PhD student in education sciences at Tallinn University and her research interests are preschool quality, leadership development and professionalism of preschool teachers.

Joanna Phillips, has experience in both the New Zealand and Australian Early Childhood sectors. She is completing her PhD at Swinburne University and is currently working in early intervention. Her research areas include family–preschool partnerships, teacher professional development, early intervention and children's social and emotional development.

Sivanes Phillipson is Professor of Education and Associate Dean International at the Faculty of Health, Arts and Design, Swinburne University of Technology. She is also the Routledge Series Editor for Evolving Families. With 20 years in higher education sector, she is currently consulting and working on a number of national and international projects on families and children education.

Brooke Richardson completed her Social Science and Humanities Research Council-funded PhD in Policy Studies, Social Policy stream at Ryerson University, Canada in 2017. She is currently pursuing a Social Science and Humanity Council of Canada funded Postdoctoral Fellowship in the Department of Sociology at Brock University, Canada. Her research interests include the discursive representation of child care in social policy debates, the critical examination of the pan-Canadian childcare movement, care as political practice and the relationship between childcare auspice and ethical care. She is also the current President of the Association of Early Childhood Educator's of Ontario.

SoJung Seo is Professor in the Department of Child & Family Studies at Kyung Hee University in Korea. Her main research areas span a range of issues related to quality of Early Childhood Education and Care (ECEC). She is currently working on research into teachers' teaching efficacy and its impacts on teachers and young children in ECEC settings in Korea.

Sonja Sheridan is Professor Emerita in Education, University of Gothenburg, Sweden. Her research is oriented towards Early Childhood Education, focusing on quality issues related to conditions for children's learning and preschool teacher competence. She has been a consultant for several authorities, led research projects and authored a wide range of books and articles.

Igor Shiyan is PhD in psychology, Chairperson of the Laboratory of Child Development, Deputy Director of the Institute of System Projects of Moscow City University. His main interests are cognitive development of children and adults, and preschool education quality.

Olga Shiyan is PhD in education, Leading Scientific Researcher of the Laboratory of Child Development of the Institute of System Projects of Moscow City University. Her main interests are preschool education quality, cognitive development of children.

Melpomeni Tsitouridou is Professor of ICT in Education at the Faculty of Education and Head of the Master's Degree Program in Learning Technologies of Aristotle University of Thessaloniki. Her research examines digital literacies; digital educational environments and learning analytics; educational robotics; computational thinking; young people and communication technologies; digital technology in children's everyday life; and social media in higher education.

Svein Erik Tuastad is Associate Professor at the Department of Social Studies, the University of Stavanger, Norway. He is a political scientist. His research interests include three main areas: political theory, constitutionalism and democratic processes; Norwegian post-war politics; and welfare policies, in particular in the field of school policies and child protection.

Gaye Tyler-Merrick is a Senior Lecturer in Education Studies and Early Years at the Nottingham Institute of Education at Nottingham Trent University. She holds a PhD in Education. Her research interests include young children's social emotional development and developing parent/teacher partnerships.

Aino Ugaste is Professor at the Institute of Educational Sciences at Tallinn University, Estonia. Her field of research has been connected with the study of the early childhood education, the teacher's professional development and children's play. More recently, she has investigated intercultural education in the early childhood.

Aleksander Veraksa is Doctor of Psychology, Corresponding Member of the Russian Academy of Education, and Head of Department of Psychology of Education and Pedagogy at Faculty of Psychology, Lomonosov Moscow State University. He is a Vice-President of the Russian Psychological Society. His main interests focus on preschool cognitive development and educational process.

Nikolay Veraksa is Doctor of Psychology, Professor, Head Scientific Researcher at Moscow City University, Professor of Moscow State Pedagogical University and Leading Researcher at Russian Academy of Education. For more than 40 years he is carried out theoretical and empirical research in child psychology and education.

Pia Williams is Professor in Child and Youth studies at the University of Gothenburg, Sweden. She has authored a wide range of publications in the field of Early Childhood Education and Care. Current research involves studies of conditions for children's wellbeing, learning and development in preschool, preschool teachers' competence and the impact of group size on children's learning.

Yvonne Yu-Feng Liu is Assistant Professor of Early Childhood Education at the National Pingtung University, Taiwan. She holds a BA and MA in Early Childhood Education and a PhD in International & Comparative Education. Her research interests are comparative early childhood education and preschool teacher education.

Preface

This book is the third and final volume in the miniseries Early Childhood Education and Care in the 21st Century. The first book provided an overview of 19 countries' perspectives on early childhood education and care. The second volume extended the perspectives of the 19 countries with a specific focus on teachers' and families' contribution in early childhood education and care. In this final volume, we explore practice and policy in the 19 countries with key components of teacher education and family practices that impact early learning and care.

We would like to thank a number of people involved in the production of this final book. First, we would like to thank all of the contributing authors who shared important insider perspectives of their own country around early childhood education. The countries represented are diverse and allow much reflection by the reader.

Next, we would like to thank both internal and external reviewers from all of the countries in this book who acted in the peer reviewer process. The reviews allowed constructive feedback for all chapters. We would like to note our sincere and heartfelt appreciation to the following external reviews for their time and effort: Helena Bergstrom, Linnea Boden, Sofia Frakenberg, Anette Hellman, Tarja Karlsson Häikiö, Lisbeth Kitson, Alicja Renata Sadownik, Tina Yngvesson and Yan Zhang. We would also like to thank Gerarda Richards for her editorial assistance with this miniseries project.

Finally, we would also like to thank the readers of the volumes for taking an active interest in early childhood education and care. Through reading and reflecting across the different countries, advocacy for early childhood education and care can grow. Through stronger advocacy, support for the development of children learning and wellbeing becomes a central focus for communities and governments.

Last but not least, we would like to dedicate this book, the final in the miniseries to our respective brilliant partners in life, Andrew and Shane, who have listened, debated and stood by us as advocates of early childhood education and care for the 21st century.

Humbly,
Susie and Sivanes

1 Introduction to policification of early childhood education and care

Susanne Garvis and Sivanes Phillipson

Introduction

The last 20 years has seen a strong focus around the world on early childhood services to support children and their families. Many governments have invested heavily into early childhood education by creating more opportunities in early learning to provide children with the best start in life. Such provision has meant that many parents, especially mothers, have been able to return to work earlier (Conboye & Romei, 2018). In line with this progress, some governments in Europe especially have put in place further support to encourage parents to return to work as quickly as possible. Whereas in some countries such as the UK and Australia, governments have reformed welfare support and tax systems to provides incentives for parents to return to paid workforce, in some Asian countries, increasing pressure from changing society sees government paying more attention to early childhood education and services (Phillipson, Koh, & Sujuddin, 2018). These types of government investments and policy moves have meant the introduction of frameworks, curricula and legal provision for young children, with explicit and implicit implications for children's early education and care. Importantly and fortunately, the majority of decisions by these governments have been based on informed research within early childhood education and care (Organisation for Economic Cooperation and Development (OECD), 2017).

In this introductory chapter, we outline the main thread of research and discussion of the 19 countries' chapters of this book. The chapters are intended to align with the key components of teaching and family practices that impact young children's education and care across the globe. Prior to this third volume, the first two volumes showed how each of the 19 countries showcased, though diverse in their status of early childhood education and care (ECEC), has a common goal of providing for the young children. What is important to remember in reading this third volume is that the 19 countries in this book represent a range of low to high economic statuses with a variety of government systems and cultures. Also, it is vital to highlight that no matter the country and cultural contexts, both teachers and families in the 19 countries share a desire to create opportunities for young children's better learning and developmental outcomes.

Outline of this book

This book focuses on research highlights of early childhood education and care from 19 countries internationally. The book provides a platform for each chapter to discuss and debate the implications of research findings on current practices that reflect policies of each country. The chapters present research that spans from challenges in teacher training to case studies and observational data of child play and family practices in relation to early child development to problematise the key components of teacher education and family practices that impact young children education and care. By problematising the key issues, chapter authors discuss the shifting paradigm of early childhood education and the importance of continuous research in informing these changes. The chapters include:

- As we have witnessed, social media dominates our lives more and more. Fittingly, the second chapter authors, Clarke and Phillipson, investigate the mentoring practices of beginning teachers using Facebook in Australia. The chapter outlines the current situation for graduates of early childhood education once they begin teaching careers with a significant lack of effective leadership and mentoring. The authors provide suggestions for future policy change to initial teacher education courses to include mentoring programmes that support future early childhood teachers.
- The context of policy in Canada is presented in Chapter 3. We learn from Richardson and Langford issues surrounding the political representation of child care policy in the lead up to the elections and how it is positioned as a 'problem' within the public sphere. Drawing on the theoretical foundation of 'caring democracy', the authors propose that all citizens have a responsibility to expand the terms of engagement with child care policies.
- Authors from Chile, Cárcamo and García-Riquelme present two debates about early childhood education and care (Chapter 4). The first debate is around the issue of quality of child care centres for all children. The second debate presented is about the issues of early literacy and the introduction of teaching practices into the preschool years. The authors suggest that quality and equity require a stronger focus in public policy to try and assist equal starting conditions for all children.
- Chapter 5 explores the political processes connected to a stronger focus on learning outcomes in Danish day care institutions. Chapter author Grumløse discusses how this focus has led to a shift in paradigms from care to learning. The shift has been predominantly influenced by international tendencies to give stronger attention to the development of academic skills. Children's day care is shown to persist as a political and pedagogical battleground in Denmark.
- Estonian preschool education policy has supported the improvement of work conditions, qualifications and training for teachers and helped to engage families and community. Chapter 6 authors, Peterson, Õun and Ugaste, provide an overview of early childhood education policy, teacher

professionalism and family practices in Estonia. Through this overview, we learn of the efforts of Estonian teacher policy for 2014–2020 to support and develop the professionalism of teachers.

- Chapter 7 authors from Finland, Kangas, Harju-Luukkainen, Brotherus, Kuusisto and Gearon, outline the importance of play in the curriculum from the viewpoints of operational cultures and the learning environment. From observational data, the importance of the child as an active agent in learning emerges, however this may also create problems for adults who are unaware of elements of play that may be taking place.
- In Chapter 8, Kasüschke and Faas reflect on current developments and challenges, especially in Germany, relating to national early childhood education systems and practices in the context of globalisation and transnational education policy. It is based on the assumption that international developments and reform movements are not adopted directly in real-world educational practice, but rather are received, adapted and implemented against a background of historically developed, culture-specific structures and contexts governing action and meaning.
- In Chapter 9, Birbili and Tsitouridou draw on their experiences as teacher educators and empirical studies from the Greek context to discuss how the lack of integrated policies weakens the teacher education continuum to educate reflective professionals. The chapter provides a historical overview of Greek early childhood education before discussing current challenges set by a centralised system and the economic crisis.
- In Chapter 10, Iceland author, Dýrfjörð raises how the early childhood profession in Iceland can regain control of the sector's educational policy. Importantly, she discusses how business-related think tanks have had a role in changing both discourses as well as the legal system surrounding preschools, especially in relation to deregulation and accountability. The chapter also presents the analysis of the development of two literacy policy documents that show how preschool teachers have been set aside in favour of experts from other disciplines. Such a move, the author laments, has led to educational policies that are driven by standardised and measurable outcomes.
- Chapter 11 author, Seo, reviews the current status of early childhood education and care services in Korea while addressing provocative issues surrounding the ramifications of ECEC policies for primary stakeholders. The move to equal starts for children began in 2012 and 2013, when a free child care policy was introduced for all children aged 0 to 5 years, regardless of family income. Around the same time, a national curriculum was also introduced. Future directions for research, practice and policy are also provided.
- In Chapter 12, the Aotearoa/New Zealand early childhood revised curriculum *Te Whāriki* is explored by Tyler-Merrick, Cherrington, McLaughlin, McLachlan, Aspden and Phillips. A specific focus is made on providing quality infant and toddler education and care, literacy and digital technologies within *Te Whāriki*. Future directions are also given to help teachers

understand the curriculum through professional learning opportunities and the research of specific teacher practices.

- The struggles over quality, play and preschool in Norway is explored in Chapter 13. Authors, Tuastad, Bjørnestad and Alvestad discuss the core elements and long-lasting controversies that are deep rooted in Norwegian historical underpinnings. Using data from various projects, the investigation shows clear links between policy and society in relation to what is best for the child. The authors conclude that Norwegian policy that focuses on both child-centrism and social investment in a united model is an important step forward.

- Staying with the theme of quality, Shiyan, Shiyan, Veraksa and Veraksa (Chapter 14) share findings from a large quality-based study of preschools in Russia. The authors compare findings with the Federal State Educational Standard and preschool teacher education to reveal areas of future development to provide optimal conditions for children's learning and development.

- In Chapter 15, Bogovac and Miškeljin discuss the current tensions and problems in initial teacher education and professional learning in Serbia. They note that there are numerous challenges with ECEC in Serbia including low coverage, inequality in access, lack of facilities and uneven geographical distribution. The authors suggest that it is necessary to initiate a change in provision of professional development by supporting alternate forms of professional development. These can involve researching teacher practice, professional networking, project development and collaborative actions.

- Authors of Chapter 16, Monk and Phillipson, problematised Singaporean in-service teachers' struggle with their own professional identity with elements of professionalisation that they were experiencing. Using visual metaphors to highlight personal, interpersonal and institutional aspects of professionalism alongside the professionalisation of the early childhood sector, the authors present an optimistic argument for the balancing act of shifting sands of ECEC in Singapore.

- Chapter 17 continues with the theme of quality by presenting three studies from various time periods in Sweden. The chapter authors, Sheridan, Garvis, Williams and Mellgren show a gap between children and teachers' perspectives and between policy intentions and the preschool practice. Critical factors are shared around quality that directly influence the professional and policy development, including aspects of learning within preschool contexts.

- In Chapter 18, Lin and Liu share insights about the new age of educare, highlighting challenges as well as the contextual support structures needed for the future of ECEC in Taiwan. The chapter reviews government policies around child care since 2000, showing the significant steps the Taiwanese government have made towards creating a better child care environment.

- Chapter 19 author, Duursma, discusses the changes in Dutch laws to strengthen the position of parents in ECEC. This includes the provision of language requirements for educators that is aimed at increasing the quality of overall care as well as parental engagement. Educators are expected to engage parents more directly and offer opportunities for parents and educators to work together to create communities of care.

- In Chapter 20, Çetin focuses on Turkish social policies that aim to increase enrolment in early childhood education. Various reports are analysed to show the effectiveness of social policies towards improved outcomes for child development. Overall the situation in Turkey appears to be improving, however it is still below desired levels.
- In Chapter 21, editors of this volume, Phillipson and Garvis, conclude this book by synthesising the main themes found across the chapters. Using a verbatim sorting method, the main concepts synthesised are presented as what we understand as the norm of policification internationally. This final chapter submits to the reader the challenges faced in teacher practices and family engagement in the face of shifting paradigms and policies in the 21st century.

Conclusion

This final book in the Early Childhood Education in the 21st Century series is designed to share with the reader the diversity of early childhood education and care around the world, presenting 19 countries that are located in different regions – Asia Pacific, Europe, North America and South America. These countries have different ideologies and systems of governance. The ultimate aim of this third volume is for readers to engage in policification of childhood within the early childhood caucus. We hope that readers will gain some vital insights from each of these countries on how they engage with the shared issues faced within early childhood education and care. More importantly, it is hoped that readers are able to relate to the shifting paradigms debated internationally, as well as see positive ways forward in the reforms and investments of the multiple governments across the globe in the 21st century.

References

Conboye, J., & Romei, V. (2018, 9 October). The rise of working mothers. *Financial Times*. Retrieved from www.ft.com/content/c3bd628a-6f2e-11e8-92d3-6c13e5c92914.

Organisation for Economic Cooperation and Development (OECD). (2017). *Starting Strong 2017: Key OECD Indicators on Early Childhood Education and Care*. OECD Publishing: Paris. Retrieved from http://dx.doi.org/10.1787/9789264276116-en.

Phillipson, S., Koh, E., & Sujuddin, S. (2018). Academic or else: Singapore parents' aspirations for their children's early education. In S. Phillipson & S. Garvis (Eds.), *Teachers' and Families' Perspectives in Early Childhood Education and Care: Early Childhood Education in the 21st Century Vol II* (pp. 191–209). London/New York: Routledge.

2 Facebook mentoring of beginning teachers

Implications for ECEC teacher training in Australia

Sharryn Clarke and Sivanes Phillipson

Introduction

This chapter details research undertaken to investigate the mentoring practices that occur for beginning early childhood teachers through open dialogue on Facebook in Australia. The research explores the perceptions of both early childhood beginning teachers and online mentors regarding the influences and dependencies that they are currently experiencing with this social media platform. This study goes on to find out how the influences and dependencies may be impacting on them in relation to their sense of professional efficacy and identity, how they understand their role as a teacher and how their understanding translates to their work in the ECEC sector in Australia. This chapter therefore outlines the current situation for graduates of early childhood teachers as they begin their careers and face complexities in a sector currently experiencing momentous change and reform, where historically, there has also been a significant lack of effective leadership and mentoring. Consideration for further policy change both in initial teacher education courses and graduate mentoring programmes are discussed.

Mentoring during times of reform

The Australian Early Years Reform has seen significant shifts in policy and practice for early childhood settings (Grieshaber & Graham, 2017; Kilderry, Nolan, & Scott, 2017; Ortlipp, Arthur, & Woodrow, 2011; Thomas, 2012). These reforms have implicated more than just regulatory changes but shifts in theoretical lenses and pedagogical approaches to learning and teaching young children. The changes have a stronger focus on children's rights and social justice than on understanding and using aspects of child development theory. The reforms include the introduction of a national learning framework, known as *Belonging, Being and Becoming: The Early Years Learning Framework for Australia* (EYLF) and benchmarks of practice that must be achieved through a mandated assessment and rating process evaluating the performance of services against the *National Quality Standard* (NQS), both of which impact strongly upon perspective and practice. It has also impacted upon the delivery and content of curriculum in higher education institutions such as universities and other registered training organisations, to ensure that new graduates are equipped with the knowledge of the new legislation, frameworks and standards, including teaching standards. The process in which these changes occurred lie heavily within the political landscape of Australia that also saw a change of federal government in the midst of implementation.

Grieshaber and Graham (2017) argue that the EYLF is an aspirational document with 'low-definition' (p. 97) that can have multiple interpretations without specific 'how-to' prescriptive statements making it difficult at times for educators to enact or know if they are enacting it according to the policy intentions. Grieshaber and Graham also highlight that mentoring practices in the early childhood sector may never have been experienced by educators, which makes enacting new policy or shifting pedagogical lenses even more problematic.

Therefore, with change, there has been both hope and despondency as educators continue to engage in a reflective discourse of what they thought constituted good practice and quality teaching compared with what the EYLF and the NQS now suggest such discourse actually is (Kilderry et al., 2017). The reforms have also seen a workforce crisis as there is now more need for Bachelor-trained early childhood teachers than ever before. Yet with the introduction of the dual degree (early years/primary) in tertiary institutes we are seeing more graduates moving into the school sector (Gibson, 2013; Nolan & Rouse, 2013), opting for better work conditions, remuneration and professional identity (with a more prescriptive curriculum to align this identity).

Change is something that can be inspiring for some but challenging for others and consequently there has been a significant proportion of the workforce also departing the profession, with approximately a third leaving each year and the majority being beginning teachers (Fenech, 2013; Ortlipp et al., 2011). The reforms have brought about evidence-based change that has caused pedagogical confusion through multiple discourses that are constantly challenging early childhood teachers and their professional identity (Thomas, 2012), and therefore perhaps not providing solidarity in their positioning as teachers. Teacher registration processes are currently different in each state and territory of Australia, despite teaching regulatory bodies working together in an attempt to make the process of registration across states more seamless by the use of national teaching standards (Australian Institute of Teaching & School Leadership (AITSL), 2011). The teaching standards use a different language to the EYLF and NQS, for instance using 'student' instead of 'child', 'teacher' instead of 'educator', and most significantly using the term 'manage student behaviour' rather than 'being responsive to children' (AITSL, 2011; Department of Education, Employment & Workplace Relations (DEEWR), 2009). Additionally, there are continued inconsistent approaches to mentoring, particularly in relation to mentoring early childhood teachers. It is this inconsistent terminology and these mentoring approaches that may also contribute to the confusion in professional discourse online and offline.

The State of Victoria has only recently introduced registration processes for beginning early childhood teachers with September 2015 being the first period initiating registration. This process involves a push for beginning teachers to engage in a professional inquiry project for their two-year provisional period where they are required to be supported by an official mentor (Victorian Institute of Teaching (VIT), 2017), yet good mentors are hard to find. Morrissey and Nolan (2015), in their study of various types of mentoring programmes in Victoria, found that participants are time-poor to attend meetings while individual mentoring at times make mentees feel intimidated or judged, indicating a strong need for better training in effective mentoring practices for the early childhood sector.

Recognising the issue around mentoring, the registration process in Victoria now requires official mentors to receive specific training in mentoring early childhood beginning teachers, known as *The Effective Mentoring Program* (EMP) (VIT, 2017). Official mentors eligible to participate in the EMP training must be fully registered early childhood teachers themselves (VIT, 2017). This requirement means that beginning teachers may need to seek mentors outside their workplace and perhaps even their type of setting (e.g. seeking a mentor from a primary school setting) to even experience the mentorship required to complete their application for full registration. While systematic mentoring is a positive move, this system is problematic as many early childhood teachers who do choose employment in the early years may be allocated to long-day care. In the long-day care context, they may find themselves to be the most qualified employee on premises and not have easy access to an official teaching mentor onsite. As a result, beginning teachers are potentially moving through their provisional years with little mentoring and finding quick ways to just 'tick the boxes' to get through, and so they turn to social media, such as Facebook, for support and guidance in their everyday teaching practice (Clarke, 2018).

The impact of Facebook dependency

Simultaneously apparent with the problematic issue of shifting early childhood policy, practice and mentoring, is the rise of Facebook dependency or in some cases, addiction. Facebook has become a global phenomenon that has changed the manner in which people connect with each other as well as who they connect with. Founded in 2004, Facebook has rapidly grown to embed itself within the daily lives of humans. In 2017, Facebook was considered one of the most widely used social networking sites (SNS) reporting 2.07 billion monthly users and 1.37 billion daily users which equates to an average increase of 16 per cent utilisation of the platform each year and totalling over ten billion US dollars in revenue (Facebook, 2017). Facebook now shapes how we communicate and connect resorting to messages, threads, links and posts to share our thoughts, photos and videos that represent our daily lives and personalities as we want them to be seen by others. Our need to know and share becomes amplified, the more we engage and scroll through posts, moving towards an addiction of Facebook notifications and connectivity with others through this medium.

'Facebook addiction' is now a term that has captured the attention of the scientific world to determine why users develop addictions, how the addiction impacts upon their health and wellbeing, and which scales can be developed to accurately measure addiction on Facebook (Andreassen & Pallesen, 2014). Vishwanath (2014) uses the term *habitual media use* to define the addictions and overuse of social media that demonstrates limited self-regulation in this communicative form, applying motivational components of self-gratification and automacity. This definition means that a large population of humanity now feel the need to access their social media sites frequently to satisfy their social and emotional needs, which has become habit-forming for many social media users. There is particular concern in the way social networking sites such as Facebook are impacting upon the human psyche and sense of self-efficacy or self-worth, and while active Facebook users are often in the spotlight in relation to the type of engagement that occurs, research suggests that it is the wellbeing of the passive Facebook users that are more at risk (Kimpton et al., 2016).

A study conducted by Verduyn et al. (2015) explored ways passive Facebook users were affected when they simply scrolled through Facebook posts rather than participating in active conversational engagement or creating posts. They found that passive use, rather than active use, contributed negatively to a user's wellbeing and found that feelings of envy were enhanced. They also discovered that most people participate in passive Facebook usage rather than active Facebook usage, which means that more people subjected their wellbeing to these negative effects more frequently and more significantly. The authors further suggested that a possible reason for this phenomenon is that studies have shown that Facebook and other social networking sites are addictive and that the feeling one experiences when connecting with others in some way, outweighs the negative outcome of their wellbeing (Verduyn et al., 2015).

Kimpton et al. (2016) also explored Facebook addiction using four various scales including *The Bergen Facebook Addiction Scale* (developed by Andreassen, Torsheim, Brunborg, & Pallesen, 2012) to discover patterns and causes for Facebook addiction in 273 participants who were students in an Australian university. They discovered that passive use was more strongly linked with Facebook addiction but that males and females had different types of addictions. For instance, 'females [were] more likely to use Facebook for … maintenance of existing and long distance relationships … and impression management through use of photos' (p. 63) while males tended to develop more Facebook addictive behaviours in gaming. Of concern were results relating to the prevalence of passive Facebook addiction, which was higher in females than in males.

Combining the Verduyn et al. and Kimpton et al. studies, it may be implied that females are more likely to engage in passive Facebook use and experience high levels of addiction, which places them more at risk to negative effects for their wellbeing. Therefore, Facebook, in terms of socioemotional stability, may be somewhat problematic for female-dominated workforces if they are inclined to engage with social networking sites for personal or professional reasons. One of the workforces that is prevalently female dominated is the Australian early years education and care sector.

Early childhood Facebook forums

Usage of social media for the purposes of professional engagement in Australian-based early childhood Facebook forums (ECFF) has seen rapid growth in the last few years. At the time of writing, forums such as *Early Childhood Teachers Victoria*, an early years Facebook forum administered and moderated by the Victorian Branch of the Australian Education Union, saw a membership of 13,162, an increase of over 2100 members in a matter of approximately 12 months since the previous recording. While this seems a large number of members, it is minor compared to forums such as the *EYLF/NQF – Ideas & Discussions forum* that currently has 85,311 members. Interestingly, some Australian-based early childhood leadership groups have mixed membership with the *Educational Leaders Unite* forum only having 1048 members while the *Educational Leaders Network and Support Group* has 12,645 members. In addition, specialist interest groups, such as the *Social Justice in Early Childhood* (SJEC) group, which is a not-for-profit organisation, has a minor online Facebook membership of 4858.

The membership number can depend upon many aspects including whether the group is 'closed' or 'public' for membership. For example, the *EYLF/NQF – Ideas and Discussions* group (forum) is a public group that could explain the membership number. However, the *Educational Leaders Unite* group is a 'closed group', which means that members have to apply to administrators of the group to be accepted and cannot post comments or receive notifications without this acceptance. It is therefore at the administrator's discretion as to whether member applications are accepted or not, which can indicate a strong level of power held by the administrators of that group. For instance, some groups, such as the SJEC Facebook group (forum) have particular expectations of group members to follow the ethos of their political lens and therefore require members to answer two questions or their application will not be approved. This group also has very strict guidelines in the types of questions that may be asked including only allowing researchers to promote their work or seek participants if the research aligns with issues of social justice, and students are not permitted to ask for guidance in relation to their assignments which minimises the ability for this group to mentor pre-service teachers and post-graduate students in issues of social justice related to their specific learning. Furthermore, only the administrators are freely permitted to advertise their publications or professional development training which at times has caused dissonance among its members.

Shifting mindsets for mentoring beginning teachers

Mentoring, particularly ad-hoc mentoring in both virtual and real-time spaces can both be positive and problematic (Clarke, 2018). Good mentoring has been seen to support beginning teachers to address feelings of anxiety and improve their professional practice and self-efficacy (Nolan, 2017). However, 'judge-mentoring' a term coined by mentoring expert, Andrew Hobson (2016), and defined as 'an enactment of mentoring found to be detrimental to beginning teachers' professional learning, development and wellbeing' (p. 87), can be particularly damaging for beginning teachers. Hobson further states that rather than engage in 'judgementoring' it is better for the mentor to be 'ONSIDE' (p. 91) (see description below). Hobson has developed a framework of practice surrounding the concept that mentors need to consider and be able to support the wellbeing of a beginning teacher, not just their professional practice and learning. He suggests that mentoring should be 'offline' (as in, non-hierarchal which is unrelated to being 'offline' on social networking sites), 'non-evaluative', 'supportive', 'individualised', 'developmental' and 'empowering' (p. 101).

'Judgementoring', on the other hand, according to Hobson and Malderez (2013), includes particular traditional actions of mentoring such as hierarchal mentor-led feedback sessions and negative critique where mentors 'also act as assessors and gatekeepers to the profession' (p. 101) ensuring that the typical teaching norms are maintained rather than developed further. They suggest that 'judgementoring' is caused by both a lack of appropriate mentor training, mentor selection and 'lack of consensus on what mentoring in teacher education is' (p. 102) and potentially leads to 'learned helplessness' (p. 101), reduced self-reflection and lowered sense of wellbeing. Nolan (2017) also suggests that when the relationship between the mentee and the mentor is not on an expert/novice basis and is of a more reciprocal nature where mentees and mentors exchange and share knowledge (which is similar to the way it is shared on Facebook), the mentorship is

> not seen as burdensome – 'yet another task to do,' but instead was [is] positioned as a way of assisting mentees to achieve some of their goals, and work to overcome some challenges they were currently facing with support from a mentor who was responsive to their needs.
>
> (p. 281)

These contentions imply that it is the nature of engagement in mentoring that is of crucial importance as mentoring impacts upon a beginning teacher's development and sense of efficacy which also include how the mentoring is conducted through online social media forums such as Facebook.

Considering the multiple aspects discussed so far, including Facebook addiction, difficulties for beginning early childhood teachers in accessing effective mentoring programmes, exclusivity of some online Facebook groups, 'judgementoring' and the nature in which participants engage with each other, a curious question emerged that became the foundation for this phase of the phenomenological research study:

> According to beginning teachers and mentors who use early childhood Facebook forums for mentoring, what impact is the engagement and dialogue having on their sense of efficacy in teaching and professional identity?

Methods

This chapter discusses the findings of the third (and final) phase of a larger research study that used phenomenology as an initial approach, followed by quantitative methods to apply the initial findings to a wider participant body. Phenomenology is a research design that allows freedom of exploration throughout the data phases, particularly those of a qualitative nature and uses an interpretivist approach to ascertain meaning. It focuses upon the 'lived experience' both of the participants and of the researcher that allows for rich descriptions of contextual data (Creswell, 2014). As the research unfolded in the first two phases, the evidence became clearer and the research process became more structured, finally leading to this quantitative phase. Data emerging from the previous phases were analysed using thematic analysis to form *five factors* that were investigated in this phase being:

- Factor 1: Dependency on Facebook
- Factor 2: Facebook Mentoring
- Factor 3: Self-Efficacy
- Factor 4: Retention
- Factor 5: Professional Identity

The five factors therefore created a basis for questioning that was then applied to a wider audience through the online survey to answer the research question.

Mentoring through Facebook survey

The *Mentoring through Facebook* survey was divided into five sections that aligned with the five factors and asked participants to consider the manner in which they engaged with others on Facebook particularly in relation to beginning teachers. The first group of questions were directly related to ascertaining who the respondents were and how often they engaged on Facebook. The next group of questions explored their thoughts in relation to how they see mentoring on Facebook for beginning teachers, which assisted in distinguishing the differences between professional conversations and mentoring. The third group focused upon how the engagement on Facebook has impacted upon them (for other mentors and beginning teachers) relating to future engagement on Facebook and the impact upon their daily practice and professional efficacy. The fourth group of questions focused upon the usefulness of engagement on Facebook and their future career or contribution to retention in the early childhood teaching field. Finally, the fifth group of questions related to the impact they felt current engagement on Facebook was having on the overall professional identity of early childhood teachers.

The questions used a four-point Likert scale ranging from 'strongly disagree' to 'strongly agree', with the exception of several background questions that required multiple-choice answers. The latter questions were mainly related to contextual data such as the type of teaching qualification they had, workplace setting and years of employment. The survey was initially piloted with six participants who were known to the researchers and active Facebook users with equal representation of beginning teachers and mentors. Learning from the responses from the pilot participants, several alterations were made including adding questions to ascertain the level of engagement respondents had, as well as adding a selection for mentors who were not currently working as teachers in the field, yet still provide mentorship.

Participants

Participants were recruited from a selection of ECFFs that allowed free advertisement for research participants and had at least 1000 members. Some sites were specifically chosen as they had a targeted audience such as beginning teachers or educational leaders. Members were asked a series of questions which were reviewed after the original pilot and testing as the initial survey required mentors to be working at least 20 hours per week in an early childhood setting. As many early childhood teachers currently work in part-time positions, this significantly restricted participation and so this requirement was lifted and replaced with a single requirement (other than a teaching qualification) that they had to be working as a teacher for at least four years if they were to be classified as a mentor.

Analysis

Two main analyses were completed for this chapter using SPSS Version 22. First, descriptive analysis and cross tabs analysis were conducted to provide an overall description of the data collected regarding the beginning and mentor teachers. Second, correlation analysis was used to identify the relationships that exist between variables for both beginning and mentor teachers.

Results

Overall, 101 respondents participated with 38 respondents considering themselves a 'beginning teacher' while 63 respondents considered themselves 'mentor (accomplished teachers)'. However, only 85 of these respondents responded as participants of the early childhood Facebook forums, which brought the valid number of respondents to 32 beginning teachers and 53 mentors.

A total of 37.6 per cent (*n* = 38) of both beginning and mentor teachers graduated between 2014 and 2017. There was an even spread of teachers graduating across the years from 1990 to 2010. Only three teachers graduated as early as 1980–1989. Most of the teachers were either employed as teachers in a funded kindergarten/preschool programme (32.7 per cent) or as educational leaders with a teaching role (20.8 per cent). Table 2.1 shows the cross tabulation of the valid number of responses for beginning teachers and mentor teachers according to their qualifications and employment roles/positions.

Only one mentor teacher and one beginning teacher check the Facebook forums more than seven times a day (see Figure 2.1). A total of 32.1 per cent of the 32 beginning teachers check the forum every few days while 47.2 per cent of the beginning teachers check the forum daily. The percentage is reversed for the mentor teachers, with 31.3 per cent of the 53 mentor teachers checking the Facebook forum daily with 46.9 per cent of the mentors checking every few days. Six of the beginning teachers check one to three times a day while five mentor teachers do the same. More of the beginning teachers (four) than the mentor (only one) check their Facebook forum four to six times a day.

A number of significant correlations were found between the responses provided by the beginning and mentor teachers. A total of 62.6 per cent beginning teachers turned to Facebook to receive mentoring. However, only 50 per cent of all beginning teachers turned to Facebook for moral support after they have had negative experiences in teaching ($r = 0.54$, $p = 0.001$). Teachers who turned to Facebook for moral support also tended to be those who believe Facebook

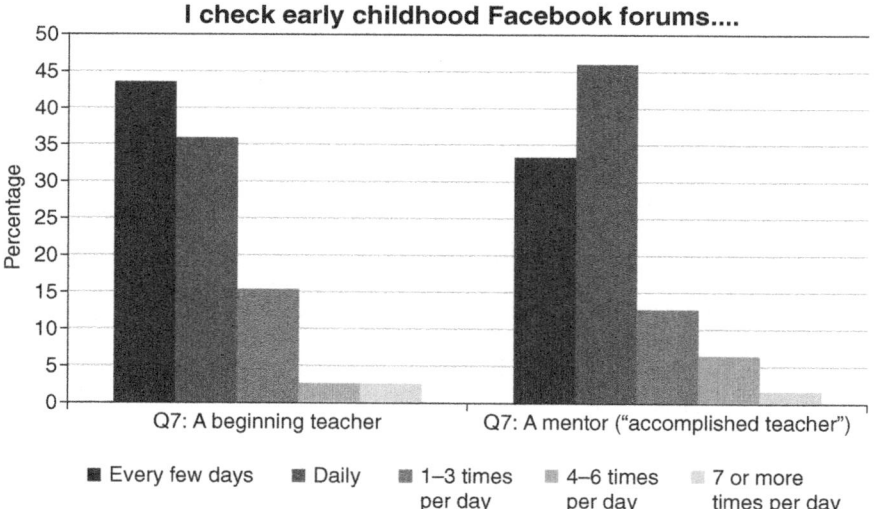

Figure 2.1 Facebook addiction across beginning and mentor teachers.

Table 2.1 A cross tabulation of type of teachers against their highest qualifications and their employment status

Highest qualification	Beginning or mentor teacher	Employed as a teacher in a funded kindergarten/preschool programme	Employed as an educational leader with a teaching role (contact time)	Employed as an educational leader without a teaching role (no official contact time with children)	Employed as a qualified assistant/co-educator	Employed as a manager/coordinator/team leader of a service or across multiple services with early childhood teaching qualifications	Employed as a consultant, tertiary teacher/lecturer/coach with early childhood teaching qualifications	Employed in local government, state government or a non-government agency (EC focused)	Unemployed	Total
Diploma of Teaching (Early Childhood) or equivalent	A beginning teacher	1	1	2	3	1	0	0	0	8
–	A mentor	1	1	0	2	1	2	0	1	8
–	–	2	2	2	5	2	2	0	1	16
Bachelor of Early Childhood Studies or equivalent	A beginning teacher	1	3	0	0	2	0	0	2	8
–	A mentor	3	2	1	0	1	2	3	0	12
–	–	4	5	1	0	3	2	3	2	20
Bachelor of Early Childhood Education or equivalent	A beginning teacher	7	3	0	1	1	0	0	1	13
–	A mentor	7	5	0	0	3	0	3	1	19
–	–	14	8	0	1	4	0	3	2	32

Continued

Table 2.1 Continued

Highest qualification	Beginning or mentor teacher	Employed as a teacher in a funded kindergarten/preschool programme	Employed as an educational leader with a teaching role (contact time)	Employed as an educational leader without a teaching role (no official contact time with children)	Employed as a qualified assistant/co-educator	Employed as a manager/coordinator/team leader of a service or across multiple services with early childhood teaching qualifications	Employed as a consultant, tertiary teacher/lecturer/coach with early childhood teaching qualifications	Employed in local government, state government or a non-government agency (EC focused)	Unemployed	Total
Graduate Diploma in Early Childhood or equivalent	A beginning teacher	2	0	0	1	0	0	0	0	3
–	A mentor	3	4	1	0	0	2	1	1	12
–	–	5	4	1	1	0	2	1	1	15
Masters of Teaching (Early Childhood or Early Childhood/Primary) or equivalent	A beginning teacher	4	1	0	0	1	0	0	0	6
–	A mentor	4	1	0	0	1	4	2	0	12
–	–	8	2	0	0	2	4	2	0	18
Total	A beginning teacher	15	8	2	5	5	0	0	3	38
–	A mentor	18	13	2	2	6	10	9	3	63
–	–	33	21	4	7	11	10	9	6	101

mentoring is more effective than face-to-face mentoring ($r=0.56$, $p=0.001$). Nevertheless, it must be noted that only 21.9 per cent of the beginning teachers agreed that Facebook mentoring is more effective than face-to-face mentoring. Beginning teachers who think Facebook is more effective also tended to use the practice ideas and suggestions in their daily teaching ($r=0.38$, $p<0.05$).

Beginning teachers who used Facebook to receive mentoring for pedagogical reasons mainly found the forums helpful and supportive ($r=0.65$, $p<0.001$). A total of 81.3 per cent of the beginning teachers felt that they received mentoring that helped them understand their role as teachers when using Facebook as a mentoring channel ($r=0.55$, $p=0.001$). On the other hand, 84.4 per cent of the beginning teachers found that some mentors were opinionated and dogmatic about their ideas. A total of 25.1 per cent of the 32 beginning teachers felt that such mentors contributed to their negative experience on the Facebook forums ($r=0.46$, $p<0.001$). These teachers' interaction with such mentors made these beginning teachers think that they should not be teachers ($r=0.47$, $p<0.001$).

Moreover, 62.5 per cent of the beginning teachers thought they had the potential to be a great teacher, judging from the responses they received from Facebook mentors. The outcome of this kind of thinking seems to have an effect on how the beginning teachers viewed the role of mentoring on Facebook as improving the professional identity of early childhood teachers ($r=0.47$, $p<0.001$). A bigger effect is seen on the professional identity when the beginning teachers (81.3 per cent) thought that the mentors helped them to understand their role as teachers ($r=0.64$, $p<0.001$).

A total of 77.4 per cent of mentor teachers turned to Facebook as a platform to mentor other teachers. However, only 30 per cent of mentors turned to Facebook to offer moral support to beginning teachers who had had negative experiences ($r=0.45$, $p=0.001$) and the mentors preferred Facebook as it meant they did not have to meet the beginning teachers in person ($r=0.56$, $p<0.001$). A small percentage of mentors (17 per cent) felt that they were challenged unfairly when supporting beginning teachers who have had negative experiences in teaching ($r=0.39$, $p=0.004$). This is in contrast to 67.9 per cent of mentors who used Facebook to mentor beginning teachers who believed mentors are effective in improving the professional identity of the early childhood teachers ($r=0.53$, $p<0.001$). Mentors who mentor beginning teachers who have had a negative experience also supported them to have a better understanding of ethical conduct through the Facebook forums ($r=0.44$, $p=0.001$).

The majority of the mentors (77.3 per cent) believed that their interactions with the beginning teachers improved their professional identity ($r=0.54$, $p<0.001$) with only 22.7 per cent of the mentors disagreeing that mentoring through Facebook is effective and supportive for beginning teachers ($r=0.63$, $p<0.001$). Obviously 73 per cent of mentors, who have had positive feedback in relation to their advice and posts on the forum, also felt competent at giving advice and continuing with the mentoring of the beginning teachers on the Facebook forum ($r=0.53$, $p<0.001$). Those mentors (50.9 per cent) who felt less competent were also hesitant to make a comment on Facebook for fear of what other early childhood teachers might respond ($r = -0.50$, $p < 0.001$). However, 24.6 per cent of mentors who have experienced career opportunities as a result of mentoring others on Facebook are also those who see themselves as competent mentors ($r = 0.46$, $p < 0.001$). A total of 60.8 per cent of mentors who reported themselves as competent also felt that they have helped teachers understand their role as a teacher through the Facebook mentoring ($r = 0.46$, $p < 0.001$).

A total of 66.1 per cent of mentors believed that some mentors are self-promoting rather than helpful as mentors on Facebook and as a result 71.1 per cent of mentors were concerned about the impact comments made by mentors on Facebook might have on beginning teachers' career ($r = 0.47$, $p < 0.001$). This concern was raised because self-promoting mentors were also seen to squabble among themselves when responding to Facebook posts ($r = 0.43$, $p < 0.001$). Such self-promoting mentors and their conduct were also seen to have negative effect on their ability to improve the professional identity of early childhood teachers ($r = -0.46$, $p = 0.001$). It is apparent that 66 per cent of mentors who are seen to engage in ethical conduct when posting also believe their mentoring can improve the professional identity of early childhood teachers ($r = 0.44$, $p = 0.001$). The mentors who engaged in ethical conduct were also those who believe they were competent to give advice on Facebook to beginning teachers ($r = 0.43$, $p = 0.002$).

Discussions

Facebook is a communicative tool that is frequently used by both early childhood beginning teachers and mentors to engage both in mentoring opportunities and professional dialogue. The time of graduation seems to also impact upon this level of frequency as the most recent graduating teachers, from 1990 onwards, seemed to participate more. It is evident that over the last few years, the level of membership to Facebook and frequency of usage has increased rapidly (Clarke, 2018; Facebook, 2017; Good, 2012) and this is also indicative through the significant rise in membership of ECFFs. Reasons for this vary according to whether the participant is a mentor or a beginning teacher, however the results highlight that Facebook mentoring is desirable because of its accessibility and instantaneous nature particularly for teachers who had previously felt they were under too much time constraint to engage in regular face-to-face mentoring meetings (Morrissey & Nolan, 2015). The participants of this study indicate that Facebook mentoring is valued, although there are certain aspects that impact both positively and negatively on them.

Dependency on Facebook and mentoring

While dependency upon Facebook was not initially a part of the initial enquiry, it became a significant factor that has contributed to the level of impact Facebook engagement has for beginning teachers, being that many of them were dependent upon Facebook for mentoring purposes with the number of times they were checking the forums. This also meant that the more beginning teachers were dependent upon Facebook for mentoring, the more susceptible they were to any negative experiences. More specifically, it seemed that beginning teachers were looking for mentoring from others more than mentors were there to give. It was interesting to note that mentors tended to be less responsive to beginning teachers than what was needed yet there were more mentors who responded to the survey used in this study. This may indicate that dependency to receive mentorship is more prevalent in the beginning teacher, however they are not necessarily receiving advice and mentoring when they need it or as often as they need it.

The results explore some of the reasons why beginning teachers use Facebook for their mentoring, including how Facebook helps them in their role. Despite beginning teachers more frequently seeking mentoring on Facebook, it is not their first preference in how they receive it, preferring face-to-face engagement with experienced others. In saying this, those who have had negative experiences in teaching and are seeking moral support to help them through this situation, do actually prefer using the social media platform that can also give a sense of anonymity when seeking this support. This relates to an interesting phenomenon that exists within the early childhood sector, being that perhaps mentoring is not something that beginning teachers readily have access to in their place of work, particularly where a great deal of the workforce have not had the training in both pedagogy and mentoring to enact the frameworks they must work with (Grieshaber & Graham, 2017). Unlike the primary or secondary sector where schools are filled with Bachelor-trained and experienced teachers, early childhood beginning teachers often work in settings where they may be the most qualified working with a document (i.e. EYLF) that is aspirational and interpretive (Grieshaber & Graham, 2017), rather than concrete or tangible and with perhaps leaders who have not received mentoring themselves. Beginning teachers also have good reason to turn to Facebook, particularly in Victoria where a part of their registration process requires them to seek mentorship from a certified official mentor (VIT, 2017) which may not be accessible to them directly in their place of work. Facebook can therefore be used to seek an official mentor.

Impact on self-efficacy and retention

Of particular interest in the findings is the nature of professional engagement that occurs between beginning teachers and mentors as well as between mentors themselves with perceptions of appropriateness and ethical conduct varying. For instance, it was evident that positive mentoring experiences impacted positively on beginning teachers where the engagement was more reciprocal and helpful, contributing to the beginning teacher's sense of efficacy and better understanding of their role (Nolan, 2017). However, mentoring that included dogma and/or self-promotion was not considered positively by either the mentors and the beginning teachers and indeed contributed to a reduced sense of self-efficacy on behalf of the mentor as they were then reluctant to provide mentoring or advice on Facebook for fear of being unfairly challenged. This aligns with the research from Kimpton et al. (2016) where their results found that 'impression management' (such as self-promotion) was something of an addiction particularly to female users, which is relevant due to the early childhood sector being a female-dominated workforce and that addictions contributed to a lower sense of wellbeing. Additionally, considering the high level of beginning teachers who felt that many mentors presented their advice as dogma indicates that there tends to be a level of frequency in discourse that perhaps leads to a misunderstanding of best practice and a lack of understanding on behalf of the mentors in how to engage more effectively in discourse online. Such a phenomenon promotes a tendency towards a traditional sense of mentorship, which involves aspects of 'judgementoring' which is detrimental to the wellbeing of the beginning teacher and their sense of efficacy (Hobson, 2016). This type of mentoring sees the mentors as the 'gatekeepers of knowledge', which is amplified both by beginning teachers seeking the advice from mentors, and mentors using dogma to give it. Despite this, there seemed to be an overall sense that beginning teachers could filter the 'dogma', as there remained many who still found that mentors did in fact help them better understand their role as a teacher and that their positive interaction helped to improve their belief that they would be a great teacher one day.

The impact Facebook mentoring has upon self-efficacy, as described before, can also impact upon whether the teacher feels that they are competent in their role and developing a strong sense of professionalism in the sector. This phenomenon was evident in the results as many beginning teachers had experienced positive engagement with mentors who had helped them to understand their role, ethical conduct, a sense of professionalism and responded in a way that made them feel competent as a teacher. This finding is encouraging as Facebook can therefore possibly be used as a tool for greater retention of early childhood teachers, potentially addressing the workforce issue that is currently experienced. Despite this positivity, there continues to be a small portion of teachers who experienced negativity that led to a sense of inadequacy and motivation to leave the profession. Facebook mentoring may therefore have the power of influence; however, it is the users (i.e. mentors) who are the influencers. Some accountability then lies with mentors in being enablers for beginning teachers where the training of the mentor needs further consideration. In addition, the ability for beginning teachers to identify a good mentor is also equally as important.

How Facebook mentoring impacts professional identity

The professional identity of early childhood teachers is important to the profession in being able to raise their profile nationally and internationally. As described earlier, the Australian early childhood profession has undergone considerable disruption to its traditional discourse with interpretive documents such as the EYLF and the NQS framing what is now considered best practice (Kilderry et al., 2017) potentially motivating political dogma on Facebook as teachers try to make sense of them. Perceptions of the participants in this study indicate that Facebook mentoring and professional dialogue has the potential to raise or lower the professional identity of the early childhood sector with many mentors and beginning teachers believing that it can be raised, so long as the experience is positive.

Implications for future teacher mentoring

Facebook mentoring holds considerable impact for many beginning teachers and mentors when they engage in professional dialogue. Some key aspects to consider are that Facebook is a relatively new way of mentoring and that current mentoring training practices or initial teacher education courses may not address this practice to the level that it is currently needed. Facebook mentoring will continue to influence society in our engagement and thinking. Embracing this tool as a positive method of mentoring and engaging in professional dialogue may in fact raise the professional profile of the sector and indeed retention of early childhood teachers, but this is dependent upon the users. Two main considerations for policy initiatives therefore are:

- support mentors in using good mentoring practices when they are engaging as mentors on Facebook; and
- include rigorous course content for pre-service teachers in their initial teacher education programmes so that they are able to learn how to filter through dogma and identify good mentoring practices.

References

Andreassen, C. S., & Pallesen, S. (2014). Social network site addiction – an overview. *Current Pharmaceutical Design*, *20*(25), 4053–4061. doi:http://dx.doi.org.ezproxy.lib.monash.edu.au/10.2174/1381612811319999061.

Andreassen, C. S., Torsheim, T., Brunborg, G. S., & Pallesen, S. (2012). Development of a Facebook addiction scale. *Psychological Reports*, *110*(2), 501–517. doi:10.2466/02.09.18.PR0.110.2.501-517.

Australian Institute of Teaching & School Leadership (AITSL). (2011). *Australian Professional Standards for Teachers*. Carlton, Australia: Education Services Australia Retrieved from www.aitsl.edu.au/docs/default-source/apst-resources/australian_professional_standard_for_teachers_final.pdf.

Clarke, S. (2018). *Facebook Mentoring and Early Childhood Teachers: The Controversy in Virtual Professional Identity*. Oxford: Taylor & Francis.

Creswell, J. W. (2014). *Research Design: Qualitative, Quantitative and Mixed Methods Approaches* (4 edn). Thousand Oaks, CA: SAGE Publications.

Department of Education, Employment & Workplace Relations (DEEWR). (2009). *Belonging, Being & Becoming; The Early Years Learning Framework for Australia*. Barton, ACT Australia: Commonwealth of Australia.

Facebook. (2017). Facebook Reports Third Quarter 2017 Results [Press release].

Fenech, S. (2013). Leadership development during times of reform. *Australasian Journal of Early Childhood*, *38*(1), 89–94.

Gibson, M. (2013). 'I want to educate school-age children': Producing early childhood professional identities. *Contemporary Issues in Early Childhood, 14*(2), 127–137. doi:http://dx.doi.org/10.2304/ciec.2013.14.2.127.

Good, K. D. (2012). From scrapbook to Facebook: A history of personal media assemblage and archives. *New Media & Society, 15*(4), 557–573. doi:10.1177/1461444812458432.

Grieshaber, S., & Graham, L. J. (2017). Equity and educators enacting The Australian Early Years Learning Framework. *Critical Studies in Education, 58*(1), 89–103. doi:10.1080/17508487.2015.1126328.

Hobson, A. J. (2016). Judgementoring and how to avert it: Introducing ONSIDE Mentoring for beginning teachers. *International Journal of Mentoring and Coaching in Education, 5*(2), 87–110. doi:10.1108/IJMCE-03-2016-0024.

Hobson, A. J., & Malderez, A. (2013). Judgementoring and other threats to realizing the potential of school-based mentoring in teacher education. *International Journal of Mentoring and Coaching in Education, 2*(2), 89–108. doi:10.1108/IJMCE-03-2013-0019.

Kilderry, A., Nolan, A., & Scott, C. (2017). 'Out of the loop': Early childhood educators gaining confidence with unfamiliar policy discourse. *Early Years, 37*(4), 341–354. doi:10.1080/09575146.2016.1183595.

Kimpton, M., Campbell, M., Eliza, L. W., Orel, A., Wozencroft, K., & Whiteford, C. (2016). The relation of gender, behavior, and intimacy development on level of Facebook addiction in emerging adults. *International Journal of Cyber Behavior, Psychology and Learning (IJCBPL), 6*(2), 56–67. doi:10.4018/IJCBPL.2016040104.

Morrissey, A.-M., & Nolan, A. (2015). Just another meeting?: Investigating mentoring for early childhood teachers in Victoria. *Australasian Journal of Early Childhood, 40*(2), 40–48.

Nolan, A. (2017). Effective mentoring for the next generation of early childhood teachers in Victoria, Australia. *Mentoring & Tutoring: Partnership in Learning, 25*(3), 272–290. doi:10.1080/13611267.2017.1364800.

Nolan, A., & Rouse, E. (2013). Where to from here? Career choices of pre-service teachers undertaking a dual early childhood/primary qualification [online]. *Australian Journal of Teacher Education (Online), 38*(1), 1–10.

Ortlipp, M., Arthur, L., & Woodrow, C. (2011). Discourses of the Early Years Learning Framework: Constructing the early childhood professional. *Contemporary Issues in Early Childhood, 12*(1), 56–70. doi:http://dx.doi.org/10.2304/ciec.2011.12.1.56.

Thomas, L. (2012). New possibilities in thinking, speaking and doing: Early childhood teachers' professional identity constructions and ethics. *Australasian Journal of Early Childhood, 37*(3), 87–95.

Verduyn, P., Lee, D. S., Park, J., Shablack, H., Orvell, A., Bayer, J., ... Kross, E. (2015). Passive Facebook usage undermines affective well-being: Experimental and longitudinal evidence. *Journal of Experimental Psychology: General, 144*(2), 480–488. doi:http://dx.doi.org/10.1037/xge0000057.

Victorian Institute of Teaching (VIT). (2017). Effective mentoring program. Retrieved from www.vit.vic.edu.au/registered-teacher/how-to-train-as-a-teacher-mentor.

Vishwanath, A. (2014). Habitual Facebook use and its impact on getting deceived on social media. *Journal of Computer-Mediated Communication, 20,* 83–98. doi:10.1111/jcc4.12100.

3 Citizen engagement in child care policy

Examining child care policy problematisations in Canadian newspaper articles from 2008 to 2015

Brooke Richardson and Rachel Langford

Introduction

Canada has a long way to go to meet its international obligation to ensure all families and young children have access to affordable, high-quality child care services. While Canada is a federated country where responsibility for child care services formally falls within provincial and territorial jurisdiction, there is widespread consensus from child care advocates and policy researchers that to address the 'consistently inconsistent' patchwork of child care services across the country the federal government must play a key leadership and funding role (Richardson & Langford, 2018, p. 20). Historically and currently, the federal Canadian government has made and continues to make promises to address the lack of access to quality child care services for Canada's families and youngest citizens. Yet in 2018, few of these policy promises have come to fruition, typically sidelined, reduced or abandoned for political, rather than rational, empirically informed reasons.

The most recent promise in Canada for a national child care system occurred during the 2015 federal election campaign. The end of 2014 into early 2015 was a time of heightened federal, political attention to the child care issue when the official opposition, the New Democratic Party, proposed a national child care system following a decade-long child care policy drought under Prime Minister Stephen Harper's Conservative government. This chapter is part of a broader research project that examined the political representation of child care policy in newspapers in the years leading up to and during the 2015 election through Bacchi's what-is-the-problem-represented-to-be (WPR) approach to policy analysis (Bacchi, 1999, 2009). A fundamental assumption in the project is that citizens/voters come to understand, situate themselves and engage with policy issues based on the information readily available to them – typically mediated texts. This chapter specifically examines how the child care policy 'problem' was conceptualised and publicly discussed in three Canadian newspapers available online from 2008 to 2015.

Bacchi (1999) argues that the purpose of policy analysis is 'to create space to consider competing constructions of issues addressed in the policy process, and the ways in which these constructions leave other issues untouched' (p. 4). In other words, citizens cannot talk or think about policy problems and solutions without talking/thinking about how they are represented in the public domain such as the media. Devoting public resources (or not) to the child care problem in Canada can be presented in a variety of ways: from a solution to alleviating poverty to a promising economic stimulus, from a basic human right for women and children to a human capital investment. According to Bacchi (2009) and embraced here, is the idea that how a problem is articulated defines the parameters of possibility for potential policy solutions. If the lack of child care in Canada is a problem for human capital reasons, services will likely reflect an outcome-based model where early academic skills are the focus of programmes. In contrast, if achieving children's rights is the goal, programmes will likely be more holistic, community-based and be accessible to all. The fundamental question this chapter answers is: What child care policy problematisations emerged/ did not emerge in the Canadian media prior to and during the 2015 federal election and how might this impact citizens' ability to engage with child care policy? Drawing on the theoretical foundations of a 'caring democracy' (Tronto, 2013), we propose that all citizens including parents, advocates, children and the media have a responsibility to expand the terms of engagement with child care policies.

Social/political context

From 2006 until late 2014 child care was off the federal political agenda and seldom reported on in the media. The Conservative government took the position that caring for/educating young children is a solely private, familial problem to be solved without government 'interference'. Logically flowing from this position, federal involvement in child care policy was limited to the tokenistic, cash-for-care Universal Child Care Benefit (UCCB) that did nothing to increase the quality, affordability or accessibility of child care. Heading into the 2015 federal election campaign, the official opposition – left of centre New Democratic Party (NDP) – proposed a national child care policy as a central plank of their campaign platform. The NDP promised to create 'one million quality child care spaces at a cost [to parents] of no more than $15 a day' (New Democratic Party of Canada, 2015, p. 6). The Conservative government's response to this proposal was to modestly increase and promote the UCCB as well as to slightly enhance a separate tax deduction parents would be able to claim for fees spent on child care-related expenses. Following this policy change by the Conservative government, the NDP promised to keep both the increased UCCB and expanded tax deduction *and* implement their $15/day national child care system. The Liberals remained notably silent on the child care issue throughout the 2015 election campaign, although there was a promise 'to ensure that affordable, high-quality, fully inclusive child care is available to all families who need it' (Liberal Party of Canada, 2015, p. 13).

In the end Justin Trudeau's Liberal Party won the 2015 federal election with a landslide victory. As of 2018, substantial investment achieving the Liberal's goal to ensure child care for 'all families who need it' has not materialised. Instead, $100 million has been allotted to develop 'new and innovative [early learning and child care] practice across the country', $95 million to 'close data gaps' in the sector and $360 million (spread out over three years) for creating an Indigenous Early Learning and Child Care Framework (Government of Canada, 2018, p. 50). The federal government's 2018 budget also reaffirmed the Government's 2017 commitment to investing $7.5 billion over 11 years into the sector. However, these funds are dependent on electoral victories in 2019 and 2023 and are therefore not a key component of the current government's mandate. Because a national ECEC system was not realised after the 2015 election, it is worth questioning the role that child care policy problematisations, disseminated widely through newspapers, may have played in this outcome – particularly during a period of heightened political attention to child care as a policy issue.

Research method

An analysis of newspaper articles published online by Canadian newspapers illuminated the parameters of possibility for child care policy during a critical child care policy juncture. This chapter focuses on newspaper articles from three major Canadian newspapers during two periods: from 2008 to 2014 (Period A) and during the 2015 federal campaign (Period B). The year 2008 was chosen as a starting point for analysis because this is where other researchers studying the representation of child care in Canadian newspapers left off (Albanese et al., 2010; Rauhala et al., 2012). Data consists of newspaper articles discussing child care policy in Canada's (only) two national newspapers, *The National Post* and *The Globe and Mail* and the high circulation, Greater-Toronto/Ontario-Area-based *The Toronto Star*. These papers also embrace different political orientations with *The Post* described as right-leaning, *The Globe* central in the political spectrum and *The Star* the most left-leaning (Rauhala et al., 2012).

While recognising there are other ways to examine parameters of political discourse (i.e. though advocacy organisation materials, political party platforms), this study is particularly focused on online newspaper articles because of the increasing presence and circulation of information available through digitised and popularised sources. The scope of democratic deliberation in contemporary Canada is increasingly limited to online articles available and consumed through personal electronic devices (laptop, tablet, phone). Citizens are likely to come to their political ideas or opinions through reading articles available on their preferred newsfeed. Appreciating what was available to citizens through reputable/ established media outlets (in this case online newspaper articles) is therefore a valuable way to grasp the scope of political discussion of the child care policy problem. Analysing newspaper content gives a sense of what information/ways of thinking were 'out there' in the world at a time when child care was and was not a focus of governments/political parties.

To identify relevant articles, the terms 'child care' OR 'child care' OR 'day care' OR 'early learning' AND 'policy' were searched in the *ProQuest Newsstand*

New Platform database between 2008 and 2015 (each year searched separately). 'Policy' was included as a separate but necessary search term, given this study's specific interest in child care on the public policy level. Opinion pieces (including letters to the editor and comments) were explicitly included given they illustrate what representations of the issue were available to the public. A stratified sample of articles published during Period A (97 out of a total of 355 articles) and the entire population of Period B (183) was included in the WRP analysis. Stratification was based on adequate representation from each paper, diversity of voice and type of article (i.e. editorial, column, news, opinion) and article length.

Prior to data analysis, a coding guide was developed which identified 16 potential conceptualisations of the child care policy problem in Canada (see Table 3.1). Each of these problematisations instantiates policy solutions in different directions while also situating people in particular ways (citizens, consumers, parents, employers, employees, dependents, etc.) (Bacchi, 2009). The coding process was therefore a deductive rather than an inductive grounded

Table 3.1 The coding guide used to identify childcare policy problems that emerged from the data

Lack of childcare in Canada is a …	*Description*
Broad public problem	Caring for children is a public responsibility, rather than something that falls to the market, parents or families
Market problem	Childcare is a commodity like any other, supply will meet demand and market will regulate cost
Private/family problem	Childcare is the responsibility of parents/families/mothers
Women's equity problem	Childcare is necessary for women's full participation in society
Family equity problem	Childcare is necessary for families' full inclusion in society
Child well-being problem	Quality care is a basic right of children
Labour market problem	Childcare is necessary for optimal labour market functioning (utilising skills/education of workers)
Human capital problem	Childcare services is an investment in the future productivity of people
Poverty reduction problem	Childcare is necessary to reduce poverty; a lack of childcare perpetuates poverty
Generational equity problem	Childcare is necessary for younger generations to have the same opportunities as previous generations
Economic problem	Childcare is an essential financial investment
Social solidarity problem	Childcare is necessary for a cohesive, multicultural, inclusive society
Early childhood workforce problem	Childcare policy is necessary for the workforce to gain adequate remuneration and employment
Population growth problem	Childcare is necessary to keep the population reproducing
Other	Childcare is necessary for a reason not listed above
Childcare is not a problem	Childcare policy and services are not necessary.

theory approach as the possible child care problematisations were predetermined by the researchers. To ensure the categories were exhaustive and that there was space should anything unexpected arise, an 'other' category was included. All articles were printed and coded manually. The presence/absence of each problematisation in each article was then inputted into an excel workbook organised by newspaper and year and listed by article title.

Findings

Findings Period A

Figure 3.1 illustrates that across all newspapers there was a wide variety of problematisations included in Period A. Table 3.2 provides textual examples of the problematisations from the newspapers. The most common were the labour market supply (44 per cent of articles), market (43 per cent) and private/family (41 per cent) problematisations. In about a third of articles the family equity (35 per cent), public (34 per cent), women's equity (34 per cent) and children's wellbeing (34 per cent) were identified. Less commonly, the poverty (24 per cent), not a problem (23 per cent), economic (21 per cent), human capital (20 per cent) and early childhood professionals (19 per cent) problematisations were available while the social solidarity (8 per cent), generational equity (7 per cent), population growth (7 per cent) and 'other' (1 per cent) remained marginal. Overall, a wide variety of problematisations emerged during Period A indicating that a diverse representation of the child care policy issue was available to citizens. However, across the newspapers a relatively small number of articles pertained to child care policy.

When data were delineated by newspaper in this period, other interesting trends emerged. *The Star*, the left-leaning newspaper, was most likely to consistently problematise the issue from a variety of perspectives – 11 problematisations were evident at least a quarter of the time (Figure 3.2). In comparison, *The Post*, a right-leaning newspaper, appears to have largely limited the scope of the discussion to the private family (48 per cent) and free market problematisations (45 per cent) while also frequently denying that there was a child care policy problem at all (35 per cent) (Figure 3.3). *The Globe* consistently discussed the issue from a variety of contradictory perspectives, though it mostly focused on the tension between child care as a private family (52 per cent) and free market (48 per cent) problem and/or a labour market support (52 per cent) and women's equity issue (42 per cent) (Figure 3.4). *The Star* was the only paper that discussed the lack of child care in Canada as a problem in the 'other' category – in this case, from an inclusion of Indigenous Canadian children and families.

Findings Period B

Figure 3.5 shows that in Period B, the federal election, the most common problematisations shifted slightly while the diversity of problematisations noticeably

Table 3.2 Text examples of each of the problematisations

Lack of childcare in Canada is a …	Example
Broad public problem	*'Child care is not a women's issue. It's not even a family issue. Like health care or education, it's an all-of-us-in-it-together issue'* (McLaren, 2015)
Market problem	*'*[the UCCB's method of cash to parents] *is individual empowerment versus the Liberals' faith in a big government solution'* (Gunter, 2010)
Private/family problem	*'giving money to* [childcare] *institution building at this stage in Canada's development hinders parents; it doesn't help'* (Mrozek, 2011)
Women's equity problem	*'For myself and my friends, we're professional, educated women who want to do the jobs we were trained for and think we are good at … .if we don't have access to care, we can't contribute'* (Anderssen, 2013)
Family equity problem	*'if we really want to have good quality early education and care programs for children and families, there has to be public policy and public money'* (Bailey, 2008).
Child well-being problem	*'young children can and do thrive in enriching environments outside their homes'* (Rothman, Scott, & Friendly, 2011)
Labour market problem	*'When parents pursue paid employment, training or education outside the home, they want and need high quality, affordable services to support their child-rearing'* (Anonymous, 2011)
Human capital problem	*'Do we want kids to feel they have a running start?'* (Renzetti, 2014)
Poverty reduction problem	*'child care is now recognised as a fundamental plank of the anti-poverty movement'* (Monsebraaten, 2014)
Generational equity problem	*'young Canadians are falling further behind their parents and grandparents and grandparents in income and opportunity'* (McKenna, 2015)
Economic problem	*'Early learning makes business sense'* (Goar, 2009)
Social solidarity problem	*'universal daycare would do a lot more to benefit society as a whole than a bribe to families'* [referring to income-splitting] (*The Globe and Mail*, 2014)
Early childhood workforce problem	*'If the government invested in a system where child-care workers are valued, where children's well-being is valued, and – this is crucial – women's ability to work without bankrupting themselves or losing their sanity is also valued …'* (Renzetti, 2012)
Population growth problem	*'Do we actually want young people to keep procreating?'* (Renzetti, 2014)
Other	*'the programs met federal policy that requires they be 'reasonably comparable' to provincial standards, as well as 'culturally appropriate' so that aboriginal children won't lose their identity'* (Diebel, 2009)
Childcare is not a problem	*'universal preschool is a "windfall" for middle-class families who are fine on their own'* (Alcoba, 2009)

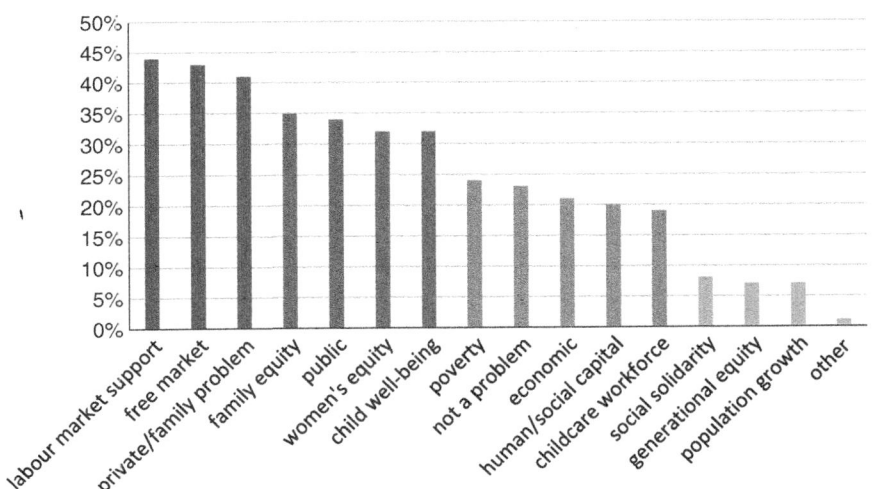

Figure 3.1 Frequency of policy problematisations in all newspapers in Period A.

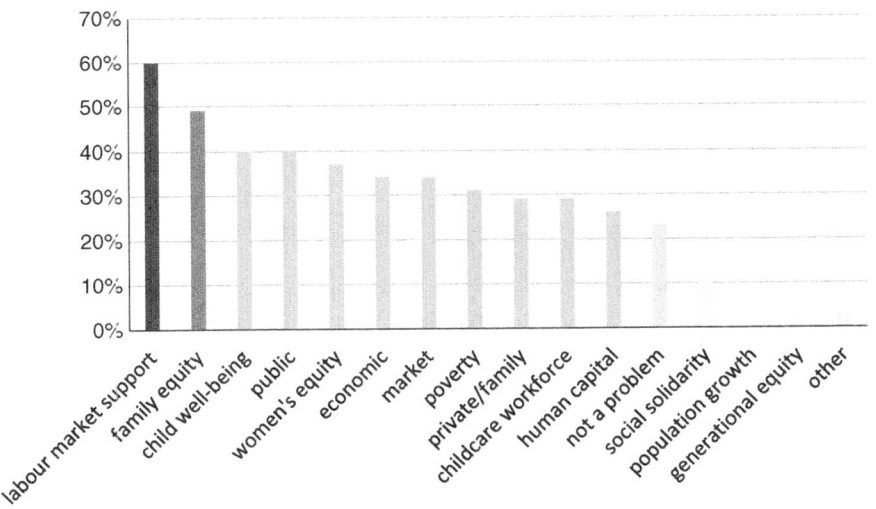

Figure 3.2 Frequency of policy problematisations in the *Toronto Star* in Period A.

diminished. Both the market (60 per cent) and private family (38 per cent) problematisations remain dominant, while the public problematisation rose to being present in 62 per cent of articles (likely due to the emergence of the NDP's $15/day plan). The labour market and women's equity were available about 20 per cent of the time, while all other problematisations were evident

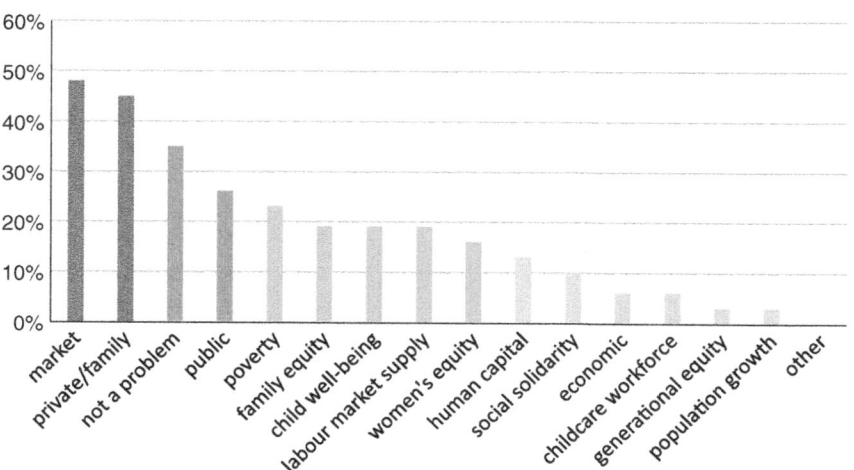

Figure 3.3 Frequency of policy problematisations in *The Post* in Period A.

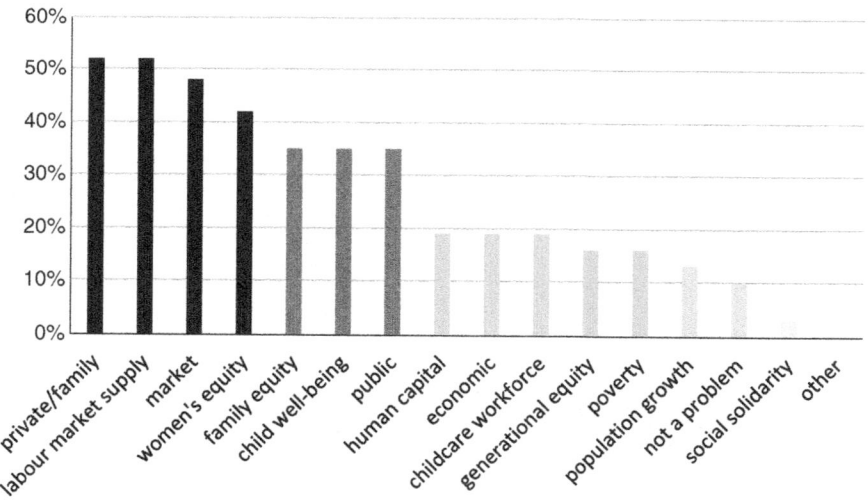

Figure 3.4 Frequency of policy problematisations in *The Globe and Mail* in Period A.

less than 12 per cent of the time. This indicates a general shift in the conceptualisation of child care policy to the bigger picture – that there should be some sort of national system of child care – rather than focusing on specific reasons why child care policy is a priority and therefore what directions policy should take. At the same, this shift indicates a much narrower scope of possibility for understanding child care policy during a federal election campaign that included discussion on the issue.

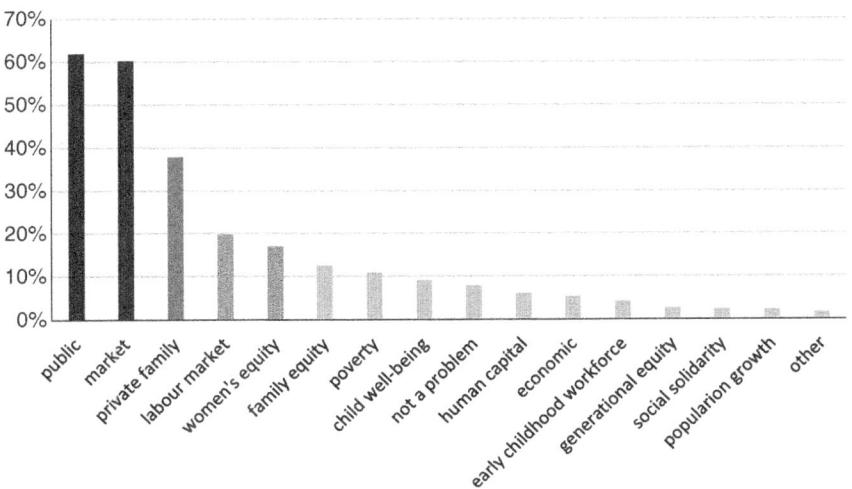

Figure 3.5 Frequency of policy problematisations across all newspapers in Period B.

The public problematisation was overwhelmingly present in articles published in *The Star* (85 per cent), a clear majority of articles in *The Globe* (65 per cent) and a slight minority in *The Post* (40 per cent). At the same time, the market problematisation was dominant in articles published by *The Post* (73 per cent) and *The Globe* (63 per cent) and a slight minority of articles published in *The Star* (45 per cent). Interestingly, when the public problematisation was included in *The Post* it was almost always rejected (i.e. publicly funded child care positioned as a barrier rather than a support for parents). A women's equity problem had all but disappeared. Overall, the diversity of representations decreased considerably during the federal election as the papers appeared to be engaging with child care as a policy issue on similar terms and through a similar narrower perspective.

The dominance of the public and market problematisations in Period B is somewhat puzzling given these problematisations appear to contradict each other. The public problematisation would suggest that child care is a public responsibility rather than a free market commodity, yet both problematisations were evident in most articles. Upon further analysis, it became apparent that the NDP's broad claim that child care should be a public, social resource funded by the government relied on language/representation that commodified child care in the process. For example, newspaper coverage of the NDP's plan was focused on the $15/day price tag and the number of child care spaces that could be created. The price tag and number of spaces are consistent with the commodification of child care in the free market that is perceived as providing child care spaces quickly at little cost to governments. Crucial aspects of child care services, such as quality, pedagogy and system sustainability, were overlooked in newspaper articles covering the NDP's platform and in the NDP's platform itself.

Discussion

The findings from this piece of research illustrate two broad insights that are relevant to Canadian children, families, child care advocates and citizens more broadly. First, during a federal election and an opportune time for political/policy change, newspapers' narrow discussion of the child care problem limited the possibilities of citizen engagement with child care policy. Second, the ideological trends associated with each newspaper raise serious questions about how citizens can learn about differing policy solutions. Joan Tronto's (2013) theoretical work around a 'caring democracy' as well as Hennessey and Leebosh's (2011) empirical research that examined parents' contemporary understanding of the child care policy problem points to potential ways to expand public discussion regarding child care policy solutions

In Period A, a time of little federal child care policy attention, Canadian citizens were less likely to have the opportunity to read about and engage with child care policy in the sense that there were relatively few articles published on the topic. However, when articles were published, a variety of perspectives were available. These perspectives included a focus on women's equity, family equity and children's wellbeing. In contrast, when the stakes were high and political attention returned to child care during the 2015 federal election campaign, citizens frequently had the opportunity to read about child care policy, but without alternative perspectives or depth of discussion. Instead, articles reported mainly on the NDP's $15/day child care price tag without getting at the type of programmes that would be supported, how these programmes would support parents/families/children/women/citizens. People, in this case parents, were solely conceptualised as individual market consumers – even in articles that favoured a public child care system. Keeping the discussion limited to spaces and out-of-pocket cost to parents allowed key policy solutions, such as high-quality programmes where staff are well educated and remunerated, as well as concrete rationales justifying generous public spending, to be ignored.

The Canadian media's market understanding of the child care issue is understandable given society's deep entrenchment in neoliberal thinking. Economic bottom lines and a hyper-individualistic attitude make it difficult to understand social policy issues beyond one's immediate, personal/economic interests. The reality is that most citizens are not parents of young children, so most voters do not see an immediate material benefit to publicly funded child care services. Furthermore, parents of young children are a constantly shifting group (i.e. parents require care for a limited time) and children, who are the group most impacted by child care policy, have no voice in our formal political system (i.e. voting).

Second, the findings revealed imbalanced, ideological trends in reporting despite the democratic mandate of the media to present diverse perspectives – particularly during the federal election in Period B. Citizens reading the politically right-of-centre *National Post* were presented with the narrowest understanding of the child care policy issue, whereby the care of children was almost always limited to a private familial or private market issue. Though the public problematisation was also frequently mentioned, it was usually only superficially acknowledged and then rejected. The left-leaning *Toronto Star* arguably appeared to make the most effort to provide a diverse and nuanced discussion of the issue – though this was ironically more pronounced in Period A than in Period B when depth of discussion was desperately needed. Finally, *The Globe* took a middle ground approach where the articles still discussed a more limited number of problematisations, but they tended to engage more critically with these problematisations (articles took contradicting positions on the issue).

Joan Tronto (Tronto, 2013, 2015) provides an alternative to neoliberalism's harsh, individualistic, market-entrenched approach to the care needs and well-being of citizens. Contrary to neoliberal thinking that conceptualises some as 'in need' (with an undertone of weakness or laziness), Tronto begins from the premise that all humans/citizens both rely on the provision and receipt of care to be well. In her vision of a 'caring democracy', it is recognised that human beings are fundamentally interdependent, at times caring for others and at times being cared for (at the beginning and end of life in particular). Instead of conceptualising the value of care through an economic lens as the market problematisation does, Tronto (2015) repositions public care as that which makes our lives meaningful and our society functional. She warns of the imminent threat to democracy when care is seen as a weakness, a barrier and a burden rather than an inevitable part of human life for which we, as democratic citizens, all bear a basic level of responsibility.

Tronto's alternative ideological orientation could expand the scope of understanding of the child care issue through focusing on issues of equity (women, children, family) – particularly when partnered with the public problematisation. It is not enough to say that we need a public/publicly funded system of child care or that child care should cost $15/day. Rather the case needs to be made that child care is a fundamental requirement of a functioning society and democracy. The motivation to provide this care is not because of future economic gains or human capital returns, or even increased labour market productivity of women, but because all children, by virtue of existing and being human, deserve high-quality care experiences. In a caring democracy, it is not only parents of children who take on the responsibility to care about and for children, but all citizens, including the media who provide a key space for public, democratic deliberation.

The question then becomes, what might the possibilities be if citizens in a democracy had an opportunity to engage with the child care issue from a variety of different perspectives? We know that 77 per cent of Canadians agree the lack of child care in Canada is a 'very or somewhat serious problem' (Environics Research Group, 2008, p. 1), yet little research has been done to engage citizens in how they conceptualised the problem. One small study on this topic carried out focus groups with parents in five Canadian cities (spread out across the country). The study revealed that child care services were understood to provide custodial care largely within institutional settings. Based on parents' own experiences finding and observing child care, they assumed that there was no other alternative than for child care services to be extremely costly and of basic quality (Hennessey & Leebosh, 2011). When information (including a video) was shared illustrating child care programmes from other countries their opinion of child care services and policy significantly shifted. For example, when viewing a video of child care programmes in Sweden, participants were surprised that child care programmes could be responsive to children (i.e. an open-ended pedagogical approach) and family's immediate care needs (i.e. hours that parents required, adequate number of educated staff, universal). Participants were even more surprised that parents did not bear the full responsibility of ensuring programmes were financially viable. Therefore, there appears to be value in educating, illustrating and communicating (including through the mass media) the possibilities of high-quality child care policy and services not just to parents but to all citizens.

Understandably, parents and citizens alike do not want to place young children in many existing, poor-quality child care centres. If a high-quality system could be envisioned with adequately paid staff, purpose-built facilities (indoor and outdoor) and an engaging pedagogy there would likely be more public support for creating it. Research both expanding on and updating this study is urgently needed both to broaden the horizon of possibilities of child care in Canada. The mass media is a key, if not *the* key, vehicle to deliver policy messaging to broaden the breadth and depth of possibility for a child care system in Canada. Other important players are child care advocates who also have a responsibility to move beyond instrumental market-entrenched messaging (i.e. cost and spaces) to a vision and possibilities for high-quality child care programmes (Langford et al., 2013).

Conclusion

Canadian child care policy and programmes have long lagged compared to other wealthy nations. This chapter has drawn attention to the important role that the media plays in representing the child care policy problem and solution – particularly during an election when child care emerged in the political consciousness of the nation. That a very narrow understanding of the issue was available through media sources to citizens on which to base their opinion and vote is problematised in a context where the provision and accessibility of quality child care remains poor and overwhelmingly dependent on market mechanisms. It became apparent that parents, as well as citizens more broadly, simply do not have the opportunity to engage with child care policy in a diverse, nuanced and meaningful way. Moving forward it has been suggested that there must be a greater effort by all, including reputable media outlets, to ensure child care is not only a focus of political discussion but also that diverse perspectives are available to citizens. Without a more expansive field of possibility for child care policy and services in Canada heading into the 2019 federal election, child care policy will remain limited to the status quo – a private (market and family) problem that occludes the necessary public financing and leadership for the wellbeing of all citizens, most importantly children and families.

References

Albanese, P., Rauhala, A., Ferns, C., Johnstone, J., Lam, J., & Atack, E. (2010). Hiding the elephant: Child care coverage in four daily newspapers. *Journal of Comparative Family Studies, 41*(5), 817–836.

Alcoba, N. (2009, 20 June). What's best for children?; Advocates, critics of early education agree the Finns seem to have the most success. *The National Post*. Retrieved from http://search.proquest.com.ezproxy.lib.ryerson.ca/docview/330899895/C466EDCD88634304PQ/10?accountid=13631.

Anderssen, E. (2013, 21 October). The case for publicly funded child care. *The Globe and Mail*. Retrieved from http://search.proquest.com.ezproxy.lib.ryerson.ca/docview/1039334173/EE310F34A16B4AA1PQ/29?accountid=13631.

Anonymous. (2011, 12 February). The daycare disconnect. *Toronto Star*. Retrieved from http://ezproxy.lib.ryerson.ca/login?url=http://search.proquest.com/docview/851362207?accountid=13631.

Bacchi, C. (1999). *Women, Politics and Policy: The Construction of Policy Problems*. Thousand Oaks, CA: Sage.

Bacchi, C. (2009). *Analysing Policy: What's the Problem Represented to Be?* Melbourne, Australia: Pearson Australia.

Bailey, S. (2008, 11 April). Regulated child-care spaces way down, report says. *The Globe and Mail*. Retrieved from http://search.proquest.com.ezproxy.lib.ryerson.ca/docview/382727468?accountid=13631.

Diebel, L. (2009, 17 March). Bureaucrats indifferent to Indian Affairs fiasco; at hearings about the funding of First Nation child-care services, civil servants had few answers. *The Toronto Star*. Retrieved from http://ezproxy.lib.ryerson.ca/login?url=http://search.proquest.com/docview/439570669?accountid=13631.

Environics Research Group. (2008). Attitudes towards child care. Retrieved from https://ccaacacpsge.files.wordpress.com/2014/09/2008environicsreport_attitudes_toward_child_care.pdf.

Goar, C. (2009, Jun 22). Early learning makes business sense. *Toronto Star*. Retrieved from http://ezproxy.lib.ryerson.ca/login?url=http://search.proquest.com/docview/439570235?accountid=13631.

Government of Canada. (2018). *Equality Growth: A Strong Middle Class*. Ottawa, ON: Government of Canada Retrieved from www.budget.gc.ca/2018/docs/plan/budget-2018-en.pdf.

Gunter, L. (2010, 7 July). From Pearson to Ignatieff, the party of elitism; On his surprisingly candid blog, a Liberal MP identifies his party's real problem. *The National Post*. Retrieved from http://search.proquest.com.ezproxy.lib.ryerson.ca/docview/605728666/AB1EA39EE46244C0PQ/15?accountid=13631.

Hennessey, T., & Leebosh, D. (2011). *Focus Groups Summary and Analysis: Public Perceptions of Early Childhood Education and Care*. Ottawa, ON. Retrieved from http://eys3.ca/media/uploads/more-files/hennessy-leebosh-early_learning_and_child_care_focus_group_summary.pdf.

Langford, R., Prentice, S., Albanese, P., Summers, B., Messina-Goertzen, B., & Richardson, B. (2013). Professionalization as an advocacy strategy: A content analysis of Canadian child care social movement organizations' 2008 discursive resources. *Early Years*, *33*(3), 302–317.

Liberal Party of Canada. (2015). *Real Change: A New Plan for a Strong Middle Class.* Ottawa, ON: Liberal Party of Canada.

McKenna, B. (2015, 16 February). It's time to help young Canadians bear the burden of higher costs. *The Globe and Mail.* Retrieved from http://search.proquest.com. ezproxy.lib.ryerson.ca/docview/1655217514/5AEFB0B56CCE4C5APQ/15?accoun tid=13631.

McLaren, L. (2015, 4 September). For parents, daycare is the real money pit. *The Globe and Mail.* Retrieved from http://ezproxy.lib.ryerson.ca/login?url=http://search.proquest. com/docview/1709328483?accountid=13631.

Monsebraaten, L. (2014, 3 November). Key election battle looming over child care. *Toronto Star.* Retrieved from http://search.proquest.com.ezproxy.lib.ryerson.ca/ docview/1619272080/E06D45E9D45E4703PQ/105?accountid=13631.

Mrozek, A. (2011, 14 February). Four votes against national daycare. *The National Post.* Retrieved from http://search.proquest.com.ezproxy.lib.ryerson.ca/docview/851914776/ A15C63C1C4B54AE8PQ/9?accountid=13631.

New Democratic Party of Canada. (2015). *Building the Country of Our Dreams: Tom Mulcair's Plan to Bring Change to Ottawa.* Ottawa, ON: New Democratic Party of Canada.

Rauhala, A., Albanese, P., Ferns, C., Law, D., Haniff, A., & Macdonald, L. (2012). What says what: Election coverage and sourcing of child care in four Canadian dailies. *Journal of Child and Family Studies*, *21*(1), 95–105. doi:10.1007/s10826-011-9481-0.

Renzetti, E. (2012, 11 February). From the House to crèche, women are still juggling bebé and work. *The Globe and Mail.* Retrieved from http://search.proquest.com. ezproxy.lib.ryerson.ca/docview/920992853/EE310F34A16B4AA1PQ/5?accoun tid=13631.

Renzetti, E. (2014, 25 October). Daycare is a tough electoral sell, but kids are about more than politics. *The Globe and Mail.* Retrieved from http://ezproxy.lib.ryerson.ca/ login?url=http://search.proquest.com/docview/1616015467?accountid=13631.

Richardson, B., & Langford, R. (2018). Early childhood education and care in Canada: consistently inconsistent childcare policy. In G. Richards, S. Phillipson, & H. Harju-Luukkainen (Eds.), *International Perspectives on Early Childhood Education and Care* (Vol. 1, pp. 20–33). London: Routledge.

Rothman, L., Scott, K., & Friendly, M. (2011, 11 February). Why we need a national daycare program. *The National Post.* Retrieved from http://search.proquest.com. ezproxy.lib.ryerson.ca/docview/851442385/A15C63C1C4B54AE8PQ/7?accoun tid=13631.

The Globe and Mail. (2014, 8 November). Talking Point: A helping hand for families? Nods all around – good idea, as Canadian as motherhood and maple syrup. But what kind of hand? Which families? Readers, print and digital, enter the debate on income splitting and universal daycare. *The Globe and Mail.* Retrieved from http://search. proquest.com.ezproxy.lib.ryerson.ca/docview/1621691027/6A6FCAA805484DD5P Q/49?accountid=13631.

Tronto, J. (2013). *Caring Democracy: Markets, Equality, and Justice.* New York, NY: New York University Press.

Tronto, J. (2015). Democratic caring and global care responsibilities. In M. Barnes, T. Brannelly, L. Ward, & N. Ward (Eds.), *Ethics of Care: Critical Advances in International Perspective* (pp. 21–30). Bristol: Policy Press.

4 Current research on early childhood education in Chile

The quality of the services and early literacy

Rodrigo A. Cárcamo and Alejandra García-Riquelme

Research impact in the quality of child care centres in Chile and early literacy

Current research in early childhood education and care (ECEC) in Chile has increased considerably in the last decade (Cárcamo, Van der Veer, Vermeer, & Van IJzendoorn, 2014a). On the one hand, the authorities have improved the conditions for doing scientific research by supplying grants for international training, knowledge exchange, conference visits, etc. On the other hand, there is increasing concern for issues of education and child care: the recent government policy to improve the coordination of services and benefits for families with young children from pregnancy to school age has been very successful and put the issue of children's wellbeing high on the agenda (Cárcamo et al., 2014a).

Until the 1990s, practically all the research about early childhood was focused on issues of physical health. Child mortality in Chile was still much higher than in the developed countries and insufficient nutrition and inadequate health care facilities frequently resulted in cases of stunted growth and suboptimal mental development. It is only natural, then, that the government's efforts were focused on keeping infants alive and insuring conditions for healthy growth and development. Fortunately, these efforts proved surprisingly successful and, when the country achieved an infant mortality rate and nutritional status of its population comparable to that of developed countries, the focus shifted towards the enhancement of psycho-emotional aspects of children's development and environment, both at home and at school (Cárcamo et al., 2014a).

The last decade has been marked by an exponential growth of the scientific interest in aspects like quality of the child care environment (Cárcamo, Vermeer, De la Harpe, Van der Veer, & Van IJzendoorn, 2014b; Herrera, Mathiesen, Manuel, Merino, & Recart, 2005; Leyva et al., 2015; Villalón, Suzuki, Herrera, & Mathiesen, 2002) and cognitive and socioemotional development (Cárcamo, Vermeer, Van der Veer, & Van IJzendoorn, 2016; Lohndorf, Vermeer, Cárcamo, & Mesman, 2018; Noboa-Hidalgo & Urzúa, 2012;

Santelices, Olhaberry, Pérez-Salas, & Carvacho, 2009; Seguel et al., 2012), however Chilean studies of these aspects are still underrepresented in the academic literature. Moreover, some of this research in the field, focusing on child development and risk factors in preschoolers, was just spread locally.

In the present chapter, two debates will be covered. First, the debate about the issue of the quality of child care centres in Chile, i.e. their current status and the strengths and weaknesses. Second, the debate about the issue of early literacy and the introduction of teaching practices in the preschool years. It will be argued that the quality of child care centres is reasonably high but that a consistent emphasis on children's emotional needs requires the continuous monitoring of both the children's wellbeing and the professional level of the staff. This is also true for the situation at preschool: the understandable wish to stimulate toddlers' cognitive development and in so doing possibly compensate for inadequate home conditions should be in harmony with children's need to play and interact with social others and, in general, to develop at their own pace. The need to find the right balance in these matters will determine the research agenda for the years to come.

Research on child care quality

Early child care attendance is nowadays an important topic of discussion within the families. Despite the fact that in Chile the maternity leave was recently extended until the child is six months old, for an important part of the population the use of private and public child care services remains inevitable. Whether an early preschool starting age is beneficial or may have negative effects is still a hotly debated issue. Several aspects of day care attendance have been investigated in the Chilean context, and the findings can be summarised as follows.

Cárcamo et al. (2016) in a low–middle income sample, studied two different ethnic groups of children attending early full-time child care centres, and one of the main findings was that early child care attendance can be beneficial in socioemotional terms, especially for those children from a more vulnerable socioeconomic background. On the other hand, Cortázar (2015), who investigated the long-term positive effects of attending early public child care centres for Chilean children, found that beneficial effects on academic achievement later on, are more pronounced in middle-low socioeconomic status (SES) groups than in the lowest SES groups.

Noboa-Hidalgo and Urzúa (2012) analysed data from a longitudinal study and found positive effects of child care attendance on cognitive and emotional regulation outcomes, but negative effects on child–adult interactions. These authors stressed the importance of quality of care for child outcomes, especially in infant classrooms. Seguel et al. (2012) analysed the differential effects of child care attendance on children's development and learning. The authors concluded that children who had attended child care did not differ on cognitive outcomes compared with children who had received maternal care exclusively. However, they found a positive effect on cognitive development when children were enrolled in child care after three years of age. According to the authors, the high quality of the professional caregiver–child interactions is the most likely explanation for this positive effect (Seguel et al., 2012). Santelices et al. (2009) found that early childhood experience in day care centres can be positive for children thanks to the fact that it improves the qualitative exchange between caregivers and children and promotes cognitive functioning more than at home, where mothers or other primary caregivers principally develop affective aspects.

In view of these results, it seems clear that in child care quality matters, and in the Chilean context, that the quality of the interactions of the professional caregivers with the child appears as an important factor. Fortunately, we now have more reliable data about Chilean child care quality and it appears that it is relatively stable across the years. Cárcamo et al. (2014b), for example, showed that quality in Chilean child care centres did not even change considerably after the implementation of the enormous increase in its coverage and remains at a moderate level. Cárcamo et al. (2014b) included the three available Chilean studies that made use of an internationally accepted robust measure for global process quality, notably the Environment Rating Scales (ERS; Harms, Cryer, & Clifford, 2006). Moreover, from their comparative analysis, the average Chilean day care quality is seen to be only slightly lower than the international overall mean (Cárcamo et al., 2014b).

Further results showed that the majority of the day care centres for 0–2 year olds (Herrera et al., 2005) and the preschools (Villalón et al., 2002) do not reach a quality level above the low or mediocre level, with a tendency for better results in private centres. For the four to five year old the state day care centres on average reached better results than the private ones. However, the centres of highest quality were all privately owned. In both infant/toddler and preschool classrooms it was concluded that the process quality of care in Chile was at a moderate level.

Some years later, Cárcamo et al. (2014b) measured the quality of public child care centres, using the Infant/Toddler Environment Rating Scale Revised (ITERS-R) scale, and found that the quality remained as a moderate level, i.e. the same as in the previous studies, however with significant differences in several subscales. For instance, while the 'personal care' and 'routines' subscales decreased significantly as compared to the two previous studies (Herrera et al., 2005), the quality of the 'listening and talking', 'activities' and 'interaction' subscales improved significantly. This increase can be explained by the current implementation of public policies at all levels of the early childhood care by the government, which impacted the type of training that professional caregivers received in their formative programmes, but also by the guidance that the government offers to increase the expertise of the caregivers. Overall, the current focus in Chile, which determines the research agenda and pedagogical practice in day care and early childhood education, is very much on the importance of the child's socioemotional development and takes its inspiration from the Bowlby–Ainsworth attachment theory.

Early literacy and academic skills in the context of Chilean preschool classrooms

Academic success has been linked to the early development of academic skills, such as early literacy, but the question can be raised whether these academic skills result from an early exposition to teaching methodology, named 'schoolification' (Bingham & Whitebread, 2018), or whether similar or even better results for language development and academic skills might be reached in a play-based curriculum.

The research carried out in Chile up to the present time does not allow us to answer this question conclusively, since on the one hand research has still been scarce and, on the other hand, it has not been focused on answering this specific question. Apparently, the dominant idea in educational circles is that academic skills should be acquired at an early age to ensure success later on, at the elementary level. Thus, research in preschool contexts in Chile has tried to identify the practices that best ensure the very early training of these academic skills and did not ask the more global question about the possible negative or positive long-term effects for the child of such an early acquisition in a schooled environment.

In this respect, Leyva et al. (2015) found a mean score in the middle range of emotional support and organisation in Chilean classrooms, i.e. somewhat lower than the middle–high range for studies conducted in the United States and Finland (Leyva et al., 2015), and at the same time, they found low instructional support in pre-kindergarten classrooms. However, it was found that the quality of the interactions and the classroom environment can be improved by an intervention, called 'Un Buen Comienzo' (UBC; Yoshikawa et al., 2015), and as a result of this intervention, an increase in the child outcomes (language, academic and executive functions) can be evidenced (Bowne, Yoshikawa, & Snow, 2016; Leyva et al., 2015; Yoshikawa et al., 2015).

The lack of explicit teaching strategies in early childhood education classrooms was also reported previously by Strasser and Lissi (2009). They were interested in the time distribution of activities in preschool centres in Chile. The authors showed that the main activities in preschool classrooms from different socioeconomic status were unstructured ones, for example, most of the time children were engaged in free play and enjoying mealtime, or the caregiver was disciplining the children. These findings were considered to be not very positive and it was suggested that the amount and quality of the instruction in pre-primary education in Chile still needs some improvement. This brings us to the debate about the role of academic instruction in preschools.

In Chile, Dominguez, Merino, Mathiesen, Soto, and Rodríguez (2016), implemented a programme focused on early literacy, including oral language, phonological awareness and print knowledge. They found an effect of this programme on classroom quality, as well as on the language and literacy skills, and print knowledge and early writing, especially for pre-kindergarten classrooms as compared to kindergarten groups (Dominguez et al., 2016). On the basis of their findings, they stressed the idea that interactions and guided pedagogical activities are more important for the development of language and academic skills than the amount and variety of the available materials (Dominguez et al., 2016).

Another study conducted in Chile by Villalón et al. (2011) previously showed a similar result. They measured an intervention programme, called Early Learning Programme for Reading, Writing and Mathematics (AILEM), developed to promote early literacy through specific teaching activities for children of five years old. Villalón et al. (2011) found evidence that the intervention to improve early literacy in children attending preschool classrooms was successful. Notably, they found a significant effect on children's knowledge of the alphabet, emergent writing and word identification, and concluded that training and coaching of teachers in the early childhood education system is essential (Villalón et al., 2011).

Pallante and Kim (2013), also tested the effectiveness of an intervention programme, called Collaborative Language and Literacy Instruction Project (CLLIP; Pallante & Kim, 2013), to promote language and early literacy in Chilean kindergartens. Their study confirmed the positive effects of a multicomponent literacy instruction model on the language and literacy achievement for both low- and high-income groups. However, children in high-SES schools made more progress on some of the tasks that predict early literacy acquisition (Pallante & Kim, 2013).

Several of the Chilean results on early literacy acquisition and academic skills point to the potential effect of context as a factor determining the acquisition of academic skills and early literacy. Indeed, in a country like Chile, it is of the utmost importance to consider the possible differences in the socioeconomic background of children for the development of academic skills and language development. Characteristic of Chilean society is a high level of inequality and a mixed public and private system for early childhood education.

Balladares, Marshall and Griffiths (2016) found evidence from Chile that language skills are strongly associated with socioeconomic status, and that children from high SES scored significantly higher in several language abilities. They also suggested that we must be very cautious in attributing the diagnosis of 'language impairment' to Chilean children from low SES groups (Balladares et al., 2016). A comparison between urban and rural areas also finds this type of inequality. Forster and Rojas-Barahona (2014), for example, showed evidence that urban preschoolers scored higher on language measures of literacy skills as compared to rural children. However, this result was contradicted by the later findings of Rojas-Barahona, Forster, Moreno-Rios and McClelland (2015). These authors also measured academic skills and the improvement of early literacy and found no differences in the performance between preschool children from rural or urban environments. Similarly, Lohndorf et al. (2018) showed in a Chilean sample that ethnicity does not yield a different performance on receptive and expressive vocabulary, but that these skills are better explained by the indirect effect of their socioeconomic status on the home environment.

In regard to the main practices in preschool classrooms, several researchers have reported that instructional activities at this level are scarce. Strasser and Lissi (2009) found that in Chile, children at preschool levels are exposed to very few literacy experiences. Teachers at the preschool level dedicate less time to language and literacy instructions than their colleagues in developed countries (Strasser & Lissi, 2009). And more recently, Strasser, Darricades, Mendive and Barra (2018), mentioned that at most of the early childhood education centres in Chile, the activities are dominated by non-instructional time, i.e. time which is not especially used for teaching purposes or language development (Strasser et al., 2018).

Policy making around the issue

The current situation of ECEC in Chile can be characterised as a mixed system between private and public child care centres, where the coverage has been increasing enormously and the government guarantees free and full-time access to the 60 per cent of the most vulnerable population in Chile (Rojas, 2010). However, preschool attendance is not yet compulsory and forms a topic of debate. In principle, from 2013 compulsory attendance forms part of the Constitution, but as yet there is no change in the law for its implementation.

The age range of the children is from three months to six years old, arranged in three different levels of two years each. Early nursery is for children up to one year; late nursery is for one-year to two-year-old children. Then the middle grades, divided by early for 2–3-year-old and late–middle to 3–4-year-old children; and finally, the pre-K for children ages four to five years old and kindergarten for five- to six-year-old children (Cortázar, 2015). In terms of the coverage, the number of day care centres for children from 6 months old has quintupled between 2006 and 2009 and, as a result, in 2009 approximately 37.4 per cent of the preschoolers received non-maternal care and most of them from 35 to 45 hours per week (Medrano, 2009), depending on their age.

According to the Organisation for Economic Co-operation and Development (OECD, 2013), around 42 per cent of the children in Chile under the age of three years and 77 per cent of the children at the age of four years now attend pre-primary education. Despite these positive developments, the annual expenditure per child in pre-primary education is still one of the lowest in the OECD countries, slightly more than half of the average annual expenditure in OECD countries (OECD, 2013). However, the government is still trying to enrol more children in these levels of education, based on the conviction that this policy can break down the circle of poverty, because mothers can participate in the labour market while their children receive adequate stimulation, particularly those children from vulnerable contexts. The envisioned result is that Chilean children develop in conditions of greater equity than previous generations (Ministerio de Educación (MINEDUC), 2013). The quantitative increase is well documented but we know still too little about possible qualitative changes in Chilean child care.

Concerning early childhood, Chile has undergone a great change in the last decade. Since democracy was restored in 1990, a series of reforms in education have taken place. The goal was to increase the coverage and improve the quality and equality in public education in general. These changes were accompanied by a series of reforms of the curriculum, and for the first time, the curricula include diverse ethnic contents representing all the indigenous people. From the beginning of the 21st century a reform of early childhood education began, based on a new curricular basis, and one of its important features is the trust given to the teachers as professionals who together with the community can promote the children's learning (Umayahara, 2006). The theoretical background is based on the sociocognitive paradigm, which emphasises the active role that children must play in their own learning process, taking into account the sociocultural context where it occurs (Friz, Carrera, & Sanhueza, 2009).

However, as we have seen, the Chilean curriculum is still insufficient to develop early literacy skills, especially because for preschool teachers it is difficult to shift from traditional practices to more novel ones (Meneses, Rodino, & Mendive, 2017). Moreover, there is a lack of clearly defined goals related to early literacy acquisition in the current curriculum and the learning objectives at this level are too general. Fortunately, in the context of the early child care education system in Chile, the Ministry of Education in 2015 has created the Under-Secretariat of ECEC, which highlights the relevance of this educational stage and has the responsibility to elaborate appropriate plans (Castillo & Lobos, 2017).

Meanwhile, it is not entirely clear what parents expect from these services. The public policy tends to increase the preschool coverage, under the assumption that it is a crucial element to reduce the gaps in social inequality. The most vulnerable families get the opportunity to increase their economic income, especially by the entry of women in the labour world, who traditionally fulfilled the role of caregiver of their children in their first years of life. A significant percentage of the Chilean population are composed of single-parent families, dependent on the income of women. On the other hand, the early entry of children to child care centres provides a more equitable development, compared with children from the most socioeconomically advantaged families, by the provision of a rich environment for early stimulation.

There are several challenges for ECEC in Chile concerning the need to improve its quality. Based on the reviewed literature, it seems that children are positively affected when the activities in preschool classrooms are well oriented and not only based on non-instructional activities. Thus, the new organisation for ECEC created under the umbrella of the Ministry of Education should design a curriculum that provides better details about what learning goals, especially concerning early literacy, are expected to achieve in each level of early childhood education. Moreover, recent research also mentioned the obstacles for better language development that a large number of children in preschool classrooms are confronted with (Strasser, Mendive, Vergara, & Darricades, 2018). The latest is probably an important but also a very complicated situation, because of the investment behind any solution. However, the rapid increase in the investment in ECEC in Chile could also take different orientations, not just in the improvement of the quality of the teaching and coverage, but also in some structural arrangements.

Future directions

Fortunately, there is widely spread agreement in Chile about the need to invest as never before in ECEC. Nowadays, such problems as infant mortality, malnutrition and stunted growth belong to history and no longer form a priority in public policy. As other authors have emphasised, early childhood education needs new steps to improve its level, coverage has been increased, but quality and equity have been relegated to a second place (Peralta, 2008; Umayahara, 2006). Despite all the efforts, child care and education services seem not to have the same effect on children from different socioeconomic levels. Therefore, another important aspect for future educational public policies, and for research as well, is to address these differences in the impact of services and to generate designs or adaptations that allow different groups (ethnic, social, etc.) to receive what they require.

Future research is indeed desirable to improve our understanding of child development in the Chilean context and evaluate the impact of the latest policies in early childhood education. It might be also important to evaluate the quality of early childhood education, especially in the vulnerable context where the current public policy is trying to provide better and equal starting conditions.

As Bowne, Yoshikawa and Snow (2016) have mentioned, one approach to improve the quality of early childhood education is through the training of teachers, for instance, in the use of language instructions techniques, which needs to be integrated in what is already in use.

In research on early childhood education in Chile, more longitudinal studies are needed, and the sources are available. For instance, there is an enormous and freely available open data set with longitudinal measures of young children, taking into account the use of services, family characteristics and several child outcomes (*Encuesta Longitudinal de la Primera Infancia;* ELPI). The ELPI data can also help to understand the convenience of early starting in child care centres in Chile. However, different and new research designs are needed to clarify the issue of the introduction of early teaching versus non-instructional or play-based activities for better academic achievement in preschool levels and after that. What can also be desirable is the inclusion of control groups for academic outcomes comparison. The limitation of this type of design is the difficulty to avoid bias in the selected sample (e.g. about the decision to start or not attending the preschool system at early years).

Another aspect to be considered for research and implementation in the ECEC in Chile is related to the preparation of the teacher in this particular system. Several studies have already shown that the quantity and complexity of the teacher's language did not prove to be a particularly fruitful aspect of instruction in supporting vocabulary (Bowne et al., 2017). And there is a concern that teaching at early years would make preschool education too much like formal school (Mendive, Weiland, Yoshikawa, & Snow, 2016), but at the same time, the interventions programmes that have been studied in the Chilean ECEC context have shown to be effective for better results in child outcomes.

Finally, the situation of ECEC in Chile is nowadays favourable in some aspects. First and foremost, there is now significant political agreement about its importance and the need of major investment in this early stage. The improvement of the child care system and especially the increase of its coverage is clearly visible, but additional efforts to improve its quality and to gain better understanding of what children in this context need are still under discussion.

References

Balladares, J., Marshall, C., & Griffiths, Y. (2016). Socio-economic status affects sentence repetition, but not non-word repetition, in Chilean preschoolers. *First Language*, *36*(3), 338–351. doi:10.1177/0142723715626067.

Bingham, S., & Whitebread, D. (2018). School readiness in Europe: Issues and evidence. In: M. Fleer, & B. van Oers (Eds.), *International Handbook of Early Childhood Education* (pp. 363–391). Dordrecht: Springer International Handbooks of Education.

Bowne, J. B., Yoshikawa, H., & Snow, C. E. (2016). Experimental impacts of a teacher professional development program in early childhood on explicit vocabulary instruction across the curriculum. *Early Childhood Research Quarterly*, *34*(1), 27–39. doi:10.1016/j.ecresq.2015.08.002.

Bowne, J. B., Yoshikawa, H., & Snow, C. E. (2017). Relationships of teachers' language and explicit vocabulary instruction to students' vocabulary growth in kindergarten. *Reading Research Quarterly*, *52*(1), 7–29. doi:10.1002/rrq.151.

Cárcamo, R. A., Van der Veer, R., Vermeer, H. J., & Van IJzendoorn, M. H. (2014a). From foundling homes to day care: A historical review of childcare in Chile. *Cadernos de Saúde Pública*, *30*(3), 461–471. doi:10.1590/0102-311x00060613.

Cárcamo, R. A., Vermeer, H. J., De la Harpe, C., Van der Veer, R., & Van IJzendoorn, M. H. (2014b). The quality of childcare in Chile: Its stability and international ranking. *Child & Youth Care Forum*, *43*(6), 747–761. doi:10.1007/s10566-014-9264-z.

Cárcamo, R. A., Vermeer, H. J., Van der Veer, R., & Van IJzendoorn, M. H. (2016). Early full-time day care, mother–child attachment, and quality of the home environment in Chile: Preliminary findings. *Early Education and Development*, *27*(4), 457–477. doi:10.1080/10409289.2016.1091971.

Castillo, F., & Lobos, M. (2017). Early child care education: Evidence from the new law in Chile. *Journal of Pedagogy*, *8*(1), 121–135. doi:10.1515/jped-2017-0006.

Cortázar, A. (2015). Long-term effects of public early childhood education on academic achievement in Chile. *Early Childhood Research Quarterly*, *32*(3), 13–22. doi:10.1016/j.ecresq.2015.01.003.

Dominguez, P., Merino, J., Mathiesen, M., Soto, M., & Rodríguez, C. (2016). Efecto de un programa de desarrollo profesional docente sobre la calidad de la literacidad temprana [Effects of a teacher professional development program on early literacy skills quality]. *Psicología y Educación: presente y futuro*, Universidad de Alicante, España. ACIPE-Asociación Cienofica de Psicología y Educación, 967–976.

Forster, C. E., & Rojas-Barahona, C. A. (2014). Niños preescolares vulnerables de sectores rurales: importancia de las practicas del hogar y la asistencia a jardin infantil en el desarrollo de habilidades de alfabetizacion temprana [Disadvantaged preschool children from rural areas: the importance of home practices and nursery attendance in the development of early literacy skills]. *Cultura Y Educacion*, *26*(3), 476–504. doi:10.10 80/11356405.2014.973668.

Friz, M., Carrera, C., & Sanhueza, S. (2009). Enfoques y concepciones curriculares en la educación parvularia [Curricular approaches and concepts in pre-school education]. *Revista de Pedagogía*, *30*(86), 47–60.

Harms, T., Cryer, D., & Clifford, R. M. (2006). *Infant/Toddler Environment Rating Scale-Revised*. New York: Teachers College Press.

Herrera, M. O., Mathiesen, M. E., Manuel, J., Merino, J. M., & Recart, I. (2005). Learning contexts for young children in Chile: Process quality assessment in preschool centres. *International Journal of Early Years Education*, *13*(1), 13–27. doi:10.1080/09669760500048253.

Leyva, D., Weiland, C., Barata, M., Yoshikawa, H., Snow, C., Trevino, E., & Rolla, A. (2015). Teacher-child interactions in Chile and their associations with prekindergarten outcomes. *Child Development*, *86*(3), 781–799. doi:10.1111/cdev.12342.

Lohndorf, R. T., Vermeer, H. J., Cárcamo, R. A., & Mesman, J. (2018). Preschoolers' vocabulary acquisition in Chile: The roles of socioeconomic status and quality of home environment. *Journal of Child Language*, *45*(3), 559–580. doi:10.1017/S0305000917000332.

Medrano, P. (2009). Public Day Care and Female Labor Force Participation: Evidence from Chile. Working paper No. 306 (December). Department of Economics, University of Chile. Retrieved from http://econ.uchile.cl/uploads/publicacion/25d848f1-0435-4691-9623-b20cff7a36aa.pdf.

Mendive, S., Weiland, C., Yoshikawa, H., & Snow, C. (2016). Opening the black box: Intervention fidelity in a randomized trial of a preschool teacher professional development program. *Journal of Educational Psychology*, *108*(1), 130–145. doi:10.1037/edu0000047.

Meneses, A., Rodino, A. M., & Mendive, S. (2017). Lessons from Costa Rica and Chile for early literacy in Spanish-speaking Latin American countries. In N. Kucirkova, C. E. Snow, V. Grøver, & C. McBride (Eds.), *The Routledge International Handbook of early Literacy Education*. Abingdon: Routledge, 27 March, Routledge Handbooks Online.

Ministerio de Educación (MINEDUC). (2013). Campaña para incentivar la matrícula de pre-kinder y kínder [Campaign to promote enrollment in pre-kinder and kinder]. Retrieved from www.mineduc.cl/contenido_int.php?id_contenido=25000&id_portal=1&id_seccion=4657.

Noboa-Hidalgo, G. E., & Urzúa, S. S. (2012). The effects of participation in public child care centers: Evidence from Chile. *Journal of Human Capital*, *6*(1), 1–34.

Organisation for Economic Co-operation and Development. (2013). *Education at a Glance: OECD Indicators 2013*. OECD Publishing. http://dx.doi.org/10.1787/eag-2013-en.

Pallante, D. H., & Kim, Y. S. (2013). The effect of a multicomponent literacy instruction model on literacy growth for kindergartners and first-grade students in Chile. *International Journal of Psychology*, *48*(5), 747–761. doi:10.1080/00207594.2012.719628.

Peralta, M. V. (2008). Quality: Children's right to appropriate and relevant education. *Early Childhood Education*, *110*, 3–12.

Rojas, J. (2010). *Historia de la Infancia en el Chile Republicano, 1810–2010* [History of Childhood in Republican Chile, 1810–2010]. 2nd ed. Chile: Ocho Libros Editores.

Rojas-Barahona, C. A., Forster, C. E., Moreno-Rios, S., & McClelland, M. M. (2015). Improvement of working memory in preschoolers and its impact on early literacy skills: A study in deprived communities of rural and urban areas. *Early Education and Development*, 26(5–6), 871–892. doi:10.1080/10409289.2015.1036346.

Santelices, M. P., Olhaberry, M., Pérez-Salas, P., & Carvacho, C. (2009). Comparative study of early interactions in mother–child dyads and care centre staff-child within the context of Chilean crèches. *Child: Care, Health and Development*, 36(2), 255–264. doi:10.1111/j.1365-2214.2009.01032.x.

Seguel, X., Edwards, M., Hurtado, M., Bañados, J., Covarrubias, M., Wormald, A., ... Sánchez, A. (2012). ¿Qué efecto tiene asistir a sala cuna y jardín infantil desde los tres meses hasta los cuatro años de edad? Estudio longitudinal en la Junta Nacional de Jardines Infantiles [What is the effect of attending nursery school between three months and four years of age? A longitudinal study in the National Preschool Association]. *Psykhe*, 21(2), 87–104.

Strasser, K., Darricades, M., Mendive, S., & Barra, G. (2018). Instructional activities and the quality of language in Chilean preschool classrooms. *Early Education and Development*, 29(3), 357–378. doi:10.1080/10409289.2018.1429765.

Strasser, K., & Lissi, M. R. (2009). Home and instruction effects on emergent literacy in a sample of Chilean kindergarten children. *Scientific Studies of Reading*, 13(2), 175–204. doi:Pii 910138664 10.1080/10888430902769525.

Strasser, K., Mendive, S., Vergara, D., & Darricades, M. (2018). Efficacy of a self-monitoring tool for improving the quality of the language environment in the preschool classroom. *Early Education and Development*, 29(1), 104–124. doi:10.1080/10409289.2017.1287992.

Umayahara, M. (2006). *Early childhood education policies in Chile: From pre-Jomtien to post-Dakar*. Background paper prepared for the Education for All Global Monitoring Report, 2007. Paris: UNESCO.

Villalón, M., Förster, C. E., Cox, P., Rojas-Barahona, C. A., Valencia, E., & Volante, P. (2011). Resultados de la enseñanza de estrategias de lectura y escritura en la alfabetización temprana de niños con riesgo social [Results of teaching reading and writing strategies on early literacy of children at-risk]. *ESE. Estudios sobre educación*, 21, 159–179.

Villalón, M., Suzuki, E., Herrera, M., & Mathiesen, M. (2002). Quality of Chilean early child-hood education from an international perspective. *International Journal of Early Years Education*, 10, 49–59. doi:10.1080/09669760220114845.

Yoshikawa, H., Leyva, D., Snow, C. E., Trevino, E., Barata, M. C., Weiland, C., ... Arbour, M. C. (2015). Experimental impacts of a teacher professional development program in Chile on preschool classroom quality and child outcomes. *Developmental Psychology*, 51(3), 309–322. doi:10.1037/a0038785.

5 From caring to learning

The transformation of Danish day care institutions in the 21st century

Sine Penthin Grumløse

Introduction

This chapter explores political processes connected to the intensified focus on learning outcomes in Danish day care institutions. It begins by describing the broad lines of development of Danish day care institutions from 1960 to the present. Even though the Danish day care institutions are older than this, an understanding of how Danish day care developed in the 1960s and the decades that followed forms the baseline for viewing the key transformation in the Danish early childhood education. We shall see that it is a shift in the political paradigm related to Danish day care institutions from *caring* to *learning*.

Throughout the last 15 years, Danish politicians have increasingly focused on the education of the youngest children. Influenced by international tendencies, Danish day care institutions have been in political focus with major attention placed on the development of academic skills. The aim has been to raise the educational level of society by beginning as early as possible. Hence, the focus on improving the day care (Juhl, 2018; Togsverd, 2015). This early childhood education policy has led Danish day care institutions to place increasing emphasis on enhancing children's academic skills rather than on ontogenesis, on children's play and their general wellbeing (Juhl, 2018; Marschall, 2018). Some observers have expressed concern that the increasing focus on schooling in the day care environment could overshadow or even eliminate the values upon which Danish day care institutions were founded, thereby neglecting the everyday realities of being a young child. As Juhl states in Volume I of this series, the focus on learning '[introduces] a hierarchical difference between academic learning activities and holistic approaches to children's learning and development' (Juhl, 2018 p. 42). Like Juhl, Marschall also points out the endangered position of the holistic approach to children in Danish day care institutions (Marschall, 2019).

Based on an analysis of Danish family policy (1960–2010), and on a study of changing definitions of 'a good life for children' (Grumløse, 2014), this chapter explores how Danish day care institutions have developed from a focus on helping families (by providing care) to helping society (by providing learning). I will demonstrate how policy-making concerning Danish day care, in the light of early childhood education, has challenged the historical understanding of 'good day care'.

A study of Danish family policy

This chapter draws upon a research project on Danish family policy (from 1960 to 2010) and the changing discourse of 'a good life for a pre-school child' (Grumløse, 2014). The empirical data for this study comes from parliamentary debates, bills, legislation, commission statements, reports, regulations and administrative directives. In Denmark, these documents are available at the Legal Knowledge Centre at the University of Copenhagen.

Based on Foucault's concept of the discourse (Foucault, 2001; 2005) the documents are analysed in order to identify statements, decisions, concepts and social changes (e.g. the scale of day care institutions) that are part of the same discursive formation (Foucault 2005, p. 44). The core questions posed by this study are: How does the Danish policy-making process articulate 'a good life for a preschool child'? What conditions have made it possible for different perceptions of the good life of preschool children to arise? How are these perceptions reflected in society e.g. as day care institutions?

Based on the concept of discourse procedures, defined as the mechanisms that operate in the discourse (Foucault, 2001), this chapter examines how statements about children work together to form an understanding of conventional knowledge about young children, but also how this conventional truth sometimes changes and is replaced by other truths. In addition, the regulation of access to the discourse is investigated. Who or which organs are informing the policy? By examining the discourse over time, it has been possible to discover that not only do the prevalent understandings of 'the good life for the child' change during time. So does the access to the discourse e.g. when different persons are chosen as experts and asked to contribute to the policy-making.

This analytical framework provides the possibility to work simultaneously with a synchronic and diachronic focus (Fogh Jensen, 2013, p. 27) in so far as it examines both *how* the different statements battle for definition *in* time, and *how* the understanding of a good life for a preschool child may change *over* time. Thus, inspired by Foucault, I investigate how the politics of Danish day care reflect specific rationalities and how these rationalities change during time.

The establishment of the Danish child care institutions in the 1960s went hand in hand with the expansion of the Danish welfare state.[1] As day care facilities expanded in the 1960s and 1970s, becoming a part of everyday life for families, the professional day care staff – the pedagogues – focused on *caring* for children and on cultural education, the latter defined as those social skills related to the child growing up to be a Danish citizen. Through a gamut of pedagogical activities, the day care institutions sought to develop children's social skills and to transmit the cultural habitus of Danish society (Ellegaard, 2000).

Until 1969, admission to become educated as pedagogue required the applicant to have worked at least six months as an au pair in a Danish or foreign household (Folketingstidende [Official Report of Parliamentary Proceedings] 1968–1969, Forhandlingerne III, p. 6254). In 1969, the entry requirement changed. However, the day care institutions remained 'family substitutes', providing children with care while the parents were at work. The institutions were publicly funded with parents paying a part of the costs through user fees (Børne- og Ungdomsforsorgens pædagogiske Nævn [Child and Youth Care Educational Board], 1963).

In the need of care

In the 1960s, Danish family life was undergoing rapid change (Christoffersen, 2004), and this led the government to increase its interest in the everyday life of preschool children (Grumløse, 2014). More mothers were entering the labour market – not because they *had to* due to economic conditions, but because they *wanted to* (Ministeriet for familiens anliggender [Ministry of Family Affairs], 1967, p. 13; Commission Concerning the Position of Women in Society [Kommissionen vedrørende kvindernes stilling i samfundet], 1974). While the equality of men and women in the labour market and in the educational system was improving in Denmark, the care of children while their mothers were at work became a political issue.

The fact that more women with young children were entering higher education or taking up employment led to new issues regarding how their children should be cared for. Where should these children be? Who should care for them? These questions about children were new in the political field, and led to new investigations and discussions about what was perceived as 'a good family' and 'a good everyday life' for the preschool child. Some of these discussions were addressed by the government's Kommissionen vedrørende kvindernes stilling i samfundet [Commission Concerning the Position of Women in Society] (1966, 1967, 1970, 1972a, 1972b, 1974), while others were addressed by the Ministeriet for familiens anliggender[2] [Ministry of Family Affairs] (1967). Formerly, policy-making with regard to family life had concerned itself solely with conditions for poor people and their children (e.g. Børneloven [Children's Act], 1905; Befolkningskommissionen [Commission Concerning the Population], 1936, 1937, 1938; Ellegaard, 2000; Grumløse, 2017).

In order to answer the questions about children's needs, leading pediatricians were consulted in the 1960s. In a discourse–analytical sense, the pediatricians *gained access* to the discourse. Their conclusions were quite close to the contemporary psychological paradigm (e.g. Bowlby, 1952). A child younger than three years, they concluded, should be at home with their mother. Mothers were given a special position, in the belief that a child establishes *one* strong attachment. In policy-making, this scientific understanding of the unique relation between mother and child was therefore reproduced by politicians. Hence, the Conservative politician Asger Jensen, who was the party's social policy spokesman, declared:

Some time ago, we of the Conservative People's Party clearly stated that greater financial support should be given to families or mothers with children younger than three years old. Such families are subject to a massive financial burden at a time when mothers are unable to go out and work. Actually, we do not think it is right that they should go out and work, since various experts have now clearly shown that at no other point in its life does any human being crave a mother's care as much as in the first years of life.

(Folketingstidende [Official Report of Parliamentary Proceedings] 1965–1966, Forhandlingerne II, p. 3982)

The same definition of 'how to take care of children' was supported by the left-wing parties. Alternative ways of structuring everyday life (e.g. having the child in a nursery while being at work) were considered less desirable or simply inappropriate for children. What seems to have been important was the prevalent idea that children's biological needs required them to stay at home with their mothers. Indirectly, this attitude was supported by the idea that with the current changes in society, there was a risk that preschool children would be *lacking care*. In the mid-1960s, the Danish Parliament examined the possibility of paying mothers who remained at home an allowance in order to ensure that children got the care they needed. However, the bill never passed, mostly because of disagreements about the financial conditions (Grumløse, 2014, pp. 78–79). Furthermore, a labour shortage during the 1960s had become a huge problem requiring the 'calling a labour reserve of married women into the labour market' (Børne- og ungdomsforsorgens pædagogiske nævn [Child and Youth Care Educational Board], 1963, p. 14). In order to understand the development of Danish day care institutions, this cultural and historical setting is important.

The expansion of Danish day care

While there was a political consensus that a child below the age of three years should be cared for by their mother at home – and while social policy sought to support this family structure – a child older than three years could attend a half-day kindergarten. In half-day kindergartens, the children could play with other children in a secure and pedagogical setting. It was a conventional understanding that children should spend no more than four to five hours a day in the kindergarten. According to both politicians and the early childhood experts of the time, longer hours in day care were to be avoided (Børne- og Ungdomsforsorgens pædagogiske Nævn [Child and Youth Care Educational Board], 1963; Kommissionen vedrørende kvindernes stilling i samfundet [Commission Concerning the Position of Women in Society], 1974). Under the predominance of this view, part-time kindergartens were established in large numbers, and nurseries remained few. In fact, as the social policy spokesman of the Social Democrats put it in 1964, nurseries had deliberately not been established:

The first stage in terms of childcare institutions is nurseries for children a few months old up to 2–3 years. There is a great shortage of these institutions, most probably because there has been a deliberate tendency not to create more nurseries than absolutely necessary. As far as possible, children in their earliest years belong at home with their mothers, both for health and psychological reasons.

(Folketingstidende [Official Report of Parliamentary Proceedings], Folketingstidende 1963–1964: Forhandlingerne II, p. 220)

In the second half of the 1970s, the conventional knowledge about 'the good life for a preschool child' was challenged by new ideas of how to take care of children. Other researchers were invited into the discourse and were asked to contribute to the policy formation process. One fundamental new conclusion was that peers were essential for a child to develop 'the right way' (Børnekommissionen [Children's Commission], 1981; Grumløse, 2014, 2017). Following the changes in the discourse about preschool children in the 1970s, it is seen that this new understanding of children's wellbeing required the establishment of more day care institutions. It also provided a legitimation for lowering the acceptable age in which children could be placed in day care. In the wake of this new knowledge informing the policy-making process, a large number of day care institutions were established to take care of the youngest children. Thus, Bowlby's attachment theory (Bowlby, 1952), and thereby the central position of the mother, was challenged by this new understanding that children needed peers and professional pedagogues as essential elements of their everyday life. Nevertheless, the assumption that a child's development could be defined in terms of universal principles remained. It was only the guiding principles that had changed (Grumløse, 2014, 2017).

By the end of the 1970s and throughout the 1980s, we can observe a veritable war between the 'old' and 'new' understandings of how the good life for preschool children should be defined and reflected in society (Grumløse, 2014, 2017). Some politicians held on to the idea that the youngest children needed to be at home with a parent; these politicians refused to support the establishment of nurseries. Other politicians supported the establishment of both nurseries and kindergartens, subscribing to the idea that being with peers was necessary for the child's healthy development. Both sides proposed a number of bills supporting their respective understandings of a good everyday life for preschool children. The right-wing parties wanted to pay the parents to take care of their youngest children at home. The left-wing parties sought to reduce parent's working hours *and* to ensure that the nurseries were multiple in numbers. With this 'war' between the two political groups, not many bills were passed. However, in the 1990s, the right of guaranteed day care was enacted into law (Law no. 1140 of 21 December 1994). Municipalities were now obliged to offer day care to *all children* from the age of 26 weeks.[3] Today, access to day care is now guaranteed by the Danish state.

Thus, the Danish politicians have been occupied with solving the problem 'where should the children be when the parents are at work?' Adults working in the day care institutions were not considered 'preschool teachers' and their job not formulated in school terms.

We are therefore facing a quite new agenda when ideas of early childhood education come into Danish day care institutions, changing the very meaning of day care. One way to unfold the seriousness is to point out how the history of Danish day care is in conflict with ideas that promote school-related substance in day care. Another aspect is the fact that early childhood education goes hand in hand with a radically different political management of the Danish day care institutions. In the following, I will focus on the political processes related to the early childhood education agenda and unfold the cultural and historical obstacles involved.

Day care institutions offering learning support to children

As we have seen, throughout the 1960s, 1970s and 1980s the political focus of the Danish day care system was on the expansion of Danish day care institutions. With more parents working, often full time, more nurseries and kindergartens were built. From the 1980s, most Danish parents were employed in the labour market (Christoffersen, 2004), and the proportion of children in day care increased markedly (see Figure 5.1).

Throughout the 1990s, there was very little political attention to the everyday life *inside* the day care institutions. The development of day care culture was not a political issue but a pedagogical task. Supporting this understanding, the strengthening of the Danish day care institutions was carried out by improving the education of the pedagogues. In the early 1990s, the pedagogical curriculum was extended from three to 3.5 years (Law no. 370 of 6 June 1991).

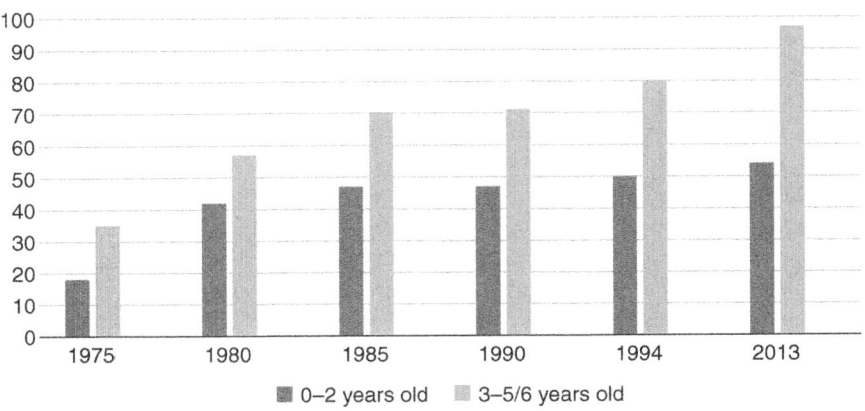

Figure 5.1 Proportion of Danish children in day care, 1975–1994 (as percentage of all children).

Data source: Statistics Denmark.

During the 1990s, the overall education of the population became a major international issue. Inspired by international institutions such as the Organisation for Economic Co-operation and Development (OECD) and the European Union (EU), the political focus on school development intensified in Denmark as well (Ministry of Social Affairs in consultation with the Ministry of Education, 2000). In 1993, a Danish school reform was passed by the parliament (Law no. 509 of 30 June 1993). The aim was to qualify the teaching by using differentiated teaching. The differentiated teaching included evaluation of the children's benefit of teaching and dialogues between the teacher and the child as part of teaching. With this school reform, the politicians moved closer to *the teaching* e.g. by enforcing continuous evaluation as part of teaching. This move is comparable to the implementation of a national education curriculum in day care (passed in 2003), and must be understood as part of the same rationality. With an intensified focus on learning outcomes *combined with* the idea of day care institutions as school-supporting institutions, the very meaning of Danish day care changed. Care had become learning. Day *care* had become preschool.

This new focus on school-related learning in day care institutions became legislation in 2003. In this curriculum logic, the child's performance during the day care period should involve acquiring skills that would be put to use when they entered school (Grumløse, 2014; Plum, 2014). This trend was concurrent with the first PISA test (in 2000) on the basis of which OECD emphasised that the Danish primary school was not showing adequate results (PISA is the OECD's Programme for International Student Assessment. Every three years, the programme tests 15-year-old students from all over the world in reading, mathematics and science). It was also stressed by the OECD that Danish schools were not sufficiently effective in eliminating the reproduction of class barriers, what in Scandinavia is known as 'the negative social heritage'.

In the political negotiations, it was argued that playing and learning had to go hand in hand. By defining children's activities in day care as learning resources for later work in schools, rather than 'just' as a learning resource related to growing up, the new agenda was articulated in terms of schooling (Law no. 224 of 31 March 2004).

Even though some politicians were very much in doubt about the legitimacy of this new school-focused agenda (members of some of the left-wing parties and the Danish Social–Liberal Party), it was widely accepted that children's day care experiences should be measurable in terms of learning output that would be relevant to their later school practice. In other words, there should now be a measurable connection between being in day care and becoming a clever learner in school. Day care was to be preschool. It was also widely accepted that policy-making related to day care institutions should support the development of the kind of tools that could document the quality of day care and the learning taking place in these institutions (Plum, 2014; Togsverd, 2015). The question was not *if* the day care institutions should support the schools but *how* they could do it most effectively. The predictable result of this performance-based policy was more management and more political control of children's everyday lives.

In the political debates, politicians framed the new focus on learning outcomes as part of a national strategy. A Liberal Party MP responsible for education policy, for example, declared:

> One of the elements of the government's strategy is to introduce into kindergartens and day care institutions what we call 'early curriculum'. This has nothing to do with the idea that children should start reading and counting at an early stage in day care institutions. The point is that all children develop by learning some basic skills, and we have to make sure that this is being taken care of. (...) To put it in a nutshell: play and learning must go hand in hand.
>
> (Folketingstidende [Educational policy spokesman of the Liberal Party in: Official Report of Parliamentary Proceedings] 2003–2004, Forhandlingerne I, p. 535)

Thus, in 2004, the day care institutions were faced with the task of developing an educational curriculum for children aged six months to two years of age, plus another one for children from age three years to school age. The curriculum had to describe learning outcomes, as well as the relevant activities and methods. The objectives of activities and the evaluation of learning processes became core concepts in an educational approach based on learning outcomes. Another new requirement was that educational learning processes within the sphere of daily activities had to be comparable and measurable. As Juhl argues, this was a rather new definition of quality in Danish day care institutions (Juhl, 2018). Whereas quality had formerly been assessed in terms of a child's well-being as judged by the pedagogues, the quality of the day care experience was to be measured in terms of a child's performance relate to the learning outcomes.

Thus, although the political focus was still on the children and their development, the existing controversy over whether the child was best served by being with the mother or being with peers had faded from view. Instead, priority was placed on the learning processes in terms of preparedness for school. Day care institutions were now a 'training ground' for school. By using a national educational curriculum, the framework of professional work in Danish day care institutions reflected a preschool logic that had been unfamiliar to Danish institutions and to the pedagogues working in them. As a result, the focus on early childhood education posed a challenge to the pedagogue profession. The pedagogues were confronted with the need to acquire new tools and carry out new tasks. At the same time, pedagogues were offered new opportunities in terms of understanding and defining themselves as professionals who 'work with' preschool children and not simply care for them while their parents were at work (Aabro, 2018). On the one hand, the emerging professionalisation of the pedagogues had been questioned by the politicians. On the other hand, by being expected to raise the children's educational standards, i.e. to prepare them for school, the pedagogues were given an important task in framing the Danish welfare state. The pedagogues were now the ones who would ensure that:

> All children, regardless of their background, should be given opportunities, and we actually see this question of educational curriculum in the kindergarten as the approach that enables us to offer children opportunities they do not have at home.
>
> (Minister of Social Affairs, Henriette Kjær in: Folketingstidende [Official Report of Parliamentary Proceedings], Tredje behandling af Lovforslag nr. L 124: Forslag om lov til ændring af lov om social service (Pædagogiske læreplaner i dagtilbud til børn), 2004)

Thus, there were two arguments for implementing a national educational curriculum into Danish day care institutions. One was elevating children from families with poor school skills (similar to the argument for the American Head Start Program). Another was to give a boost to all children (based on the idea of empowering the nation by empowering the education of the population). In other words, those problems that the schools had not been handling successfully were now to be tackled earlier, by the day care institutions (Kofod, 2019).

In terms of this latter argument, curriculum, evaluation schemes, tests and other assessment technologies used in children's day care could easily be considered as techniques designed to compensate for inadequate parenting. At the same time, however, these measures were an attempt to raise the educational level of the nation by using a more instrumental approach to policy-making. In this case, the professional staff were nudged in a particular direction. When Danish politicians intervened at the level of pedagogical practice in day care institutions with the intention of raising the academic level in schools, they reformulated the very meaning of the Danish day care. Day care children were now to be considered 'school children in the making'.

Conclusion

In this chapter, I I have paid attention to the political level arguing how the idea of early childhood education in day care challenged the well-established understandings of Danish nurseries and kindergartens. Using a discourse analytic approach, it was shown how ideas of early childhood education came to challenge the existing understanding of a holistic and child-centred approach for pedagogical work in Danish day care. The analysis offers an understanding of why early childhood education has not been a 'plug and play' endeavour in Denmark given the historical and cultural context.

However, investigating the political framework, it seems to have been easier to establish the legal basis for day care as a school-supporting institution than it was to implement the legislation into day care practice. Even though not all political parties emphasised the idea of a national education curriculum in 2003, the national education curriculum bill was passed with a clear majority. The bill was considered as good politics, in sync with the international attention to education. At present, the political debates about the national educational curriculum have addressed the quality of the curriculum. In 2018, this emphasis resulted in a reformulation of the legislation (Law no. 554 of 29 May 2018). There seems to be a disillusionment with the 'learning outcomes' approach, and the ideological pendulum regarding day care seems to have swung back to a broader understanding of 'being a child in day care'. As Jakob Sølvhøj (spokesman for The Red-Green Alliance) put it during the negotiation:

> We make a clear break with the preschool and learning thinking, which until recently has been politically dominant, in favor of a childhood vision that highlights childhood as a value in itself.
>
> (Folketingstidende [Official report of parliamentary proceedings]:
> 1. Behandling af lovforslag nr. L 160, 28 February 2018)

The 'new and strengthened' national educational curriculum (Law no. 554 of 29 May 2018) is an attempt to play down the acquisition of academic skills as the primary element of children's day care. The goal now is to allow room for at least some elements from 'the old day care'. In the new national educational curriculum, child-initiated play is recognised as an important part of day care activities. However, Danish day care is still organised by six areas of learning (Law no. 554 of 29 May 2018). The question remains as to how the 'new and strengthened' national educational curriculum will affect the everyday life of day care institutions, both the daily activities of the children and the work tasks of the pedagogues. Regardless of these changes, children's day care persists as a political and pedagogical battleground.

Notes

1 Day care institutions have a long history in Denmark. In terms of legislation targeting poor people, the care of children formed part of poverty relief (Ellegaard, 2000; Grumløse, 2017). Later kindergartens based on ideas and theories of Froebel and also Montessori were established (Ellegaard, 2000). Thus, there was a wide variation in the early Danish day care institutions.
2 The Ministry of Family Affairs was established in 1966, and for the next two years, the country's Minister of Family Affairs was a Social Democrat, Camma Larsen-Ledet (1915–1991). The Ministry of Family Affairs was abolished in connection with the Social Democrat Jens Otto Kragh's transfer of power to the right-wing government in 1968. Subsequently, family policy issues were administered by the Ministry of Social Affairs. In 2004, the Ministry of Family and Consumer Affairs was established. It was abolished in 2007.
3 According to this: In 2014 18 per cent of the children aged 0–1 years were in day care. Some of these children were in small units with a few children in private homes. In Danish terms: "dagpleje" (Danmarks Statistik, 2015).

References

Aabro, C. (2018). *Koncepter i pædagogisk arbejde*. Copenhagen: Nota.

Befolkningskommissionen. (1936). *Foreløbig betænkning vedrørende børnehave spørgsmålet m.v.* Befolkningskommissionens Betænkninger nr. 1.

Befolkningskommissionen. (1937). *Laan til Boligbyggeri og Huslejefradrag for mindrebemidlede børnerige familier.* Befolkningskommissionens Betænkninger nr. 2.

Befolkningskommissionen. (1938). *Moderens rettigheder i anledning af fødsel samt angaaende seksualoplysning.* Befolkningskommissionens Betænkninger nr. 3.

Bowlby, J. (1952). *Maternal Care and Mental Health*. Geneva: World Health Organization.

Børne- og Ungdomsforsorgens pædagogiske Nævn. (1963). *Betænkning fra Børne- og Ungdomsforsorgens pædagogiske Nævn om Børnehaveproblemer.* Betænkning nr. 337.

Børnekommissionen. (1981). *Børnekommissionens betænkning.* Betænkning nr. 918.

Børneloven. (1905). Lov nr. 72 om behandling af forbryderske og forsømte Børn og Unge Personer. Stadfæstet af H.M. Kong Christian IX. Den 14. April 1905.

Christoffersen, M. N. (2004). *Familiens udvikling i det 20. århundrede: demografiske strukturer og processer.* Copenhagen: Socialforskningsinstituttet.

Ellegaard, T. (2000). *Én institution – forskellig barndom: sociale forskelle i børnehaveliv.* Copenhagen: Nota.

Danmarks Statistik (2015): *Nyt fra danmarks Statistik.* 1. April 2015. nr 162.

Fogh Jensen, A. (2013). *Mellem ting: Foucaults filosofi.* Copenhagen: THP.

Foucault, M. (2001). *Talens forfatning.* Copenhagen: Hans Reitzels Forlag.

Foucault, M. (2005). *Vidensarkæologien.* Århus: Philosophia.

Grumløse, S. P. (2014). *Den gode barndom: dansk familiepolitik 1960–2010 og forståelsen af småbarnets gode liv.* Doctoral dissertation, Roskilde University.

Grumløse, S. P. (2017). *Den gode barndom.* Copenhagen: Hans Reitzel.

Juhl, P. (2018). Early childhood education and care in Denmark: The contested issue of quality in children's everyday lives. In S. Garvis, S. Phillipson, & H. Harju-Luukkainen (Eds.), *International Perspectives on Early Childhood Education: Early Childhood Education in the 21st Century* (*Vol. 1*). London: Routledge.

Kofod, K. K. (2019). Daginstitutioner under forandring: Glidninger i organisation, ledelse og styring. In: Moos, Lejf (Ed.), *Glidninger 'usynlige' forandringer inden for pædagogik og uddannelser* (pp. 88–106). Århus Universitet, DPU.

Kommissionen vedrørende kvindernes stilling i samfundet. (1966). *Forsørgerbegrebet. Studier i familiens retlige problemer.* Betænkning nr. 440.

Kommissionen vedrørende kvindernes stilling i samfundet. (1967). *Bilag 1. psykologiske kønsforskelle. En gennemgang af den psykologiske litteratur om forskelle mellem kvinder og mænd.*

Kommissionen vedrørende kvindernes stilling i samfundet. (1970). *Betænkning vedrørende Familiens og børnenes tilpasning.* Betænkning nr. 575.

Kommissionen vedrørende kvindernes stilling i samfundet. (1972a). *Betænkning vedrørende kvinders stilling på arbejdsmarkedet.* Betænkning nr. 668.

Kommissionen vedrørende kvindernes stilling i samfundet. (1972b). *Betænkning vedrørende ligestilling.* Betænkning nr. 673.

Kommissionen vedrørende kvindernes stilling i samfundet. (1974). *Betænkning vedrørende kvindernes stilling i samfundet.* Betænkning nr. 715.

Marschall, A. (2019). Children's well-being – a joint effort? Collaboration about children's well-being across the contexts of family life and kindergarten. In Garvis, S., & S. Phillipson (Eds.), *Early Childhood Education in the 21st Century – engaging families and communities.* (Vol. 2) (pp. 47–58). London: Routledge.

Ministeriet for Familiens anliggender. (1967). *Betænkning vedrørende økonomisk støtte til mødre med spædbørn*. Betænkning nr. 464.

Ministry of Social Affairs in consultation with the Ministry of Education. (2000). *Early Childhood Education and Care Policy in Denmark – Background Report*. Retrieved from www.oecd.org/education/school/2475168.pdf.

Plum, M. (2014). *Den pædagogiske faglighed i dokumentationens tidsalder: læreplaner, dokumentation og styring på daginstitutionsområdet*. Frederikshavn: Dafolo.

Togsverd, L. (2015). *Da 'kvaliteten' kom til småbørnsinstitutionerne*. Doctoral dissertation, Roskilde University.

6 Early childhood education policy, teachers' professionalism and family practices in Estonia

Tiina Peterson, Tiia Õun and Aino Ugaste

Introduction

The aim of the chapter is to provide an overview of how the education policy, qualification, work conditions and training of Estonian preschool teachers as well as their partnership with parents affect the professionalism of preschool teachers and the quality of preschool education in a multicultural context. Several contextual changes have taken place in the Estonian preschool system in the past ten years. After the regaining of independence, the educational system began to be democratised. The individuality of each child and the creation of an environment that would support development began to be emphasised instead of collectivist education also in preschool education (Kööp, 2013). The approach to learning has changed both in the national curriculum of preschool child care institutions as well as in the organisation of kindergartens and local municipalities. Early childhood education and care (ECEC) professional work is closely connected to society functions (Bronfenbrenner & Morris, 2006; Tudge, Mokrova, Hatfield, & Karnik, 2009). In connection with the development of the society and the change in the national curriculum, the focus in Estonian kindergartens has shifted from teachers to learners and children are viewed as active learners, and teachers are viewed as the creators of the educational environment and the supporters of children's individuality (*Koolieelse lasteasutuse riiklik õppekava*, 2008).

The central strategical aim of education in Estonia is to apply in all educational stages an approach that supports the individual and social development of every learner. The attainment of this aim requires competent and professional teachers (*Eesti elukestva õppe strateegia 2020*, 2014). The professionalism of preschool teachers is influenced by the national curriculum in Estonia, the system of teacher education, in-service training and motivation, the conditions for providing preschool education as created by local municipalities, the leadership and work organisation in preschool child care institutions. The teachers can develop their professionalism and apply their knowledge in specific practical situations in cooperation with children, parents and colleagues. Professionalism then can be understood as an attribute of the entire system, developed in its reciprocal relationships (Urban, 2010). Understanding the complexity of professional knowledge and practice is an important step for all practitioners wishing to improve the quality of their practice (Dayan, 2010).

Directions of educational policy in early childhood education in Estonia

Research demonstrates that participation in early childhood education programmes can have a positive impact on children's academic achievements at school (Belfield, Nores, Barnett, & Schweinhart, 2006). High-quality early childhood education is necessary for the child for the participation in further lifelong education, for social integration and for self-development. Increasing the quality of early childhood education everywhere in the EU is of primary importance in ensuring sustainable and inclusive economic growth (European Commission, 2014). Based on the Estonian Lifelong Learning Strategy, flexible opportunities need to be developed for all children to participate in preschool education. According to Estonian Education Information System (EHIS), 93.6 per cent of children aged 4–6 years and 77 per cent of children aged 1.5–3 years attended institutions of early childhood education in 2017. An additional 10 per cent of 1.5–3 year olds and 2 per cent of 4–6 year olds were covered by child care. Brannen and Moss (2003) have emphasised that the quality of preschool education depends primarily on the education of teachers and on their skills to employ theoretical knowledge in practice. Based on the 'Proposal for Key Principles of a Quality Framework for Early Childhood Education and Care' report by the European Commission (2014), professional standards for preschool teachers and childminders in Estonia are being established. Standardisation, including the evaluation criteria for the quality of child care and preschool education, at the level of local governments is in process. Priority is given to the improvement of the national curriculum for preschool institutions and better integration of pre-primary and primary education for the smooth transition from kindergarten to school. The purpose is to investigate how well the objectives and content of learning and education in different subject fields and the expected outcomes of the development of 6–7-year-old children are connected with the national curriculum of basic schools.

Preschool curricula should be based on the child-centred approach, where the focus is on the needs, interests and experiences of children, and where teachers use child-centred teaching methods which support the comprehensive development of children (European Commission, 2014). Several researches have focused on interaction between teachers, children and parents (Kuisma & Sandberg, 2010; Sheridan, Williams, & Sandberg, 2013; Sheridan, Williams, Sandberg, & Vuorinen 2011; Vuorinen, Sandberg, Sheridan, & Williams, 2014). The national curriculum of Estonian preschool institutions supports child-centred teaching practice, but studies have demonstrated (Tuul, Mikser, Neudorf, & Ugaste, 2015) that even though most teachers, in their own opinion, have adopted the principles of child-centred education, there are also such teachers who prefer detailed instructions and given guidelines to the decision making freedom. A study on the teaching approaches of teachers in Estonia has demonstrated that in their activities, teachers pay more attention to creating a positive atmosphere in the group and to making the material taught understandable for children than to creating opportunities for children to make choices, study independently or interact each other, Teachers in general follow the principles of the child-centred approach presented in the national curriculum; however, they also use the adult-led approach (Kimer, Tuul, & Õun, 2016). Thus, in implementing the national curriculum, teachers should pay more attention to the process of interaction, children's initiative, communication between children and the implementation of child-centred principles.

Teachers' work conditions, qualification and professionalism

The work conditions and the qualification of preschool teachers have the greatest influence on the quality of preschool education and on whether changes in training, leadership or conditions of employment make the most significant differences to children and the outcomes of ECEC. Several documents emphasise that for ensuring high-quality preschool education, teacher education must rely on child-centred approaches, and the learning process and the learning environment organised by teachers should be child-centred (United Nations Educational, Scientific and Cultural Organization (UNESCO), 2000b). The development of high expectations requires all staff to be trained for their role and responsibilities. This includes training to work in multidisciplinary teams, to work with parents and members of the community, and to recognise their own competences and skills through a process of reflection and discussion (European Commission, 2014).

In Estonia, the qualification requirements of preschool teachers include higher education (Bachelor's degree). Sixty-seven per cent of teachers and 98 per cent of principals have a higher education degree equivalent to the Bachelor's degree. Universities provide higher education in the specialised subject area of early childhood education for Bachelor's, Master's and doctorate studies, and pursue research in educational sciences. In teacher education, it is recommended to avoid educating narrow and one-sided technical experts who only teach certain subjects and prepare children for school (Oberhuemer, 2005; Van Laere, Peeters, & Vandenbroeck, 2012). In teacher education and in ensuring pedagogical quality, the development of moral and philosophical beliefs also plays a major role (Dahlberg & Moss, 2005). By relying on the Estonian Qualifications Framework, teachers' professional standards based on competencies are being developed. All teacher training graduates can undergo an induction year during which they are supported by their colleagues and mentors, and they have the opportunity to participate in the support programme offered by the institutions of higher education.

According to the Preschool Child Care Institutions Act (*Koolieelse lasteasutuse seadus*, 1999) and with the objective of ensuring a safe educational environment for children, the work organisation of the staff of a preschool institution is based on the following principle. Teachers have 35 work hours in their work week, including the time for preparation and reflection with their team. During the whole work time of a preschool group there is a person employed in the field of learning and teaching or an employee assisting a teacher for up to seven children. This means a maximum ratio of 1:8 in nursery groups and 1:12 in kindergarten groups. According to Dennis and O'Connor (2013), the teacher–child ratio, a measure of structural quality, is also associated with process quality, as measured by better teacher–child interactions, less restrictive teacher behaviour, and children engaging in more complex language interactions and play, and with more sensitive and responsive teachers. Higher staff ratios are more likely to facilitate positive and responsive interactions among adults and children on an individual and a group level (European Commission, 2014). In Estonian kindergarten groups, two ways of organising work are used. First, there is one teacher and two teacher's assistants. Second, there are two teachers and one teacher's assistant. The studies of work organisation have demonstrated that teachers do not feel that they are the pedagogical team leaders. Teachers need more competence concerning pedagogical leadership, including teamwork in the group, how to enable children to make choices, communicate with children individually and support smaller adult–child ratios, and how to involve teachers' assistants in the learning process (Peterson, 2017; Peterson et al., 2016).

The professionalism of teachers in Estonia is described by seven processes: interaction, family involvement, the planning of education and the evaluation of children's development, the use of teaching strategies, the support for professional development, the creation of a growth environment and the development of values (Peterson et al., 2016). The same aspects are important in the 'Quality Framework for Early Childhood Education and Care' report by the European Commission (2014). According to the studies (Peterson et al., 2014, 2016; Tuul, Õun, & Botvina, 2018) there are two main areas that should be focused on more in terms of educational policy. First, there are an increasing number of families in Estonia who have a different cultural and language background. Teachers lack cooperation experience with such families. Studies have also revealed that the existing experiences of kindergarten teachers regarding cooperation with families also need to be developed. Estonian teachers need more knowledge and skills in how to encourage family members to participate in educational activities, how to create possibilities for families to learn and to support one another, and how to promote family involvement in the community (Peterson et al., 2016). Thus, the challenges related to multicultural preschool education and to cooperation with families in Estonia will be addressed more thoroughly.

The implementation of multicultural preschool education

In preschool education, the appreciation of a multicultural educational environment and the development of tolerance in preschool age are increasingly prioritised

(UNESCO, 2000a). The aspect of multicultural education is an important area in teacher education, in the preschool curriculum, in teaching and in cooperation with parents. It is emphasised in the EU that high-quality pre-school education is supportive of social inclusion and diversity and that the needs and culture of different families are respected (European Commission, 2014). In preschool education, there should be a culturally responsive approach to respect the diversity of learner characteristics and backgrounds. The education of teachers is stressed in connection with this aspect – qualified teaching staff know how to be empathic towards the families' and children's cultural backgrounds when these were different from their own (European Agency for Special Needs and Inclusive Education, 2016).

According to the national curriculum of preschool child care institutions in Estonia, in planning and performing educational activities teachers take into consideration children's special characteristics such as capabilities, linguistic and cultural background, age, etc. Teachers also pay attention in teaching both to the appreciation of Estonian cultural traditions as well as to the consideration of the peculiarities of other cultures. If the child's native language is not Estonian, studies of Estonian are offered to him/her at the preschool, which take place by separate language teaching, by integrating language learning with other activities or by using the methods of language immersion (*Koolieelse lasteasutuse riiklik õppekava*, 2008). In earlier studies on the implementation of the curriculum, the implementation of the principles of multicultural education in Estonian kindergartens has also been studied as an aspect. In 2009, observations of the quality of the learning environment in preschool classrooms were made in 30 preschool classes (Õun, 2009). The results revealed that the principle set in the national curriculum – introducing other nationalities and cultures – had been paid little attention in the environment of the studied preschool classes. In 2008, a written survey was conducted among 308 Estonian preschool teachers. It appeared from the survey that in teachers' own assessment they seldom organised events introducing various cultures in their kindergarten and they do not always know how to take the specificity of the family into consideration (Õun, Ugaste, Tuul, & Niglas, 2010). Thus, in Estonia, in teacher education special attention should be paid to multicultural education, the specificities of the multicultural learning environment should be explained and suitable teaching methods should be introduced.

In multicultural preschool education, language studies are one of the primary areas, since children's knowledge of the language supports their cognitive development. Language studies are supported by various bilingual educational programmes that help children to cope with the acquisition of several languages and at the same time support the adjustment with the other culture (Derman-Sparks & Ramsey, 2009). In order to ensure Estonian language studies to all non-Estonian-speaking children they have to be enabled a place in a child care institution. In 2013, a study was conducted among children of new immigrants, their teachers, parents and classmates, to learn about their assessments regarding social relationships at school and coping with their studies (Kasemets, Asser,

Hannust, & Rahnu, 2013). The study revealed that the views of new immigrant parents, their children and the children's classmates about the atmosphere at school and in the class were positive. On the positive side, the new immigrants stressed factors related to school and learning. On the negative side, unpleasant issues related to the strange language and cultural environment were mentioned. In summary, the study revealed that the school and the positive experience gained from the school could serve as an important support mechanism for students from other countries and could mitigate the difficulties related to being in a strange cultural environment. According to the OECD report (2017), the challenges of preschool education lie in the partnership of the early child care institution with parents and the community.

Engaging families and communities

The family is the most relevant and natural educational environment where children grow and develop, because it is the task of parents to ensure the wellbeing and development of each and every child. Estonian families are characterised by increasing socioeconomic, cultural and religious diversity. Families have to cope with new challenges in the society (unemployment, migration, poverty). Parents often feel helpless in solving various problems related to children's upbringing. However, at the same time it has been noted in recent years that the assessments of parents regarding the time spent with their children have become higher and parents (especially fathers) spend more time with their children (Hansson & Ugaste, 2012).

According to the development plan for children and families, the children and family policies up to now have focused primarily on alleviating the symptoms of various problems while dealing with the causes of the problems has not been adequately addressed (*Laste ja perede arengukava*, 2011). To support the sustainability of the society, one of the strategic aims states that Estonia is a country supportive of positive parenting where necessary support is offered in children's upbringing and in being a parent, in order to improve children's quality of life and future prospects in life. In the new implementation plan for the years 2015–2018, an important measure involves available and high-quality preschool education and child care service that would enable the combination of work and family life. The aim is to create new child care facilities and to support the offering of services to children aged 0–7 years and to develop preschool education and the child care system.

Parents have the right and obligation to make decisions regarding their child's preschool education. According to the Preschool Child Care Institutions Act (*Koolieelse lasteasutuse seadus*, 1999), Estonian child care institutions support the child's family, contribute to the raising and development of children and to the consideration of the children's individuality. According to the National Curriculum of Preschool Child Care Institutions (*Koolieelse lasteasutuse riiklik õppekava*, 2008), one of the key principles in conducting educational activities is the cooperation between the home and the child care institution.

Preschool teachers usually have a specific type of communicative competence that enables children and parents to feel confident in talking to them (Sheridan et al., 2013). The cooperation between preschool teachers and parents should be based on a dialogue, on mutual trust and respect. Teachers regularly inform parents about the development of their child and about the organisation of educational activities. Parents in their turn are allowed to participate in the planning and implementation of the educational process and to provide feedback to the child care institution.

Studies have revealed that Estonian preschool teachers find the involvement of parents in the everyday life at preschools increasingly important, and they also emphasise the communication among parents (Veisson & Suur, 2011). The results demonstrated that teachers are the key people in cooperation the aim of which is to support parents and advise the family in educational issues. Parents wish teachers to contact them, talk to them individually and advise them on various educational issues. The development interview is views as a good form of cooperation and the interview is conducted at least once a year with the child's parent(s) about the development of the child and a suitable form of cooperation is also meetings. It has appeared in research that principals and teachers assessed higher than parents the involvement of the latter in the educational process (Suur & Veisson, 2012). Teachers also valued highly open door days, training seminars and educational activities for parents. Principals placed higher value on the use of various IT means in communication, while teachers and parents preferred face-to-face communication. Compared to teachers and principals, parents are more critical of the organisation of educational activities.

The assessments of teachers regarding the cooperation between the preschool and the family have been compared internationally (Veisson et al., 2010). It appeared that teachers in Estonia and Iceland see the need for cooperation and communication, while in Finland they see the need for trust and respect, and in Portugal the need to consider the child's individuality and wellbeing. Teachers in Finland, Iceland and Estonia considered parents' meetings to be an important method of cooperation while teachers in Portugal considered individual conversations important. It is noted in the OECD report (2017) that it remains a challenge for preschool education to establish a partnership of the child care institution with parents and the community, so that cooperation could be strong and interested parties could be informed about the activities of the child care institution. The involvement of the community as also being responsible is also important for cooperation because the community could be viewed as the connecting link between the child care institution and the family.

Conclusion

According to the European Commission (2014), from the educational policy perspective it is relevant to ensure the availability and quality of preschool education that is supported by staff training and development and good leadership.

Good work conditions create well-motivated individuals who have the time and resources they need to support children and to work with their parents and members of the community. It is important to adapt training to meet the needs of the staff who are working with children from low-income families and minority ethnic backgrounds, as this significantly benefits children.

In Estonia, preschool education is ensured to most of children aged 3–6 years, and there are requirements established concerning the education of kindergarten teachers as well as a national curriculum to ensure the quality of primary education. At the same time, studies have revealed several aspects that more attention needs to be paid to in the organisation of preschool education in Estonia, in the work of the staff and in the content of pedagogical activities. The teacher assistants and childminders of kindergarten and child care institutions need better training in supporting the general skills of children. The professionalism of preschool teachers needs more support regarding the avoidance of cultural stereotypes in learning and educational activities, enabling children to take personal responsibility for creating a caring growth environment and enabling the children's smooth transition from kindergarten to school. Teachers and principals need more support to enhance their competence in addressing pedagogical leadership and human resource management issues. Family involvement is a challenge in the development of the quality of preschool education. Teachers need more knowledge and skills in how to encourage family members to participate in learning and in educational activities, create possibilities for families to learn and to support one another, and promote family involvement in the community.

The professionalism and the professional development of teachers are priorities of the Estonian teacher policy for 2014–2020. Programmes at Estonian universities have undergone significant changes in the recent past, and these changes seem to be of a positive nature. The universities have a common platform that unites the effort across the university and provides the opportunity for an interdisciplinary approach. The methods and forms of preschool teachers' initial training are modern and multifaceted, with an emphasis on student-centred approaches, and teaching and learning are supported by current technologies. Better integration of pre-primary and primary education is important in improving the national curriculum of preschool child care institutions so that the transition from kindergarten to school is smooth. Ensuring a smooth transition is also a challenge for the initial and in-service training of preschool teachers and primary teachers. According to the Estonian Lifelong Learning Strategy 2020 (*Eesti elukestva õppe strateegia 2020*, 2014), the role of preschool teachers is of key importance in carrying out changes. Their image in society needs to change as well: salaries must be more competitive and work organisation must be such that working as a preschool teacher would be highly valued in society. The objective in Estonian educational strategy is to make the evaluation and compensation of teachers and leaders in early childhood education proportional to their professional qualifications and their effectiveness in performing their tasks.

Funding

The study is a part of the research project launched in Estonia and led by Ivor Goodson, IUT18-2 'Teachers' professionality and professionalism in changing context' (2014–2019).

References

Belfield, C. R., Nores, M., Barnett, S., & Schweinhart, L. (2006). The high/scope Perry Preschool Program. *Journal of Human Resources 41*(1), 162–190.

Brannen, J., & Moss, P. (2003). *Rethinking Children's Care*. Philadelphia, PA: Open University Press.

Bronfenbrenner, U., & Morris, P. A. (2006). The bioecological model of human development. In W. Damon & R. M. Lerner (Eds.), *Handbook of Child Psychology* (pp. 793–828). New York: Wiley.

Dahlberg, G., & Moss, P. (2005). *Ethics and Politics in Early Childhood Education*. Oxford: Routledge Falmer.

Dayan, J. (2010). Towards professionalism in early childhood practicum supervision – a personal journey. In C. Dalli & M. Urban (Eds.), *Professionalism in Early Childhood Education and Care. International Perspectives* (pp. 153–170). New York: Routledge.

Dennis, S. E., & O'Connor, E. (2013). Reexamining quality in early childhood education: Exploring the relationship between the organizational climate and the classroom. *New York Journal of Research in Childhood Education 27*(1), 74–92.

Derman-Sparks, L., & Ramsey, P. G. (2009). A framework for culturally relevant, multicultural, and antibias education in the twenty-first century. In J. L. Roopnarine & J. E. Johnson. (Eds.), *Approaches to Early Childhood Education* (pp. 120–146). Upper Saddle River, NJ: Pearson.

Eesti elukestva õppe strateegia 2020. (2014). [The Estonian Lifelong Learning Strategy 2020]. Tallinn: Sotsiaalministeerium.

European Agency for Special Needs and Inclusive Education. (2016). *Inclusive Early Childhood Education: An Analysis of 32 European Examples.* Denmark: Odense.

European Commission. (2014). *Proposal for Key Principles of a Quality Framework for Early Childhood Education and Care.* Brussels: European Commission.

Hansson, L., & Ugaste, A. (2012). Social change and Estonian parents' time allocation to their children. *Journal of Comparative Family Studies, 43*(4), 583–599.

Kasemets, L., Asser, H., Hannust, T., & Rahnu, L. (2013). *Uusimmigrantõpilaste akadeemiline ja sotsiaalne toimetulek Eesti üldhariduskoolis* [Academic and social success of the newly-migrant students in the Estonian school]. Tallinn: Mind Park.

Kimer, M., Tuul, M., & Õun, T. (2016). Implementation of different teaching approaches in early childhood education practices in Estonia. *Early Years 36*(4) 368–382. doi:10.10 80/09575146.2015.1118443.

Koolieelse lasteasutuse riiklik õppekava. (2008). [National Curriculum of Preschool Child Care Institutions]. Riigi Teataja I, 23, 152.

Koolieelse lasteasutuse seadus. (1999). [Preschool Childcare Institutions Act]. Riigi Teataja, 27, 387.

Kööp, K. (2013). Estonia: Socio-historic and political influences on the early childhood education and care system. In J. Georgeson & J. Payler (Eds.), *International Perspectives on Early Childhood Education and Care* (pp. 64–75). Maidenhead: Open University Press.

Kuisma, M., & Sandberg, A. (2010). Preschool teachers' and student preschool teachers' thoughts about professionalism in Sweden. In C. Dalli & M. Urban (Eds.), *Professionalism* in *Early Childhood Education and Care. International perspectives* (pp. 186–195). New York: Routledge.

Laste ja perede arengukava 2012–2020. (2011). [The Development Plan for Children and Families 2012–2020]. Tallinn: Sotsiaalministeerium.

Oberhuemer, P. (2005). Conceptualising the early childhood pedagogue: Policy approaches and issue of professionalism. *European Early Childhood Education Research Journal, 13*(1), 5–16.

Organisation for Economic Co-operation and Development (OECD). (2017). *Early Learning Matters.* Paris: OECD Publishing.

Õun, T. (2009). Quality of learning environments in Estonian preschools. *Problems of Education in the 21st Century, 15,* 118–124.

Õun, T., Ugaste, A., Tuul, M., & Niglas, K. (2010). Perception of Estonian preschool teachers about the child-centered activities in different pedagogical approaches. *European Early Childhood Education Research Journal, 18*(3), 391–406.

Peterson, T. (2017). Professionalism of Estonian preschool teachers in the European context. In T. Geraint (Ed.), *Professionalism: Perspectives and Practices of the 21st Century,* (pp. 123–144). New York: Nova Science Publishers.

Peterson, T., Veisson, M., Hujala, E., Härkönen, U., Sandberg, A., Johansson, I., & Kovacsne Bakosi, E. (2016). Professionalism of preschool teachers in Estonia, Sweden, Finland and Hungary. *European Early Childhood Education Research Journal, 24*(3), 136–156.

Peterson, T., Veisson, M., Hujala, E., Sandberg, A., & Johansson. I. (2014). The influence of leadership on the professionalism of preschool teachers in Estonia, Sweden and Finland. In A. Liimets & M. Veisson (Eds.), *Teachers and Youth in Educational Reality* (pp. 119–142). Frankfurt am Main: Peter Lang Verlag.

Sheridan, S., Williams, P., & Sandberg. A. (2013). Systematic quality work in preschool. *International Journal of Early Childhood 45*(1), 123–150. https://doi.org/10.1080/03004430.2014.929861.

Sheridan, S., Williams, P., Sandberg, A., & Vuorinen. T. (2011). Preschool teaching in Sweden – a profession in change. *Educational Research 53*(4), 415–437. https://doi.org/10.1080/00131881.2011.625153.

Suur, S., & Veisson, M. (2012). Teacher-principal-parent understanding of partnership in early childhood education: A comparative study. In J. Mikk, M. Veisson, & P. Luik (Eds.), *Lifelong Learning and Teacher Development* (pp. 58–77). Frankfurt am Main, Berlin, New York, Oxford, Wien: Peter Lang Verlag.

Tudge, J. R. H., Mokrova, I., Hatfield, B. E., & Karnik. R. B. (2009). Uses and misuses of Bronfenbrenner's bioecological theory of human development. *Journal of Family Theory & Review 1*(4), 198–210.

Tuul, M., Mikser, R., Neudorf, E., & Ugaste, A. (2015). Estonian preschool teachers' aspirations for curricular autonomy – the gap between an ideal and professional practice. *Early Child Development and Care 185*(11–12): 1845–1861.

Tuul, M., Õun, T., & Botvina, U. (2018). Hea Alguse programmi rakendavate ja mitterakendavate rühmade õpetajate hinnangud oma tegevusele lapsekeskse kasvatuse kontekstis. Eesti Haridusteaduste Ajakiri [Perception of step by step and non-step by step preschool teachers about the child-centred activities]. *Eesti Haridusteaduste Ajakiri, 6*(1), 102–135.

United Nations Educational, Scientific and Cultural Organization (UNESCO). (2000a). *Framework for Action on Values Education in Early Childhood.* Paris: UNESCO.

United Nations Educational, Scientific and Cultural Organization (UNESCO). (2000b). The Dakar Framework for Action: Education for All: Meeting Our Collective

Commitments 2000. Adopted by the World Education Forum, Dakar, Senegal, 26–28 April. Paris: UNESCO.

Urban, M. (2010). Dealing with uncertainty: Challenges and possibilities for the early childhood profession. In C. Dalli & M. Urban (Eds.), *Professionalism in Early Childhood Education and Care. International Perspectives* (pp. 4–21). New York: Routledge.

Van Laere, K., Peeters, J., & Vandenbroeck, M. (2012). The education and care divide: The role of the early childhood workforce in 15 European countries. *European Journal of Education, 47*(4), 527–541.

Veisson, M., Einarsdottir, J., Gardarsdottir, B., Gaspar, F. M., Hujala, E., & Suur, S. (2010). A cross-cultural qualitative study of parent-teacher partnership in child care in Estonia, Finaland, Iceland and Portugal. In J. Mikk, M. Veisson, & P. Luik (Eds.), *Teacher's Personality and Professionalism* (pp. 31–52). Frankfurt am Main, Berlin, New York, Oxford, Wien: Peter Lang Verlag.

Veisson, M., & Suur, S. (2011). Estonian preschool teachers' vision about cooperation with parents. In M. Veisson., E. Hujala., P. K. Smith., M. Waniganayake., & E. Kikas (Eds.), *Global Perspectives in Early Childhood Education: Diversity, Challenges and Possibilities* (pp. 367–382). Frankfurt am Main, Berlin, New York, Oxford, Wien: Peter Lang Verlag.

Vuorinen, T., Sandberg, A., Sheridan, S., & Williams, P. (2014). Preschool teachers' views on competence in the context of home and preschool collaboration. *Early Child Development and Care 184*(1), 149–159. https://doi.org/10.1080/03004430.2013.773992.

7 Playing to learn in Finland

Early childhood curricular and operational contexts

Jonna Kangas, Heidi Harju-Luukkainen, Annu Brotherus, Arniika Kuusisto and Liam Gearon

Introduction

In this chapter, we outline the definition of play-based learning in both Finnish and international literature as well as describe how Finnish early childhood education and care (ECEC) curriculum guidelines describe play. Further, we describe play activities in early childhood education practices from the viewpoints of operational cultures and the learning environment. We use both content analysis of the national curriculum as well as observational data in order to illustrate the national play-based learning context. We use mixed methods design, where various types of data sets are in a dialogue to complement and confirm the findings from each other. This provides wider and more in-depth information of play-based learning orientation in the Finnish ECEC context. Finally, we take a critical perspective on the Finnish operational cultures and suggest developmental objects.

Curriculum for ECEC guides the practical implementation of the caring and education of young children's growth and overall development. It also guides how, for example, children's play and further play-based pedagogy is viewed. During the recent years, the Organisation for Economic Cooperation and Development (OECD) has taken the initiative to explore the contrasts and complexities of the different national policies and approaches to ECEC. In this examination, Bennett (2005) has distinguished two broad categories between the national settings, particularly visible in Europe, as the pre-primary tradition (e.g. Belgium, France, Ireland, UK and the US) focusing on cognitive goals and 'readiness for school' as important aims, and the social–pedagogic tradition (e.g. Nordic countries, many parts of Central Europe) focusing more on children's play and social development with an emphasis on children's agency. This latter approach defines the developmental aims more broadly, enabling the staff to tailor the ECEC programme to local settings and to base assessment on more varied objectives than set results. This same notion can be found in the latest research by Toom and Husu (2016), claiming teachers are considered as autonomous and trusted when choosing, designing and implementing their teaching methods and pedagogical activities. As such approaches are directly linked to different perceptions of childhood, the OECD and researchers (Bodrova, 2008) have expressed concerns that there is a risk of too much emphasis on formal teaching and other 'schoolification'. Referring to the United Nations convention on the Rights of the Child, the OECD advocates an understanding of the curriculum in which the children should have a high degree of initiative and agency, and stresses the reinforcing of 'those aspects of curriculum that contribute to the wellbeing and involvement of the child' (Bennett 2005, 7; also Dahlberg 2005, pp. 228–229; Rainio, 2010).

Definitions of play-based learning

Recent research has found that social competence is a requirement for successful play, because play includes active carrying out of negotiations and agreements between facts and fiction. Therefore, play has been seen as a dynamic and dialogical process in an imaginary environment (Møller, 2015). According to Wood (2010), pedagogical play refers to the use of play in early childhood education in promoting the learning of young children (see also Lester & Russell, 2010; Sefton-Green et al., 2015). Playful activities and free play are shown to have a role in the development of children's self-regulation skills. Skills such as enactment into learning activities through creativity and goal-setting for learning through independent initiatives and choice making were shown to be developing in the context of play-based learning environment with the participatory teaching approach of teachers (Kangas, Ojala, & Venninen, 2015).

International research and policy documents (Hedges & Cooper, 2018) also suggest that teachers should practice pedagogy that facilitates learning through play. Further, that there is a discrepancy concerning play and how it should be implemented in educational practices (McInnes, Howard, Miles, & Crowley, 2011). The empirical data from research on developmental psychology are consistent with the neo-Vygotskian analysis of the role of adult mediation in the development of children's motives for play.

Finnish ECEC context

In Finland, every child (ten months to six years old) has a subjective right to participate in public ECEC (Finnish Law of Early Childhood Education, 2018). One of the key principles of the ECEC system is universalism, meaning that everyone should have access to good-quality services (Paananen, Repo, Eerola, & Alasuutari, 2018). In 2015 68 per cent of four year olds, 76 per cent of five year olds and almost 100 per cent of six year olds participated in ECEC (Karila, Kosonen, & Järvenkallas, 2017; Organisation for Economic Cooperation and Development (OECD), 2015). In the working team there is at least one teacher with an academic Bachelor's degree and one to three adults with lower educational degrees. Teachers' commitment to the learning situation creates sensitivity towards children's feelings and personal wellbeing. Children are considered active agents when the staff implement educational activities and assessment on more varied objectives than set results through participatory pedagogy (Kangas et al., 2015). The role of parents in early education is also considered strong, and staff should practice open and dialogic education to emphasise parents' participation in the services (Finnish national core-curriculum of ECEC, 2016). It is however argued that teachers have a limited understanding of how to address people with different family, social and ethnic backgrounds (Layne & Dervin, 2016) and Lastikka and Lipponen (2016) have proposed new reflectional models to support parents' participation, including a twice-yearly discussion about the child's interest, strengths and competencies (Finnish Law of Early Childhood Education, 2018).

The role of children in the curriculum (2016) is described as active agents and composers of meaningful learning experiences (Karila 2008). When implementing the Finnish national core-curriculum of ECEC (2016) teachers must ensure that children's initiatives and actions are taken into account. It suggests that teachers support and guide children to become conscious of their own learning. Teachers are advised to listen to children, provide them with opportunities to show initiatives, let children decide on their activities, explore, draw conclusions and express their thoughts (Kangas et al., 2015).

Research methods

In this chapter we use both content analysis on the national curriculum as well as observational data in order to illustrate the national play-based learning context. In a research aiming to shed light into child perspectives, utilising merely a singular method is often insufficient for grasping a holistic view on the examined phenomena. Mixed methods designs (e.g. Tashakkori & Teddlie, 1998), where various types of data are set in a dialogue to complement and confirm the findings from each other (Brooker, 2001; Denzin & Lincoln, 2000), can work to provide wider and more in-depth information.

In terms of ethical considerations, our study was committed into adhering to both national and international guidelines on research ethics, including those set by the Finnish National Advisory Board on Research Ethics (2002), with special considerations to research with young children.

Curriculum data

The curricula document was analysed through qualitative content analysis (e.g. Cohen, Manion, & Morrison, 2011, pp. 564–569). In all, documents provide a rich though often underused source of data for educational research. Documentary research holds a critical position in the development of social science. Research on document sources has particular applicability in educational sciences, as educational systems consistently produce excessive amounts of documentary data (Punch & Oancea, 2014). In the field of curriculum research, critical theory has held an influential role. Cohen, Manion and Morrison (2011, p. 35) write: 'It has been argued for many years that the most satisfactory account of the curriculum is given by a modernist, positivist reading of the development of education and society.' As the curricular expression of this, they refer to Tyler's (1949) influential rationale for the curriculum, including four questions:

- What educational purposes should the school [here the ECEC] seek to attain?
- What educational experiences can be provided that are likely to attain these purposes?
- How can these educational experiences be effectively organised?
- How can we determine whether these purposes are being attained?

(Cohen et al., 2011, p. 36)

The policy document level and the day-to-day implementation may not always meet in the way the policy makers have aimed for. Therefore, in connection to curriculum studies, it is also notable to ask, to what extent do these document-level guidelines actually become practical-level reality in the early childhood education settings and, even more so, local settings. Yang and Li (2018) have examined cultural ideology matters in early childhood education curricula across cultural settings by utilising a three-level model by Adamson and Morris (2014), including (1) the intended curriculum, (2) the implemented curriculum and (3) the curriculum ideology.

Observational data

As a second data for this chapter, we use observational data. The data was gathered in 2014–2015 through observation (field notes, photos, video recordings) and interviews related to children's play-related activities in a context of three ECEC centres located in a large Finnish municipality. The sample included 30 3–6-year-old children (16 girls and 14 boys). The video-recorded data (almost 23 hours) was transcribed. Also, separate space–time paths were transcribed for each of the participating child. Finally, based on the photos (240 pictures), ECEC unit-specific visual maps were created for the operational environments representing the physical contexts of the play. The video-recorded observation in the ECEC took place in the mornings (8.00–11.30) and afternoons (13.30–15.00). One video camera was permanently located in a separate play room which was for the children's use only, generally with no teacher or adult presence. This might be seen a setting more free from adult rules, enabling more child agency in organising and carrying out their own free play (Riihelä, 2007). The other camera was set in the general operational spaces. Besides video-recorded observance data, the researchers made notes in field diaries (six notebooks) based on non-participative observation in each of the ECEC centres and took photos of children's play-related activities.

Findings

How is play defined in ECEC curriculum in Finland?

In the Finnish national core-curriculum of ECEC (2016) the word 'play' occurs 55 times, however, only twice as a chapter heading. The conception of play from the national core-curriculum (2016) is that play creates joy and pleasure and thus is a motivating activity and not a tool to achieve learning goals. In relation to the main concept of learning, the core-curriculum states:

> The concept of learning is based on the conception about a child as an active agent of her own learning. Play is therefore seen as meaningful for the learning of children. The concept of learning is based on holistic approach and learning happens when children play, explore, move around, take care of the learning environment as well as through self-expression and creativity.
>
> (p. 20)

However, when playing children are not learning through cognitive assignments but more through the way of being, living and perceiving the world. The elements that are combined through play are enthusiasm, cooperation and challenging personal skills and competences. Play itself is seen as a motivating and joyful action, where children are learning different skills and knowledges. Children are naturally curious and they are willing to learn (Finnish national core-curriculum of early childhood education and care, 2016, p. 14.)

A core-curriculum emphasises that play has an intrinsic value for children, but has an essential role in pedagogics to support learning, wellbeing, and development. In this the play is described as an element where learning and action are the foundation. The curriculum defines the concept of guided play, where teachers use play as a medium of learning, but also it emphasises the concept of self-initiated play to describe children's free activities. Kangas et al. (2015) have identified guiding principles for early years based on the national curriculum. These principles are the autonomy, exploration, social competence, self-expression, self-control and participation emerging through play and action.

The role of play is also emphasised in the context of learning communities as following:

> An operational culture that encourages children to play recognises the significance of play for a child's well-being and learning. The staff recognises factors that set limits to play and develop approaches and learning environments that promote playing. The children and staff have the opportunity to experience the joy of doing things together and playing together.... Room, time and peaceful settings are given to children's initiatives for playing, experiments and experiences. Playing children and adults are given an opportunity to concentrate on play.
>
> (Finnish national core-curriculum of early childhood education and care, 2016, p. 29)

Practices of play

In the following we describe the play activities in ECEC practices from the viewpoints of operational cultures and the learning environment.

Operational cultures have been defined in the Finnish national core-curriculum of ECEC (2016, p. 46) as 'historically and culturally evolving way of doing things, which develops in the interaction of the community'. The operational culture in the Finnish ECEC context is therefore the holistic practice of implementing early education within one preschool. The concept of the operation culture is defined in the national core-curriculum of ECEC (2016, p. 48) and is described to be 'culture that encourages children to play recognises the significance of play for a child's well-being'. Characteristic of the operational culture in Finland is an alternation of both guided and non-guided activities but also (according to our finding from the observations of this study) that children don't expect adults to participate in play-based activities if they happen in classroom or outside.

Viewed from the organisational culture, the conception of the child as an active agent who are masters of play, mastering of the play was visible. Children could quite freely enter play-based activities, and negotiate and solve problems on their own. They seemed to be competent in testing their skills and understanding. In case 1, children are testing their skills of building machines together and solving social problems.

Case 1: Our team (9:32 am at class)

Five four and five-year-old boys have created constructions with H-blocks. Soon they have set up two artillery lines facing each other. They start shooting the other line with loose blocks (see Figure 7.1).

Figure 7.1 Artillery lines in action (picture image Finland).

However, they discover that the side with three players is always winning and the other side is always losing and therefore that side is giving up. Then 5-year-old Aron begins the problem solving. He switches from one side to the other, balancing the power distribution of the play. All players seem to be pleased with the solution and the 'losing' side warmly welcomes Aron to join their side (Video-observation, ECEC centre 1, class of three to five year olds).

Play activities are sometimes considered to have less meaning to children's learning. Traditional ways of implementing ECEC are shown to happen when the time-schedule for the day is planned by teachers and the focus is on the preset flow of learning goals (see Kangas & Brotherus, 2017). Both Aras (2016) and Leinonen, Brotherus and Venninen (2014) have shown that teachers let children play self-initiated games before classes to increase their motivation towards teacher-initiated classroom activities.

The conception of learning here might be suggestive as something more – there is, for example, evidence to suggest that play is itself foundational to the formation of patterns of social activity and relationships (Riihelä, 2007). Such learning takes place with and without adult supervision. Learning through play happens both among young peers with or without adults in the vicinity. Riihelä's (2007) notion of play as an important originating source of social activity seems therefore to be in need of refinement from the data collected here. In our conceptualisation of playing to learn, this indicates a complex interaction of early childhood peer learning along with adult (here teachers') supervisory guidance. Bondioli (2001) thus similarly suggests 'the adult as a tutor in fostering children's symbolic play'. According to the observations, children would sometimes require more teacher participation in their play. Children made regular contact with teachers and showed them meaningful play episodes and items. Sometimes they also sought guidance, like in the case 2 below, where two four-year-old boys were getting only verbal guidance from their teachers who were not in the same room.

Case 2: Whose house is this? (08:40 am at class)

Tommy and Timothy are entering to a block play with legos. They are observing and exploring a big box of legos. The teacher who is sitting next to the door is brushing the hair of a girl and reminds them to build a representation of their own home.

TOMMY: Hey, teacher, My house is ready?
TEACHER [DON'T LOOK AT THE BOYS]: Did you finished the house already?
TOMMY: yeee … Timothy: I am not ready yet.
TOMMY: Me neither!
TIMOTHY: Why did you ask for the teacher then?

Boys continue building. Tommy adds several pieces in his constructions and is the whole time calling somebody to look at his work saying 'look at me, look at me'.

TOMMY: Hey, teacher, My house is ready!
TEACHER [IN THE OTHER ROOM]: Bring it to me.

Teacher and Tommy stop for a moment in front of his house.

TEACHER: Who could live in this house?
TOMMY GOES BACK TO TIMOTHY AND SAYS: I have to put a family in here.

Timothy breaks his house and starts again. It has to be higher for a family.
                              (Observation diary, ECEC centre 1, class of 3 to 5 year olds)

While the teachers were absent it was also common that children didn't have
the skills to involve themselves in play. Children could wander around the play
area and spend time. Children were lightly observing toys or chatting with
each other. Building a long-lasting play would require making plans and implementing them in peaceful conditions, for three and four-year-old children
teachers' engagement and participation would create more meaning and help
to create long-lasting play. A few times during our observations the children
were involving themselves in play fully and were within their imaginary world.

Case 3: New proposal (9:12 am behind the classroom)

Henry has entered the classroom with his mother and the teacher is greeting
him warmly. Henry looks around and the teacher seems to be guessing what he
is looking for.

TEACHER: Would you like to play with James and Benjamin? They are in the
     second room [behind the classroom]. You can join them, if you wish?

Henry smiles and nods happily. He waves to his mother and runs to his friends
who have been constructing a castle with wooden blocks.

HENRY: Hey! What are you doing?

Boys explain about the castle but do not seem enthusiastic about it. Henry
looks a moment on the construction.

HENRY: We have to tear it down! (see Figure 7.2.)

The unexpected proposal seems to inspire the boys. All three jump on the castle
and start kicking it down and laughing. The noise summons an assistant teacher
to them.

ASSISTANT TEACHER: Henry! What are you doing?
JAMES AND BENJAMIN: No, no! This was our decision. It is a construction work.

Figure 7.2 We should tear it down! (picture image Finland).

Boys laugh and assistant teacher accepts the explanation and leaves boys to their play.

(Video-observation, ECEC centre 2, class of 3 to 5 year olds)

The new curriculum is setting goals for views on children as competent particip-ants of self-initiated play activities. While the results from our research show that the play activities are secondary related to teacher-initiated and routine activities, in future teachers will need to pay more attention to these existing routines and ideas about play, and develop, through reflective practices, existing pedagogical supports to play-based activities (see Kangas & Brotherus, 2017; Kangas et al., 2015). This will support children's active agency and participation as a whole.

The learning environments of the Finnish early childhood education have been designed to support the daily schedules in the classrooms. The national curriculum of ECEC (2016) defines that education is not only teaching and cognitive processes, excluding other activities. This holistic approach means that the entire day is meaningful for the child. Therefore three warm meals are served to children and they have a chance to sleep in their classrooms after lunch. These care activities are a part of the Finnish ECEC and they set require-ments for classroom design. On the other hand, research findings suggest that learning environments are designed for both guided and non-guided activities. There are several corners, small rooms and secret spots for self-initiated play for children in Finnish ECEC centres, while the guided activities are often com-pleted within circle-time (sitting on the floor) (see Kangas & Brotherus, 2017). However, Kangas and Brotherus (2017) have shown that children have to learn to play and use their environment (materials, places and time) without the support of teachers and that there are rules to justify ways of play. A common item in Finnish classrooms is the 'wall of play' where children find the available activities and they choose one activity with their name tag (Figure 7.3).

Figure 7.3 A typical 'wall of play' in a classroom in Finland (picture image Finland).

During the observation period from April 2014 to November 2015, the play environment didn't change or it was not developed in the ECEC centres. It was designed to be safe for children's play and to make room for independent initiatives and learning, but children's personal skills and competences were not taken into account. During drama play there are always the same dresses despite the popular media and children's culture, and the home play corners were from the 1950s, without microwave ovens or dishwashers. During the observation period we found a couple of environments set by teachers, like in case 4 below. Every time teachers made an effort to plan and set up an environment, children became inspired about the play possibilities.

Case 4: Airport in the classroom (9.50 am in classroom)

Five children aged three and four years have been left behind in the classroom to wait their turn to go to the gym hall. On the other side of the wall the teacher is focusing on the drawing activity with older children, but three of children are restless and don't want to focus on this. They take their papers and come to classroom. With them is a young trainee assistant who is on his second day in the classroom.

TRAINEE ASSISTANT: Do you know how to make paper airplanes? Do you want me to show to you?
CHILDREN: Airplanes? Wow! Can we really?

Trainee makes a couple of planes and shows the children how to use them. The children try to make their airplanes fly, but aiming high enough is challenging and the planes end up crashing each time.

LIDIA: We need … something up?
CALVIN: Like, like … like airport!
TRAINEE ASSISTANT: Could this table serve as an aircraft carrier [pulls the table in the middle of the room]?

Children are confused about the concept of aircraft carrier, but Lidia ventures to stand up on the desk. She holds the hand of trainee assistant, focuses and throws the airplane. Plane flies beautifully to the other side of classroom.

The children are soon involved in the play. They are climbing up to the desk, aiming and throwing the planes and then picking them up to start over again (see Figure 7.4). The play develops further.

(Video-observation, ECEC centre 3, class of 3 to 5 year olds)

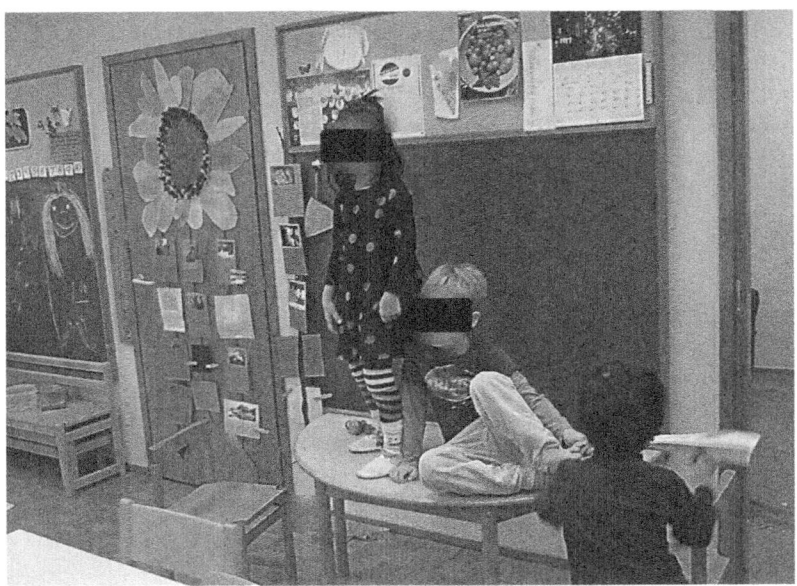

Figure 7.4 Aircraft carrier (picture image Finland).

Conclusion

Even though play-based learning is understood to be one of the key factors in Finland, it does not seem to have a strong presence in the National Curriculum Guidelines for ECEC (mentioned as a word only 55 times). However, the concept of play-based learning and teaching is quite new in Finnish teacher education, where previously play has been mainly a focus of observation that gives information about children's competences and skills. Teachers' competencies need to supported so that they see themselves as active enablers and supporters of children's play activities. Therefore, up-to-date research from the Finnish context is also needed.

According to our observations, play-based activities were often seen as a self-initiated activity of children where teachers didn't participate that actively. However, teachers were responsible for setting up the environment and controlling the routines and schedules in the background. The national curriculum of ECEC (2016) describes the significance of play for children's wellbeing. However, this did not fully emerge through existing practices and the balance between non-guided and guided activity requires more critical reflection and development. Play creates shared joy and motivation and should not emerge only as a tool to achieve learning goals. Children were considered as active agents of their learning. They had freedom to involve themselves in self-initiated activities of play that created chances to solve problems meaningfully and, therefore, teachers' presence was not needed. This, however, might lead to situations where adults may even be quite unaware of many elements of play that are taking place in the children's 'subculture' in the ECEC context (Köngäs, 2018).

Based on our research findings we suggest that play-based activities in ECEC are considered through participation, wellbeing and learning of both an individual child and children in joint meaning making. Different experiences in play offer possibilities to construct thinking processes and practice different skills. The ECEC operational culture should therefore be further developed through constructing new approaches and solutions into the pedagogical environments for play. These would better enable or support and enrich the pedagogical practice of play as learning. Furthermore, the practices and routines related to supporting children's play in the ECEC could thereby be re-evaluated and further developed in order to develop the quality of play as an environment for and of learning. Merely focusing on the further development of physical structures is not, however, enough. The key to change into better support for children's play seems to derive from renewing the cultural practices and structures in the ECEC which view play as part of children's learning, not only of instrumentalist knowledge and skills as learners in institutional contexts but as a zone of peer-to-peer engagement which is quite foundational to their ability to survive and thrive in later life. This provides a chance for critical development but also a more complex enrichment in the understanding of limited, pragmatic models of play in narrow instrumental terms. By developing teachers' involvement in play-practices it is possible to develop a better quality of play as learning in early childhood curriculum settings. It provides yet further opportunities for exploring the insights of play as a function of personal and social life too across a range of disciplines.

References

Adamson, B., & Morris, P. (2014). Comparing curricula. In M. Bray, B. Adamson, & M. Mason (Eds.), *Comparative Education Research: Approaches and Methods* (pp. 309–332). Hong Kong: Comparative Education Research Centre, University of Hong Kong; Springer.

Aras, S. (2016). Free play in early childhood education: A phenomenological study, *Early Child Development and Care, 186*(7), 1173–1184. doi.org/10.1080/03004430.2015.1083558.

Bennett, J. (2005). Curriculum issues in national policy-making. *European Early Childhood Education Research Journal, 13*(2), 5. doi.org/10.1080/13502930585209641.

Bodrova, E. (2008). Make-believe play versus academic skills: A Vygotskian approach to today's dilemma of early childhood education. *European Early Childhood Education Research Journal, 16*(3), 357–369. doi.org/10.1080/13502930802291777.

Bondioli, A. (2001). The adult as a tutor in fostering children's symbolic play. In A. Göncu & Klein, L. (Eds.), *Children in Play, Story, and School* (pp. 107–131). New York: Guilford Press.

Brooker, L. (2001). Interviewing children. In G. McNaughton, Rolfe, S., & I. Siraj-Blatchford (Eds.), *Doing Early Childhood Research: International Perspectives on Theory and Practice* (pp. 162–177). Buckingham: Open University Press.

Cohen, L., Manion, L., & Morrison, K. (2011). *Research Methods in Education*. London: Routledge.

Dahlberg, G. (2005). *Ethics and Politics in Early Childhood Education*. London: Routledge.

Denzin, N. K., & Lincoln, Y. S. (2000). *Handbook of Qualitative Research*. Thousand Oaks, CA: Sage Publications.

Finnish Advisory Board on Research Ethics. (2002). *Good Scientific Practice and Procedures for Handling Misconduct and Fraud in Science*. Hyvä tieteellinen käytäntö ja sen loukkausten käsitteleminen. Finnish Advisory Board on Research Ethics. Retrieved from www.tenk.fi/sites/tenk.fi/files/HTK_ohje_2012.pdf.

Finnish Law of Early Childhood Education. (2018). 540/2018, set in Helsinki 13th of July, 2018.

Finnish national core-curriculum of early childhood education and care. (2016). Määräykset ja ohjeet 2016: 17. Tampere: Finnish National Agency for Education.

Hedges, H., & Cooper, M. (2018). Relational play-based pedagogy: Theorising a core practice in early childhood education. *Teachers and Teaching, 24*(4), 369–383. doi.org/10.1080/13540602.2018.1430564.

Kangas, J., & Brotherus, A. (2017). Osallisuus ja leikki varhaiskasvatuksessa: 'Leikittäisiin ja kaikki olis onnellisia!'. In A. Toom, M. Rautiainen, & J. Tähtinen (Eds.), *Toiveet ja todellisuus: Kasvatus osallisuutta ja oppimista rakentamassa* (pp. 197–223). Turku: Finnish Educational Research Association.

Kangas, J., Ojala, M., & Venninen, T. (2015). Children's self-regulation in the context of participatory pedagogy in early childhood education. *Early Education and Development, 26* (5–6), 847–870. doi.org/10.1080/10409289.2015.1039434.

Karila, K. (2008). A Finnish viewpoint on professionalism in early childhood education, European *Early Childhood Education Research Journal*, *16*(2), 210–223. doi. org/10.1080/13502930802141634.

Karila, K., Kosonen, T., & Järvenkallas, S. (2017). *Varhaiskasvatuksen kehittämisen tiekartta vuosille 2017–2030. Suuntaviivat varhaiskasvatuksen osallistumisasteen nostamiseen sekä päiväkotien henkilöstön osaamisen, henkilöstörakenteen ja koulutuksen kehittämiseen. Opetus- ja kulttuuriministeriön julkaisuja* [The roadmap for developing early childhood educatiin Finlanda 2017-2030. A framework for increasing the participation rate in early education services and the development of the professional skills, teacher ratios and teacher education programs. Finnish Ministry of Education and Culture] 2017:30. Helsinki: Lönnberg Print & Promo.

Köngäs, M. (2018). *'Eihän lapsil ees oo hermoja': etnografinen tutkimus lasten tunneälystä päiväkotiarjessa. Rovaniemi: Lapin yliopisto* ['Kids don't have nerves': Ethnographic research about children's emotional intelligence in early childhood education settings]. Doctoral thesis. Acta Universitatis Lapponiensis 368.

Layne, H., & Dervin, F. (2016). Problematizing Finland's pursuit of intercultural (kindergarten) teacher education. *Multicultural Education Review, 8*(2), 118–134.

Lastikka, A. L., & Lipponen, L. (2016). Immigrant parents' perspectives on early childhood education and care practices in the Finnish multicultural context. *International Journal of Multicultural Education, 18*(3), 75–94. doi.org/10.1080/2005615X. 2016.1161290.

Leinonen, J., Brotherus, A., & Venninen, T. (2014). Children's participation in Finnish pre-school education – identifying, describing and documenting children's participation. *Nordisk Barnehageforskning, 7*(8), 1–16. doi.org/10.18251/ijme.v18i3.1221.

Lester, S., & Russell, W. (2010). *Children's Right to Play: An Examination of the Importance of Play in the Lives of Children Worldwide.* The Hague, The Netherlands: Bernard van Leer Foundation.

McInnes, K., Howard, J., Miles, G., & Crowley, K. (2011). Differences in practitioners' understanding of play and how this influences pedagogy and children's perceptions of play. *Early Years, 31*(2), 121–133. doi.org/10.1080/09575146.2011.572870.

Møller, S. J. (2015). Imagination, playfulness and creativity in children's play with different toys. *American Journal of Play, 7*(3), 322–346.

Organisation for Economic Cooperation and Development (OECD). (2015). *Starting Strong IV: Monitoring Quality in Early Childhood Education and Care.* Paris: OECD Publishing.

Paananen, M., Repo, K., Eerola, P., & Alasuutari, M. (2018). Unravelling conceptualizations of (in) equality in early childhood education and care system. *Nordic Journal of Studies in Educational Policy*, 1–11.

Punch, K. F., & Oancea, A. (2014). *Introduction to Research Methods in Education.* London: Sage Publications.

Rainio, A. P. (2010). *Lionhearts of the Playworld: An Ethnographic Case Study of the Development of Agency in Play Pedagogy*, Doctoral Dissertation. University of Helsinki.

Riihelä, M. (2007). Children's play is the origin of social activity. *European Early Childhood Education Research Journal, 10*(1), 39–53. doi.org/10.1080/13502930285208831.

Sefton-Green, J., Kumpulainen, K., Lipponen, L., Sintonen, S., Rajala, A., & Hilppö, J. (2015). *Playing with Learning. The Playful Learning Center.* University of Helsinki. Retrieved from http://plchelsinki.fi/.

Tashakkori, A., & Teddlie, C. (1998). *Mixed Methodology Combining Qualitative and Quantitative Approaches* (Vol. 46). Thousand Oaks, CA: Sage Publications.

Toom, A., & Husu, J. (2016). Finnish teachers as 'makers of the many': Balancing between broad pedagogical freedom and responsibility. In Niemi, H., Toom, A., & Kallioniemi,

A. (Eds.). *Miracle of Education. The Principles and Practices of Teaching and Learning in Finnish Schools* (pp. 41–55). Rotterdam: Sense Publishers.

Tyler, R. W. (1949). *Basic Principles of Curriculum and Instruction, revised edition.* Chicago, IL: University of Chicago Press.

Wood, E. (2010). Developing integrated pedagogical approaches to play and learning. In P. Broadhead, J. Howard, & E. Wood (Eds.), *Play and Learning in Education Settings.* London: Sage.

Yang, Y. and Li, H. (2018). Cultural ideology matters in early childhood curriculum innovations: A comparative case study of Chinese kindergartens between Hong Kong and Shenzhen. *Journal of Curriculum Studies,* 50(4), 560–585. doi.org/10.1080/00220272.2018.1428367.

8 Beyond transformations and transnational reform movements in educational policy and practice

'Culture' as a framework for critical reflections

Dagmar Kasüschke and Stefan Faas

Introduction: beyond a global culture of education in ECEC

In recent years, national education systems from early childhood education to higher education have increasingly found themselves under intense pressure to reform. Against this background, many countries implementing educational reforms and changes in the education system are making reference to international research findings and trends in order to create a 'new pedagogy' that meets these trends. Some new approaches, such as results-based teaching and learning as well as learning based on prescribed standards, especially in the areas of reading, writing, arithmetic and science, have been applied, although there have been some objections and resistance (Hargreaves, Earl, Moore, & Manning, 2001; Hargreaves & Shirley, 2011; Ramberg, 2014). Many of these strategies and developments are similar in principle (Gogolin, Baumert, & Scheunpflug, 2011) and can be summarised as general aspects of international education reform movements and transnational education policies (Sahlberg, 2011). In other words, the further developments of national education systems and educational policies are becoming increasingly more similar – despite existing criticism and scepticism (see Faas, Wu, & Geiger 2017).

Such adaptations and transformations are often perceived in educational analyses as steps towards a universalisation of education. However, comparative education does not recognise this as a short-term development, but as a long historical process of converging national education systems, which began in the 18th century and experienced various phases of acceleration (Adick, 1992; Amos, Keiner, Proske, & Radtke, 2002). International organisations, such as the Organisation for Economic Cooperation and Development (OECD), have a significant role to play in this regard – not only via the development of programmes and concepts, but also through the prioritisation of these by means of agenda-setting activities, publications and other dissemination strategies. Accordingly, educational standards are discussed worldwide, competence models are used and states participate in student assessment. This process of adaptation has been initiated and furthered in recent years in the field of early childhood education and care, largely thanks to the 'Starting Strong' study commissioned by the OECD. The orientation towards early learning, in particular the concentration on language promotion and early contact with mathematical and scientific content, must be acknowledged in this context (Amos, 2014).

In an effort to explain such processes of universalisation from a neo-institutionalist perspective, reference is made in particular to the ever-present interconnectedness of national states with overarching political, economic and religious developments. For education in particular, this implies a tendency towards interdependence. This explanatory approach is linked to a specific concept of culture, which is theoretically substantiated in the context of world cultural theory (Meyer, 1999; Meyer, Kamens, & Benavot, 2017).

This approach to research and reflection, which focuses primarily on the question of how certain education programmes are disseminated and legitimised, has often been criticised as too simplistic compared to approaches based on aspects such as system theory and phenomenology. Such criticism relates both to the underlying concept of culture and to the neglect of local conditions and culture-specific adaptation processes (e.g. Schriewer, 2003; Steiner-Khamsi, 2004).

Beyond this controversy, there has also been substantial criticism relating to the observable tendencies towards universalisation in the various national education systems – especially in the field of early childhood education and care (e.g. Dahlberg, Moss, & Pence, 2013). There are growing accusations that this universalisation represents a unilateral and ethnocentric perspective in international early childhood education and care (ECEC) policy and programmes. Among other things, this approach is also being discussed as a new form of postcolonialism:

> However, despite growing awareness of the misleading potential of ethnocentric thinking, and the increasing number of publications addressing this issue, much of current developmental research tends to ignore the argument that 'childhood' and 'child development' are cultural constructs, and remains steadfastly ethnocentric.
>
> (Rosenthal, 1999; see also e.g. Andreotti, 2011; Cannella & Viruru, 2004; Nieuwenhuys, 2013; Rizvi, 2007)

It is not possible to resolve these controversies within the context of this chapter, nor is this the aim. Also, on closer inspection, these different approaches are not mutually exclusive but indeed somewhat complementary: they are all able to explain the transformation of national education systems, policies and practices to a certain extent, albeit from very different perspectives and/or with respect to different dimensions (see Amos, 2014). However, it is noticeable that in each discourse the term 'culture' seems to play a key role, although its meaning differs within the wide range of arguments that are pursued.

Against this backdrop, the chapter below focuses on different concepts of culture and its various foundations related to content, theory and research. This is intended to enable the development of an approach or a framework for critical and cultural-sensitive reflection on early childhood education and transnational developments and changes in this context. The chapter describes two selected empirical studies or research perspectives, with the aim of concretising the argument that transnational educational concepts and the results of international comparative longitudinal studies are not simply transferred to national or local contexts. On the basis of these studies, the necessity of clarifying and interpreting general concepts and quantitative empirical results against the background of specific social, cultural and institutional structures and practices shall be demonstrated. The chapter concludes with a discussion of the theoretical and empirical findings.

Concepts of 'culture' – theoretical foundations, reflections and conclusions

In recent decades, the field of cultural studies has been developed as a cross-sectional undertaking within social and educational sciences on an international level. The so-called 'cultural turn' describes the establishment of interdisciplinary research perspectives and the opening up of a wide range of theoretical references and subject fields. Although it is impossible to definitively categorise cultural studies, its importance in relation to (self-)critical educational science cannot be overlooked. As we cannot cover all lines of discussion within cultural studies in the following sections, we will instead sketch out three arguments concerning the interdependence of culture and migration, culture and identity, and culture and 'doing difference'. This discussion will then be transferred to the context of ECEC and conceptually developed as a reflection framework – for the abovementioned target area.

Culture. Dimensions of meanings of a term

Cultures, migration, society and rules of human cohabitation appear to be developing into the most important challenges facing European community life. Migration movements into European countries are discussed in terms of the changes seen in democratic values and rules, while conflicts in the context of migration are identified as a problem of national affiliation or ethnicity. Recent sociological research has underpinned the importance of clarifying the term ethnicity in order to describe social processes within the context of migration and globalisation. In this chapter, ethnicity as a concept takes on crucial significance when it comes to explaining conflicts and misunderstandings in early childhood education settings.

Wimmer distinguishes four understandings of culture, which can be derived from different scientific approaches (cf. Wimmer, 2013). The first statement is related to cultural anthropology and describes 'ethnicity' as a national affiliation, which understands culture as a consistent system of rules and values belonging to a closed society. The second approach is based on Foucault's theory and represents the key message of theoretical discourses of power in different socio-logical disciplines with respect to aspects such as gender, race and class. In this case, cultural discourse takes place by means of language. The range of terms either broadens or limits our ability to consider the issues at hand. The third additional discourse is initially drawn from neo-institutional economic research, with neo-institutional economic theories arguing that trade relationships are determined by actions and interaction processes between business partners. This is referred to as a 'game of cooperation', meaning that all interacting partners make use of strategies in order to achieve the most success without jeopardising their cooperation. These strategies are known as informal rules that function as a kind of unspoken guide that is not openly discussed, but is nevertheless observed on a social level. In this context, culture is viewed as a set of informal rules for cooperation strategies (Wimmer, 2005). When we look at culture as a system of informal rules for cooperation strategies, we can explain cultural change: whenever cooperation strategies cease to be effective, a new foundation must be established. These considerations lead to a different perspective on culture, which is pursued by this chapter. This approach focuses on the inter-actional processes between people representing themselves in communication. Ethnicity is hereby understood as a changeable concept that takes on varying forms in each new context.

'Culture'. A process of negotiation in interaction

The fourth approach is represented by Jenkins (2008) and Wimmer (2013), ref-erencing Max Weber's *Economy and Society* (1978), who developed their con-cepts of ethnicity in contrast to a closed national or racial concept. In this case, culture is a process of negotiation in interaction. Jenkins (2008) provides the following detailed summary of his 'basic social anthropological model of ethnicity':

- 'Ethnicity is a matter of cultural differentiation – although identification always involves a dialectical interplay between similarity and difference.
- Ethnicity is centrally a matter of shared meanings – what we conven-tionally call "culture" – but is also produced and reproduced during interaction.
- Ethnicity is no more fixed or unchanging than the way of life of which it is an aspect, or the situations in which it is produced and reproduced.
- Ethnicity, as an identification, is collective and individual, externalised in social interaction and the categorisation of others, and internalised in per-sonal self-identification' (p. 14).

Ethnicity is thus explained as an interactive process between individuals and groups. Culture can be illustrated as an action and performance involving people, and can be described as fluid, fuzzy and non-static. This approach refers to social actions and behaviour, but fails to consider processes within the individuals themselves: the next step must therefore be to address how individuals' identification with ethnic affiliation can account for the phenomena that are observed.

In general, identity is understood as a stable personal condition of self-awareness. Since the time of G. H. Mead's theory of symbolic interactionism at the latest, identity has been defined as a balancing process between demands and interpretations of the individual and the social environment (Ziebertz & Herbert, 2009). This begs the question: How is it possible for a person to remain the same in light of the various changes and discrepancies that occur throughout their life cycle? Provided that these problems are reinforced in modern multicultural societies, we can thus ask how people build their identities in social interactions.

Nieke (2011) distinguishes between a collective and an individual identity. From the perspective of human history and developmental psychology, the collective identity evolved prior to the individual identity but is increasingly shorn of its anthropological role in modern societies. The anthropological functions of the collective identity are a sense of purpose and a notion of belonging to a group. In this context, 'sense of purpose' refers to the adherence to and positive socialisation within the system of values and rules belonging to a collective body, while 'belonging to a group' describes processes of allocation to one group and separation from other groups. The collective identity itself is also part of self-awareness.

This collective identity is an unconscious framework established in the early years of childhood. The child's experiences of family values, education and treatment form its collective orientation patterns, which serve as the basis for personal identity. This identity of a person consists of various collective orientation patterns according to gender, age, race, family, peer group, job and living environment. Described by Nieke as the identity rosette, these collective orientation patterns are universal but their specific shape will be formed by socialisation.

These observations can be used to explain clashes between different cultures, especially if the practice of belonging to a specific minority group differs from the values of the majority in a given society. The more the pattern of a family's collective orientation differs from societal values, the more exclusion and separation will be performed on both sides. This model can explain the phenomena of exclusion, separation, integration or inclusion as a double-sided process during socialisation.

The next step is to combine both perspectives, which will enable us to address processes of globalisation and the growing criticism of what some consider to be the new face of postcolonialism in ECEC.

'Culture'. A framework for critical reflections

The conclusion drawn from the preceding sections is to focus on processes of formation, as well as the performance of self-presentation and representation of the counterpart in interaction. Two of the earliest researchers to deal with this approach were West and Fenstermaker in their article 'Doing Difference' (1995). Arguing from a gender studies perspective, they reasoned that difference should not be viewed as a characteristic of individuals but rather as an ongoing interactional performance. In addition, they advocated extending the theoretical reference framework to accommodate an intersectional perspective and noted that these changes of perspective were associated with a variety of different implications.

> First, and perhaps most important, conceiving of these as ongoing accomplishments means that we cannot determine their relevance to social action apart from the context in which they are accomplished. While sex category, race category and class category are potentially omnirelevant to social life, individuals inhabit many different identities, and these may be stressed or muted, depending on the situation.
>
> (West & Fenstermaker, 1995, p. 30)

The second implication is that this perspective does not need any categories for describing differences. It also offers a multifaceted perspective on the actions of individuals, since the same activity can be interpreted separately from the individuals involved. An intersectional perspective at least enables an understanding of the performance of aspects such as gender, ethnicity and class 'as constituted in the context of the differential 'doings' of the others' (West & Fenstermaker, 1995, p. 32). McCall (2005) states that if the nature of differential categories is socially constructed, then

> a wide range of different experiences, identities, and social locations fail to fit neatly into any single 'master' category. Indeed, the premise of this approach is that nothing fits neatly except as a result of imposing a stable and homogenising order on a more unstable and heterogeneous social reality.
>
> (p. 1777)

Based on these lines of argumentation, culture can be considered a process of 'doing ethnicity'. One of the most debated publications in the field, which discusses this subject with reference to Foucauldian discourse analysis and Derrida's deconstruction theory, is Homi K. Bhabha's book *The Location of Culture* (1994). In order to develop our considerations of culture as a means of 'doing difference', it is necessary to highlight some of Bhabha's thoughts on culture and identity. From his point of view, neither culture nor the individual exist per se and the starting point is that of difference itself. Cultures and individuals bear the otherness, the experience of foreignness and the need for translation by themselves beyond the encounter with others (Göhlich, 2010; see also e.g. Drichel, 2008). This otherness is not based in the identities of individuals but will be created as the individual acquires an existence in relation to an otherness. The negotiation in interaction is described as a space of (potential) identification or animosity. Although the encounter with an otherness opens up a space of difference, there is space for negotiation, redistribution and ultimately reconstitution of agency.

What conclusions can we draw from this in relation to ECEC? Against the background of difference-based theoretical approaches, culture can be described as 'doing difference' by means of 'doing ethnicity'. But 'doing ethnicity' is neither a system of characteristic features nor a racial or national belonging to a group. Instead, it can be described as a performance between people representing self and otherness in interaction. Early childhood settings, as well as structures of the education system and policies addressing them, need to be analysed as complex and differentiated cultural contexts from a multifaceted perspective. This refers, among other things, to the need to supplement internationally comparative, quantitative and mostly deductively constructed empirical studies with research and reflection that is inductive and therefore suitable for understanding given structures and practices in the context of cultural negotiation processes. This does not require a specific research method.

Empirical concretisations

The research perspective outlined here takes into account the complexity of education or educational contexts and goes hand in hand with the argument that transnational educational concepts and the results of international comparative longitudinal studies are not simply transferred to national or local contexts. Indeed, it appears necessary to classify general concepts and quantitative empirical results according to specific social or institutional practices and interpret them against this background. Only then will it be possible to understand the proposed changes and their significance for national and local educational contexts, which will in turn enable scientific substantiation of educational policy and conceptual decisions (Moss & Urban, 2010). In the following, two selected studies are presented that refer to this research perspective.

Cultures of parenting in early childhood

The first study is a large cross-cultural study from Germany that researches the different cultural variations of the universal concept of 'attachment', conceptualised by Bowlby (Keller, 2007). Herein, after the background of the study, the research design and methods will be briefly mentioned and their findings will be discussed against the backdrop of our thesis on culture as a process of negotiation in interaction.

Background of the study

Over a period of more than ten years, Keller and her research team studied different cultural contexts of parenting – primarily in two countries; specifically Western middle-class families in Germany and Nso farming families based around the small city of Kumbo in the North-western Province of Cameroon. They analysed different parenting models in order to develop cultural parenting patterns. These results were proofed by additional data collected in Germany, India, Japan, Cameroon and other countries and compared with research studies all over the world (Otto & Keller, 2014).

Research design and methods

This study utilised method triangulation, which centred on participatory observation and standardised questioning. They developed an infancy assessment concerning the social context, the sociocultural orientation, socialisation goals and parenting ethno-theories (Keller, 2007, p. 53). On the basis of the results of the pilot scheme, the research group developed scales for the questioning which extended between two prototypes of educational styles: the 'traditional rural family' type which is oriented towards deep relationships and a hierarchical structure, and the 'urban middle class' type focused on autonomy, self-responsibility and democratic structures. The prototype of autonomy is defined as the mental skill to monitor one's own lifestyle and actions and to lead one's life in self-responsibility. It represents the parenting ideology of Western middle-class families, who focus on the education of an individual personality. Educational goals are to accept the child as it is, to appreciate its wishes and to acknowledge its needs. The priorities of parenting are to promote the child's cognitive skills. Parents treat a child as an autonomous human that has its own wants and desires from the beginning. In this model, the transfer of values follows a horizontal pattern that sees parents asking friends and experts for advice. The idea of asking older people for advice would be considered non-individual and old-fashioned.

In contrast to this model, the prototype of relatedness describes the mental and/or economical relationships and dependencies between people. This prototype promotes fellowship skills and regards the infant as part of a complex relationship matrix, which itself consists of a close network of expectations and obligations. Relationships are organised hierarchically along the lines of age and gender – and they are obligatory. Autonomy is important inasmuch as it refers to the needs and the expectations of the collective. The parenting model, which considers the child to be a trainee, promotes social togetherness. Senior members are treated with obedience and respect. The knowledge and values of the older people, and the transfer of these aspects, is respected and not criticised.

Parents from different countries and different socioeconomic backgrounds were interviewed with this infancy assessment.

Findings

For our object of investigation, two findings are interesting. First cultural differences do not concern national or ethnic affiliation, but can be explained significantly by the factors 'number of children', 'status of formal education', 'economic status' and 'urbanisation level'.

In this case, the concept of culture has nothing to do with an allocation to nations, countries or continents, not to mention concepts of race. Culture is a shared system of interpretation patterns and behaviour patterns that are adapted to the social and economic resources of the environment in which people live.

Second the results of this study show impressively that globalisation of institutional education in early childhood seems to disregard patterns of thinking, acting and communication about education beyond Western industrial societies. This explanatory research sees Keller (2007). (Otto & Keller, 2014) as a critique of the majority discourse in relation to parenting, which is dominated by the prototype of autonomy. Although they indicate that these prototypes are explanatory poles and do not represent the reality of families, it seems obvious that there is an inherent danger of individualist and collectivist parenting patterns being ordered into a hierarchy of sorts – a concept that has been the subject of much criticism in recent decades (Kâğitçibaşi, 1994). Perhaps discussions of this kind, which contrast middle-class families in Western industrial countries with rural families in non-Western rural countries, further illuminate this complex subject more than comparisons between the empirical aspects of 'number of children', 'status of formal education', 'economic status' and 'urbanisation level' as recorded in one country (Sinha & Tripathi, 1994). In any case, the importance of this research into theoretical considerations of cultures of education and 'doing culture' as a process of negotiating meanings, establishing boundaries and agency can no longer be ignored in a changing world.

Educational concepts and practices in different cultural contexts

The second study to be presented here is an investigation by Shu-Chen Wu, Stefan Faas and Steffen Geiger (2018) on the importance of 'learning at play' in various cultural contexts. The qualitative study investigated Hong Kong and German early childhood education professionals' and parents' conceptions and understandings of learning at play. The findings reveal different social and cultural concepts and reflections on educational activities between Hong Kong and Germany. The following account outlines the background to the study, explains the manner in which the research was designed and the methods used, and concludes with the presentation and discussion of the core results.

Background of the study

In Germany, where the first-ever kindergarten was founded, the concept of 'free play' – understood as the opportunity for children to spontaneously choose activities according to their own desires and psychological needs (Flitner, 1972) – is of great importance. In this context, playing is the main activity undertaken by children in kindergartens and the central aspect of early childhood learning. However, this conceptual orientation was critically questioned with the publication of the initial results of the OECD Programme for International Student Assessment (PISA), which put Germany below the PISA average (Gruber, 2006). From an educational and scientific perspective, the subsequent debate centred on whether the kindergarten system in effect in Germany at the time adequately prepared children for school (Oberhuemer, 2012).

Adopting a broader perspective, it is interesting to compare the German model with a completely different cultural setting – in this case, the situation in postcolonial Hong Kong, where pedagogy functions as a hybrid of traditional Chinese teaching methods and contemporary early childhood education (Rao, Ng, & Pearson, 2009). Although traditional Chinese ideas and values play an important role in educational practice (Biggs, 1996), the imported approach of play-based learning in early curriculum policy has been repeatedly endorsed since the 1980s. However, it has been noted that there is a discrepancy between what happens in practice and the educational policies that are adopted (Cheng, 2011), as kindergartens in Hong Kong continue to focus primarily on teaching pre-academic skills (Wu & Rao, 2011).

Research design and methods

Against this background, the empirical study by Wu, Faas and Geiger (2018) described below investigated the following central issues:

1   What characterises the understanding and perceptions of learning at play among pedagogical professionals and parents in Hong Kong and Germany?
2   What are the commonalities and differences?

To clarify these research questions, the kindergartens to be examined, two in Hong Kong and two in Germany, were selected according to the following specified criteria: they are (a) run by non-profit agencies; (b) recognised as ordinary kindergartens in their societies; and (c) comply with curriculum guidelines for mainstream programmes.

It should be noted that 80 per cent of kindergartens in Hong Kong are operated on a non-profit basis (Education Bureau, 2017). The two selected kindergartens were located among public housing in Kowloon and New Territories, where 45.6 per cent of the inhabitants of Hong Kong live (Hong Kong Housing Authority, 2016). On the other hand, in Germany, 33.1 per cent of children's day care centres are publicly owned, 63.9 per cent are non-profit organisations (e.g. churches), and 3 per cent are other independent organisations (i.e. for-profit organisations). In the federal state of Baden-Württemberg, the two publicly owned kindergartens examined in the study are located in an urban area, where 41.9 per cent of the kindergartens are publicly owned, 56.3 per cent are non-profit organisations, and 1.8 per cent are private for-profit organisations (www.laendermonitor.de).

From these four kindergartens, a total of 28 early childhood education professionals and 12 parents participated in the study. In an initial step, 12 kindergarten professionals (six German and six Chinese) were interviewed and observed as they explored their understanding of 'learning at play' in semi-structured interviews. During the observations, the researchers followed the professionals' instructions to film what they regarded as episodes of learning at play. After watching the videos together, the educational staff confirmed the content of the episodes. The researchers edited the video clips accordingly. Four representative three-minute videos from Germany and Hong Kong containing most elements of 'learning at play' were selected. These video clips were subsequently shown to 16 other kindergarten professionals (eight German and eight Chinese) and two parents without a specific migration background (six German and six Chinese) in focus groups as part of a video-based multivocal ethnography (Tobin, Hsueh, & Karasawa, 2009) aimed at eliciting their perspectives on and understanding of learning at play.

Before the videos were shown, however, the pedagogical approach in day care centres in Hong Kong had to be introduced to the German participants and vice versa. Afterwards, the Hong Kong groups first saw and discussed the videos recorded in the kindergartens in Hong Kong, then those from the German kindergartens, while their German counterparts viewed and discussed the videos in reverse order (see Wu et al., 2018).

Findings

An analysis of the data collected demonstrates the pronounced divergences between the practical examples of 'learning at play' as selected by early childhood professionals in Germany and Hong Kong respectively, pointing to fundamental differences in the underlying concepts of learning and playing. These differences correspond to or result from the traditional pedagogy of each country. For example, all the video sequences selected by the Hong Kong experts referred to group activities that were focused on collective learning goals. All children were involved in the respective activities, with each child being supervised by a teacher. Given that both rules and competition are clearly visible, the tightly structured activities can still be identified as playing or as a game. The Chinese teachers emphasised a systematic learning approach focused on learning objectives, the rules of play/games and a specific course of play. In contrast, the German examples were mainly characterised by the dominance of individual activities or activities in small groups. When tasked with selecting 'learning at play' situations in their own pedagogical practices, the German professionals focused on daily activities and less attention was paid to specific learning situations. Furthermore, they emphasised the importance of the environment and the children's own initiative and self-awareness. Their role as educational professionals was shaped by the response to curiosity and autonomy on the part of the children.

However, the results of the group discussions did not demonstrate such clear differences between the German and Chinese participants: the German professionals and parents reiterated the importance of children's own activities and explorations during play, rating the Chinese play activities as too teacher-oriented. They stated that such a concept was not applicable to German kindergartens, especially since they considered making decisions as an autonomous individual to be an important learning factor.

In contrast, the statements of the Chinese teachers and parents were inconsistent: while emphasising the learning approach and the importance of teachers' interventions and guidance during play, they also saw the importance of children's self-initiative and self-experience – aspects that were not shown in their children's play episodes, but which did appear in those of their German counterparts. Even though this led them to provide a somewhat positive assessment of the German play activities, they also voiced critical opinions concerning their transferability to early childhood education as practiced in China. The early education professionals were particularly sceptical about the transferability of German methods (see Wu et al., 2018).

Conclusion

In this chapter, the term 'culture' was discussed with reference to the international globalisation of educational systems and the increasing criticism of this unilateral and ethnocentric development. By discussing different approaches to the term 'culture', this contribution has demonstrated that culture is neither a racial or national affiliation, nor is it something that can be attributed to an individual character or groups of people – instead, it is a social process of representation and negotiation in encounters with otherness.

The anthropological approach of Keller (2007) demonstrates that the explanatory power of empirical items such as 'number of children', 'status of formal education', 'economic status' and 'urbanisation level' are more important in terms of explaining similarities of cultural values and rules of education than any affiliation to a nation or continent. The results of the qualitative study conducted by Wu, Faas and Geiger show that the interpretation and discussion of pedagogical concepts in different cultural contexts, in this case Germany and Hong Kong, is very different in certain areas but also features similarities in other respects. However, the research results make it clear that international developments are primarily assessed within the context of national educational traditions and structures.

In light of these findings, it can be argued that – despite some assimilations and tendencies towards universalisation – international developments and transnational educational concepts have different effects on different educational systems and educational practices, in the context of social and cultural negotiation processes (Faas et al., 2017). It is important that this be taken into account in the context of critical reflection on educational policy developments and changes in education systems and in educational practice. Therefore, in addition to international comparative longitudinal studies, cross-cultural qualitative research focusing on the reception, assessment, implementation and transformation of international trends in national and regional practice is needed. The results of cross-cultural qualitative studies allow a much broader debate on national education systems, in terms of historical developments and normative discourses, which then better serves the complexity of international comparisons. Insights of this kind are also important for a well-considered policy design in this context; when it comes to putting transnational policies and trends in an appropriate relationship to national developments and local practice.

References

Adick, C. (1992). Modern education in 'non-Western' societies in the light of the world systems approach in Comparative Education. *International Review of Education, 38*(3), 241–255.

Amos, S. K. (2014). Globalisierung der Bildung, Bildung der Globalisierung und die Wirkungen einer globalen Perspektive auf die pädagogische Historiographie. In S. Faas & M. Zipperle (Eds.), *Sozialer Wandel. Herausforderungen für Kulturelle Bildung und Soziale Arbeit* (pp. 13–24). Wiesbaden: Springer Verlag.

Amos, S. K., Keiner, E., Proske, M., & Radtke, F.-O. (2002). Globalisation: Autonomy of education under siege? Shifting boundaries between politics, economy and education. *European Educational Research Journal, 1*(2), 193–399.

Andreotti, V. (2011). *Actionable Postcolonial Theory in Education*. Basingstoke: Palgrave Macmillan.

Bhabha, H. K. (1994). *The Location of Culture*. New York: Routledge.

Biggs, J. (1996). Western misperceptions of the Confucian-heritage learning culture. In D. Watkins & J. Biggs (Eds.), *The Chinese Learner: Cultural, Psychological, and Contextual Influences* (pp. 45–67). Hong Kong: CERC & ACER.

Cannella, G. S., & Viruru, R. (2004). *Childhood and Postcolonization: Power, Education, and Contemporary Practice*. New York & London: Routledge-Falmer.

Cheng, P.-W. D. (2011). Learning through play in Hong Kong: Policy or practice? In S. Rogers (Ed.), *Rethinking Play and Pedagogy in Early Childhood Education: Concepts, Contexts and Cultures* (pp. 100–111). London: Routledge.

Dahlberg, G., Moss, P., & Pence, A. (2013). *Beyond Quality in Early Childhood Education and Care: Languages of evaluation*. New York: Routledge.

Drichel, S. (2008). The time of hybridity. Philosophy & social criticism. *Sage, 34*(6), 587–615.

Education Bureau. (2017). Kindergarten education. Retrieved from www.edb.gov.hk/en/about-edb/publications-stat/figures/kg.html.

Faas, S., Wu, S. C., & Geiger, S. (2017). The importance of play in early childhood education: A critical perspective on current policies and practices in Germany and Hong Kong. *Global Education Review, 4*(2), 75–91.

Flitner, A. (1972). Playing—learning. Interpretation of children's play. In Institute for Scientific Cooperation (Ed.), *Education. A Biannual Collection of Recent German Contributions to the Field of Educational Research* (Vol. 7) (pp. 32–46). Tübingen: Göbel.

Gogolin, I., Baumert, J., & Scheunpflug, A. (2011). 'Transforming education'. Large-scale reform projects and their effects—German and international experience. In. I. Gogolin, J. Baumert, & A. Scheunplug (Eds.), *Transforming Education. Umbau des Bildungswesens. Large-scale Reform Projects in Education System and their Effects*. Bildungspolitische Großreformprojekte und ihre Effekte. Zeitschrift für Erziehungswissenschaft. Sonderheft 13, (pp. 1–8). Wiesbaden: VS.

Göhlich, M. (2010). Homi K. Bhabha: Die Verortung der Kultur. In B. Jörissen & J. Zirfas (Eds.), *Schlüsselwerke der Identitätsforschung* (pp. 315–330). Wiesbaden: VS Verlag für Sozialwissenschaften.

Gruber, K. H. (2006). The German PISA-shock: Some aspects of the extraordinary impact of the OECD's PISA study on the German education system. In H. Ertl (Ed.), *Cross-national Attraction in Education: Accounts from England and Germany* (pp. 195–208). Oxford: Symposium Books.

Hargreaves, A., Earl, L., Moore, S., & Manning, S. (2001). *Learning to Change. Teaching beyond Subjects and Standards*. San Francisco, CA: Jossey-Bass.

Hargreaves, A., & Shirley, D. (2011). *The Far Side of Educational Reform*. Ottawa, Ontario: Canadian Teachers' Federation.

Hong Kong Housing Authority. (2016). Housing in figures 2016. Retrieved from www.housingauthority.gov.hk/en/common/pdf/about-us/publications-and-statistics/HIF.pdf.

Jenkins, R. (2008). *Rethinking Ethnicity. Arguments and Explorations*. London: Sage.

Kâğitçibaşi, Ç. (1994). A critical appraisal of individualism and collectivism: Toward a new formulation. In U. Kim, H. C. Triandis, Ç. Kâğitçibaşi, S.-C. Choi, & G. Yoon (Eds.), *Cross-cultural Research and Methodology Series, Individualism and Collectivism: Theory, Method, and Applications* (Vol. 18) (pp. 52–65). Thousand Oaks, CA: Sage Publications.

Keller, H. (2007). *Cultures of Infancy*. New York: Psychological Press.

McCall, L. (2005). The complexity of intersectionality. *The University of Chicago Press, 30*(3), 1771–1800.

Meyer, J. W. (1999). The changing cultural content of the nation-state: A world society perspective. In G. Steinmetz (Ed.), *State/Culture: State-formation after the Cultural Turn* (pp. 123–143). Ithaca, NY; London: Cornell University Press.

Meyer, J. W., Kamens, D., & Benavot, A. (2017). *School Knowledge for the Masses: World Models and National Primary Curricular Categories in the Twentieth Century* (Vol. 36). London: Routledge.

Moss, P., & Urban, M. (2010). *Democracy and Experimentation: Two Fundamental Values for Education*. Gütersloh: Bertelsmann Stiftung.

Nieke, W. (2011). Kollektive Identitäten als Bestandteil von Selbst-Bewusstsein – eine bisher systematisch unterschätze Kategorie im deutschen bildungstheoretischen Diskurs. In J. Bilstein, J. Ecarius, & E. Keiner (Eds.), *Kulturelle Differenzen und Globalisierung* (pp. 51–69). Wiesbaden: Verlag für Sozialwissenschaften.

Nieuwenhuys, O. (2013). Theorizing childhood(s): Why we need postcolonial perspectives. *Childhood, 20*(1), 3–8.

Oberhuemer, P. (2012). Balancing traditions and transitions: Early childhood policy initiatives and issues in Germany. In T. Papatheodorou (Ed.), *Debates on Early Childhood Policies and Practices: Global Snapshots of Pedagogical Thinking and Encounters* (pp. 17–26). London: Routledge.

Otto, H., & Keller, H. (Eds.). (2014). *Different Faces of Attachment. Cultural Variations on a Universal Human Need*. Cambridge: Cambridge University Press.

Ramberg, M. R. (2014). What makes reform work? – School based conditions as predictors of teachers' changing practice after a National Curriculum reform. *International Education Studies, 7*(2), 46–65. doi:10.5539/ies.v7n6p46 .

Rao, N., Ng, S. S. N., & Pearson, E. (2009). Preschool pedagogy: A fusion of traditional Chinese beliefs and contemporary notions of appropriate practice. In C. K. K. Chan & N. Rao (Eds.), *Revisiting the Chinese Learner: Changing Contexts, Changing Education* (pp. 255–280). Hong Kong: The University of Hong Kong, Comparative Education Research Centre/Springer Academic.

Rizvi, F. (2007). Postcolonialism and globalization in education. *Cultural Studies, Critical Methodologies, 7*(3), 256–263.

Rosenthal, M. (1999). Child care research: A cultural perspective. *International Journal of Behavioral Development, 23*(2), 477–518.

Sahlberg, P. (2011). The fourth way of Finland. *Journal of Educational Change, 12*(2), 173–185. doi:10.1007/s10833-011-9157-y.

Schriewer, J. (2003). Globalisation in education: Process and discourse. *Policy Futures in Education, 1*(2), 271–283.

Sinha, D., & Tripathi, R. C. (1994). Individualism in a collectivist culture: A case of coexistence of opposites. In U. Kim, H. C. Triandis, Ç. Kâğitçibaşi, S.-C. Choi, & G. Yoon (Eds.), *Cross-cultural Research and Methodology Series, Individualism and Collectivism: Theory, Method, and Applications* (Vol. 18) (pp. 123–136). Thousand Oaks, CA: Sage Publications.

Steiner-Khamsi, G. (Ed.) (2004). *The Global Politics of Educational Borrowing and Lending*. New York: Teachers College Press.

Tobin, J., Hsueh, Y., & Karasawa, M. (2009). *Preschool in Three Cultures Revisited: China, Japan, and the United States*. Chicago, IL; London: The University of Chicago Press.

Weber, M. (1978). *Economy and Society*. Berkley and Los Angeles, CA: University of California Press.

West, C., & Fenstermaker, S. (1995). Doing difference. *Gender & Society, 9*(1), 8–37.

Wimmer, A. (2005). *Kultur als Prozess. Zur Dynamik des Aushandelns von Bedeutungen*. Wiesbaden: Verlag für Sozialwissenschaften.

Wimmer, A. (2013). *Ethnic Boundary Making. Institutions, Power, Networks*. New York: Oxford University Press.

Wu, S. C., Faas, S., & Geiger, S. (2018). Chinese and German teachers' and parents' conceptions of learning at play–similarities, differences, and (in) consistencies. *European Early Childhood Education Research Journal, 26*(2), 229–245.

Wu, S.-C., & Rao, N. (2011). Chinese and German teachers' conceptions of play and learning and children's play behaviour. *European Early Childhood Education Research Journal, 19*(4), 471–483.

Ziebertz, H., & Herbert, M. (2009). Plurale Identität und interkulturelle Kommunikation. *Interculture journal: Online Zeitschrift für interkulturelle Studien, 8*(7), 11–30. Abgerufen am 12 May 2018 von http://neu.interculture-journal.com/index.php/icj/article/view/74.

9 Early childhood teacher education in Greece

Challenges and opportunities in a centralised education system

Maria Birbili and Melpomeni Tsitouridou

Introduction

Policy-making regarding teacher education is not a straightforward issue of 'establishing "best" policy and practice' (Cochran-Smith, 2013, p. 3). It is a process that is inextricably linked with all other levels of education and one that involves the negotiation of conflicting beliefs about issues such as curricula, the role of schools in society, accountability and the persons and structures that should govern and regulate all these (Cochran-Smith, 2005).

Teacher education's link with 'the complex and contradictory historical enterprise of public mass schooling' (Green, Reid, & Brennan, 2017, p. 40) calls for thinking about the preparation of future teachers as part of a continuum – the starting point of the continuum of the teaching profession. The notion of a continuum of learning implies a coherent, integrated approach to the different levels of education and phases of teacher development (The Teaching Council, 2011). From a policy-making perspective, this should be a collaborative process among all stakeholders based on 'a shared vision, understanding and ownership' (ET2020 Working Group on Schools Policy, 2015, p. 17). Such collaboration would not only ensure that all phases connect but also that different perspectives are heard.

As the teaching profession is increasingly regarded as a continuum, policy makers are faced by bigger challenges in national education systems where the phases of teacher education and development have traditionally been poorly connected. This is the case of Greece. In this chapter, we draw on our experience as teacher educators and empirical studies from the Greek context to discuss how lack of integrated policies and regulations can weaken the teacher education continuum and teacher education departments' effort to educate reflective professionals. We use student field experiences as a case example to demonstrate how Schools and Departments of Early Childhood Education (SECE) try to connect with public kindergartens within a framework of uncoordinated policy making. We begin with a historical overview of Greek early childhood teacher education and a look at the current situation, and we conclude with a discussion on how SECE have responded to the challenges set by both a centralised system and the economic crisis. We argue that difficulties can push teacher education departments to change old practices and seek new ways of supporting students but, without the support of the system, learning to teach will be viewed as a destination rather than the beginning of professional development.

Preparing early childhood professionals: a historical overview

In order to understand the current situation of early childhood teacher education in Greece it is useful to consider its history. By looking at key developments in the field, we can gain an insight into the steps teacher education institutions have taken to 'emancipate' themselves from the past and move forward. We can also identify similarities with other European teacher education systems as we follow the evolution of the Greek system from the first teacher training schools to university departments and Schools of Early Childhood Education (Zgaga, 2013).

Teacher education in Greece goes back to 1837 when missionaries and philanthropists established the first schools for young children and the first all-female training schools for primary teachers (Charitos, 1998). Kindergarten teachers were, in reality, primary teachers who have chosen to 'specialise in nursery education' (Charitos, 1998, p. 252). Candidates were trained for a few months 'in theoretical issues and the kindergarten method' and complemented their knowledge by observing experienced teachers (Charitos, 1998, p. 252). They were taught either the peer-tutoring method (a technique used in the French infant schools of the time) or the Froebelian method or a combination of both. The choice of these two methods reflected the influence of the French and German systems of education either through the foreigners who opened schools in the country or through the first Greek teacher educators who studied abroad (Birbili & Christodoulou, 2018). Although candidates took exams for obtaining a 'specialisation', these were not officially recognised by the state. As Bouzakis, Tzikas and Anthopoulos (1998) note 'preschool teacher training and the recognition of qualifications and titles delayed in as much as the institutionalisation of early childhood education' (p. 42). In the educational legislation the first reference to kindergarten, as part of the public schooling system, was made in 1895. It was not until 1897 that the state recognised the degrees given to those who studied early childhood education (ECE) (Charitos, 1998).

In 1904, the Greek state realised for the first time the need to establish 'schools' exclusively for the preparation of kindergarten teachers. Their programme included courses in 'psychology, didactics, pedagogy, the Froebel method, children's health and the subjects taught in "kinder-gardens"', namely knowledge of the social and physical world, singing, rhythmic games, arts and crafts' (Bouzakis et al., 1998, p. 44). These first training schools were named 'Didaskalia' and their orientation was highly practical. 'Didaskalia' functioned largely unchanged until 1956 when they were developed into 'Higher Schools for kindergarten teachers', institutions that resembled the Pedagogic Academies that had developed 20 years earlier (in 1933) for the preparation of primary teachers. Comparing preschool teachers' education with that of primary teachers, Bouzakis et al. (1998, p. 59) point out that progress regarding preschool teacher education policy was slow and decisions were taken in an offhand way.

In Greece, the year 1982 became a turning point in the education of both primary and preschool teachers. After years of 'struggles and insistence' for more and better teacher training by the national Teachers' Union, the then socialist government transferred teacher education to the universities (Tourtouras, Kyridis, & Karamouzas, 2018, p. 107). It was a change that was also brought on by the movement towards the elevation of teacher education to higher education status in the 1980s around the world (Zgaga, 2013). Until 1988–1989 the old Pedagogic Academies and Higher Schools for kindergarten teachers ran in parallel to university departments.

In a critical review of initial teacher education in Greece, Bouzakis et al. (1998) argued that the abolishment of the old Pedagogic Academies and Higher Schools for Kindergarten teachers marked the end of teacher education's direct dependence on the state. As they explained, until then, teacher training was used by the state to prepare teachers who would serve the current political ideology (p. 79). The state's embracement of teacher education also made it vulnerable to the changing sociopolitical circumstances. As a result, it experienced an uneven course of development: stagnation, modernisation and regression (p. 79). The closure of the old institutions and their replacement with university departments also signalled a change in the mission of Greek teacher education: The era of preparing teachers on the basis of a 'sterile hoarding of information, without scientific identity' was over (Stamelos, 1999, as cited in Tourtouras et al., 2018, p. 108).

Since their inception, teacher education departments – both preschool and primary education departments – faced a number of challenges, which defined their profile (Stamelos & Emvalotis, 2001, p. 3). Some of them were generated by the fact that while teacher education was 'now' enjoying university status it still remained in the hands of one of the most centralised educational systems in OECD member countries (Dimitropoulos & Kindi, 2017). For example, the state increased too fast too soon – largely on populist politics and unionist arguments – both the number of students and the number of departments. In a decade, the first five departments of teacher education became 18, a number which was hard to justify based on the country's actual needs (Stamelos & Emvalotis, 2001, p. 3). Another set of challenges emerged from departments' history. Positioning teacher training within higher education created a 'discomfort' to the host universities and an 'anxiety' to the newly founded pedagogical departments regarding their acceptance, or not, from the university community (Stamelos & Emvalotis, 2001, p. 2). Objections and critiques meant that the departments faced pressure to demonstrate in a shorter period of time that they are academic enough to be part of universities (e.g. through recruiting PhD holders from various disciplines). The new teacher education departments also struggled for a long time to shake off half a century of traditional approaches to teacher training and shape an identity between two 'discreet sectors: educational sciences and teacher training' (Stamelos & Emvalotis, 2001, pp. 6, 7). Notwithstanding these issues, back in 1984, the new university departments constituted an important achievement, since at the time of their foundation only a small percentage of the world's teachers were educated in universities (Tourtouras et al., 2018, p. 110). Furthermore, the upgrading of teacher education into higher education increased not only the duration of the studies but also the status of the teaching profession in the country and teachers' salaries (Tourtouras et al., 2018).

While the preparation of preschool teachers goes back to the 1800s, the training of child care workers began in 1955 with the foundation of the School for Nursery Nurses known as 'Princess Sofia' (named after the young queen Sofia of Spain, who studied there). In 1984, the same year that Higher Schools for kindergarten teachers were repositioned as university departments, 'Princess Sofia', renamed as Department of Nursery Nursing, was integrated into the Technological Educational Institutes (TEI), the vocational sector of Greek higher education. This change was a policy decision grounded in the tradition of the 'split' ECE system which required countries to 'educate' kindergarten teachers in universities and 'train' child care workers in vocational institutions (Organisation for Economic Cooperation and Development (OECD), 2016).

Today, there are three Departments of Nursery Nursing in the country that train candidates to work with children from 0–6 years in child care centres and day care centres, both in the public and the private sector. These candidates go through the training for 3.5 years including six months field experience in day care and child care centres. In 2007, Departments of Nursery Nursing were renamed 'Departments of Preschool Education' in an effort to construct a different identity in the national educational context (Bucholtz & Hall, 2005). In 2018, the TEI Department of Preschool Education in Athens was transferred to the newly founded University of West Attiki.

Schools of Early Childhood Education: 30 years later

Today, there are nine Schools (or Departments) of Early Childhood Education (SECE) around the country that provide candidates with both a four-year Bachelor degree and the qualification that is required for working in public and private kindergartens, in regular and inclusive classrooms. Prospective students enter a School after participating in the highly competitive, state-controlled Panhellenic Exams (or else university entrance exams), in May or June. The majority of candidates are women, a fact that maintains the dominance of female over male early childhood educators in Greek classrooms.

Despite their common history, SECE do not have a common curriculum profile (Avgitidou & Androussou, 2013; Stamelos & Emvalotis, 2001). According to the Greek Constitution and the principle of 'university self-governance', SECE are free to design their own curriculum, both in terms of the content and the time allocated to different parts of it (Stylianidou, Bagakis, & Stamovlasis, 2004).

Although all SECE follow contemporary trends in early childhood theory and practice, which suggests a considerable degree of convergence, each one has its own academic programme influenced by the expertise (or the subject areas) of the available academic staff, staff's research interests and the history of the department's development. On the whole, as Kourti and Androussou (2013) note:

> The curriculum of university Departments of Early Childhood Education is largely dominated by a focus on pedagogy and educational sciences. Students attend courses on general pedagogical knowledge [i.e. knowledge of classroom management], on subject-specific pedagogies (for example, environmental education, special needs education and the didactics of science and mathematics) and on questioning and planning, as well as courses on psychology, social psychology, sociology, history of education and educational politics.
>
> (p. 195)

A common component of all ECE academic programmes are field experiences although there are a number of dimensions that distinguish one programme from another. For example, some programmes include field experiences (more commonly referred to as practicum) throughout the programme, while others offer them in certain semesters. Most SECE follow, in varied forms, a concurrent model of practicum on the basis that it offers a greater integration of classroom and practice. Field experiences take place in public kindergartens, a fact that, as discussed later in this chapter, plays a significant role in both the organisation of the practicum and the quality of experiences offered to student teachers.

One implication of departments' autonomy to plan their own curriculum is the risk of having prospective teachers graduating without having studied certain subjects (or topics or issues), either because they are not covered by staff's expertise and/or research interests, or because the academic programme does not include mandatory courses (Kourti & Androussou, 2013). As there are no state requirements for a common core of subjects and/or skills that all Greek kindergarten teachers should have before entering the profession (e.g. a national competence framework) early childhood education graduates enter the profession with the knowledge and the skills that their departments have provided them with. While this differentiation is in principle positive, lacking a minimum of common ground may present challenges for professionals who have to implement a national curriculum, as is the case in Greece (Birbili & Christodoulou, 2018). On the other hand, departments' autonomy on this issue allows teacher educators to offer courses that are closely linked to their research interests, a practice that is in line with the Humboldtian concept of academic freedom (Altbach, 2011). Tourtouras et al. (2018, p. 112) also make the argument that the existence of differentiating directions among teacher education departments gives each department its own identity and establishes its reputation in the field of teacher education. In the Greek system where higher education institutions 'lack the freedom to define their strategy, to set their own goals and objectives, and to develop operational and action plans' (Dimitropoulos & Kindi, 2017), being able to decide on what they will teach makes teacher educators feel a greater sense of autonomy.

Significant changes in both the curricula and the functioning of SECE were introduced in response to the Bologna Process and the European Union's objectives to improve the compatibility of study programmes and academic qualifications, increase student and staff mobility, and promote quality assurance in higher education. Like other universities in mainland Europe that followed the Humboldt approach to higher education (e.g. Germany and Italy), Greek universities underwent massive and, as Garben (2011, p. 42) puts it, 'sometimes painful reorganisations'.

Among the changes made were the restructuring of academic programmes to comply with the European Credit Transfer System (ECTS), the introduction of the diploma supplement, departments' self- and external evaluation (by the Hellenic Quality Assurance and Accreditation Agency for Higher Education) and the strengthening of the post-graduate cycle of studies. Regarding degree awards, Greek universities have so far resisted the changing of the highly respected four-year degree into the more intensive three-year degree and had already in place a three-cycle system. However, unlike other European countries (e.g. France), a Master's degree is not required for working in public education. It is still considered to be an optional advanced qualification (which unemployment is quickly turning into a highly sought-after degree).

Despite the criticism, voiced both in Greece and other countries, that some governments used the Bologna process 'to pester universities to do things [they] have wanted them to do for years' (Paul Temple, as cited in Palfreyman, 2008, pp. 249–250), the overall impression is that SECE have benefited in several, often unexpected, ways from this process. For example, they had the opportunity to reconsider their place in the European academic landscape and evaluate the existing curricula. There was also an increase in new Master's programmes that raised the quality of studies by strengthening research-based practice and attracted students from other, 'non-teacher' study areas. At the same time, as was feared by 'Bologna-sceptics', the Bologna agenda generated more bureaucracy in an already bureaucratic higher education system (Haukland, 2017; Traianou, 2013). According to some academics, it has also strengthened state control over Greek higher education institutions through introducing a culture of performativity, an act that is frequently described in the literature as an indirect mechanism of control (Sifakakis, Tsatsaroni, Sarakinioti, & Kourou, 2016; Tourtouras et al., 2018). Seen in the context of teacher education, a focus on performance raises the concern whether SECE will continue to struggle against Greek policymakers' habit of forgetting the social and political dimensions of education and focusing on individual effort – a view that implies that teacher quality is a static concept and a practice that conveniently exonerates the system (Mavrogiorgos, 1993; Snoek, 2016).

As SECE are reorganised according to the Bologna Declaration and tensions, ambiguities and difficulties arise, it becomes clear that the Europeanisation of teacher education is a more complex and complicated process than the Europeanisation of higher education in general (Zgaga, 2008, p. 1). One of the dimensions that makes the process more complicated is the fact that very often governments are regulating the teaching profession (Zgaga, 2013). This government involvement, as Zgaga (2013, p. 359) argues, creates a dangerous tension: Teacher education is trying to 'follow the logic of higher education and research' in a context that does not control. In the next section, we discuss this tension using as an example SECE's effort to organise student field experiences within a centralised educational context. We focus on student practicum because it constitutes a core component of SECE's academic programmes in their effort to educate reflective, inquiry-oriented professionals.

As we present the obstacles that both teacher educators and students face during this process, we show how the lack of a comprehensive teacher education policy, and appropriate structures for meaningful relationships between university departments and schools, interferes with the development of a model of initial teacher education that supports teachers across the entire professional continuum (Darling-Hammond, Hyler, & Gardner, 2017).

Finding alternatives within centralised systems: the case of student teacher practicum

In a recent article on clinical preparation in teacher education, Darling-Hammond (2014, p. 549) argues that fieldwork and the relationship between schools and universities are two important pedagogical cornerstones of successful teacher education programmes. Contemporary approaches to teacher professional learning and development view student field experiences as a critical part of teacher education not only because it helps students to integrate the distinctive contributions of the university and school but also because it provides them with the opportunity to understand teaching as a collaborative profession and schools as learning communities. As the dominant image of teachers has changed from autonomous professionals to collegial professionals, there has been a new appreciation of teachers as school-based teacher educators (Conway, Murphy, Rath, & Hal, 2009, p. 45). This perspective has in turn highlighted the need to design and provide teacher education programmes that use a partnership model (The Teaching Council, 2011, p. 10). Evidence suggests that the stronger the partnership the bigger the benefits are for the participants: teachers, pupils, parents, student teachers and teacher educators (Darling-Hammond, 2014; Darling-Hammond et al., 2017).

Of course, developing and maintaining this partnership is, as Murray (2012) says, 'demanding in terms of professional skills and energies, not least because seemingly simple structures need to be underpinned by high levels of trust, and shared values and practices' (p. 21). It also takes time. More importantly however, establishing and maintaining such partnerships requires keeping in mind that collaboration is a social practice and as such it is organised and managed through political and sociocultural discourses, norms and agendas that 'circulate' within national contexts (Chan, 2016). In order to understand what makes these partnerships possible and how they develop, we need to set both teacher education institutions and schools within the broader sociopolitical context.

Student field experiences in the Greek context

Although practicum experiences – their duration, organisation, structure and content – vary among academic programmes due to the reasons mentioned earlier, all SECE share two characteristics: (a) they place student teachers almost exclusively in public kindergartens and (b) they depend on the Ministry of Education (MoE) to provide them with people who can support teacher educators in their work. The two largest SECE in the country, in Athens and Thessaloniki, also have in common large numbers of students (ranging from 100 to 300 over the past two years). These three parameters mediate both students' experiences and teacher educators' work and influence the impact of the practicum programme on student learning. We discuss them in turn with a focus on how the policy context challenges relationships, practices and outcomes.

For nearly 20 years SECE had built a working relationship with professionals in the field mainly through their role as providers of continuous professional development. More specifically, in the past, teacher education departments run a free of charge, two-year training programme that was financed by the MoE. As Hudson et al., (2015, p. 1) point out, providing professional development to teachers is considered an effective activity for making and sustaining partnerships. Since the abolishment of the programme in 2012 by the MoE, the connection between teacher education departments and teachers in the field has weakened. Nowadays, kindergartens and universities liaise formally through a legislation that almost forces practitioners to accept student teachers in their classroom (a case example is the SECE at Aristotle University of Thessaloniki and public kindergartens in the wider area of Thessaloniki and the Department of ECE at the University of Thessaly – Pimenidou & Kakana, 2013). At the same time, 'cooperating' kindergarten teachers have no motivation for participating in student practicum other than the satisfaction that they are helping someone who is going through the same process they went through years ago. There are no incentives like accreditation, certification or professional development credits, which can encourage kindergarten teachers, or whole school units, to see their relationship with the university from a different perspective.

For years the connection between SECE and kindergarten teachers has been maintained through an additional channel. Since 1984, when teacher education obtained university status, student field experiences were supported by experienced kindergarten teachers who left their classrooms for a year to be appointed by the MoE as 'teachers seconded to the university'. Although the framework of their role was never officially clarified by the MoE, and that occasionally created problems, these teachers formed a 'triad' with teacher educators and students which supported prospective teachers to make connections between field/school experiences and academic/university coursework (Gregoriadis & Birbili, 2009; Kominia & Avgitidou, 2013). They also functioned as a link between universities and their colleagues in kindergartens (Gregoriadis & Birbili, 2009). Due to their role in students' support, these teachers are often referred to as 'mentors' in the Greek literature, even though their duties do not fully correspond to the role of mentors as defined in the international literature.

Since 2010, the initial large numbers of 'mentors' were gradually reduced by the MoE (e.g. at the SECE at Aristotle University of Thessaloniki, there was a ratio of 1 'mentor' per 30 students in the academic year 2016–2017). Despite protests by university chancellors, teacher educators and student themselves, ministers of the last eight years refused to release active teachers from their duties or consider other solutions suggested by SECE (e.g. the employment of permanent assistant personnel that would save departments from the 'whims' of governments (Chrysafidis, 2013)). The ease with which a practice of so many years was abandoned reflects the discrepancy between ministerial rhetoric on the importance of practicum and policy implementation.

Last but not least, the issue of student numbers. The number of students allowed to enter university departments is defined centrally after recommendations made by the departments themselves (numerus clausus). The battle between SECE and the MoE concerning the number of prospective students is an old one and one that, as mentioned in the historical overview, has been fought since kindergarten teacher training was transferred to universities. The importance that Greek society assigns to university education coupled with political parties' populist practices lead to large numbers of students without consideration of the capabilities and infrastructure of the departments (Papoulia-Tzelepi, 1993).

Furthermore, the initial number of students almost doubles every year due to the policy of 'transfer' introduced by the MoE: students are allowed to transfer from one university to another on health, social and financial grounds. Despite the good intentions, this practice fills central universities with more students than they can handle and weakens those on the periphery. In combination with the decreasing number of tenured university faculty – due to a large number of retirements and the recent stagnation in hiring new faculty members – the ratio of university teachers to students in Schools of ECE has increased to 1:80 or 1:90 in the largest universities, in Athens and Thessaloniki (Androussou, Kortessi-Dafermou, & Tsafos, 2012). Large numbers of student teachers, as the literature has long established, easily lead to traditional teaching methods, limit dramatically the opportunities students have for communication with their peers and university teachers, and make feedback and guided experiences in schools a challenging process (Androussou et al., 2012; Sapelli & Illanes, 2016).

Brought together and put in the context of the current situation in Greece, the abovementioned factors influence early childhood teacher preparation both in direct and indirect ways. For example, as the number of student teachers increases public kindergartens are included in the practicum without consideration of the quality of the education provided or the particular conditions a kindergarten faces (for example, extremely small classrooms that cannot host student teachers) (Pimenidou & Kakana, 2013). As students venture out in their practicum without the valuable support of a reflective mentor, teachers in kindergartens often feel that they are asked to step into a role they are not familiar with (or remunerated for) or that students are not properly supervised during their presence in kindergarten. Other consequences include:

1   students' limited access to out of classroom activities (unsupervised students find it hard to be involved in activities such as parent–teacher meetings);
2   departments' difficulty to communicate to large numbers of practitioners communicate the nature of practicum
3   teacher educators struggle to give quality feedback to students and maintain the personal component of teaching (two aspects of teacher educators' work that, according to Ramsden (2009), are among the first to be challenged in difficult environments).

As Heyneman (1990 p. 115) argues, difficulties tend to increase our capacity to manage situations 'based upon what is feasible rather than upon precedent' and to respond creatively to constraints. The challenges experienced due to the mentioned policies and the economic crisis have been the impetus for SECE to critically examine and redefine existing ideas, practices and roles that have been 'there' for a long time (Androussou et al., 2012; Chatzopoulou & Kakana, 2013). Seeking ways to create reflective environments for large numbers of students and strengthen the relationship between SECE and kindergartens led departments to turn to each other for support and inspiration and attempt to address their problems from the inside.

In 2008, Schools and Departments of ECE formed what is called 'Network of Practicum' whose aim is to develop a 'community of practice that interacts systematically, exchanges knowledge and experiences and improves student teacher education accordingly' (Avgitidou & Androussou, 2013, p. 19). Although it has no legal status, through its annual meetings, research projects, conferences and publications the Network has so far succeeded in creating an 'arena' for the development of a common discourse on student teachers' learning, something that is often missing among people and institutions involved in teacher education (Ottesen, 2008). Sharing a vision of teaching and learning is even more important in the Greek policy context where there is no centrally provided common framework for teacher education curricula (see for example Finland).

Training 'cooperating' teachers to function as 'mentors' of student teachers has been another practice used to support both students and teacher educators. To explore its effectiveness and feasibility within the Greek higher education context, Androussou and Tsafos (2013) from the School of Early Childhood Education at the University of Athens organised a relevant seminar for two consecutive years and involved 'trainees' in students' field experiences. The results of their study showed that the amount of time devoted to training practitioners for the role of student teacher mentor is critical: kindergarten teachers needed more time to make the transition from the old role to the new one. That implies time and resources spent by both teacher educators and departments. It also requires willingness on Greek kindergarten teachers' part to collaborate with the university. Studies show that many practitioners experience their relationship with the university as one of hierarchy and power, and express a negative stance towards SECE (Pimenidou & Kakana, 2013). Research also suggests that Greek kindergarten teachers do not place themselves and their work in the wider educational context. As Pimenidou & Kakana (2013, pp. 418–419) argue, at the macro-level this attitude could be linked to policies that have encouraged 'a stance of alienation'. However, the authors also acknowledge that Schools and Departments of ECE have not always done a good job in setting the foundation for a genuine collaboration (p. 419). Their views mirror that of Androussou et al. (2012) who stress the need for the development of school-university networks, as an opportunity to shape, 'an active community that discusses, researches and reviews concepts and practices, utilising theory in order to expand its horizon and reshaping theory in order to meet the needs of specific context' (p. 209).

Although most SECE are making steps towards creating collaborative networks, these networks function on a voluntary basis – usually with small numbers of kindergarten teachers who have experienced some sort of professional development and are willing to play a more active role in student teacher learning. What is missing, however, are the resources and the policy-related mechanisms that are needed for 'rigorous training that goes beyond briefing about the structure and nature of the course, and focuses on how teachers learn and the skills of effective mentoring' (Carter, 2015, p. 12).

Lastly, efforts have been made to deal with the large numbers of the student body without compromising the goal of encouraging students to adopt a critical and reflective approach to teaching. For example, Rekalidou, Karadimitriou and Moumoulidou (2014) at Democritus University of Thrace and Gourgiotou (2017) at the University of Crete have introduced methods like the Lesson Study method and peer learning which promote a collaborative culture among student teachers and support reflective thinking while taking into consideration the particularities of the local context (e.g. in Crete, there are more student teachers than available schools).

Concluding remarks

Although the dates and the details may differ, Greek teacher education had a similar beginning to other European teacher education systems: it had to fight for its place in higher education and the status of teachers and teacher educators as professionals and academics respectively (Ellis, Edwards, & Smagorinsky, 2010). It also had to shape a new identity regarding its purpose and the knowledge it generates. While some researchers rightfully argue that Greek Schools and Departments of teacher education may still be immersed in their history – as indicated by debates over 'what and how' should be taught in undergraduate courses (Androussou et al., 2012; Kourti & Androussou, 2013; Sarakinioti & Tsatsaroni, 2015) – it is also a fact that 30 years later, SECE have developed academic programmes that prepare early childhood education teachers for both the Greek and the international education market and have reached high positions in world university rankings.

Like other countries which are hit by the economic crisis, Greek education is grappling with drastic cuts in education spending, decreasing numbers of teachers and teacher educators in the workforce (due to retirement or early retirement schemes), 'frozen' or diminishing salaries and an increasing list of teacher education graduates waiting to be recruited by the state. While lack of financial support is not unique to the Greek context – nor for that matter inadequate national regulations like the ones discussed earlier – what makes Greek education a challenging context to be in is the messages that the system gives (Zgaga, 2013). As Robinson (2006, p. 34) points out, in systems that are characterised more by 'continuity than radical change or transformation' it is difficult to imagine how things might change in the future. Similarly, in policy contexts where there is no long-term planning or stability in the political scene it is difficult to form partnerships that are genuine and secure (Burn & Mutton, 2015). While individual Schools or Departments of ECE review and update their programmes based on current theories and evidence, there has been no major reform of the teacher education framework since 1984 and Greek education policy has made few, weak efforts to co-ordinate the different components of the teacher education continuum.

Notwithstanding the difficulties, SECE continue to evolve, at least in aspects they control (e.g. academic programmes, research output etc.). Perhaps an advantage of centralised systems of education is that they encourage schools and departments to work together, to share ideas and to learn from each other in the face of common challenges and problems. Both the network of SECE and those between departments and schools constitute innovative actions (although not novel ideas – see Papoulia-Tzelepi, 1993) for the Greek political and educational context where traditionally collaboration among institutions and services is not strong. However, teacher education departments cannot continue to work on their own and, while interesting innovations may come out of difficult times, there is still an urgent need for a cohesive policy across the different phases of the teacher education continuum.

References

Altbach, P. G. (2011). The past, present, and future of the research university. *Economic & Political Weekly EPW, 46*(16), 65–73. doi:10.1596/9780821388051_CH01.

Androussou, A., Kortessi-Dafermou, C., & Tsafos, V. (2012). Educating teachers: Observation of a classroom's framework as part of the student teachers' education. *The International Journal of Learning, 18*(8), 191–212. doi:10.18848/1447-9494/CGP/v18i08/47699

Androussou, A., & Tsafos, V. (2013). Ekpedevontas ekpedeftikous os mentores mellontikon ekpedeftikon se ena dierevnitiko anastochastiko plesio [Educating teachers as mentors of student teachers in a reflective research context]. In A. Androussou & S. Avgitidou (Eds.), *I praktiki askisi stin archiki ekpedefsi ton ekpedeftikon: Erevnitikes proseggisis* [Teaching practice during initial teacher education: Research perspectives] (pp. 360–395). Athens: Diktio Praktikon Askiseon, National and Kapodistrian University of Athens.

Avgitidou, S., & Androussou, A. (2013). Isagogi [Introduction]. In A. Androussou & S. Avgitidou (Eds.), *I praktiki askisi stin archiki ekpedefsi ton ekpedeftikon: Erevnitikes proseggissis* [Teaching practice during initial teacher education: Research perspectives] (pp. 15–37). Athens: Diktio Praktikon Askiseon, National and Kapodistrian University of Athens.

Birbili, M., & Christodoulou, I. (2018). Early childhood education and care in Greece: Looking back and moving forward. In S. Garvis, S. Phillipson, & H. Harzju-Luukkainen (Eds.), *International Perspectives on Early Childhood Education and Care. Early Childhood Education in the 21st Century, vol 1*. New York: Routledge.

Bouzakis, S., Tzikas, X., & Anthopoulos, K. (1998). *I katartisi ton didaskalon-didaskalisson ke ton nipiagogon stin Ellada. I periodos ton pedagogikon akadimion ke ton scholon nipiagogon 1933–1990* [Primary and preschool teacher training in Greece. The time of Pedagogic Academies and Schools for kindergarten teachers]. Athens, Greece: Gutenberg.

Bucholtz, M., & Hall, K. (2005). Identity and interaction: A sociocultural linguistic approach. *Discourse Studies, 7*(4–5), 585–614. doi:10.1177/1461445605054407.

Burn, K., & Mutton, T. (2015). A review of 'research-informed clinical practice' in initial teacher education. *Oxford Review of Education, 41*(2), 217–233. doi:10.1080/03054985.2015.1020104.

Carter, A. (2015). Carter review of initial teacher training (ITT). Retrieved from https://assets.publishing.service.gov.uk/government/uploads/system/uploads/attachment_data/file/399957/Carter_Review.pdf.

Chan, C. (2016). *School-university Partnerships in English Language Teacher Education. Tensions, Complexities, and the Politics of Collaboration*. Hong Kong: Springer.

Charitos, X. G. (1998). *To Elliniko nipiagogio ke i rizes tou. Simvoli stin istoria tis proscholikis agogis* [The Greek kindergarten and its roots. Its contribution to the history of preschool education]. Athens, Greece: Gutenberg.

Chatzopoulou, K., & Kakana, D. (2013). Ipostirizontas to stochasmo ton ipopsifion ekpedeftikon sto plesio tis praktikis askisis. Sigritika apotelesmata meso piramatikis erevnas [Supporting reflection of initial teacher education in the Practicum. Comparative results through experimental research]. In A. Androussou & S. Avgitidou (Eds.), *I praktiki askisi stin archiki ekpedefsi ton ekpedeftikon: Erevnitikes proseggisis* [Teaching practice during initial teacher education: Research perspectives] (pp. 125–156). Athens: Diktio Praktikon Askiseon, National and Kapodistrian University of Athens.

Chrysafidis, K. (2013). Praktiki askisi fititon pedagogikon tmimaton. Anamesa ston praktikismo ke tin anapotelesmatiki theoritikologia [Teaching practice of students teachers at Departments of Education: Between practice and ineffective theorizing]. In

A. Androussou & S. Avgitidou (Eds.), *I praktiki askisi stin archiki ekpedefsi ton ekpedeftikon: Erevnitikes proseggisis* [Student practice in initial teacher education. Research approaches] (pp. 173–196). Athens: Diktio Praktikon Askiseon, National and Kapodistrian University of Athens.

Cochran-Smith, M. (2005). The politics of teacher education and the curse of complexity. *Journal of Teacher Education, 56*(3), 181–185. doi:10.1177/0022487105276411

Cochran-Smith, M. (2013). Introduction: The politics of policy in teacher education: An international perspective. *The Educational Forum, 77*, 3–4. doi:10.1080/00131725.2013.739013

Conway, P. F., Murphy, R., Rath, A., & Hal, K. (2009). Learning to teach and its implications for the continuum of teacher education: A nine-country cross-national study. Report Commissioned by the Teaching Council, Ireland. Retrieved from www.teachingcouncil.ie/en/Publications/Research/Documents/Learning-to-Teach-and-its-Implications-for-the-Continuum-of-Teacher-Education.pdf.

Darling-Hammond, L. (2014). Strengthening clinical preparation: The holy grail of teacher education. *Peabody Journal of Education, 89*(4), 547–561. doi:10.1080/0161956X.2014.939009.

Darling-Hammond, L., Hyler, M. E., & Gardner, M. (2017). *Effective Teacher Professional Development*. Palo Alto, CA: Learning Policy Institute. Retrieved from https://learningpolicyinstitute.org/sites/default/files/product-files/Effective_Teacher_Professional_Development_REPORT.pdf.

Dimitropoulos, A., & Kindi, V. (2017). Accountability in Greek education. Country case study prepared for the 2017/8 Global Education Monitoring Report. Retrieved from http://unesdoc.unesco.org/images/0025/002595/259533e.pdf.

Ellis, V., Edwards, A., & Smagorinsky, P. (2010). *Cultural-historical Perspectives on Teacher Education and Development. Learning Teaching*. London: Routledge.

ET2020 Working Group on Schools Policy (2015). Shaping career-long perspectives on teaching. A guide on policies to improve Initial Teacher Education. European Commission. Retrieved from http://ec.europa.eu/dgs/education_culture/repository/education/library/reports/initial-teacher-education_en.pdf.

Garben, S. (2011). *EU Higher Education Law: The Bologna Process and Harmonization by Stealth*. Alphen aan den Rijn, The Netherlands: Kluwer Law International.

Gourgiotou, E. (2017). Trainee teachers' collaborative and reflective practicum in kindergarten classrooms in Greece: A case study approach. *The Educational Review, USA, 2*(1), 117–128. doi:10.26855/er.2018.01.001.

Green, B., Reid, J. A., & Brennan, M. (2017). Challenging policy, rethinking practice; or, struggling for the soul of teacher education. In T. A. Trippestad, A. Swennen, & T. Werler (Eds.), *The Struggle for Teacher Education: International Perspectives on Teacher Education Governance and Reforms* (pp. 39–55). London: Bloomsbury.

Gregoriadis, A., & Birbili, M. (2009). *Exploring the Role of Student-teacher Supervisors in Greek Higher Education: Learning from the insiders*. Proceedings from the OMEP European Regional Meeting and Conference 'Current Issues in Preschool Education in Europe: Shaping the Future' (pp. 149–164). Syros.

Haukland, L. (2017). The Bologna process: The democracy–bureaucracy dilemma. *Journal of Further and Higher Education, 41*(3), 261–272. doi:10.1080/0309877X.2015.1070403.

Heyneman, S. P. (1990). Economic crisis and the quality of education. *International Journal of Educational Development, 10*(2–3), 115–129.

Hudson, P., Hudson, S., Kwan, T., Chan, C., Maclang-Vicencio, E., & Ani, A.-L. (2015). *Making connections within the Asia-Pacific region: Case study around the Mentoring for Effective Teaching (MET) program*. Paper presented to Strengthening partnerships in teacher education: Building community, connections and creativity: The Annual Conference of the Australian Teacher Education Association, Darwin, 8–10 July.

Kominia, E., & Avgitidou, S. (2013). Optikes ke roli ton sinergazomenon foreon sto programma tis praktikis askisis [Perspectives and roles of collaborating participants in the teaching practice programme]. In A. Androussou & S. Avgitidou (Eds.), *I praktiki askisi stin archiki ekpedefsi ton ekpedeftikon: Erevnitikes proseggissis* [Teaching practice during initial teacher education: Research perspectives] (pp. 424–452). Athens: Diktio Praktikon Askiseon, National and Kapodistrian University of Athens.

Kourti, E., & Androussou, A. (2013). Promoting critical awareness in the initial training of preschool teachers in Greece: Resistance and perspectives. *International Journal of Early Years Education, 21*(2–3), 192–206. doi:10.1080/09669760.2013.832946.

Mavrogiorgos, G. (1993). *Ekpedeftiki ke axiologisi* [Educators and evaluation]. Athens, Greece: Sichroni Ekpedefsi.

Murray, J. (2012). Performativity cultures and their effects on teacher educators' work. *Research in Teacher Education, 2*(2), 19–23.

Organisation for Economic Cooperation and Development (OECD). (2016). PF4.2: Quality of childcare and early education services. Retrieved from www.oecd.org/els/soc/PF4-2-Quality-childcare-early-education-services.pdf.

Ottesen, E. (2008). *Dilemmas of mentoring in teacher education: Constructing the object.* Paper presented at the 'Sociocultural Perspectives on Teacher Education and Development' conference, University of Oxford, 7–8 April 2008.

Palfreyman, D. (2008). The legal impact of Bologna implementation: Exploring criticisms and critiques of the Bologna process. *Education and the Law, 20*(3), 249–257.

Papoulia-Tzelepi, P. (1993). Teaching-practice curriculum in teacher education: A proposed outline. *European Journal of Teacher Education, 16*(2), 147–162. doi:10.1080/0261976930160206.

Pimenidou, M., & Kakana, D. (2013). Praktiki askisi ke exelixi tis epaggelmatikis kinotitas. Apopsis ekpedeftikon sta nipiagogia praktikis askisis gia ti sinergasia me to panepistimio [Practicum and the evolution of the professional community. The teacher' views on the collaboration with the university]. In A. Androussou & S. Avgitidou (Eds.), *I praktiki askisi stin archiki ekpedefsi ton ekpedeftikon: Erevnitikes proseggisis* [Teaching practice during initial teacher education: Research perspectives] (pp. 396–423). Athens: Diktio Praktikon Askiseon, National and Kapodistrian University of Athens.

Ramsden, P. (2008). The future of higher education teaching and the student experience. Retrieved from www.dius.gov.uk/higher_education/shape_and_structure/he_debate/;/media/publications/T/teaching_and_student_experience_131008.

Rekalidou, G., Karadimitriou, K., & Moumoulidou, M. (2014). Efarmogi tou Lesson Study me fitites. Sinergasia, anastochasmos ke anatrofodotisi [Implementing lesson study with students. Collaboration, reflection and feedback]. *Erevna stin Ekpedefsi, 1,* 7–31.

Robinson, W. (2006). Teacher training in England and Wales: Past, present and future perspectives. *Education Research and Perspectives, 33*(2), 19–36.

Sapelli, C., & Illanes, G. (2016). Class size and teacher effects in higher education. *Economics of Education Review, 52,* 19–28. doi:10.1016/j.econedurev.2016.01.001.

Sarakinioti, A., & Tsatsaroni, A. (2015). European education policy initiatives and teacher education curriculum reforms in Greece. *Education Inquiry, 6*(3), 259–288. doi:10.3402/edui.v6.28421.

Sifakakis, P., Tsatsaroni, A., Sarakinioti, A., & Kourou, M. (2016). Governance and knowledge transformations in educational administration: Greek responses to global policies. *Educational Administration and History, 48*(1), 35–67. doi:10.1080/00220620.2015.1040377.

Snoek, M. (2016). Teacher education as a mirror of the profession. Retrieved from www. hva.nl/kc-onderwijs-opvoeding/gedeelde-content/publicaties/publicaties-algemeen/ teacher-education-as-a-mirror-of-the-profession.html.

Stamelos, G., & Emvalotis, A. (2001). Anixnevontas to profil ton pedagogikon tmimaton [Charting the profil of teacher education departments]. *Epistimoniki Epetirida PTDE University of Ioannina, 14*, 281–292.

Stylianidou, F., Bagakis, G., & Stamovlasis, D. (2004). *Attracting, developing and retaining effective teachers.* OECD Activity, Country Background Report For Greece. Retrieved from www.oecd.org/greece/30101431.pdf.

The Teaching Council (2011). Policy on the continuum of teacher education. Retrieved from www.teachingcouncil.ie/en/Publications/Teacher-Education/Policy-on-the-Continuum-of-Teacher-Education.pdf.

Tourtouras, X. D., Kyridis, A., & Karamouzas, N. (2018). Ta pedagogika tmimata sti dini tis trechousas ekpedeftikis politikis [The Departments of Education in the maelstrom of current educational policy]. *Academia, 11*, 103–121.

Traianou, A. (2013). Greek education reform: Resistance and despair. In K. Jones (Ed.), *Education and Europe: The Politics of Austerity* (pp. 86–112). London: Radicaledbooks. Retrieved from https://radicaledbks.files.wordpress.com/2013/09/education-in-europe.pdf.

Zgaga, P. (2008). Mobility and the European dimension in teacher education. Retrieved from www.pef.uni-lj.si/ceps/knjiznica/doc/2008%20Mobility_Teachers.pdf.

Zgaga, P. (2013). The future of European teacher education in the heavy seas of higher education. *Teacher Development, 17*(3), 347–361. doi:10.1080/13664530.2013.813750.

10 How think tanks and literacy policies can be used as examples of neoliberal influences on Icelandic preschools

Kristín Dýrfjörð

Introduction

Neoliberalism has been on the horizon for decades (Hursh, 2016). As a political and ideological tool, it has shaped ideas that we used to have different viewpoints or common understanding of. Such as the fundamental importance of the democratic role public schools play as keepers of society's codes and ways of being. In the United States academics write about war on public education and how it can be looked at as a war on our understanding of society, social justice and equality, and socialisation (see for example Ravitch, 2013). Coming from a homogeneous Nordic society that has, up until now, valued public education and social welfare, it has been both interesting and frightening to watch the impact of neoliberalism in Icelandic, especially within the early childhood sector.

The philosophy and pedagogy of early childhood education in Iceland was for a long time not of much interest for policymakers (Dýrfjörð, 2011).[1] In media discourses about elections, political interest has typically been on available enrolments, the age of children when they enter the system, and how possible reforms could be politically or economically beneficial. Discussion of the actual practices and preschool pedagogy was left to the professionals in the field. This has changed in the era of neoliberalism. Schools at all levels have become a vital part of the market and important tools for changing societies from democratic to neoliberal, shifting the power away from the people and towards the market and those who run, own, and profit from it (Lissovoy, Means, & Saltman, 2015). In the world of preschools, this has resulted in principals that before had much to say about educational programmes and methods now being bound by managerial duties both from the state and municipalities and policy documents that have, in some cases, been developed by policy borrowing from transnational agencies such as the Organisation for Economic Cooperation and Development (OECD) (Dýrfjörð & Magnúsdóttir, 2016). The professional freedom to choose methods and philosophy has been buried behind curtains of newspeak and connected to bureaucracy and new managerialism (Hursh, 2016).

This chapter will do three things. First, it will show how the Icelandic preschool has become part of a new political horizon in which agencies and think tanks are powerhouses. Second, it will show how players other than preschool teachers are dismantling educators' professional powers and acquiring control over the system. Finally, it will show how those players are enacting neoliberal ideology and using means developed or promoted by transnational institutions (Grek, 2014), such as new managerialism, deregulation, standardisation and accountability, to undermine the power of the profession and take over the curriculum and methods. Relevant literature and selected data are intertwined in each section.

The result of political indifferences

This former political indifference gave preschools freedom to develop in directions based on each preschool principal and teacher's pedagogical interests. This led to different approaches and different aspects of education philosophy developing within preschools over the last three decades. For a long time, preschools were more or less the same. Very few were organised around a specific philosophy or ideology, based instead on what was thought to be good early childhood education as taught at The Preschool Teachers College.[2] When the first National Curriculum for Icelandic Preschools (NCIP) was published in 1985 (it was updated in 1999 and 2011), most schools claimed to use it as pedagogical base. However, when further training in educational leadership was first offered at The Preschool Teachers College in 1983, many preschool teachers were influenced by it, and, during the years that followed, preschools bloomed, and pedagogy branched out in different directions. Looking back, preschools before were as Osgood (2017) described: shaped and defined by particular regimes of truth and the profession's grand narratives. Many preschools embodied those grand narratives into the fabric of daily lives and claim to have later added other methods based on philosophies they consider relevant. For example, some schools on top of the NCIP are in conversation with Reggio Emilia and the philosophy of Loris Malaguzzi. Meanwhile, there is a school chain running 17 schools and preschools (with 2000 pupils) in Iceland; it is based on gender segregation and behavioural rules. Others use Highscope; p4c; behavioural cookie-cut programmes bought from American educational businesses, such as SMT PMT, SOS, and ART;[3] and green flag or eco schools (Dýrfjörð & Magnúsdóttir, 2016). The conclusion being that the political indifferences have given the preschools opportunity to develop and grow in different directions.

Hegemonic globalisation

Preschools have gone from being homogenous to polymorphic and maybe the trend is back to become homogenous, grounded in what Moss (2014) has named 'hegemonic globalisation' based on the story of quality and high returns. In this new story the tendency is to subside early childhood education to simple formulas and technicality where the pedagogy is in danger of being reduced to manuals and cookie-cutter programmes and the pedagogy becomes a market solution instead of a shared dialogue of professionals. Ideas that have been traced to neoliberalism have found their way into the forefront, with emphasis on austerity, accountability deregulations and so on (Moss 2014; Moss and Urban 2011). This hegemonic globalisation through spread of neoliberal ideology has been supported by transnational actors and agencies (Thrupp, 2018) or as Moss states:

> [T]he dominant discourse in ECE, the story of quality and high returns, has gained influence through an exceptionally strong nexus of power relations. In particular, the story has been amplified, normalised and spread through a partnership of institutional actors: international organisations (e.g. IMF, OECD, UNESCO, European Union); national think tanks and other NGOs.
>
> (Moss, 2017, p. 17)

This discourse of quality and high returns has gained traction in Iceland and has caused a power shift in the early childhood sector, away from educators and towards others, such as policymakers, educational businesses, as well as other professions such as psychologist that were previously on the sidelines of preschools (Dýrfjörð, 2011; Dýrfjörð & Magnúsdóttir, 2016). This shift has its roots in another, bigger issue, in the social imagination that has become the narrative of our time (Hursh & Martina, 2016). It can be traced to a willingness to establish universal truths about early childhood education (Penn, 2005), resulting in colonisation of ideas and methods. This is evidenced by the increased attention given to academic skills and fundamentals in early childhood, In the Organisation for Economic Co-operation and Development (OECD) report, Starting Strong (2006) for example, concern that ' "[s]choolification" have connotations of taking over early childhood institutions in a colonising manner' (p. 3) is expressed. This is indeed worrisome and not without merit, as evidenced by the discourses around preschools' place in society and how policy on literacy in preschool has developed in Iceland.

The Icelandic preschool system

For readers unfamiliar with Iceland it can be useful to get contextual description. In Iceland, the legal concept of playschool is used in all official early childhood programmes. Here, on the other hand, the more common words preschool and preschool teachers will be used. Preschool attendance in Iceland is considered universal. The starting age for children beginning preschool is supposed to be related to the parents' paid maternity leave, which is currently nine months. Most children, however, start preschool around the age of 18–24 months, with the gap between parental leave covered by family day care. There are discussions among the public and policymakers about providing more preschool facilities for the youngest children. According to Statistics Iceland (2017), around 97 per cent of children 2.5 to six years and around 80 per cent of children aged between 1.5 and two years attend preschool. All preschools have full-day classes, and most children attend school for around 7.5 to eight hours, with the longest stay at around nine hours and most have three to four classrooms (Statistics Iceland, 2017). The preschool system is mainly financed and managed by municipalities, and private preschools are financed the same way as public ones. All parents pay fees on a sliding scale according to their income; between 12 per cent and 15 per cent of the actual cost of running the schools are paid by the parents (Icelandic Association of Local Authorities, 2011). Notably, Iceland's early childhood education system is not divided by children's age, and the same laws and rules apply to all children under the age of six years. This means, for example, that the same standards for teacher education and curriculum are used for all age groups under six years.

Hijacking the system: the think tank and its impact

Around the millennium shift, early childhood education in Iceland suddenly found itself in the public eye in a way it had not previously. The business world started to show interest in the system. This interest aligned with what was already happening in the USA, Australia and England, where preschools were a fast-growing 'industry' (Moss, 2009), and the interest that Nobel prize economists such as Heckman showed towards the early childhood, but he has pointed out that money invested in early childhood is part of the saviours of the future of the global market (Heckman, 2008). From the sidelines, it seemed as though some powerful Icelandic businesspeople belonging to the Icelandic Chamber of Commerce (CfC)[4] discovered both unused business opportunities as well as chances to shape preschools' pedagogical ideology in a direction that would serve the market. According to their view, the only obstacles in their way were regulations and laws concerning preschools (Viðskiptaráð Íslands, 2006). This interest was not coincidental; it can be traced to the development of the neoliberal genre that has slowly taken over global ideology (Hursh, 2016; Lissovoy et al., 2015), though it may have taken longer to arrive in Iceland.

In 2006, the CfC assembled a think tank to draw up preferred futurist scenery for Icelandic society. Part of their vision was an interesting take on early childhood education as an upcoming market opportunity. Concepts and words close to the market (e.g. child care industry) were used to describe their desires for the future (Viðskiptaráð Íslands, 2006). According to Hursh (2016), this can be looked upon as the result of an attack on Keynesian ideology concerning the welfare state that Iceland was part of (Ólafsson, 2013). Although part of the CfC's goals concern unused marked opportunities, another part touches on the desire for a neoliberal society to create competitive citizens for the future market. A competitive citizen is adjustable or flexible, a citizen that is able to change according to the needs of the market (Apple, 2006). The aim is for the system to make good workers and followers that will, in the long run, secure capitalist interests. It could be argued that it does not serve the new ideological model for citizens to become too critical or reflective; a school system that promotes such characteristics can be looked upon as dangerous to the neoliberal worldview in which the CfC operates.

In a 2006 report, the CfC listed what they deemed to be unnecessary regulations concerning the running of the preschool system, such as the sizes of schools (they were not big enough, now they are bigger), the staff-to-child ratio (it was regulated). Currently, Iceland is one of few OECD countries that does not have any standards concerning group sizes and staff-to-child ratios; those standards were abandoned with the Preschool Act of 2008 (Dýrfjörð, 2011). The Minister of Education at the time, Þorgerður Katrín Gunnarsdóttir, seems to have taken the recommendations advocated by the CfC and carried most of them out in the new legislation at all school levels. Many of the abovementioned regulations that no longer apply in Iceland are strongly related to the educational quality of preschools (Sylva, Melhuish, Sammons, Siraj-Blatchford, & Taggart, 2011). Even though the concept of quality in the early years education is both problematised and contested, it gives indications of a chosen road (Elwick, Osgood, Robertson, Sakr, & Wilson, 2018).

The CfC then published a report in October 2014 about education in Iceland in which they recommended reorganising the educational system on a large scale. The authors are an economist and a specialist in public relations, and it is evident that their knowledge about education and educational policy is minimal, as well as that the report is written with a very clear political agenda. As an example, a big part of what the authors see as opportunity is connected to teachers' salary, linking it with student achievement (Björnsson and Gunnarsdóttir, 2014) which can be strongly linked to GERM.[5] Other examples from the new report concern the use of data, it is presented to mineralise people's beliefs and trust in the educational system and is part of an attack on teachers' unions and professionalism.

To understand how neoliberalism affects us, Lissovoy says,

> More than a matter of doctrine or policy, neoliberalism is a particular historical organisation of the meaning of human relationships and human being. The kinds of responsibility and freedom that it proposes are not meant merely to reorient systems of values.
>
> (Lissovoy, 2018, p. 189)

He relates his understanding of the concept to Foucault's notion of governmentality and homo economicus, and he points out the importance of the state's role: '[it] becomes an important arena for the enactment of neoliberal governmentality, as the market is understood as requiring intervention in order to secure its efficiency' (2018, p. 189). The conclusion is that the state has the role of protecting the market at the cost of its citizens, and the word *citizen* has acquired a new meaning in the neoliberal era. Citizens are not subjects of the state anymore but subjects of the market.

Losing the profession to others: the 'educationalisation' of the preschool

As a way of redefining the world, neoliberals have taken to heart Foucault's understanding of how discourses can be used to control and govern, how one 'truth' can replace another and become the new regime (Rose, 2016). In daily life this is done deviously by developing new vocabulary or, as Saltman claims: 'Part of this ideological journey has had, as an underlying aim, to change public discourses; change how we think and act' (Saltman, 2014, p. 9). Within preschools, this change of discourses and truths has gone hand in hand with new language, that of 'educationalisation' and attention to academic skills such as reading, writing and maths, which has led to pedagogical changes. This is demonstrated in Bassok, Latham and Rorem's (2016) research, in which they examine whether kindergarten is the new first grade and give relevant evidence that this is the case in many schools in United States. The 'old truth', learning through play, empowerment and children's agency is being swept out to implement a new regime of truth based on literacy and tests that aim to prepare the future workforce to be adaptable and disciplined.

Dýrfjörð and Magnúsdóttir (2016) describe how organisational reform at the top governmental level was conducted in Iceland and how it has changed the landscape of education:

> That was an important step of the social engineering in the system, i.e. to have a central control and overview of curriculum, evaluation and consultancy for schools, similar to Norway. Now, Iceland has one institution taking charge of the national curriculum materials, educational consultancy and production of national tests and standard evaluation instruments. [...] A part of the literacy reform is for every municipality to sign a convention with the Ministry of Education that declares that reading will be placed in the forefront of all educational reforms. The *Directorate of Education* has the role of implementing this policy and has recently hired 10 reading specialists that will promote methods that they deem appropriate and grounded on evidence based practice as well as to support screening and tests. Interestingly almost half of those specialist are preschool teachers.
>
> (Dýrfjörð & Magnúsdóttir, 2016)

This agreement between each municipality and the Ministry of Education has led to a strong emphasis on a very narrow definition of literacy in the media and among politicians at both the community and state levels. The next section will show how the struggle between different regimes' literacy at the preschool level have been carried out.

Rose (2016) writes about how Foucauldian researchers read data through discourses that are articulated through all sort of texts, and how researchers have to read between the lines – she uses the word intertextuality to describe the method. By that she means 'to the way that the meaning of any discursive image or text depend not only on that text or image, but also on the meanings carried by other images and texts'. (p. 188).

The texts that were chosen to show the influence of transnational agencies on literacy policies in Iceland are both from the biggest provider of preschool education in Iceland, the capital of Reykjavík. Because of its size the city is considered to be leader in the preschool sector. The texts were juxtaposed against each other, reading between the lines for example who are those that manufactured the texts and the ideology they are based on. The texts were also selected because they reveal clear indicators of changing policy directions and therefore are interesting to take a closer look at.

How the policy of early childhood literacy mirrors a changing regime

Reykjavík, the capital of Iceland, is the biggest provider of preschools in the country, running 62 preschools for around 6000 children and supporting 17 other preschools[6] (Reykjavíkurborg, 2018). Since the 2010 elections, the political landscape of Reykjavík has been a coalition between the left and the middle, leaning towards the middle. In January 2012, city preschool principal Þórunn Gyða Björnsdóttir, a member of the educational board, proposed that the city establish a committee of preschool teachers from the city's Department of Education and Youth (Skóla- og frístundasvið Reykjavíkurborgar, 2013) and members of the preschool teachers' unions with the aim of creating a reading policy for the city's preschools. In her proposal, Þórunn Gyða Björnsdóttir advocated for the multimodal literacy, which was well known, practiced in preschools and a part of the NCIP requirements. She also advocated in the spirit of the NCIP for the main teaching method to be learning through play, with attention to language stimulation, written language and expressions. Her proposal was approved, and a committee of four preschool teachers was formed: two from the city's educational department and two from the unions. Their aim was to become familiar with policies and curricula that other municipalities may have utilised in their preschools, as well as to observe each city preschool's literacy curriculum. They were to study existing research on language stimulation and young children's literacy, call in specialists for consultations, and write a preschool literacy policy proposal for the city.

The committee gathered information from different municipalities', met with specialists, made a relevant literature review, referred to the NCIP, and assembled the city's preschool principals and teachers into separate working groups. Both groups discussed their understanding of multimodal literacy and their expectations concerning the literacy policy. The end result mirrored the principals and teacher groups; the emphasis was on play-based learning. As part of a final report the committee recommended that each preschool create a curriculum plan in which following contents are addressed and clarified:[7]

- how learning within preschools can support emerging literacy;
- how learning is situated in each child's personal history and fields of interest;
- how teachers aim to promote children's interest and their attitude based on the idea of language as a creative tool;
- how various methods are used concerning all language acquisition, it has to be explained how children are exposed to different materials, books as well as digital media, showcased that children's books are read for children both as part of group but also for a singular child, and books read differ;
- how teachers address how they use singing, learning poems and nursery rhymes as an important part of childhood and how stories and poems are used as resources for play;
- how teachers address how they give special attention to children that need to learn Icelandic as a second language, and explain how they support children's home language in relationship with parents;
- how teachers plan to carry out systematic attention to children's language acquisition and literacy;
- to describe which early interventions programmes are available for children with, for example, languages delays;
- to describe how they involve parents in their children's learning and how parents get information about their children's learning;
- lastly, how the preschool is planning relationship with the next school level.
      (Skóla- og frístundasvið Reykjavíkurborgar, 2013 p. 10)

The policy was published as a policy for literacy for Reykjavík preschools in June 2013 as Lesið í leik (Reading in Play). The requirements mentioned above are obviously based on the Nordic early childhood system: it emphasises how children learn through different types of play, with attention to poems and nursery rhymes, which in Iceland are an old and important way of transmitting cultural values and stories between generations (Jensen, 2009). There is also significant emphasis placed on cooperation between institutions, family connections and the need for preschool teachers to efficiently recognise children's developmental delays or other problems. The authors do not appear to have been overly worried about standardised testing or screening all children within public preschools, and the most-used screening test for language in Iceland was not part of the recommendations.

However, just a year later, in September 2014, the city formed a new advisory board, the Professional Advisor-Board on Reading and Reading-Related Issues for Both the Pre- and Primary Schools (Fagráð um eflingu málþroska, lestrarfærni og lesskilnings í leik- og grunnskólum). This new advisory board was formatted differently than the previous committee on literacy in preschools. It was headed by Freyja Birgisdóttir, a developmental psychologist and associate professor at the University of Iceland, and the other members were two teachers, one from preschool and the other from primary school, and a primary school teaching specialist, all of whom worked at the city's Department of Education and Youth. The committee decided to use the transnational agency; International Association for the Evaluation of Educational Achievement (IEA) definition of literacy as a starting point:

> Reading literacy is the ability to understand and use those written language forms required by society and/or valued by the individual. Readers can construct meaning from texts in a variety of forms. They read to learn, to participate in communities of readers in school and everyday life, and for enjoyment.
>
> (PIRLS, 2016, p. 12)

In the PIRLS report, the narrow definition of reading is connected to the written texts and is focused on children after four years of schooling. As a supplement for the preschools, the advisory board recommended a definition of emergent literacy with connections to similar concepts and definition, such as phonological awareness, knowledge of the alphabet, language comprehension, decoding, word recognition and written texts (Birgisdóttir, Jónsdóttir, Rafnsdóttir, & Bentsdóttir, 2015). At a glance, it is obvious that the new advisory board made a drastic change from the previous committee's policies, moving away from multimodal literacy and towards the straight and narrow definitions connected to academic skills and schoolification. They made their recommendations, which included the following:

> About 90% children in second class shall have gotten to the minimum criteria in reading in reading screening tests and in five year gotten to step 2 by PISA. To acquire this the preschool have to step up their work. Teachers are expected to use early interventions, and then pay a special attention to the foundation of emergent literacy as mentioned above and evidence based methods shall be used. And even though the preschools have already submitted their plan of action as part of the first report, they are obligated to rewrite it with this new emphasis in mind. The preschools are requested to use criteria that appear in standardised test and evaluation tools. And that all children the last year in preschool (five – six years) shall be screened with tests [owned by a private companies] and their alphabetical knowledge shall also be tested. Additionally all children shall be screened for language delays with various recommended tools [owned by private companies].
>
> (Birgisdóttir et al., 2015)

The report was published, and preschool principals were required to carry out the decisions and requirements that were put forward, such as writing new plans of action for literacy in their preschools. This new report came at a time when working conditions in preschools were being avidly discussed, and teachers and principals were very tired after years of being underfinanced, high staff turnover and preschool teacher shortages (Dýrfjörð, 2019). The new action plan was troublesome for some of the preschools, or, as one preschool principal put it, 'it was just one more thing to do, and it ended on the shelf, where nobody have looked at it ever since. That happens when you don't have the staff and time you need' (Dýrfjörð, personal communication, 15 April 2018).

While there are similarities between the two literacy policy documents, it is also clear that neoliberal attention to the technical, measurable and evidence-based aspects of early childhood are more visible in the later document. The focus has shifted from the grand narrative and the 'classic' preschool methods to using instruments that have been developed mostly by specialists from other professions, and preschools have to both ensure that teachers are licensed to carry out the tests and pay for each test taken.

Conclusion

Recent indicators of neoliberalism in early childhood education are evident. Business-related think tanks have had a hand in changing both discourses as well as the legal system surrounding preschools, particularly in the areas of deregulation and accountability. This progression is just a part of a larger and more complicated societal shift in which new social imagery based on neoliberalism has paved the road for change and established a new paradigm. Analysis of the development of two literacy policy documents indicates that preschool teachers have been set aside in favour of experts from other disciplines and this has led to educational policy being transformed from play-based to being part of the newspeak based on standardised and measurable outcomes. Finally, the ideology behind these two policy documents indicates that the actors in the second policy paper are looking to transnational agencies to justify their claims and procedures.

It is unclear if or how the early childhood profession in Iceland can regain control of the sector's educational policy. It may be too big of a fight for one profession against the rising tide of multimillion-dollar industries and transnational agencies. Early childhood professions have often taken up fights for children in the past; that is part of their history, and they can do so again. But for that to happen, the profession must first acknowledge the neoliberal shift that has already happened; they have to map it, frame it and name it, or, as Pablo Freire said, '[reflect] and [act] upon the world in order to transform it' (Freire, 1986, p. 36).

Notes

1 In this chapter the reference to preschools changing landscapes are written from Icelandic context.
2 Iceland had one collage for preschool teacher until 1996 when the education was transferred B.ed. level.
3 Those are acronyms for programmes such as School Manag.
4 Viðskiptaráð Íslands, in this chapter I use the official English acronym CfC.
5 GERM – an acronym for Global Educational Reform Movement.
6 Those are 79 out of 242 preschools in Iceland.
7 The report had different proportions, but those are the ones I chose as a relevant for this chapter and the translation is mine.

References

Apple, M. (2006). Interviews with Michael Apple. In L. Weis, C. McCarthy, & G. Dimitriadis (Eds.), *Ideology, Curriculum and the New Sociology of Education: Revisiting the Work of Michel Apple* (pp. 219–250). New York: Routledge.

Bassok, D., Latham, S., & Rorem, A. (2016). Is kindergarten the new first grade? *AERA Open, 2*(1), 527–545. doi:10.1177/2332858415616358.

Birgisdóttir, F., Jónsdóttir, F. B., Rafnsdóttir, D., & Bentsdóttir, G. E. (2015). *Fagráð um eflingu málþroska,lestrarfærni og lesskilnings í leik- og grunnskólum –áfangaskýrsla* [Professional advisor-board on reading and reading-related issues for both the pre- and primary Schools, phase report]. Retrieved from Reykjavík: https://reykjavik.is/sites/default/files/fagrad_laesi_skyrsla_loka.pdf.

Björnsson, B., & Gunnarsdóttir, Á. (2014). *Stærsta efnahagsmálið Sóknarfæri í menntun* [The greatest economical issue, opportunities in education]. Reykjavík: Samtökum Powell and Smith atvinnulífsins og Viðskiptaráði Íslands.

Dýrfjörð, K. (2011). Áhrif nýfrjálshyggju á íslenskt leikskólastarf [Impact of neoliberalism on Icelandic preschools]. *Íslenska þjóðfélagið, 2*, 47–68.

Dýrfjörð, K. (2019). Preschool teachers' working conditions in Iceland: Crisis in the making. In Phillipson, S. & Garvis, S. (Eds.), *Teachers' and Families' Perspectives in Early Childhood Education and Care. Early Childhood Education in the 21st Century* (pp. 110–122). London: Routledge.

Dýrfjörð, K., & Magnúsdóttir, B. R. (2016). Privatization of early childhood education in Iceland. *Research in Comparative and International Education, 11*(1), 80–97. doi:10.1177/1745499916631062.

Elwick, A., Osgood, J., Robertson, L., Sakr, M., & Wilson, D. (2018). In pursuit of quality: Early childhood qualifications and training policy. *Journal of Education Policy, 33*(4), 510–525. doi:10.1080/02680939.2017.1416426.

Freire, P. (1986). *Pedagogy of the Oppressed*. New York: Continuum Press.

Grek, S. (2014). OECD as a site of coproduction: European education governance and the new politics of 'policy mobilization'. *Critical Policy Studies, 8*(3), 266–281. doi:10.1080/19460171.2013.862503.

Heckman, J. (2008). The case for investing in disadvantaged young children. *CESifo DICE Report, 6*(2), 3–8.

Hursh, D. (2016). *The End of Public School: The Corporate Reform Agenda to Private Education*. New York: Routledge.

Hursh, D., & Martina, C. A. (2016). The end of public schools? Or a new beginning? *The Educational Forum, 80*(2), 189–207. doi:10.1080/00131725.2016.1135380.

Icelandic Association of Local Authorities. (2011). *Leikskólar – gjaldskrár – reglur* [Preschools, tariff and regulations]. Reykjavík: Icelandic Association of Local Authorities.

Jensen, B. (2009). A Nordic approach to Early Childhood Education (ECE) and socially endangered children, *European Early Childhood Education Research Journal, 17*(1), 7–21. doi:10.1080/13502930802688980.

Lissovoy N. D. (2018) Pedagogy of the anxious: Rethinking critical pedagogy in the context of neoliberal autonomy and responsibilization. *Journal of Education Policy, 33*(2), 187–205. doi:10.1080/02680939.2017.1352031.

Lissovoy, N. D., Means, A. J., & Saltman, K. J. (2015). *Toward a New Common School Movement*. Boulder, CO: Paradigm Publishers.

Lynch, K. (2014). New managerialism, neoliberalism and ranking. *Ethics in Science and Environmental Politics, 13*(2), 141–153.

Moss, P. (2009). *There are alternatives! Markets and democratic experimentalism in early childhood education and care*. Working Paper No. 53. The Hague: Bernard van Leer Foundation and Bertelsmann Stiftung.

Moss, P. (2014). *Transformative Change and Real Utopias in Early Childhood Education: A Story of Democracy, Experimentation and Potentiality*. London: Routledge.

Moss, P. (2017). Power and resistance in early childhood education: From dominant discourse to democratic experimentalism. *Journal of Pedagogy/Pedagogický časopis, 8*(1), 11–32. doi:10.1515/jped-2017-0001.

Moss, P., & Urban, M. (2011). *Democracy and Experimentation: Two Fundamental Values for Education*. Gütersloh: Bertelsmann-stiftung.

Ólafsson, S. (2011). Icelandic capitalism: From statism to neoliberalism and financial collapse. *Comparative Social Research 28*, 1–51. doi:10.1108/S0195-6310(2011)0000028005

Organisation for Economic Co-operation and Development (OECD). (2006). *Starting Strong: Early Childhood Education and Care*. Paris: OECD.

Osgood, J. (2017). Opening Pandora's box: Post-modern perspectives of childhood. In (Eds.), *An Introduction to Early Childhood Studies, 4th edition*. London: Sage.

Penn. H. (2005). *Understanding Early Childhood: Issues and Controversies*. Maidenhead: Open University Press.

PIRLS. (2016). Assessment Framework. International Association for the Evaluation of Educational Achievement. TIMSS & PIRLS International Study Center, Lynch School of Education: Boston.

Ravitch, D. (2013). *Reign of Error: The Hoax of the Privatization Movement and the Danger to America's Public Schools*. New York: Vintage Books.

Reykjavíkurborg. (2018). Reykjavík í tölum [Reykjavik in numbers]. Retrieved from http://tolur.reykjavik.is/PXWeb/pxweb/en/08%20Education/08%20Education__01.%20Pre-schools/FRA01010.px/table/tableViewLayout1/?rxid=0895a024-ab8a-4a03-b122-540838af0989.

Rose, G., (2016). *Visual Methodologies (4th ed.) An Introduction to Researching with Visual Materials*. London: Sage.

Saltman, K. J. (2014). The austerity school: Grit, character, and the privatization of public education. *Symploke, 22*(1), 41–57.

Skóla- og frístundasvið Reykjavíkurborgar. (2013). *Skýrsla starfshóps um læsisstefnu leikskóla* [Report on literacy policy for preschools]. Reykjavík: Reykvíkurborg.

Statistics Iceland. (2017). *Fewer children and staff in pre-primary schools*. Retrieved from www.statice.is/publications/news-archive/education/pre-primary-schools-2016/.

Sylva, K., Melhuish, E., Sammons, P., Siraj-Blatchford, I., & Taggart, B. (2011). Preschool quality and educational outcomes at age 11: Low quality has little benefit. *Journal of Early Childhood Research, 9*(2), 109–124. https://doi.org/10.1177/1476718X10387900.

Thrupp, M. (2018). *The Search for Better Educational Standards: A Cautionary Tale*. Cham: Springer.

Viðskiptaráð Íslands. (2006). *Viðskiptaþing: Ísland 2015*. Report from CfC. Retrieved from http://vi.is/%C3%BAtg%C3%A1fa/sk%C3%BDrslur/2006_02_08%20Island_2015.pdf.

11 Unlocking Pandora's Box

Rethinking the cost, quality and outcomes of early childhood education and care services in Korea

SoJung Seo

Introduction

The Korean government has striven to tackle its extremely low fertility problem (e.g. a historic low of 1.09 in 2005, the lowest among 34 Organisation for Economic Cooperation and Development (OECD) members) over the last decade. In a very keen move to boost the extremely low fertility rate, in 2006 the Korean government began drafting a five-year comprehensive plan to provide incentives to married couples with young children in child care (Park, 2015).

A major landmark in providing unprecedented benefits for all parents with young children (aged 0 to five years) was the 'Nuri Policy', which provided free child care services in 2012, coupled with the development of the first integrated national standard curriculum for young children, entitled 'Nuri Curriculum' in 2013 (Seo, 2019). The core of this Nuri curriculum is to guide a common set of early childhood learning goals in five areas (e.g. physical, social–emotional, communication, problem solving and reasoning, and creative development) for all three- to five-year-old children who receive early childhood education and care (ECEC) services in Korea (Choi, Park, Ha, & Kim, 2016; Seo, 2019).

Since the Nuri policy was implemented in 2012, Korea's struggle with a low birth rate is not new, but chronic. Statistics of Korea (2018) announced that the total population in Korea is approximately 51,801,449, and the number of children (aged 0 to five years) is 2,720,124 (5.8 per cent of the entire population). The data on the birth rate came as a shock. There were only 357,700 new babies in 2017, and that put the average birth rate at 1.05 per woman, the lowest since data began being collected from mid-2000s. In fact, it is a critical blow to the Korean government, which has allocated much of the national budget to ECEC services to tackle the low fertility issue. Specifically, the government spent more than 150 trillion won, and ECEC expenditures from 2010 to 2014 increased from 0.52 per cent to 1.01 per cent of overall GDP, including improvements in the quality of ECEC services, such as disseminating the national standard Nuri curriculum (Park, 2015; Seo, 2019).

Ideology in ECEC politics

The differing views of the causes and remedies for poverty have profound consequences for the social policies that have been enacted in Korea. In general, conservatives blame social support policies for the absolute dependency of the poor on others rather than on themselves. Radical democrats, acting on their political beliefs that the poverty line is set too low for the poor to support themselves, strive to transform the infrastructures of the economic, political and social systems to achieve justice and equity in Korea. Also, ECEC sectors have been politicised over the last decades, and place political ideology at the centre of deliberations surrounding economic and social policies that affect the target population.

It is worthwhile to note that one of the drastic milestones in the history of ECEC policy was the Democrat Noh's administration in 2003. The Noh government recognised the impact of social disadvantages on life chances and was very eager to break the vicious cycle of poverty, in which socioeconomically disadvantaged children received poor public services and went on to experience a range of adversities over their lifetime (Park, 2015). During his five-year presidency period (2003–2008), the Noh administration had sowed the seeds for the very considerable expansion of early years services that continues today.

In 2008, President Lee set forth the promise of his new Conservative government to build non-partisan mechanisms in order to address child care policy and legislation for families of young children, so that when children start school, they are ready to learn, calling for national unity and non-partisan support for his administration (Kwon & Kim, 2012). President Lee's child care policy gained wide support that crossed party lines, even though his administration's ideology on poverty was conservative. Since Lee's administration in 2008, the provision of child care has transcended political ideology, with the belief that it will solve the low fertility problem and narrow the gap between the haves and the have-nots in Korea (Kwon & Kim, 2012). To date, the child care support policies have been predominantly focused on in-service benefits rather than on other benefits, such as the child allowances.

The ECEC policy entered a new phase when the newly elected President Moon had pledged a new 100,000 won (approximately US$100) child allowance during his presidential campaign. After his inauguration in 2017 the Child Allowance Act was enacted, and from September 2018, parents with a child up to seven years old received 100,000 won each month, regardless of their uses of ECEC services or the family's income bracket (except for the upper 10 per cent of family income brackets). Although the current Korean government is pushing ahead with the new child care policy, it seems that conflicts are inevitable, because the government does not say anything about how to finance the policy and put it into practice.

Controversies

Given that ECEC policy in Korea shifted from a selective to a universal approach, with particular attention to young children aged 0 to five years, financing of ECEC has been classified into: (1) government financial support (financial grants for local education) from the Ministry of Education, and (2) autonomously executed budgets by 17 metropolitan and provincial offices of education under the Nuri policy (Seo, 2019). The fragmented policy reflected an internal conflict between the role of government and the roles of local governments, thus skewing policy away from some of the fundamental needs of young children and families.

Korea has a dichotomised ECEC system with two distinct authorities in charge: (1) kindergartens for 3–5 year olds under the supervision of the Ministry of Education; and (2) child care centres for 0–5 year olds, under the supervision of the Ministry of Health and Welfare (Seo, 2018). After the implementation of Nuri policy, only the curriculum was integrated (Nuri Curriculum) under the divided ECEC governing system.

From the inception of the Nuri policy, several issues around this universal approach to all families with young children were under severe debate. First and foremost, the Nuri Curriculum under this divided governing system has created severe budgetary conflicts every year between regional education offices and the central government. In 2014 the Korean government ordered regional education offices to assume the burden of finding the programme due to the curriculum's skyrocketing annual state budget for expanding the programme to children aged 0 to five years (Seo, 2019). However, the regional offices have refused to support the free child care programme, claiming that they are not responsible for providing this care, especially for the day care centres, which are under the jurisdiction of the Ministry of Health and Welfare (Seo, 2019). Since kindergartens are under the control of the Ministry of Education, some municipal councils have also refused to fund their kindergartens within the same districts in the current dichotomised ECEC systems (Seo, 2019). The ECEC policy has become a hot potato in Korean society, and because of populist policies without public consensus, the conflicts and struggles among the stakeholders remain persistent. Thus, the issue of whether the universal access to ECEC sectors is in the best interests of young children in Korea is under debate.

Counting the Nuri policy

Social policy should emerge from fundamental needs of young children and families, and it should be a direct response to a target or urgent issue to be solved (Seo, 2019). The value and effectiveness of a policy depend on the underlying assumptions and intent of those who frame it and the extent to which the policy defines the problem in precise ways (Melhuish & Petrogiannis, 2006; Seo, 2019). Compared to other social problems that Korea as a nation faces, problems and needs for ECEC services clearly need to be addressed. But, reality is a whole different world, and multiple issues, seemingly unrelated, are intertwined, making the problem more difficult to solve.

Countermeasure for low fertility

As discussed earlier, over the last decade the Korean government has provided the astronomical financial support for the universal Nuri policy, along with the Nuri Curriculum for all children (under the age of five years). Accordingly, the research on its effectiveness has been conducted to investigate the following two dimensions: (1) the index of birth rates and (2) its effects on primary stakeholders. First, Korea's fertility rate is still one of the lowest (1.05 in 2018) among the OECD countries (Statistics of Korea, 2018). The Korean government has been striving to boost the low birth rate that has plagued Korea in recent years (Figure 11.1). As shown in Table 11.1, expenditures on ECEC services between 2010 and 2014 has been increased from 0.52 per cent to 1.01 per cent of overall GDP in Korea. A series of the ECEC policies, including the Nuri policy are, however, paradoxical, in that no significant progress has been reported since the implementation of Nuri policy in 2012. It seems that the provision of free ECEC services did not pay off as countermeasures for improving birth rates, and it alone cannot resolve the low fertility problem in Korea. Amid a prolonged economic slowdown, young people cannot land decent jobs and so delay marriage; hence the fact that the problem of low fertility is multifaceted must be considered (Seo, 2019).

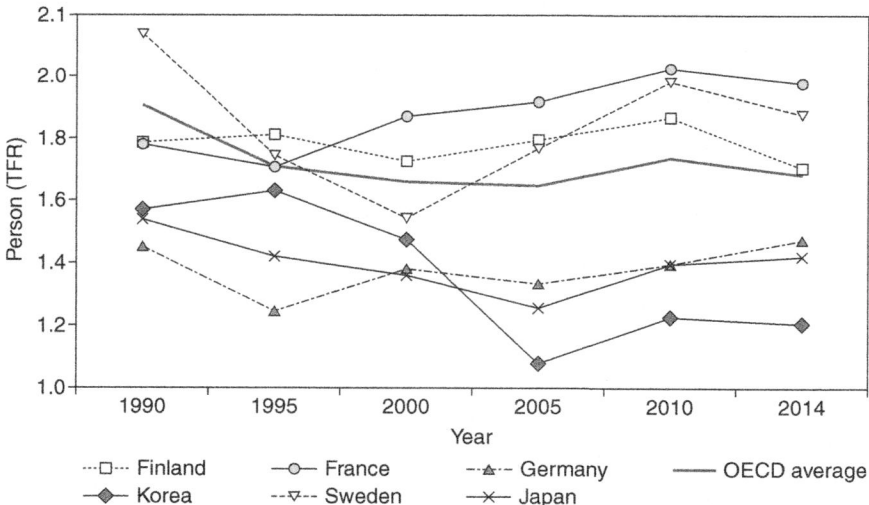

Figure 11.1 Total fertility rate in selected OECD countries (1990–2014), including OECD average.

Source: Kim (2016)

Table 11.1 Expenditure on early childhood education and care services as a percentage of GDP: 2010–2014 (unit: 100 million won (%))

	2010	2011	2012	2013	2014
Total ECEC budget	65,662	85,162	98,286	136,434	149,459
% of GDP	(0.52)	(0.64)	(0.71)	(0.96)	(1.01)

*Source: Park (2015).

Entitled but unmet needs

As addressed herein, the government has been expanding financial support policies for young children to lessen the burden on parents and to give a fair starting point to all children regardless of family income levels. Accordingly, the government had spent relatively more on in-kind services (both kindergartens and child care centres), with the lowest public expenditures on cash benefits, even though its spending on in-kind services matched that of other OECD countries during 2002–2011 (Kim, 2016; Seo, 2019). In 2016, 68.1 per cent of entire population of young children (3,153,489, aged 0–5 years) utilised either kindergartens or child care centres (22.3 per cent for kindergarten users vs. 45.8 per cent for centre-based care ones, respectively) (Statistics of Korea, 2017). Coupled with the fact that the percentage of dual-income families who utilised ECEC services increased from 41.8 per cent in 2009 to 53.2 per cent in 2015 (Korean Educational Development Institute (KEDI), 2015), the trend of child care-support policy has focused on financially supporting child care centres, recently extending child care hours.

Though the cash scheme and that of the flexible working hours have been also introduced to the arena of ECEC politics, they are still limited to child care home allowances. Despite such efforts and support measures, the effects of the Nuri policy are controversial, because parents, as one of the primary stakeholders, did not feel that their burden related to childrearing was relieved, and they are still responsible for extracurricular activities provided in ECEC services (Yang, 2014).

In the same vein, the findings from a recent study by Park (2016) substantiate the contention that the Nuri policy did not affect the daily experiences of those whom it is intended to serve. Park (2016) investigated people's perceptions about the effects of Nuri policy (0–5 years) that appeared in the news media from 2011 to 2015. He investigated centrality concepts with high frequency and the relations to other concepts by frequency analysis, cross-analysis and social network analysis. There were 104 concepts on the policy outcomes, of Nuri policy, and the five concepts were found to be central nodes. The state responsibility (15.2 per cent) appeared most frequently appeared in news articles during 2011–2015, followed by free child care for children from 0 to five years (13.0 per cent), shortage of financial resources (9.5 per cent), burden on parents (7.3 per cent) and free infant care (4.8 per cent), which accounted for almost 50 per cent of the observed frequencies. One of the profound findings was that those five focal nodes were related to negative perceptions about the effects of Nuri policy. Especially, the focal node of 'lack of public funding' was nine times more negatively perceived by the people than other categories. Those findings from Park's study (2016) push us as conscious citizens towards an investigation of the current Nuri policy, with an eye open towards underlying assumptions about people in need, with questions about what might end investment in the future, and with worries about who gains by our not choosing to do so.

Coupled with the research findings discussed earlier (Kim, 2016; Park, 2016), the free child care, Nuri policy, was doomed to failure, because of the mismatch between demands and responses to them in the first place, let alone the lack of sustainable public funding, as predicted. As reflected in the results of the national survey (Korean Educational Development Institute (KEDI), 2015), nearly 40 per cent of respondents preferred income-based support for child care and education for children (aged three to five years) to the current free care, and only 29 per cent of respondents supported the free child care programme, regardless of family income (Korean Educational Development Institute (KEDI), 2015; Seo, 2019). This finding sheds light on the contention that child care policies in Korea have been swayed by the winds of politics in the midst of the economic and political downturn, not meeting its intended goals for both increasing the chronic fertility rate and meeting the diverse needs of ECEC stakeholders in Korea (Seo, 2019).

Effects on primary stakeholders

To date there has been a dearth of research that scrutinised the effects of child care support policies on primary stakeholders, including parents, young children, and working staff or professionals in ECEC services in Korea. But recently, research efforts emerged at the time in Korean ECEC history when child care support became a public good. In this light, a related study by Yoo, Kim and Kim (2015) is worthwhile to note, in that it displays the burgeoning research interests in speculating about the extent to which the trend of ECEC policies affects the daily experiences of those whom they are intended to serve or target. Yoo et al. (2015) investigated the effects of child care support policies, specifically, those of Nuri policy in the last decade, with a sample of 1045 parents with young children nationwide and 98 experts. The parents of young children reported that financially supporting child care centres and extension of child care hours had more of an effect than other parental support measures for increasing accessibility to public child care sectors and strengthening ECEC practitioners' professionalism (Yoo et al., 2015).

With regard to parental involvement in ECEC sectors, it is suggested that incorporating the expectations and diverse needs of parents be mandatory under the Nuri policy. Given that the full-day class children spend more time in ECEC settings than at home, it is imperative to identify the diverse needs of their parents (Moon, 2010). To address this issue and drive change, a certain number of parents of the ECEC their child attends should be included in a parents' committee, and a variety of ways should be also utilised to facilitate communication between teachers and parents on a regular basis. The teachers hardly make efforts or demonstrate interests in engaging parents in the ECEC their child attends to gather information on the child's developmental status as well as family life from the parents (Moon, 2010; Yoo et al., 2015), though the issue of parental involvement in ECEC sectors is of great significance to policy makers in Korea.

Along the same line, Lee, Lee and Park (2017) investigated the current Nuri policy (1) as a universal free child care policy for all children regardless of their income levels and (2) as a standardised national curriculum for early years education and care in order to provide implications for ECEC policy in the future. There were 993 parents, 1034 working professionals (directors and teachers) in subsidised ECEC services, and 150 experts (college or university professors and civil servants) nationwide sampled as primary stakeholders. The main results found that professionals in ECEC services were in favour of the current entitled child care support, in which the same amount of subsidies are offered to all children regardless of the parents' income brackets, whereas the experts preferred differential support that depended on family's income level (Lee et al., 2017). The parent group took a stance midway between these two groups. In terms of effectiveness of the Nuri curriculum, professionals rated the Nuri curriculum higher than experts did, though all groups felt that the Nuri curriculum did not undermine the diverse curricula implemented previously at both kindergartens and child care centres. However, the experts were more likely to be against the standardised Nuri curriculum.

Finding from those studies (Lee et al., 2017; Yoo et al., 2015) underlined the need to reform the current ECEC policy in its direction towards expanding public child care sectors and improving the quality of services. There has been a strong need to narrow the pay gap between kindergarten teachers and teaching staff working at subsidised centres and contemplate its ramifications for children and families in an attempt to change the direction and stance of the Nuri policy (Seo, 2018).

Teacher qualifications and career development

It is widely accepted that ECEC quality cannot exceed the quality of the teachers who provide the education and care (Seo, 2018). In other words, teacher qualifications and career development have been directly related to the ECEC quality. When it comes to curriculum planning and pedagogy, kindergarten teachers were more skilled than their counterparts working at subsidised child care sectors (Lee et al., 2017). It is noteworthy to address that the ECEC teacher qualification is composed of the three levels for day care teachers (teacher level 1, 2, 3) and for kindergarten teachers (deputy head teacher, teacher level 1, 2). The minimum education for kindergarten teachers is the

2–3-year college degree (teacher level 2), while day care teachers are required to have at least a high-school diploma and 1-year vocation training (teacher level 3). In 2014 the percentage of teachers with 4-year college degrees for kindergarten teachers is 50.3 per cent, whereas for day care teachers it is 29.7 per cent (Park, 2015). This distinct unevenness in the initial training of teachers in the paralleled ECEC system has resulted in differing perceptions of the nature of early childhood education by the different ECEC stakeholders (Seo, 2016).

Within the Nuri policy teachers should be provided their job training opportunities for career development, findings from the limited number of studies indicated that there is still a great deal of variation in both the job training offered and what teachers are able to access (Seo, 2016; Lee et al., 2017; Yoo et al., 2015). The issues of job training and career development in ECEC sectors seem to have been neglected by researchers as well as policy makers in Korea. Thus, considering the efforts of career development for teachers would be profitable to improve ECEC quality in the future.

Effects on children

In Korea there is no national definition of ECEC quality; the only indicators for ECEC accreditation and evaluation are national (Organisation for Economic Cooperation and Development (OECD), 2015; Seo, 2018). The indicators consist of environmental dimensions, curricula (the Standardised Child care Curriculum for ages 0–2 years and the Nuri Curriculum for ages 3–5 years), interactions, health and safety, and management, and settings that meet these minimum quality criteria are accredited or pass evaluation. In the current situation of the deep-rooted conceptual and organisational divide in ECEC services, there has been a strong need for the united evaluation system with unified quality standards for both subsidised kindergartens and centres (Seo, 2018).

To improve the quality of ECEC, it was not until 2017 that the first large-scale Korean evaluation of the Nuri curriculum was conducted by Lee et al. (2017), after its nationwide implementation in 2013 in order to strengthen the nation's responsibility for ensuring a fair start from the early years of life. From this point of view, it is worthwhile to note the findings by Lee et al. (2017), who observed classes at kindergartens and child care centres across the country that were implementing the Nuri curriculum. Their study used the first united indicators across three dimensions: (1) Curriculum, (2) Environment, and (3) Professionalism as evaluation tools. As expected, among the indicators, the sub-area of teaching–learning of the first dimension of Curriculum was rated the lowest; and many teachers both in kindergartens and child care centres were unskilled at teaching practices. Given the inequality in ECEC services in Korea, this is not surprising but it is debatable if the gap between kindergarten teachers and teachers from the child care sectors remains evident, and its ramifications, specifically for children, were taken into consideration to evaluate the Nuri curriculum.

In the same vein, another study by Choi, Park, Lee, and Cho (2017) investigated the current status and pedagogy of 988 ECEC teachers who implemented the national Nuri curriculum in kindergartens and child care centres across the country. Choi et al. (2017) found that 30 per cent of teachers sampled answered that they were not efficacious in teaching and good at curriculum planning and pedagogy. Coupled with the findings pertaining to pedagogy and teaching efficacy (Choi et al., 2017; Lee et al., 2017), it is imperative to develop a professional development programme tailored for those lag-behind teachers who may impact children negatively in everyday settings of kindergartens and child care centres.

However, what is still missing in the full package of evaluation of the Nuri curriculum is a direct monitoring system for keeping track of children's outcomes, including children's views on their everyday experiences with the Nuri curriculum. Children's perceptions can not only provide useful information on their own developmental outcomes, but also ought to be required for staff evaluations about pedagogical practices, which in turn positively affect children's early development (Garvis, Ødegaard, & Lemon, 2015; Seo, 2018). As the recipients of the Nuri curriculum, children's own voices need to be heard and considered seriously, because their voices could help provide policy makers and ECEC staff with new insights into enhancing ECEC quality, as in Finland, which currently monitors children's views on their own ECEC experiences (OECD, 2015; Seo, 2018).

Moving forward

Given the research reviewed herein, there is a strong need to rationalise the Nuri policy (including the Nuri Curriculum), keep pressure for a consistent approach and conduct rigorous evaluations across all the ECEC sectors in Korea. This need is deeply rooted in the proposition that ECEC policies should affect the daily experiences of those whom they are intended to serve, given the new trend in social policy in Korea (Seo, 2016). The following is provided to present insights into and directions towards the development of ECEC policies in the future.

ECEC paradigm shift

As described in the previous section, ECEC policies focused on young children have been fragmented, reflecting a persistent struggle between the role of central government and roles of local governments within the limit of sustainable public funds. To date, the ECEC services have been highly polarised and politicised by the two distinct ideological perspectives (Conservatives vs. radical Democrat) on poverty, failing to meet the best interests of children. Even though the last two consecutive Korean administrations tried to transcend the boundary of their political ideologies in order to deal with low fertility problems via ECEC policies, the government efforts did not come to fruition.

However, in 2017 the new Child Allowance Act was enacted to take into account a changing ECEC policy landscape in Korea (Seo, 2019). Through this ground-breaking new policy, parents of young children (under age seven years) will be provided 100,000 won per month (approximately US$100) regardless of family income levels. In accordance with this benefit, the number of subsidised child care support centres in local communities increased ($n=92$, as of April 2018) to support parental childrearing practices and, in turn, promote child development (Seo, 2019).

In the midst of paradigm shift from in-service benefits towards direct child allowances, parents need more than ever to nurture children as capable caregivers. In this transitional period of ECEC history, the Korean government should create conditions that empower parents in the community in order to validate them as caregivers, help them form social networks, expand family resources, strengthen an equal and strong family–professional partnership, and improve primary stakeholders' efficacy (parent–child–professionals) (Seo, 2019). Early childhood educators and parents need to be intimately involved as partners in planning and nurturing for optimal development of young children. It is significant to be shared firmly among all of ECEC stakeholders including parents, teachers, providers and policymakers that education begins at birth and that children develop and learn in their very first years, which are crucial for their own development (Kaga, Barnnett, & Bennette, 2012).

Need for child assessment

The meaning of assessment of young children's progress in their development and learning has been broadly supported by researchers in the related field. Currently, 'assessment' tends to be used as an umbrella term for all types of measurement and evaluation (National Association for the Education of Young Children (NAEYC), 1992). Usually, the assessment is divided into two categories: (1) testing as the traditional standardised measures; (2) assessment as developmentally appropriate procedures that are used for educational decision making (Shepard, 1994). Regardless of how the assessment is defined or categorised, it should benefit the child. The uses for assessment facilitate the identification, programme planning and programme evaluation for all types of young children in all types of ECEC programmes (Seo & Chang, 2013).

Despite the importance of and purposes for assessment, there is no national system under which the children's progress in development and learning are evaluated over time. As a primary recipient of the Nuri curriculum, the child's outcome should be monitored as a key indicator of the effectiveness of the Nuri policy or the Nuri curriculum. This claim is supported by Han & Yoon (2017), who studied current assessment practices of ECEC teachers with a sample of 600 teachers from 300 kindergartens and child care centres nationwide. Only diagnostic evaluation to identify a child with special needs at the beginning of the school year was conducted (Han & Yoon, 2017). Coupled with this finding, the systematic, ongoing assessment for young children based on the Nuri curriculum should be mandated and, in turn, reflected in the individualised educational plan. To proceed with this, research findings that are large scale, broadly representative and longitudinal in nature should be documented in the future. This move will contribute to an 'evidence base' for development of ECEC policy on the likely benefits of offering this universal Nuri curriculum for all children in Korea and provide a policy rationale for the benefits of ECEC services, specifically, meeting the best interests of children.

Opportunity for professional development

As illuminated from the findings pertaining to the effects of the Nuri curriculum on teaching practices and efficacy (Choi et al., 2017; Lee et al., 2017), there is much room for improvement in teacher's professional development. As discussed by Choi et al. (2017), the welfare status of ECEC teachers was not good, in terms of long working hours and many administrative works, affecting their psycho-emotional wellbeing. Teachers reported that they were struggling with depression, frustration, work-related stress, fatigue and burn-outs, and those negative aspects of teachers' feeling and psycho-emotional struggles were found to affect their perceived levels of teaching efficacy and professionalism. Furthermore, teachers' perceived social recognition was associated with their levels of teaching efficacy and professionalism (Choi et al., 2017). The teachers with less social recognition were found to be less efficacious in teaching, and they had lower levels of professionalism than their counterparts with better recognition.

Teacher's professionalism, which often refers to their levels of perceived self-regulation and autonomy, salary satisfaction and respect for their profession, seems to be paradoxical because teaching in ECEC services cannot regulate itself, in terms of compulsory job training and ongoing career development, as specified in other professions, such as law and medicine (Seo, 2016). The time is ripe for reforming the current status and pedagogy of teachers, but the counterargument is that without opportunity for professional development, on a par with better compensation, teaching quality and optimal learning cannot be ensured. For policy-making, it is worthwhile to note that ECEC teachers and curriculum are not isolated and decontextualised. Rather, both are deeply woven into the lives of the children in kindergartens and child care centres, as well as those of their families both in and out of ECEC sectors.

Conclusions

As addressed so far, the ECEC services in Korea have been politicised over the last decade. Inside the ECEC politics the false beliefs that the provision of entitled child care services would boost the low fertility rate has guided the development of ECEC policies in Korea. On the flip side of child care policies, all the politicians in Korea, regardless of their ideology, have propagandised the child care issues to meet their political purposes. Like unlocking Pandora's box, a body of research on the effectiveness of Nuri policy is emerging that has investigated its effects on primary stakeholders. The effectiveness of the Nuri policy (Nuri Curriculum) is under severe debate, as discussed earlier.

As the ground-breaking new policy was enacted in 2017 to change the landscape in ECEC policies, the focus and direction of ECEC policy in Korea is moving towards provision of child allowances to all families with young children, in parallel with the current free in-service benefits. In the current situation, in which the Korean ECEC sectors (kindergartens and child care centres) are dichotomised, with two different authorities in charge, introduction of a new policy that would be universalistic to practice may bring about more confusion and chaos among ECEC stakeholders in Korea. Hence there is a clear momentum for a coherent, explicit and monitoring framework and standardised tools to evaluate ECEC policies in the future. This move will provide new evidence on good practice and insights for policy development, setting a stepping stone to depoliticise the ECEC issues in Korea.

References

Choi, Y. K., Park, C. H., Ha, Y. S., & Kim, H. S. (2016). *Implementing Strategies for ECEC Integration and Its Settlement in Korea*. Seoul: Korea Institute of Child Care and Education (KICCE).

Choi, Y. K., Park, J., Lee, S. M., & Cho, H. S. (2017). *Survey of ECEC Staff and Leader for Quality Improvement of Nuri Curriculum's Learning Outcomes*. Seoul: Korea Institute of Child care and Education (KICCE).

Garvis, S., Ødegaard, E., & Lemon, N. (2015). *Beyond Observations: Narratives and Young Children*. The Netherlands: Sense Publishers.

Han, S. S., & Yoon, S. J. (2017). Teachers' perception and practices about the assessment of young children based on the Nuri-Curriculum. *Korean Journal of Early Childhood Education, 37*(3), 365–387. http://dx.doi.org/10.18023/kjece.2017.37.3.017.

Kaga, Y., Barnnett, S., & Bennette, J. (2012). Integration and coordination of early childhood care and education in the Republic of Korea. *International Journal of Child Care and Education Policy, 6*(2), 1–20.

Kim, N. Y. (2016). *International Comparisons for Public Financing on ECEC (Policy Brief, Issue 8)*. Seoul: KICCE.

Korean Educational Development Institute (KEDI) (2015). *Education Statistics Service*. Korea: Ministry of Health and Welfare.

Kwon, M. K., & Kim, M. J. (2012). *Outcomes of the Early Childhood Education Policy in 2012 and Future Tasks*. Seoul: Korea Institute of Child care and Education (KICCE).

Lee, Y. J., Lee, G., & Park, E. (2017). *Evaluation of Nuri-policy and Future Tasks*. Seoul: Korea Institute of Child care and Education (KICCE).

Melhuish, E. C., & Petrogiannis, K. (Eds.). (2006). *Early Childhood Care and Education: International Perspectives on Policy and Research*. London: Routledge.

Moon, M. K. (2010). Enhancing the quality of full-day kindergarten education in Korea. *International Journal of Child Care and Education Policy, 4*(2), 55–66.

National Association for the Education of Young Children (NAEYC). (1992). Guidelines for appropriate curriculum content and assessment in programs serving children ages 3 through 8. In S. Bredekamp & T. Rousegrant (Eds.), *Reaching Potentials: Appropriate Curriculum and Assessment for Young Children* (pp. 9–27). Washington, DC: National Association for the Education of Young Children.

Organisation for Economic Cooperation and Development (OECD) (2015). *Starting Strong IV: Monitoring Quality in Early Childhood Education and Care*. Paris: OECD Publishing.

Park, C. H. (2016). Public opinion analysis about policy outcomes of the Nuri curriculum appeared on news media: Using social network analysis. *Korean Journal of Early Childhood Education, 36*(5), 399–422. doi:http://dx.doi.org/10.18023/kjece.2016.36.5.016.

Park, J. H. (2015). *ECEC Statistics of Korea: Access to Service, Participation and Financial Resources.* Policy Brief (Issue 5). Seoul: Korea Institute of Child care and Education (KICCE).

Seo, S. J. (2016). Teaching efficacy belief as a new paradigm for teacher career development and professionalism in Korea. In S. Garvis, D. Pendergast (Eds.), *Asia-Pacific Perspectives on Teacher Self-efficacy* (pp. 53–69). The Netherlands: Sense Publishers.

Seo, S. J. (2018). Early childhood education and care in Korea: History, current trends and future challenges. In S. Garvis, S. Phillipson, & H. Harju-Luukainne (Eds.), *Early Childhood Education in the 21st century: An International Perspective* (pp. 114–126). London: Routledge.

Seo, S. J. (2019). Pathways to build strong and equal family-professional partnerships in communities in Korea. In S. Phillipson & S. Garvis (Eds.), *Early Childhood Education in the 21st Century: Teachers and Families* (Vol. 2). London: Routledge.

Seo, S. J., & Chang, H. S. (2013). The reliability, validity, and usability of the on-line version for Early Development Screening Test(e-DEP) for young children. *Korean Journal of Special Education, 12*(3), 23–42.

Shepard, L. A. (1994). The challenges of assessing young children appropriately. *Phi Delta Kappan, 76*(5), 206–213.

Statistics of Korea. (2017). *Annual Korean family household research report.* Korean Government Department of Statistics.

Statistics of Korea. (2018). *Annual Korean family household research report.* Korean Government Department of Statistics.

Yang, M. S. (2014). *Multilateral Measures Required to Ease the Cost Burden of Early Childhood Education and Care (ECEC) Placed on Parents (Policy Brief, Issue 4).* Seoul: Korea Institute of Child care and Education (KICCE).

Yoo, H. M., Kim, A. R., & Kim, J. M. (2015). *The Trend of Child Care Support Policy and Its Future Challenges.* Seoul: Korea Institute of Child care and Education (KICCE).

12 Aotearoa/New Zealand early childhood education

Moving forward with intention

Gaye Tyler-Merrick, Sue Cherrington,
Tara McLaughlin, Claire McLachlan,
Karyn Aspden and Joanna Phillips

Introduction

The Aotearoa/New Zealand early childhood (EC) curriculum, *Te Whāriki*, first introduced in 1996 has been heralded as a huge success (Smith, 2015) and received international acclaim (Li, Park, & Chen, 2016). The structural features of the curriculum are represented as a *whāriki* or weaving metaphor, enabling the creation of a holistic, child-centred, inclusive curriculum that recognised New Zealand's bicultural heritage (Carr & May, 1993). In April 2017, a revised version of *Te Whāriki* was released. While the structural features of the principles, strands and goals remain the same, guidance to teachers reflects changes in society, research and practice in the last 20 years (McLachlan, 2017). Volume 1 of this series presented changes across the successive curriculum versions.

Guided by the principles, strands and goals underpinning *Te Whāriki* (Ministry of Education, 1996; 2017), teachers and practitioners are expected to weave a curriculum that reflects the values, goals and beliefs of teachers, children, families, *whānau* (extended family) and community. Thus, children's daily curriculum experiences and interactions are determined at a local community level. This presents both opportunities and challenges in ensuring that children experience a curriculum that is broad and deep but also responsive to individual interests, culture and context (Dalli, 2011; Smith, 2015).

Historically, strengths and opportunities identified in the curriculum include the positioning of children as competent and confident learners (Nuttall, 2013); the view that learning occurs through *all* experiences and interactions and the importance of relationships (Nuttall, 2003); the focus on children's interests in a child-centred, play-based approach (White et al., 2008) and the openness of the curriculum to allow for maximum teacher decision making (Brostrom, 2003).

Challenges and concerns about the implementation of *Te Whāriki* have also been raised, including several reports from the national Education Review Office (ERO, 2013, 2016, 2017) that identified varying levels of quality across the sector. Further critique has noted that the non-prescriptive nature of *Te Whāriki* relies heavily on teacher content and pedagogical knowledge (Hedges & Cullen, 2005); the potential for the openness of the curriculum to be used to justify poor or traditional practices (ERO, 2013); and the absence of guidance on pedagogy, teaching and the role of the teacher (ERO, 2013; McLaughlin, Aspden, & Snyder, 2016; Meade, 2000).

While many of the challenges outlined above remain, McLachlan (2017) has noted that the 2017 version of the curriculum 'is not business as usual with a new cover' (p. 8), highlighting a new guidance on pedagogy, learning outcomes, assessment and particularly, teachers as intentional practitioners. This increased emphasis on intentional teaching reflects international trends highlighting intentionality and the importance of teacher–child interactions (Epstein, 2014; Kennedy & Stonehouse, 2012; Siraj-Batchford, 2009) along with recognition within New Zealand that teachers need a more active role in children's learning if the promise of the sociocultural curriculum is to be realised (Cherrington, 2016; Cullen, 1996; Hedges, 2000; Meade, 2000). Thus, meaningful engagement with the revised curriculum will require a process of re-envisioning deeply embedded perspectives of child-centredness that have traditionally positioned teachers roles as non-directive and facilitative (Siraj-Blatchford, 2009). To aid teachers in this process, McLaughlin and Cherrington (2018) have highlighted useful models to help teachers explore notions of intentional teaching within play-based practice.

McLachlan, Fleer and Edwards (2018) argue that *Te Whāriki* is a *competence*-based curriculum in which learners have some control over the selection, pacing and sequencing of curriculum. This type of curriculum also requires teacher judgements of *when* and *how* to introduce new learning to children. Despite the increased emphasis on intentional teaching within the updated curriculum, there remain a number of teaching practices that are *hidden* and teacher's *perceptions* of their implementation of teaching strategies may not reflect what occurs in practice. In the following sections we examine research into teachers' experiences of, and challenges in implementing *Te Whāriki* in relation to (1) promoting children's social and emotional competence, (2) providing quality infant and toddler education and care, (3) developing children's literacy and (4) understanding the impact digital technology has on the engagement of children and families within the Aotearoa/New Zealand context.

Promoting children's social–emotional competence

Aotearoa/New Zealand EC teachers are generally aware of the pivotal role they play in supporting the social–emotional development of young children and key aspects of promoting social–emotional competence are embedded throughout the curriculum strands (Koh, 2017). Yet, a growing body of literature (ERO, 2011a, 2013, 2017; Koh, 2017; McLaughlin et al., 2016; Phillips & Tyler-Merrick, 2015; Tyler-Merrick, Hunter, van Dyk, & Soper, 2017) suggests that working with children who lack social–emotional competence skills is one of the most stressful issues teachers face. In 2017 the Education Review Office (ERO) reported that teachers said they received inadequate training to teach social–emotional competence skills during their initial teacher education (ITE) programme. This finding was also supported by professional leaders in EC services who reported that ITE programmes did not always equip teachers with the necessary skills to teach or respond to children's needs, including those children with social–emotional competence difficulties (ERO, 2017). This need for additional knowledge and skills was previously highlighted by ERO in 2011(a), when they found in 45 per cent of the services they reviewed, teachers' practices were only '*somewhat effective*' or '*not effective*' in supporting children's social–emotional competence. Issues such as poor policy implementation, lack of consistency and poor-quality teacher–child interactions were identified as the most problematic.

Despite the inclusion of social–emotional competence in the curriculum, Koh (2017) found that teachers do not refer to *Te Whāriki* (Ministry of Education, 1996) to inform their practice but they did identify similarities in their own philosophical beliefs and practices with the principles and strands of *Te Whāriki*, especially in relation to developing children's wellbeing and sense of belonging. Similarly, McLaughlin, Aspden and McLachlan (2015) found that teachers stressed the importance of building warm and trusting relationships with children and their family/*whānau* as the foundation for promoting children's learning and social–emotional competence. Koh (2017) also found teachers were less specific about naming the teaching strategies they used to support children's social–emotional competence and that the ways they taught social–emotional competence varied. In contrast, McLaughlin, Aspden and Clarke (2017) reported that specific social–emotional teaching practices were derived from teachers' descriptions of their interaction with children rather than specific naming of practices. Once named, however, teachers were able to indicate their level of use of different specific teaching practices (e.g. naming different emotion words, modelling how to enter peer play or take turns).

Collectively, these studies indicate that teachers have a general understanding about how to support the development of social–emotional competence in young children, suggesting that more specific, nuanced approaches and strategies to building competence and addressing concerns with children's social behaviours may be relatively 'hidden' (or unnamed) practices within the Aotearoa/New Zealand EC context. Research into recent professional learning programmes to support teacher practice in this area is now discussed.

Professional leaders play a pivotal role in providing guidance to teachers in their EC services by sharing and modelling appropriate strategies to support the development of social–emotional competence skills (ERO, 2016). In Aotearoa/New Zealand, research in this field is still in its infancy but professional learning opportunities on *how* to use intentional teaching practices to teach social–emotional competence skills in the daily EC programme is developing with promising results. With the use of two professional learning workshops, Tyler-Merrick et al. (2017) found increased teacher positive attention to children resulted in increased positive child behaviour and decreased challenging behaviour. The teachers anecdotally reported they were more motivated to continue to use the identified strategies as they could see positive outcomes for all children.

A more widely available professional learning programme to support New Zealand teachers' to teach social–emotional competence skills is the *Incredible Years* programme (Ministry of Education, 2018). Positive results from the National Evaluation of the programme (Wylie & Felgate, 2016) have been reported by ECE teachers, with their confidence levels in managing children's behaviour increasing from 46 per cent at the beginning of the programme to 88 per cent by the end of the programme.

These studies suggest that developing EC teachers' skills in supporting young children's social–emotional development can be achieved when hidden practices are made explicit and teachers are supported to learn about, and use, specific practices in line with *Te Whāriki's* principles and values.

Providing quality infant and toddler education and care

In outlining the nature of curriculum in New Zealand EC services, *Te Whāriki* differentiates between the characteristics, strengths and needs of infants, toddlers and young children. Recognising individual pathways of development, *Te Whāriki* identifies these three groups of children within overlapping bands: infants (birth to 18 months), toddlers (one to three years) and young children (2.5 years to school entry). Both global and national trends indicate growing numbers of infants and toddlers are attending EC services for at least part of their week and, at times, for long periods of time (Dalli et al., 2011).

Alongside growth in participation, there is increasing research evidence that intentional and specialised teaching practices are required in order to provide quality education and care for our youngest children (ERO, 2015). Such practices for infants and toddlers are necessary given infants' and toddlers' higher needs for physical and emotional support in line with attachment theory and current neurological research on early brain development (National Scientific Council on the Developing Child, 2009; Shonkoff & Phillips, 2000). *Te Whāriki* affirms the need for specialised teaching practices by making distinctions in the examples of practice for infants, toddlers, and young children.

In order for infants and toddlers to thrive, the EC environment must be built upon the foundation of rich, sensitive, responsive and individualised relationships between adults and children (Shonkoff & Phillips, 2000). *Te Whāriki* prioritises such relationships and argues that, in order to thrive and learn, an infant or toddler must establish an intimate, responsive and trusting relationship with at least one adult within the setting. New Zealand research suggests that these relationships function best in the context of an attachment-based approach (such as a primary caregiving or key teacher model), in which the organisational culture of the setting allows teachers to engage with children in individualised, responsive and flexible ways that best meet the needs of each infant or toddler (Bary, 2010; Rockel, 2010). Such models also emphasise the critical importance of close partnerships between teachers and family members, collaborative approaches and flexible routines and rituals (Dalli, Kibble, Cairns-Cowan, Corrigan, & McBride, 2009).

However, the extent to which attachment-based approaches are adopted in EC settings is varied (Carroll-Lind & Angus, 2011), compounded by systemic issues related to the lack of specialised training for infant/toddler teachers, the need for a fully qualified EC teaching workforce and limited access to targeted professional development related to infant/toddler pedagogy (Dalli et al., 2011). Implementation of specialised practices can be problematic if teachers do not understand important characteristics for each age group and the need for a more intensive relational pedagogy for very young children. Without specialised practices, professional development or appropriate qualifications teachers may implement a de facto, watered down version of curriculum for 3–5-year-old children that will not meet the needs of infants and toddlers and has the potential to be detrimental to their learning and wellbeing. Underestimating the importance of specialised teaching practices and, as a result, minimising the role of the infant/toddler teacher serves neither children nor teachers, and has potential to render such practices less visible within broader EC pedagogy.

There is also clear evidence for the need for teachers to be intentional in their interactions with infants and toddlers and provide a responsive curriculum across all areas of learning (National Scientific Council on the Developing Child, 2009). This requires having specialised practice knowledge about effective approaches for the unique characteristics of these age groups and comprehensive knowledge of development and curriculum. A recent ERO report (2015) identified that, consistent with a strong emphasis on relationships, EC services gave priority to the wellbeing and belonging stands of the curriculum with infants and toddlers yet placed less emphasis on the communication and exploration strands of the curriculum. Intentional teaching approaches are thereby critical in ensuring that within the context of sensitive and responsive interactions, teachers also attend to cognitive and language development, positioning infant and toddlers as capable and confident learners, communicators and explorers. Thus, taken together, attachment-based caregiving, specialised pedagogical knowledge and intentional teaching practices provide an important pathway to improving quality infant/toddler pedagogy across curricular and developmental domains.

Developing children's literacy in *Te Whāriki*

Internationally, research has focused on the role of the EC teacher in supporting children's literacy prior to school entry (National Early Literacy Panel, 2009; Shanahan & Lonigan, 2013). Literacy was included in *Te Whāriki* (Ministry of Education, 1996), but how teachers should promote literacy was open to interpretation (McLachlan & Arrow, 2011). For teachers with strong understandings of literacy, *Te Whāriki* offered maximum flexibility and scope, but for teachers with poor understandings, it was a recipe for few or poor literacy practices. ERO's (2011b) national evaluation of literacy in EC services suggests many teachers lacked knowledge and effective pedagogies to promote literacy in EC, with wide variation in the literacy experiences provided for children in

353 EC settings. Around 25 per cent of centres provided inappropriate literacy activities for young children, such as phonics packages with two year olds, extended mat sessions and meaningless literacy worksheet activities.

New Zealand research suggests that teachers have had difficulty in understanding their role using *Te Whāriki*, particularly in relation to literacy, given its guidance on broad rather than specific practices (Foote, Smith, & Ellis, 2004; Hedges, 2003; McLachlan & Arrow, 2013). Westerveld, Gillon, van Bysterveldt and Boyd's (2015) study of emergent literacy skills in 92 4-year-olds in kindergartens showed that, although girls did better than boys, all children scored relatively poorly on letter name knowledge and phonological awareness – literacy abilities which are predictive of later reading achievement (Tunmer, Chapman, & Prochnow, 2006). McLachlan and Arrow (2013) and McLachlan, Arrow and Watson (2014) similarly found low levels of letter name knowledge, phonological awareness and vocabulary in children in low SES child care centres and kindergartens. However, children's literacy abilities were improved after professional learning with teachers, which led to an enhanced literacy environment and intentional teaching of literacy within free play environments. Westerveld et al. (2015) and McLachlan et al.'s (McLachlan and Arrow, 2013; McLachlan et al., 2014) studies suggest teachers need to be more aware of the importance of children's literacy development and have the requisite pedagogies to be able to teach in EC.

One of the problematic issues for EC teachers is the literacy policy framework within which they teach (McLachlan & Arrow, 2011). New Zealand's current literacy strategy is a conglomeration of approaches developed by the Ministry of Education (2003) to counter the literacy gap highlighted in international studies of literacy and reading (e.g. PIRLS and PISA) and includes literacy-related professional development for primary teachers and resources for teaching (Ministry of Education, 2003, 2006). These resources do not explicitly address the role that EC teachers play in supporting children's literacy (e.g. Ministry of Education, 2006), which may contribute to EC teachers' lack of confidence and certainty about their role as teachers of literacy (McLachlan & Arrow, 2013; ERO, 2011b). Whether deliberately, or an oversight, successive documents have overlooked how literacy should be promoted in EC settings, instead focusing on dispositions for literacy. This has resulted in the knowledge and skills and associated practices being hidden from teachers or more difficult to access (Nuttall, 2013). Although dispositions for literacy are obviously important, so too are the experiences of literacy that children need in order to meet the school entry expectations of the Literacy Learning Progressions (Ministry of Education, 2012) and which are part of the literate cultural capital that predicts reading achievement (Tunmer et al., 2006).

The greater focus on outcomes in children's learning recommended by the Advisory Group on Early Learning (2015) was influential in the 2017 revision of *Te Whāriki*. Twenty learning outcomes are highlighted including three targeted at oral language and literacy acquisition. Alongside these, the revised curriculum offers stronger guidance on the role of teachers in promoting oral language and literacy acquisition and clearer expectations of what literacy learning and development will look like, so teachers can more readily assess children's literacy outcomes. Such changes have potential to build EC teachers' confidence and make their literacy teaching practices more visible.

Digital technologies, literacy and *Te Whāriki*

Research on the use of digital technologies in EC is relatively recent, although in the compulsory school sector it is long-standing (McLean, 2016). Burnett and Merchant (2013) argue that children are increasingly 'technologised', as they encounter toys with digital components from birth and this technologisation increases through childhood. While there is growing research on digital literacy practices in home, school and digital communities, including the online spaces utilised by young children (Hooker, 2015; Wohlwend, 2013), EC teacher practices in relation to supporting children learning through digital literacies are an emerging pedagogy.

In her Australian study, Hill (2010) found that children had greater 'multiliteracies' knowledge than anticipated through their engagement with digital technologies at home. When teachers built on the multiliteracies knowledge from the home in the EC setting, there was greater literacy engagement and strengthened literacy outcomes for children. McLean (2016) argues that teachers need to be aware of new literacy practices and how children engage in what Burnett and Merchant (2013) refer to as 'meaning-making in technologically–enriched contexts' (p. 577). Both Burnett and Merchant (2013) and McLean (2016) have noted the importance of teachers becoming confident with digital technologies in order that they are able to use these as part of their literacy practices, rather than separate from them. Although *Te Whāriki* 2017 refers to supporting children's engagement with digital technologies, there is still limited guidance on teachers' roles. Building on the emerging research in this area within New Zealand, including teacher-led enquiries, is necessary to strengthen our knowledge base and make more explicit effective pedagogical practices in order to promote teachers' capacities and confidence in this area.

Notably, one specific technology has received a lot of attention and uptake across the sector: digital or e-portfolios. Digital or e-portfolios enable online representations of children's assessment documentation for the purpose of making learning visible and sharing with children and families. Recent New Zealand studies (Goodman & Cherrington, 2015; Hooker, 2015) found greater engagement by families with their children and their assessment data when centres moved to using digital or e-portfolios, while Higgins and Cherrington (2017) found teacher–parent communication was enhanced. Children's engagement with their e-portfolios is somewhat more problematic. Goodman and Cherrington (2017) found that EC services adopted idiosyncratic approaches to their introduction of e-portfolios, ranging from using e-portfolios as their sole approach to documenting children's learning, through to maintaining a full or abbreviated traditional, hard-copy portfolio for children alongside e-portfolios which they used primarily for communicating children's learning to parents. In many instances, children were given little or no access to their online portfolio, raising the question that 'if documentation of children's learning is only available online, how do teachers ensure that young children are able to re-visit, reflect on and self-assess their learning?' (Goodman & Cherrington, 2017, p. 36). Their findings highlight the importance of teachers carefully thinking through the adoption of new technologies, particularly in relation to the principles, goals and learning outcomes of *Te Whāriki*. To achieve such outcomes requires the provision of appropriate professional learning to support teachers' confidence and use of intentional practices when using digital technologies, including e-portfolios, while also including children in their own learning.

Future directions

We argue that it is time to move to 'actionable behaviours' (McLaughlin et al., 2015, p. 32) to enact the philosophical and aspirational foundations of *Te Whāriki*. Across the curriculum, including the areas we have highlighted in this chapter, EC teachers in Aoteaora/New Zealand appear to struggle relating theory to practice (Alvestad, Duncan, & Berge, 2009; Koh, 2017). Moving to ensure children's learning is more visible and that teachers engage in intentional teaching practices in which the goals they have for children's learning and the strategies they use to meet those goals are made explicit may help address this issue.

The provision of more professional learning opportunities for teachers, both at the pre-service and in-service level, is required to support greater intentionality within their practice together with using adaptive and responsive approaches that are appropriate for teaching and learning in EC settings. Such professional development should draw upon the characteristics of effective professional learning and development as identified by Mitchell and Cubey's (2003) best evidence synthesis of quality professional development, in particular that 'theoretical and content knowledge and information about alternative practices' is included and that it 'helps ... change educational practice, beliefs, understanding, and/or attitudes' (p. 81).

Alongside such professional learning programmes, we advocate for ongoing research to help inform, identify and enact specific teaching practices that work in Aotearoa/New Zealand EC settings. Finally, we look forward to the evaluation of the implementation of *Te Whāriki 2017* planned by the Education Review Office over the 2018–2020 period, in particular the extent to which teachers are better able to implement the curriculum and assess 'what matters here' (Ministry of Education, 2017, p. 65) for all children.

References

Advisory Group on Early Learning. (2015). *Report of the Advisory Group on Early Learning*. Wellington, NZ: Ministry of Education.

Alvestad, M., Duncan, J., & Berge, A. (2009). New Zealand ECE teachers talk about Te Whāriki. *New Zealand Journal of Teachers' Work, 6*(1), 3–19.

Bary, R. (2010). It's all about relationships: Infant and toddler pedagogy. *The First Years: Ngā Tau Tuatahi. New Zealand Journal of Infant and Toddler Education, 12*(2), 15–18.

Brostrom, S. (2003). Understanding Te Whāriki from a Danish perspective. In J. Nuttall (Ed.), *Weaving Te Whāriki: Aotearoa New Zealand's early childhood curriculum document in theory and practice* (pp. 215–238). Wellington, NZ: NZCER Press.

Burnett, C., & Merchant, G. (2013). Learning, literacies and new technologies: The current context and future possibilities. In J. Larson & J. Marsh (Eds.), *The SAGE Handbook of Early Childhood Literacy* (2nd edn) (pp. 575–587). London: SAGE Publications.

Carr, M., & May, H. (1993). Choosing a model. Reflecting on the development process of Te Whāriki: National early childhood curriculum guidelines in New Zealand. *International Journal of Early Years Education, 9*(3), 7–21.

Carroll-Lind, J., & Angus, J. (2011). *Through Their Lens: An Inquiry into Non-parental Education and Care of Infants and Toddlers.* Wellington, NZ: Office of the Children's Commission.

Cherrington, S. (2016). Early childhood teachers' thinking and reflection: A model of current practice in New Zealand. *Early Years. An International Journal of Research and Development*, online first. doi:10.1080/09575146.2016.1259211.

Cullen, J. (1996). The challenge of Te Whāriki for future developments in early childhood education. *Delta, 48*(1), 113–125.

Dalli, C. (2011). A curriculum of open possibilities. A New Zealand kindergarten teacher's view of professional practice. *Early Years. An International Journal of Research and Development, 31*(3), 229–243.

Dalli, C., Kibble, N., Cairns-Cowan, N., Corrigan, J., & McBride, B. (2009). Reflecting on primary caregiving through action research: The centre of innovation experience at Childspace Ngaio Infants and Toddlers' Centre. *The First Years: Ngā Tau Tuatahi. New Zealand Journal of Infant and Toddler Education, 11*(2), 38–45.

Dalli, C., White, J., Rockel, J., Duhn, I., with Buchanan, E., Davidson, S., Ganly, S., Kus, L., & Wang, B. (2011). *Quality Early Childhood Education for Under-two-year-olds: What Should it Look Like?* A literature review. Ministry of Education. Wellington. Retrieved from www.educationcounts.govt.nz/publications/ece.

Education Review Office (ERO). (2011a). Positive foundation for learning: confident and competent children in early childhood service. Retrieved from www.ero.govt.nz/publications/positive-foundations-for-learning-confident-and-competent-children-in-early-childhood-services/.

Education Review Office (ERO). (2011b). Literacy in early childhood services: Teaching and learning. Retrieved from www.ero.govt.nz/National-Reports/Literacy-in-Early-Childhood-Services-Teaching-and-Learning-February-2011.

Education Review Office (ERO). (2013). *Working with Te Whāriki.* Wellington: New Zealand Government, 27 May. Retrieved from www.ero.govt.nz/National-Reports/Working-with-Te-Whariki-May-2013.

Education Review Office (ERO). (2015). *Infants and Toddlers: Competent and Confident Communicators and Explorers.* Wellington, NZ: Author.

Education Review Office (ERO). (2016). Early learning curriculum. Retrieved from: www.ero.govt.nz/publications/early-learning-curriculum/.

Education Review Office (ERO). (2017). Newly graduated teachers: Preparation and confidence to teach. Retrieved from: www.ero.govt.nz/assets/Uploads/ERO-Newly-Graduated-Teachers-December-2017.pdf.

Epstein, A. S. (2014). *The Intentional Teacher: Choosing the Best Strategies for Young Children's Learning* (2nd edn). Washington, DC: National Association for the Education of Young Children.

Foote, L., Smith, J., & Ellis, F. (2004). The impact of teachers' beliefs on the literacy experiences of young children: A New Zealand perspective. *Early Years: Journal of International Research and Development, 24*(2), 135–148.

Goodman, N., & Cherrington, S. (2015). Parent, whānau, and teacher engagement through online portfolios in early childhood education. *Early Childhood Folio, 19*(1), 10–16. Retrieved from http://dx.doi.org/10.18296/ecf.0003.

Goodman, N., & Cherrington, S. (2017). Children's engagement with their learning using e-portfolios. *Asia-Pacific Journal of Research in Early Childhood Education 11*(3), 17–38.

Hedges, H. (2000). Teaching in early childhood: Time to merge constructivist views so learning through play equals teaching through play. *Australian Journal of Early Childhood, 25*(4), 16–21.

Hedges, H. (2003). A response to criticism and challenge: Early literacy and numeracy in Aotearoa/New Zealand. *New Zealand Research in Early Childhood Education, 6*, 13–22.

Hedges, H., & Cullen, J. (2005). Subject knowledge in early childhood curriculum and pedagogy: Beliefs and practices. *Contemporary Issues in Early Childhood, 6*(1), 66–79.

Higgins, A., & Cherrington, S. (2017). What's the story? Exploring parent–teacher communication through ePortfolios, *Australasian Journal of Early Childhood, 42*(4), 13–21. doi:http://dx.doi.org/10.23965/AJEC.42.4.02.

Hill, S. (2010). The millennium generation: Teacher-researchers exploring new forms of literacy. *Journal of Early Childhood Literacy, 10*(3), 314–340.

Hooker, T. A. (2015). Assessment for learning: A comparative study of paper-based portfolios and online ePortfolios. *Early Childhood Folio, 19*(1) 17–24.

Kennedy, A., & Stonehouse, A. (2012). Victorian early years learning and development framework evidence paper: Practice principle guide 6 integrated teaching and learning approaches. Victoria Department of Education and Early Childhood Development. Retrieved from www.education.vic.gov.au/Documents/childhood/providers/edcare/practiceguide6.PDF.

Koh, G. (2017). *A Descriptive Study of How Teachers Identify and Respond to Children's Challenging Behaviour in Early Childhood Education Settings.* Master of Science thesis, University of Canterbury, Christchurch, New Zealand.

Li, H., Park, E., & Chen, J. (Eds.). (2016). *Early Childhood Policies in Asia-Pacific.* New York: Springer.

McLachlan, C. (2017). 'Not business as usual': Reflections on the 2017 update of *Te Whāriki. Early Education, 62*, 8–14.

McLachlan, C., & Arrow, A. (2011). Literacy in the early years in New Zealand: Policies, politics and pressing reasons for change. *Literacy, 45*(3), 126–133.

McLachlan, C. J., & Arrow, A. W. (2013). Promoting alphabet knowledge and phonological awareness in low socioeconomic child care settings: A quasi experimental study in five New Zealand centres. *Reading and Writing, 27*(5), 819–839. doi:10.1007/s11145-013-9467-y.

McLachlan, C., Arrow, A., & Watson, J. (2014). Partnership in promoting literacy: An exploration of two studies in low decile early childhood settings in New Zealand. In J. Duncan & L. Conner (Eds.), *Research Partnerships within Early Years Education: Relational Expertise and Knowledges in Action.* Sydney, NSW: Palgrave Macmillan.

McLachlan, C., Fleer, M., & Edwards, S. (2018). *Early Childhood Curriculum: Planning, Assessment and Implementation* (3rd edn). Melbourne, Vic: Cambridge University Press.

McLaughlin, T., Aspden, K., & Clarke, L. (2017). How do teachers support children's social-emotional competence? Strategies for teachers. *Early Childhood Folio, 21*(2), 21–27. doi/org/10.18296/ecf.0041.

McLaughlin, T., Aspden, K., & McLachlan, C. (2015). How do teachers build strong relations: A study of teaching practices to support child learning and social-emotional competence. *Early Childhood Folio, 19*(1), 31–38.

McLaughlin, T., Aspden. K., & Snyder, P. (2016). Intentional teaching as a pathway to equity in early childhood education: Participation, quality, and equity. *New Zealand Journal of Educational Studies, 51*(2), 175–195. doi:10.1007/s40841-016-0062-z.

McLaughlin, T., & Cherrington, S. (2018). Creating a rich curriculum through intentional teaching. *New Zealand Council for Educational Research: Early Childhood Folio, 22*(1), 33–38.

McLean, K. (2016). Literacy, technology and early years education: Building sustainable practice. In C. J. McLachlan & A. W. Arrow (Eds.), *Literacy in the Early Years: Reflections on International Research and Practice* (pp. 239–268). New York: Springer.

Meade, A. (2000). If you say it three times, is it true? Critical use of research in early childhood education. *International Journal of Early Years Education, 8*(1), 15–26.

Ministry of Education. (1996). *Te Whāriki: he whāriki matauranga mō ngā mokopuna o Aotearoa: Early Childhood Curriculum.* Wellington, NZ: Learning Media.

Ministry of Education. (2003). *Effective Literacy Practice in Years 1 to 4.* Wellington, NZ: Learning Media.

Ministry of Education. (2006). *Effective Literacy Practice in Years 5–8.* Wellington, NZ: Learning Media.

Ministry of Education. (2012). *Literacy Learning Progressions.* Retrieved from www.literacyprogressions.tki.org.nz/.

Ministry of Education. (2017). *Te Whāriki: he whāriki matauranga mō ngā mokopuna o Aotearoa: Early Childhood Curriculum.* Wellington, NZ: Learning Media.

Ministry of Education. (2018). Incredible years teacher. Retrieved from: http://pb4l.tki.org.nz/Incredible-Years-Teacher.

Mitchell, L., & Cubey, P. (2003). *Professional Development in Early Childhood Settings: Best Evidence Synthesis Iteration.* Wellington, NZ: Ministry of Education.

National Early Literacy Panel. (2009). *Developing Early Literacy: Report of the National Early Literacy Panel.* Washington, DC: National Institute for Literacy.

National Scientific Council on the Developing Child. (2009). *Young children develop in an environment of relationships.* Working Paper No.°1. Retrieved from www.developingchild.net.

Nuttall, J. (2003). Exploring the role of the teacher within *Te Whāriki*: Some possibilities and constraints. In *Weaving Te Whāriki: Aotearoa New Zealand's Early Childhood Curriculum Document in Theory and Practice* (pp.°161–187). Wellington, NZ: NZCERPress.

Nuttall, J. (2013). Curriculum concepts as cultural tools: Implementing *Te Whāriki*. In *Weaving Te Whāriki: Aotearoa New Zealand's Early Childhood Curriculum Document in Theory and Practice* (2nd edn) (pp.°177–196). Wellington, NZ: NZCER Press.

Phillips, J., & Tyler-Merrick, G. (2015). *The Effects of an In-service Course to Develop Early Childhood Teacher's Skill in Positive Behaviour Strategies.* Wellington, NZ: NZARE (NZ Association for Research in Education) Early Childhood Education SIG Hui, 15 May.

Rockel, J. (2010). Infant pedagogy: Learning how to learn. In B. Clark & A. Grey (Eds.), *Ata kitea te pae. Scanning the Horizon – Perspectives on Early Childhood Education* (pp.°97–110). Auckland, NZ: Pearson.

Shanahan, T., & Lonigan, C. J. (Eds.). (2013). *Literacy in Preschool and Kindergarten Children: The National Early Literacy Panel and Beyond.* Baltimore, MD: Brookes Publishing.

Shonkoff, J., & Phillips, D. (2000). *From Neurons to Neighborhoods.* Washington, DC: National Academy Press.

Siraj-Batchford, I. (2009). Quality teaching in the early years. In A. Anning, J. Cullen, & M. Fleer (Eds.), *Early Childhood Education: Society and Structure* (pp.°147–157). London: Sage.

Smith, A. B. (2015). Te Whāriki: An enduring legacy? *Swings and Roundabouts, 26,* 18–19. Retrieved from https://issuu.com/waterfordpresslimited/docs/sw2_2015_web.

Tunmer, W. E., Chapman, J. W., & Prochnow, J. E. (2006). Literate cultural capital at school entry predicts later reading achievement: A seven-year longitudinal study. *New Zealand Journal of Educational Studies, 41*(2), 183–204.

Tyler-Merrick, G., Hunter, J., van Dyk, M., & Soper, J. (2017). *The Effects of Two Data Informed Professional Development Workshops on Increasing Teacher Best Practice in Three BestStart Early Childhood Centres.* Christchurch, NZ: BestStart Regional Conference, 6 May.

Westerveld, M., Gillon, G., van Bysterveldt, K., & Boyd, L. (2015). The emergent literacy skills of four-year-old children receiving free kindergarten early childhood education in New Zealand. *International Journal of Early Years Education, 23*(4,), 339–351. doi:10.1080/09669760.2015.1033617.

White, J., Ellis, F., O'Malley, A., Rockel, J., Stover, S., & Toso, M. (2008). Play and learning in Aotearoa New Zealand early childhood education. In I. Pramling Samuelsson, & M. Fleer (Eds.), *Play and Learning in Early Childhood Settings: International Perspectives* (pp.°19–49). Netherlands: Springer.

Wohlwend, K. (2013). *Literacy Playshop: New Literacies, Popular Media, and Play in the Early Childhood Classroom.* New York: Teachers College Press.

Wylie, C., & Felgate, R. (2016). *Use of IYT learning in New Zealand: Changes for 'target' students and sustainability of learning and practice 8–9 months after the end of the IYT programme. Incredible Years Teacher programmes.* NZCER Evaluation Report 3. Wellington, NZ: NZCER Press.

13 Contested quality

The struggle over quality, play and preschooling in Norwegian early childhood education and care

Svein Erik Tuastad, Elisabeth Bjørnestad and Marit Alvestad

Introduction

Competing concepts of quality have caused deep and long-lasting controversies over core elements in Norwegian early childhood education and care (ECEC). In this chapter, we aim to analyse the background for and the contents of the controversies as the dispute may have an impact on prospective policies. We also aim to identify possible common ground in the argumentation from the contenders. This chapter, first, examines the research questions related to the content of the dispute: What is its historical background? Who are the main contenders in the controversy, and what are their basic arguments? Can novel empirical research on Norwegian ECEC cast new light on the dispute? Second, we look closer into the arguments and the positions by addressing the final research question: To what extent do the arguments on the two sides appear to be mutually exclusive?

The Nordic countries represent a separate tradition of system governance on policies affecting children, the child–political domain (Bennett, 2008; Organisation for Economic Co-operation and Development (OECD), 2006; Ringmose & Kragh-Müller, 2017). Scandinavian policies covering child care and early education were forerunners to establish widespread institutionalised care and to develop child-centrism (Frønes, 2018; Gilbert, Parton, & Skivenes, 2011; Hantrais, 2004). Viewed in this light, both scholars and politicians have conventionally cherished Norwegian child policies. For instance, in his autobiography, former Norwegian Prime Minister Jens Stoltenberg of the Labour party considered the Norwegian family policies on children – namely, ECEC and parental leave – to be among his major political triumphs (Stoltenberg, 2017, p. 532). Moreover, Inga Martha Thorkildsen, the Minister of Children and Equality, described Norway as:

> the best country in the world for mothers, the best country in the world for breastfeeding, the best country in the world for women, the best country in the world for fathers and the second best country in the world for children.
>
> (Thorkildsen, 2013) (Authors' translation)

In relation to ECEC, the political self-understanding illustrated earlier does not necessarily correspond to high rankings on comparative international quality evaluations (Bjørnestad & Os, 2018). The quality of ECEC, in recent years, has been under increased political scrutiny, signalling a political ambition of stronger monitoring and evaluation (Bjørnestad, Baustad, & Alvestad, 2019; Ministry of Education and Research, 2009, 2013, 2015, 2016; OECD, 2015). Though it began with quantity, political attention has shifted to quality (Lohmander Karlsson, Vandenbroeck, Pirard, Peeters, & Alvestad, 2009).

However, academics and professionals who work with children have contested the concept of quality. Some central academics, who have set normative premises for the scholarly debate, have even advocated eliminating the concept of quality altogether (Dahlberg, Moss, & Pence, 1999). Recently, when the minister in charge of ECEC announced a new policy that stressed quality measures and early learning, media reported a 'storm' against it among the professionals working in the field (Fladberg, 2016, 19 September). The wider social investment strategy came under attack from several scholars, as well as from observers, debaters and commentators (see for instance, Pettersvold & Østrem, 2018a; 2018b; Sandelson, 2018; Thoresen, 2018); Ulvund, 2017). It will be of wider interest to look closer into Norwegian ECEC; a political success among politicians while controversial among scholars and the professions.

In this chapter, we analyse the controversies surrounding the quality dimension in Norwegian ECEC and determine to what extent the competing arguments appear mutually exclusive. This analysis is based on two previous studies presented in Studsrød and Tuastad (2017), focusing on the polarisation and tensions in scholarly and political discussions of Norwegian ECEC (Alvestad, Tuastad, & Bjørnestad, 2017; Bjørnestad, Tuastad, & Alvestad, 2017). The controversies embody various sorts of tensions and form two major, competing positions or models in the scholarly and professional dispute over what best serves the interests of children in ECEC. It is hardly an exaggeration to speak of a trench of warfare among the contending parties.

The chapter consists of three main parts. We first review quality in Norwegian ECEC before giving an account of the two competing models. Finally, we present a novel Norwegian case study illustrating the dispute between the two competing models.

Part I. Quality in Norwegian ECEC: history, policies and findings

Since 1997, young children begin school at the age of six years in Norway. Two decades later, the debate over whether schools have sufficient concern for the special interests of young children is heated (see for instance, Haug, 2017; Myhrvold, 2018; Sandelson, 2017). The political and scholarly debate on the education system runs parallel to similar debates over the content in ECEC institutions especially for the eldest children. Both cases address the fundamental child policy issue in Norway related to how many demands and burdens society can place on children before risking the violation of their here-and-now interests (Pettersvold & Østrem, 2018b; Röthle & Moser, 2007; Størksen & Rege, 2018a). Two questions come out of this issue: *Should* ECEC, in addition to the primary role of taking care of children and providing them with social and emotional development, fulfil important societal investment as well? The latter involves aiming for the knowledge gain in society, preparing young children for school and their future educational pathway. *Can* ECEC settings and schools for young children combine the former role definition and the new aims in education?

To address these questions, initially we look at the background to these questions and outline some major traits of Norway's ECEC system, its historical background and research around the quality of the system.

History and policies

ECEC in Scandinavia draws from the German tradition, where the primary concerns around early childhood education spanned around the home, outdoor play, health and maternal care (Johansson, 2007). The first Norwegian day care centres were established in the largest cities in the country in the1920s, based on ideals of the 'common good Norwegian home' (Balke, 1995, p. 243). In 1954, ECEC fell under the Child Welfare Act and accordingly a social pedagogical framing hallmarked by protection and prevention formed the basis of the ECEC provisions (Korsvold, 2016).

The post-World War II period is known as the era of the housewife, which meant caring for their own children at home. Hence, ECEC institutions were few and somewhat invisible in the public space. In 1975, the first Kindergarten Act was introduced, under the Ministry of Children and Family Affairs. These events made ECEC institutions more ambitious and focused on professional development, resulting in the conceptualisation and genesis of the modern 'kindergarten childhood' (Korsvold, 2016). Twenty years later, the first Norwegian framework plan stated more precise aims and ambitions for kindergartens. At the same time, the school start age was lowered from seven to six years of age, and parental leave was extended. From 2000 onwards, 91.3 per cent for all Norwegian children aged one to five years had enrolled in ECEC prior to entering primary school (Statistic Norway (SSB), 2018).

Looking at the policy level, high public spending and universalism characterise Norwegian child policies, particularly the ECEC system. Scandinavian spending on family benefits is comparatively high, being more than 50 per cent above the OECD average and amounting to three to four times higher than in the United States, measured as a percentage of the gross national product (OECD, 2014). Since 2009, all children in Norway from the age of one year have a legal right to a full-time place in ordinary ECEC settings or family ECEC settings (Ministry of Education and Research, 2015). The enrolment rates in Norwegian ECEC are exceptionally high; specifically, 97 per cent of children aged three to five years and 82.5 per cent of children aged one to two years attend ECEC settings, with the majority enrolled full time. In no other OECD country do so many toddlers attend ECEC (SSB, 2018).

Beyond public spending, universalism is a common feature in Norwegian welfare and educational policies; with ECEC, policies addressing universalism concern both financing and institutional shape (Hatland, Kuhnle, & Romøren, 2018). Arguably, the universal shape of the policy is even more important than the quantitative numbers on enrolment rates and public spending. In Scandinavia, ECEC settings are heavily subsidised, holding an annual maximum price of 32,000 kroner (€3200). Additionally for one year olds, parents can choose a cash benefit (*kontantstøtte*) instead of a place in the ECEC setting (Norwegian Directorate for Education and Training, 2017b).[1] Both municipals and private enterprises offer ECEC settings. The system results in draining of a separate market segment for better-off families in which quality might be higher than in the more affordable day care institutions (Tuastad, 2014). Hence, the universal system includes children from both higher and lower social strata in the same ECEC settings; normally, the inclusion of children from upper social ranks in common public institutions results in pressure towards quality for all.

Quality discussions in Norwegian policies on ECEC

What might look good from a political perspective does not necessarily correspond to high quality at a professional level. In this subsection, we outline the discussion about quality dimensions in ECEC before presenting some empirical data on those dimensions in the next section. We analyse the various national framework plans and the reactions they received.

The first national framework plan in 1995 accentuated that childhood had its own intrinsic value as a specific period in the life cycle (Ministry of Child and Families, 1995). Compared to the Swedish plan, which was distinguished by a social and cognitive perspective, the Norwegian plan was characterised by a more traditional social and developmental orientation (Alvestad & Pramling Samuelsson, 1999). At this time, scepticism towards formal learning was expressed both in the framework plan and in the field of practice because this was seen as part of the school and the school tradition (Alvestad, 2004; Röthle, 2007).

In 2005, responsibility for ECEC as a policy area shifted from the Ministry of Child and Family Affairs to the Ministry of Education and Research. This move signalled a new era in which cognitive learning outcomes received stronger attention. At the same time, the second framework plan in 2006 marked a change in Norwegian policies on ECEC (Ministry of Education and Research, 2006). Topics and aims in ECEC settings began including clearer links to school subjects in the primary school. For instance, the learning areas in the plan now included the new learning area number, spaces and shapes. Furthermore, the plan also emphasised children's participation even more than the first plan did (Ministry of Education and Research, 2006).

The 2006 framework plan seemed to epitomise the quality in Western educational policies, including those addressing ECEC (Segerholm, 2012). What started as a tendency in 2006 became more manifest in the 2011 revision and the new 2017 framework plan (Norwegian Directorate for Education and Training, 2017a). In the public documents, quality measures and the OECD comparisons become indicators of the degree of success for national policies. Against this backdrop, the 2006 framework plan became a target for criticism. Critics held that the plan represented a move towards school preparation and away from the Nordic tradition and many of its social–pedagogical ambitions (Moser & Röthle, 2007). Obviously, the shift towards the 2017 framework plan did not silence the critics. In the 2017 framework plan, the Nordic ECEC tradition and play seemed to be ensured, and the attitudes of both scholars and trade unions towards the latest new plan was positive overall (for more information see Alvestad et al., 2017). However, the public debate proceeded.

Empirical data on quality and expectations

Despite the controversies and disputes related to the quality discussion, few large-scale studies have measured or monitored quality in ECEC, particularly at the national level. The OECD (2015) has criticised the lack of process quality monitoring in Norway. In their report, *Early Childhood Education and Care Policy Review Norway*, the OECD recommended that Norway carefully monitor process quality by using international measurement tools such as Environment Rating Scales (ERS) like the Infant/Toddler Environment Rating Scales – Revised (ITERS-R). In the following, based on findings from the longitudinal study Better Provision for Norway's Children in ECEC (BePro),[2] we present some novel empirical data related to global quality for toddlers at the centre level and expectations of quality from parents' and centre leaders' survey responses. These data hint at rising expectations among core actors in the child–political field and present a case for the importance of model synthesis as well.

BePro is the first large-scale study in Norway using the ITERS-R to assess the quality of Norwegian ECEC for toddlers. The ITERS-R is a global quality scale measuring different aspects of children's learning environments (Harms, Cryer, & Clifford, 2006). Inspired by socioecological, attachment and constructionist models and theories, the ITERS-R and other ERS 'measure quality in terms of children's access to enriching activities, supportive teacher-child interaction, and a healthy and safe environment' (Burchinal, 2018, p. 4). The scale was developed in an Anglo-American context and needed to be carefully adapted to the Norwegian context before use. The scale has been widely criticised as being too superficial and global, as well as lacking the core element of interaction quality. In spite of these potential shortcomings, Bjørnestad et al. (2019) conducted a comparative document analysis of the Norwegian framework plan and the ITERS-R, and they found significant similarities between the documents, both at the ideological level and in terms of pedagogical activities. Importantly, they noted the importance of carefully contextualised assessment tools. The ITERS-R gives an overall picture of quality, and it especially provides information about the strengths and weaknesses of the Norwegian ECEC context. Using the global assessment tool ITERS-R[3] for the first time in Norway allowed us to compare Norwegian quality standards to standards in other countries (for detailed descriptions of ITERS-R, see Bjørnestad et al., 2019; Bjørnestad & Os, 2018).

The ITERS-R consists of seven main areas: (1) Space and Furnishings, (2) Personal Care Routines, (3) Listening and Talking, (4) Activities, (5) Interaction, (6) Programme Structure and (7) Parents and Staff. Each area has been further divided into 39 sub-areas in total. Table 13.1 presents ITERS-R comparative data from Norway, the Netherlands, the United Kingdom (UK) and Portugal.

The quality scales rank from 1 (low) to 7 (high). Altogether, the quality scores were low, except for the 2017 UK results. As in the Norwegian case, most scores circled around 3 or 4. In ITERS-R terminology, these scores imply minimal quality standards. In the Norwegian case, no sub-areas reached the 'good' standard.

Comparatively, Norwegian ECEC for toddlers scored about one point higher than their Dutch and Portuguese counterparts. However, the UK study from 2017 showed considerably higher quality than in Norway, and nearly all sub-areas scored above 5 (good quality). In total, the Norwegian score was, at

Table 13.1 ITERS-R scores from Norway, United Kingdom (2012, 2017), Netherlands (2015) and Portugal (2010)

	Norway N = 206	*UK 2012* N = 247	*UK 2017* N = 402	*Netherlands* N = 55	*Portugal* N = 160
	M (SD)	*M (SD)*	*M (SD)*	*M (SD)*	*M (SD)*
Space and Furnishings	3.8	3.9 (0.90)	5.5 (1.06)	2.7 (.63)	3.3 (0.74)
Personal Care Routines	3.5	3.6 (1.2)	5.3 (1.15)	–	1.7 (0.53)
Listening and Talking	4.3	4.6 (1.1)	5.1 (1.25)	3.5 (1.09)	3.4 (0.98)
Activities	3.5	3.5 (1.0)	4.8 (1.01)	2.3 (0.56)	2.44 (0.56)
Interaction	4.7	5.1 (1.2)	5.6 (1.14)	3.8 (1.25)	3.7 (1.10)
Programme Structure	4.4	4.5 (1.3)	5.4 (1.24)	3.5 (1.18)	2.56 (.65)
Total	**3.9**	**4.0 (0.90)**	**5.3 (0.99)**	**2.9 (0.60)**	**2.8 (0.48)**

Sources: Barros and Aguiar, 2010; Helmerhorst, Riksen-Walraven, Vermeer, Fukkink, & Tavecchio, 2014; Mathers, Singler, & Karemaker, 2012; Melhuish & Gardiner, 2017.

best, at a medium level. According to the ITERS-R scale, the quality was overall not satisfactory. Compared to other nations, Norwegian scores were average and far behind the UK 2017 scores. These results hardly fit with self-perceptions within the Norwegian child–political domain.

Hints of new cleavages

In Alvestad et al. (2017), we analysed the first reactions from various central actors in the 'trench war' over what best serves children's interests in the preparatory work prior to and in the immediate aftermath of the 2017 framework plan. We found that, while the parental organisation and the profession's interest organisation clearly stated opposition to the preliminary draft of the 2017 framework plan and the discussion of systematic educational work and learning, the owners of the ECEC institutions to a larger degree appreciated the new tones they heard in it, as did several researchers within the political economy tradition. In fact, the new framework plan continued the child-oriented and play-based traditions, as already mentioned. However, we would like to draw attention to some of the earlier findings from the surveys carried out in the BePro project. Some particularly interesting results might reveal new cleavages in the debate over ECEC. The results (see Table 13.2) document how the political initiatives to promote quality work and school preparation have support from both the directors and the parents.

Nine out of ten participants in both groups held children's learning as the most important aspects. Moreover, both groups stated that the staff should have an active supporting role. The claim that children should do what they want to do produced the lowest scores (54.9 per cent of parents; 48.8 per cent of

Table 13.2 Parents' and directors' opinions of elements of a good kindergarten

A good day-care centre is where …	Parents n = 1079 %	Directors n = 90 %
Children's play is the most important thing	99.2	100
Children's learning is the most important thing	93.0	90.2
The staff works with children's social competence	99.6	100
The staff works with letters and numbers with the children	91.3	62.7
The staff works with promoting children's creativity	97.1	94.0
The staff decides what the children should do	72.0	77.8
Children decide what they wish to do	54.9	48.8
The staff and the children together determine what to do	95.6	100
Children express their own ideas and opinions	99.7	100
The staff encourages children's social curiosity	99.5	100

directors), but there is no doubt that both groups envisioned play, creativity and co-decisions as core elements in a good ECEC setting.

We find the most interesting results to be those where the discrepancy was largest. The statement that a good day care centre is one where 'the staff works with letters and numbers with the children' resulted in a difference of nearly 30 per cent. While nine out of ten parents thought numbers and letters should be introduced in the toddler groups, only six out of ten directors agreed. This statement might provide the clearest indication of a difference in attitudes towards the educational role of ECEC. Parents may expect these sorts of activities to take place to a larger degree than what professionals (presumably) and directors intend.[4] In these results, we see an emerging cleavage where parents support the political initiatives without corresponding back-up among the professionals.

This finding became even more interesting when we looked closer into which parental groups supported the claim most strongly. At first glance, there were few differences between parents' statements and their educational levels. A closer look revealed two striking findings. First, when we combined educational background with how often parents read to and played with letters with the children we found that the parents with higher education (Bachelor's degree and higher) were those who most often read to/with the children (Bukhart, 2016).

This group (the 'readers') signals a learning home environment with parents who might give their children a better start in their educational careers than parents who do not read with their children (Esping-Andersen, 2016). However, we found that parents with lower levels of education most often supported the claim that the day care centre should include working with letters and numbers. In this way, they apparently joined sides with the advocates of the social investment strategy (as we will return to in Part II of this chapter).

In the long term, children of the readers would already have a strong start in the emerging educational selection race, as their parents would prepare them well for it (cf. Esping-Andersen, 2009, 2016; Frønes, 2018). Children of parents reading less and offering a less supportive home environment might benefit the most from stimulating ECEC settings. Apparently, those latter parents are the ones most strongly supporting activities akin to school preparation.

Part II. Two competing models

In this part, we further analyse conceptions of what should lie at the heart of Norwegian ECEC as they unfolded in the previous descriptions. First, we situate the development in Norway in the scholarly debate and in an international context. Next, building on the former, we suggest two new concepts that may cover the Norwegian case more accurately.

Different models

Analyses of ECEC systems have conventionally contrasted the pedagogical content of ECEC settings and their political organisation (Lister, 2008; Pettersvold & Østrem, 2018a; Ringmose & Kragh-Müller, 2017). Scholars who describe and analyse sets of values and pedagogical ideas have contrasted the Anglo-American or school-preparing model with the Nordic social–pedagogical model (Bennett, 2008; Pettersvold & Østrem, 2018a). Including contrasting systems of governance, comparative researchers have further distinguished between French–English/continental split systems (between child care and educational systems) and the Nordic integrated system (Lister, 2008; Ringmose & Kragh-Müller, 2017).

At the heart of the Nordic social–pedagogical integrated model lies priority for the children's wellbeing here and now. The Nordic model holds that ECEC should promote what is good for children during childhood. Childhood has its own value; this period in life is not merely instrumental to fulfil other societal aims or to prepare for the future individual career. The ECEC settings' pedagogical work should reflect this ideal. Consequently, ECEC settings are not political tools for overall societal aims such as economic progress or female equality. Scholars have used phrases such as 'promoting good childhood' or even 'the good childhood model' to describe their positions on ECEC (Lister, 2008). This basic idea implies scepticism towards a school-preparation role for ECEC settings. Such a role can disturb the organisation of ECEC to protect the worth of childhood, which day care centres should be responsive to.

At the concrete level, the basic attitudes of the Nordic model towards childhood and the mission of ECEC emphasise what children themselves like to do. The staff should adjust for spontaneity and play. The collective aspects of childhood receive attention in the model; social competence is a major aim. The position consists of educationalists, the profession as well as of the research tradition leaning on smaller qualitative studies.

The Anglo-American/French–English or split governance model emphasises the importance of early learning (Bennett, 2008; Lister, 2008; Pettersvold & Østrem, 2018a; Ringmose & Kragh-Müller, 2017). According to the adherents of this model, ECEC should have clear learning outcomes and a school-preparation role, which involve testing to identify which children are at risk (Bennett, 2008). The identification of those at risk allows them to receive extra resources earlier to combat their weaker starting points in their educational careers. According to this line of thought, school preparation must start in ECEC to achieve central political aims such as equal opportunities. Among the central spoke-persons for this viewpoint are developmental psychologists, political economists and politicians.

Summing up, we find that the Nordic model is based on research related to developmental psychology, sociology and sociocultural theories. This model focuses on intrinsic values of childhood, child participation and the collective rather than the individual. When it comes to learning, the focus in the Nordic model is on everyday activities and children's play. Professionals, educationists and researchers conducting small qualitative studies have often supported this model (see for instance, Frønes, 1989, 2018; Sommer, 2012). The school-preparation model builds on large-scale effect studies of the benefits of early investment as conducted by economists, psychologists and researchers. These studies have focused on developmental psychology and individual learning, and adherents believe ECEC should prepare children for school by focusing on systematic learning (see for instance Havnes & Mogstad, 2011; Heckman, 2011).

A novel formulation of the models

It appears paradoxical that many adherents of the school-preparing model, the second model described earlier, emphasise aims such as equality, which are traditionally values of the political left. This second model – the school-preparing model, which for the Norwegian context acts as a social investment strategy in children – is frequently framed as a neoliberal and right-wing line of thought in the political and scholarly debate (Lister, 2008; Olsen, 2012). However, as we see it, the former presentation of these models does not quite cover the Norwegian context. Proponents of this model do not oppose the overall aims of the child-centred model, as the subsequent analysis reveals. These circumstances might suggest an alternative way of characterising the positions in the Norwegian context. Hence, we suggest a slightly different way of conceptualising these models in the Norwegian case. The positions then become more open and closer to the self-understanding of the protagonists.

First, we conceptualise the Nordic tradition/the social–pedagogical view as *a child-centred model*, in this way linking to the wider child–political field (Frønes, 2018; Gilbert et al., 2011). The second model, which we conceptualise as *a social investment model or strategy*, is probably the model in which we find it most urgent to present and formulate the thinking in a slightly different way to address the Norwegian case (Esping-Andersen, 2016; Frønes, 2018).

The theoretical reasoning behind a social investment strategy in welfare consists of one child-oriented part and one social investment part. Anton Hemerijck, a prominent defender of the social investment strategy internationally, has contended that, since life chances 'are so overdetermined by what happens in childhood, a comprehensive child investment strategy with a strong emphasis on early childhood is imperative' (Hemerijck, 2013, p. 381). Conversely, societal gains are clearly present in the argument as well, as the child-centred social investment strategy 'is needed to ensure that children become lifelong learners and strong contributors to their societies' (Hemerijck, 2013, p. 382).

We interpreted the recent writings of Esping-Andersen (2009, 2016), the reputable Scandinavian welfare researcher behind the modern formulation of the major welfare models in comparative welfare research, in a similar vein. Esping-Andersen (2009, 2016) has provided central inputs to the social investment strategy in children. To Esping-Andersen, Scandinavian child policies count among the major successes of the Scandinavian welfare states. According to

Esping-Andersen (2009, 2016), a crucial learning for scholars and politicians is that early intervention is of utter importance to equalise life chances. If quality day care centres for all providing some early learning did not exist, then the child's home learning environment would decide nearly all the child's prospects. That would imply fewer correcting mechanisms to obtain equal opportunities. As seen in Part I (Table 13.2), it is interesting to note that the most relevant parent groups might share this idea about early intervention.

As we see it, Esping-Andersen's main concern is to help equalise life chances. By pointing at societal gains as well, Esping-Andersen's argument is more pragmatic than ideological, acknowledging that politicians do not necessarily listen to justice arguments about equal life chances but may be more likely to listen if the argument addresses massive efficiency gains.

Consequently, the social investment model theoretically represents different traditions. One tradition is the general political concern of having competitive economies, and some adherents of this tradition may advocate neoliberal political solutions and New Public Management policies. With respect to the Norwegian case, we will emphasise the other tradition, exemplified by the above-referenced welfare researchers, who have protected the traditional aims of the Nordic welfare state models. They are not neoliberals; instead, they write in the tradition of political economy. The terminology in the latter discipline should not be

Table 13.3 Competing models of the Norwegian ECEC field

	The child-centred model	*The social investment in children model*
Overall aims	The intrinsic value of childhood Participation in decisions	Re-distribution Societal efficiency
Theoretical foundation	Sociology of children and developmental psychology	Developmental psychology
Perspectives on learning	Social competence	Individual learning
Accentuated aspects in childhood	Collective	Individualised childhood
Cooperation ECEC – school	Scepticism towards the school-preparation role	ECEC should prepare for school
Knowledge base/ perspectives on knowledge	Everyday activities follow the child's interests; spontaneity, play and children's culture Observation and adaption to child	Adapted systematic training over time; scholarly and professionally oriented Testing and mapping
Protagonists	The profession; educationalists; researchers within the qualitative and constructivist traditions	Economists, psychologists and politicians; researchers within the quantitative tradition
Research tradition	Small qualitative studies	Effect research; large national and international studies

confused with normative aims in the former position. Consequently, in the Norwegian context, it might be worthwhile to describe the second model in a way that does not exclude child-centrism and is distinguishable from the split governance or French–English model, see Table 13.3 above.

Based on this outline, in the Norwegian context, the competing positions might be less antagonistic than they appear to be. This understanding might call for a more fine-tuned analysis. Hence, the discussion should concern whether ECEC and schooling for five-year-olds can *combine* child-centrism and wider societal aims. While proponents of the child-centred model have argued that such a combination is difficult, scholars representing the social investment in children model have maintained that societal aims such as social equality and social mobility can be reached only if policies intervene in early childhood.

We will now turn to a closer analysis of the two models described above, including the nature of the social investment strategy. Next, we look at the possibilities of combining the two models.

Part III. A Norwegian case study: illustrating the dispute

In a novel literature study, we looked closer at a Norwegian case that illustrates how adherents from the two positions could possibly juxtapose or complement. Building on a background gathered from media, we conducted a systematic literature search to identify the media debate on this query (Thagaard, 2013). We searched for the word 'barnehage' (kindergarten/ECEC) in the media-database search engines, limiting our search to the six-month period when debates around this issue took place in the regional newspapers (*Stavanger Aftenblad*). The search returned a total of 175 hits and included all articles on kindergartens/ECEC for the six-month period from 25 November 2017 to 25 April 2018. We excluded articles that indirectly addressed the core debate, such as articles on budgets or tariff negotiations, and articles in which discussions about ECEC were secondary aspects of other main issues. In total, we read closely 19 articles that formed the basis for the analysis in this empirical study.

In the following sections, we draw on quotes from the media texts as we present our analysis, interpretations and descriptions. We have followed the required national ethical guidelines (The National Committee for Research Ethics in the Social Sciences and the Humanities (NESH), n.d.)

Findings from the analysis

The dispute took place in the wake of the presentation of the framework plan 2017, in a regional newspaper that covered ECEC and children's policies quite closely, including in the debate and commentary section. This controversy was particularly interesting to us because typical examples of an implemented social investment strategy (i.e. the Agder project and the Stavanger project, both located in Norway at the University of Stavanger) came under attack. The subsequent case study showed that the Agder project was considerably more debated than the Stavanger project (www.uis.no/agderprosjektet). The charge was that the ideas and principles in the Agder project threatened the Nordic model of ECEC.

The leaders of the Agder project and the Stavanger project were among the participants in the debate. On the other side, were core groups defending the traditional child-centred model, among those both national leaders and regional leaders of the profession's trade union. Scholars and researchers participated as well.

The main topic of the media dispute concerned whether the ideas in the Agder project, introducing play-based learning, would introduce preschooling and violate the main principles in the traditional Nordic model for ECEC. In the latter model (see Table 13.3, Part II), spontaneous play is central, and play and learning supposedly go hand in hand while minimising adult-governed activities for learning purposes. Four topics were crystallised during the dispute: the possible conflict between learning and play, competing conceptions of co-decisions for children, the nature of early intervention, and the possible breach with the traditional Nordic model, emphasising play.

The arguments from the child-centred position

It was one of the Stavanger Aftenblad editors (Sandelson, 2017) who initiated the debate, at first regarding young school children before expanding to include ECEC. She addressed the costs of early intervention, stating, 'I have seen first graders cry before celebrating Christmas because they are afraid their reading skills are too poor' (our translations from Norwegian). According to Sandelson (2017), the testing regime was behind that anxiety; in fact, she reported that she had heard worried young school children discuss why they did not reach the 100 per cent score in tests. Consequently, her main target was New Public Management with its principles of detailed learning outcomes 'for each class, each week, each pupil', which she claimed lay behind the first graders' fear (Sandelson, 2017). The leader of the biggest local trade union for the profession confirmed that local headmasters of schools and ECEC setting directors shared the same frustration over the testing and ranking systems (Haraldsen, 2017).

The Union of Education Norway (UE) organises ECEC professionals, too. The national UE leader, Steffen Handal, took part in the controversy. He identified preschooling in ECEC, which he strongly opposed, as a main principle in the Agder project. According to Handal (2018b), play-based learning, a central part of the Agder project, would imply less play and more adult-governed learning. Having five-year-old children dedicated for two hours a day, four days a week, to learn language, arithmetic and more would mean they had less time with friends outside the learning group. Overall, Handal (2018a, 2018b) argued that such an approach represented a form of preschooling that replaced the emphasis on play and spontaneity traditionally characterising Norwegian ECEC settings.

Some scholars read the Agder project as a way of instrumentalising child-hood to benefit societal economic outcomes. One scholar wrote, 'Children are made into investment objects to improve the competitiveness of the country' (Thoresen, 2018, p. 27). Two scholars apparently accused the Agder project leaders of opportunism, changing 'in the direction which the wind blows' (Pettersvold & Østrem, 2018b, p. 27). The scholars' contribution was interesting as it described their perception of play-based learning. According to them, play-based learning was not real play. They noted that 'what generally characterises play, is being initiated by the child and that it would not have any purpose to be exploited outside the play-situation' (Pettersvold & Østrem, 2018b).

The question raised is how adherents from the opposite model responded. Moreover, to what extent did the responses leave the two positions irreconcilable?

The adherents of the social investment strategy

The project leaders of the Agder project and the Stavanger project held that they strongly supported the traditional Norwegian child-centred thinking, which included combining play and co-decisions from the children, while they opposed the continental preschooling tradition. They agreed that 'a school-like approach does not belong in the ECEC' (Størksen, Reikerås, & Rege, 2018, p. 26). According to these researchers, the here-and-now interests of the children were decisive, and ECEC should not include aims to make children clever. Hence, the project leaders claimed their project 'walks hand in hand with the Norwegian ECEC tradition in which there is much room for free play' (Størksen & Rege, 2018b, p. 36).

The empirical nature of adult-governed play might be the most important aspect of the controversy. According to the Agder project and the Stavanger project researchers, their projects did not involve teaching young children mathematics. They aimed to identify which children might struggle to understand rules and premises for games. Identifying them would allow them to receive help and be included rather than excluded (Størksen et al., 2018, p. 26). The alternative to early intervention, as they saw it, would be to ignore those who would need the most support.

The project leaders elaborated on their conception of play-based learning (Størksen & Rege, 2018a). They situated this American learning tradition as an alternative approach to instruction learning and traditional formal preschooling (see Størksen et al., 2018) Moreover, they held that play-based learning fits well to young children, as documented by former research (see Hirsh-Pasek, Golinkoff, Berk, & Singer, 2009). They argued that play-based learning consists of both free play and adult-guided play. Moreover:

> In adult-guided play, the staff prepare funny games for the children while accentuating interplay and co-deciding with the children during the games

and activities. In many ways, we can say that to work according to the documented research results on play-based learning fits well with the Norwegian tradition and the framework plan.

(Størksen & Rege, 2018a, p. 30) (Authors' translation)

Two directors at two ECEC settings that participated in the Agder project pointed at similar school-preparation groups in earlier ECEC settings; as such, they argued that the Agder project did not represent a new idea in bringing in some sort of school preparation (Wiig & Hobbestad, 2018). However, they held that the Agder project was a better way of doing it; in fact, they argued that the Agder project did not dispose the same character of preschooling that their former activities did.

A synthesis

We suggest the above analysis of the dispute between the social investment case and the child-centred model can present a possible way of combining the two competing positions (see Table 13.3) in an integrated model. In the right column of Table 13.4, we present a possible synthesis of the two former models.

Table 13.4 Models and possible synthesis for Norwegian ECEC

	The child-centred model	*The social investment model*	Synthesis
Overall aims	The intrinsic value of childhood Participation in decisions	Re-distribution Societal efficiency	**Not one or the other: Children's co-decisions, the worth of childhood and attention to individual children's future interests can be combined**
Theoretical foundation	Sociology of children and developmental psychology	Developmental psychology	**Multi-disciplinary approaches**
Perspectives on learning	Social competence	Individual learning	**Learning in groups; individual follow-up**
Accentuated aspects in childhood	Collective	Individualised childhood	**Artificial contradiction: both collective and individual**
Cooperation ECEC – school	Scepticism towards the school-preparation role	ECEC should prepare for school	**Closer cooperation is necessary**

continued

Table 13.4 continued

	The child-centred model	The social investment model	Synthesis
Knowledge base/ Perspectives on knowledge	Everyday activities follow the child's interests; spontaneity, play and children's culture Observation and adaption to child	Adapted systematic training over time; scholarly and professionally oriented Testing and mapping	**Combinations of the two perspectives are necessary; success depends on implementation procedures**
Protagonists	The profession; educationalists; researchers within the qualitative and constructivist traditions	Economists, psychologists and politicians; researchers within the quantitative tradition	**Barriers between traditions should be broken down**
Research tradition	Small qualitative studies	Effect research; large national and international studies	**Combinations of qualitative and quantitative approaches; multi-disciplinary research**

Concluding remarks: social investment and child-centrism combined?

The synthesis we suggest in Table 13.4 signals the possibility of a bridge uniting the former models. The above case study identified the empirical premises holding that play-based learning and early intervention were at the heart of the dispute. We will not take sides: Whether play-based learning involves time for free play or not is an empirical question.

However, we note a possible need for reformulation on some other points. Resistance against early intervention may seem unfounded if it is based on a principle stating that it is wrong for ECEC to pay attention to the long-term interests of the child. That would not be a sound principle as long as it is possible to avoid sacrificing entirely the here-and-now interests (and we have no reason to believe such avoidance is not possible). Hence, a moderate version of the above-cited principle might be better: To pay attention to individual future interests of children in ECEC might be wrong if it changes ECEC so that it is no longer child-centred.

Such a charge – that it sacrifices children's here-and-now interests – could hardly be raised against the principle of early intervention itself. Theoretically, it is possible to combine much room for free play, spontaneity and so forth while still having early opportunities to identify children at risk of marginalisation. To develop systems to detect the latter would arguably not require the abandonment of the tradition of child-centred ECEC. Consequently, we conclude in an optimistic manner: Perhaps it is, in fact, possible for prospective Norwegian child policies to combine aims and insights from the best of both worlds – child-centrism and social investment – in a united model.

Notes

1 From 1 August 2018, it is possible to combine part-time place in kindergarten with graduated cash benefits (www.nav.no/no/Person/Familie/Barnetrygd+og+kontantstotte/Nyheter/forslag-til-endringer-i-kontantst%C3%B8tteordningen-fra-1.august-2018).
2 Key Investigators in BePro: Elisabeth Bjørnestad, Jan Erik Johansson and Lars Gulbrandsen (Oslo and Akershus University College); Marit Alvestad and Eva Johansson (University of Stavanger); Liv Gjems and Thomas Moser (University of Southeast Norway); Edward Melhuish (Oxford University); and Jacqueline Barnes (Birkbeck University of London).
3 ITERS-R data were collected in collaboration with the project 'Searching for Qualities'.
4 Note that ordinary staff and directors, for instance, join the same trade union, indicating common basic attitudes.

References

Alvestad, M. (2004). Preschool teachers' understanding of some aspects of educational planning and practice related to the National Curricula in Norway. *International Journal of Early Years Education, 12*(2), 51–64.

Alvestad, M., & Pramling Samuelsson, I. (1999). A comparison of the National Preschool curricula in Norway and Sweden. *ECERP Journal, 1*(2), 1–12.

Alvestad, M., Tuastad, S. E., & Bjørnestad, E. (2017). Barnehagen i ei brytningstid. Spenninga mellom samfunnsnytte og barndommen sin eigenverdi [Kindergarten in a time of tensions between the societal and childhood's intrinsic value]. In I. Studsrød & S. E. Tuastad (Eds.), *Barneomsorg på norsk: Samspill og spenning mellom hjem og stat* [Child care in Norwegian: Interaction and tensions between home and state] (pp. 154–172). Oslo, Norway: Universitetsforlaget.

Balke, E. (1995). *Småbarnspedagogikkens historie. Forbilder for vår tids barnehage* [The history of toddler pedagogy]. Oslo, Norway: Universitetsforlaget.

Barros, S., & Aguiar, C. (2010). Assessing the quality of Portuguese child care programs for toddlers. *Early Childhood Research Quarterly, 25*(4), 527–535. doi:10.1016/j.ecresq.2009.12.003.

Bennett, J. (2008, 13 August). Early childhood education and care systems in the OECD ccountries: The issue of tradition and governance. *Encyclopedia on Early Childhood Development*. Retrieved from http://citeseerx.ist.psu.edu/viewdoc/download?doi=10.1.1.527.9774&rep=rep1&type=pdf.

Bjørnestad, E., Baustad, A. G., & Alvestad, M. (2019). To what extent does the ITERS-R address pedagogical quality, as described in the Norwegian framework plan? In S. Phillipson & S. Garvis (Eds.), *Teachers and Families' Perspectives in Early Childhood Education and Care: Early Childhood Education and Care in the 21st Century* (Vol. 2). London: Routledge.

Bjørnestad, E., & Os, E. (2018). Quality in Norwegian childcare for toddlers using ITERS-R. *European Early Childhood Education Research Journal, 26*(1), 111–127. doi: 10.1080/1350293X.2018.1412051.

Bjørnestad, E., Tuastad, S. E., & Alvestad, M. (2017). Kvaliteten i norske barnehagar: Eit nytt PISA-sjokk? [Quality in Norwegian ECEC: The new PISA-chock?]. In I. Studsrød & S. E. Tuastad (Eds.), *Barneomsorg på norsk. I samspill og spenning mellom hjem og stat* [Child care in Norway: Interaction and tensions between home and state] (pp. 173–190). Oslo, Norway: Universitetsforlaget.

Bukhart, L. (2016). *Norwegian home and preschool environments reflected in early vocabulary developments. A theoretical and empiric study.* (Master of Philosophy in Pedagogy Master), University of Oslo, Oslo. Retrieved from www.duo.uio.no/bitstream/handle/10852/52493/Master-LBurkhart-Word2010.pdf?sequence=1&isAllowed=y Available from University of Oslo DUO database.

Burchinal, M. (2018). Measuring early care and education quality. *Child Development Perspectives, 12*(1), 3–9. doi:10.1111/cdep.12260.

Dahlberg, G., Moss, P., & Pence, A. (1999). *Fra kvalitet til meningsskaping – morgendagens barnehage* [From quality to meaningmaking – tomorrow's kindergarten]. Oslo, Norway: Kommuneforlaget.

Esping-Andersen, G. (2009). *The Incomplete Revolution: Adapting to Women's New Roles.* Cambridge: Polity Press.

Esping-Andersen, G. (2016). *Families in the 21st Century.* Stockholm, Sweden: SNS-förlag.

Fladberg, K. L. (2016, 19 September). OECD vil lage barnehage-PISA. *Dagsavisen.* Retrieved from www.dagsavisen.no.

Frønes, I. (1989). *Den norske barndommen* [The Norwegian childhood]. Oslo, Norway: J.W. Cappelens forlag AS.

Frønes, I. (2018). *Den krevende barndommen. Om barndom, sosialisering og politikk for barn* [A demanding childhood. Childhood, socialization and policies for children]. Oslo, Norway: Cappelen Damm Akademisk.

Gilbert, N., Parton, N., & Skivenes, M. (2011). *Child Protection Systems. International Trends and Orientations.* Oxford: Oxford University Press.

Handal, S. (2018a, 3 February). Er Agderprosjektet feilplassert? [Has the Agder project been situated in the wrong place?]. *Stavanger Aftenblad.*

Handal, S. (2018b, 12 February). Barnehagen trenger ikkje en førskole [ECEC do not need any pre-school]. *Stavanger Aftenblad.*

Hantrais, L. (2004). *Family Policy Matters. Responding to Family Change in Europe.* Bristol: Policy Press.

Haraldsen, I. G. (2017, 24 November). Vi må heie på rektorene og styrerne [We need to cheer on both the headmasters and the kindergarten directors]. *Stavanger Aftenblad,* p. 38.

Harms, T., Cryer, D., & Clifford, R. M. (2006). *Infant/Toddler Environment Rating Scales Revised Edition.* New York: Teachers College Press.

Hatland, A., Kuhnle, S., & Romøren, T. I. (2018). *Den norske velferdsstaten* [The Norwegian welfare state]. Oslo, Norway: Gyldendal.

Haug, P. (2017). Seksårsreformen 20 år etter: – Gi seksåringene førskolen tilbake [The six-year olds reform 20 years after – Give the preschool back to the six-year-olds]. Retrieved from www.barnehage.no/artikler/seksarsreformen-20-ar-etter-gi-seksaringene-forskolen-tilbake/427214.

Havnes, T., & Mogstad, M. (2011). No child left behind: Subsidized child care and children's long-run outcomes. *American Economic Journal: Economic Policy, 3*(2), 97–129. doi:10.1257/pol.3.2.97.

Heckman, J. J. (2011). The economics of inequality: The value of early childhood education. *American Educator, 35*(1), 31–35.

Helmerhorst, K. O. W., Riksen-Walraven, J. M., Vermeer, H. J., Fukkink, R. G., & Tavecchio, L. W. C. (2014). Measuring the interactive skills of caregivers in child care centers: Development and validation of the caregiver interaction profile scales. *Early Education and Development, 25*(5), 770–790. doi:10.1080/10409289.2014.840482.

Hemerijck, A. (2013). *Changing Welfare States.* Oxford: Oxford University Press.

172   *Svein Erik Tuastad et al.*

Hirsh-Pasek, K., Golinkoff, R. M., Berk, L. E., & Singer, D. G. (2009). *A Mandate for Playful Learning in Preschool. Presenting the Evidence.* New York, NY: Oxford University Press.

Johansson, J. E. (2007). Familj, natur och fabrik, verkstad eller laboratorium – vart går barnehagepedagogiken i dag? [Family, nature and industry, workhop or labratory – to where are the kindergartens heading?]. In M. Röthle & T. Moser (Eds.), *Ny rammeplan – ny barnehagepedagogikk?* [New Framvork plan – new ECEC pedagogy] (pp. 41–55). Oslo, Norway: Universitetsforlaget.

Korsvold, T. (2016). *Perspektiver på barndommens historie* [Perspectives on the history of childhood]. Bergen, Norway: Fagbokforlaget.

Lister, R. (2008). Investing in children and childhood: A new welfare policy paradigm and its implications. In A. Leira & C. Saraceno (Eds.), *Childhood: Changing Contexts (Comparative Social Research)* (Vol. 25) (pp. 383–408). Bingley: Emerald Group Publishing.

Lohmander Karlsson, M., Vandenbroeck, M., Pirard, F., Peeters, J., & Alvestad, M. (2009). New developments: New developments in Belgian childcare policy and practice. *European Early Childhood Education Research Journal, 17*(3), 407–424.

Mathers, S., Singler, R., & Karemaker, A. (2012). Improving quality in the early years—A comparison of perspectives and measures. Retrieved from www.education.ox.ac.uk/wordpress/wp-content/uploads/2012/03/Early-Years-Quality-Research-Brief.pdf.

Melhuish, E., & Gardiner, J. (2017). *Study of Early Education and Development (SEED): Study of Quality of Early Years Provision in England.* London: Department for Education.

Ministry of Child and Families. (1995). *Rammeplan for barnehagen (Q-0903 B)* [Framework plan for kindergarten]. Oslo: Ministry of Child and families.

Ministry of Education and Research. (2006). *Framework Plan for the Content and Tasks of Kindergarten.* Oslo, Norway: Ministry of Education and Research.

Ministry of Education and Research. (2009). *Meld. St. [White paper 41] (2008–2009). Kvalitet i barnehagen* [Quality in kindergarten]. Oslo, Norway: Ministry of Education and Research Retrieved from www.regjeringen.no/contentassets/78fde92c225840f68bce2ac2715b3def/no/pdfs/stm200820090041000dddpdfs.pdf.

Ministry of Education and Research. (2013). *Meld. St. [White paper 24] (2012–2013). Framtidens barnehage* [Future kindergarten]. Oslo, Norway: Ministry of Education and Research. Retrieved from www.regjeringen.no/no/dokumenter/meld-st-24-20122013/id720200/.

Ministry of Education and Research. (2015). *OECD – Thematic Review of Early Childhood Education and Care Policy in Norway. Background Report.* Retrieved from Oslo, Norway: www.regjeringen.no/contentassets/6372d4f3c219436e990a5b980447192e/oecd_rapport_2015_kd_web.pdf.

Ministry of Education and Research. (2016). *Meld. St. [White paper 19](2015–2016). Tid for lek og læring: Bedre innhold i barnehagen* [Time for Play and Learning: Better Content in Kindergarten]. Oslo, Norway: Ministry of Education and Research Retrieved from www.regjeringen.no/contentassets/cae152ecc6f9450a819ae2a9896d7cf5/no/pdfs/stm201520160019000dddpdfs.pdf.

Moser, T., & Röthle, M. (2007). Prolog – Ny rammeplan, ny barnehage, nye utfordringer? [Prologue – New framwork plan, new kindergarten, new challanges?]. In M. Röthle & T. Moser (Eds.), *Ny rammeplan – ny barnehagepedagogikk?* [New framework plan – new ECEC pedagogy?] (pp. 13–22). Oslo, Norway: Universitetsforlaget.

Myhrvold, L. M. (2018, 12 April). Skolen er ikke barnemoden [The school is not child readiness]. *Dagbladet.*

Norwegian Directorate for Education and Training. (2017a). *Rammeplan for barnehagen – innhold og oppgaver* [Framework plan for kindergarten – content and tasks]. Oslo, Norway: Norwegian Directorate for Education and Training.

Norwegian Directorate for Education and Training. (2017b). Foreldrebetaling [Parental fee]. Retrieved from www.oecd.org/social/expenditure.htm.

Organisation for Economic Co-operation and Development (OECD). (2006). *Starting Strong II: Early Childhood Education and Care*. Paris, France: OECD.

Organisation for Economic Co-operation and Development (OECD). (2014). Social Expenditure Database (SOCX). Retrieved from www.oecd.org/social/expenditure.htm.

Organisation for Economic Co-operation and Development (OECD). (2015). Early childhood education and care policy review Norway. Retrieved from www.oecd.org/ norway/Early-Childhood-Education-and-Care-Policy-Review-Norway.pdf.

Olsen, B. (2012). Markedsliberalisme og modstand. På strejftog i Trondheim og i børne-havepædagogikken [Marketliberalism and resistance. Rambling in Trondheim and in the ECEC pedagogy] *Nordisk barnehageforskning, 5*(13), 1–14.

Pettersvold, M., & Østrem, S. (2018a). *Profesjonell uro* [Professional unrest]. Oslo, Norway: Cappelen damm akademisk.

Pettersvold, M., & Østrem, S. (2018b, 19 February). Verken for barnehage eller skole [Neither for schools nor kindergartens]. *Stavanger Aftenblad*.

Ringmose, C., & Kragh-Müller, G. (2017). *Nordic Social Pedagogical Approach to Early Years*. Heidelberg, Germany: Springer.

Röthle, M. (2007). Norsk barnehagepedagogikk – et historisk og komparativt perspektiv [Norwegian ECEC pedagogy – a historical and comparative perspective]. In M. Röthle & T. Moser (Eds.), *Ny rammeplan – ny barnehagepedagogikk?* [New framework plan – new ECEC pedagogy?] (pp. 57–73). Oslo, Norway: Universitetsforlaget.

Röthle, M., & Moser, T. (2007). *Ny rammeplan – ny barnehagepedagogikk?* [New framework plan – new ECEC pedagogy?]. Oslo, Norway: Universitetsforlaget.

Sandelson, S. G. (2017, 17 November). Kven skal slå dørene opp [Who is going to open the doors?]. *Stavanger Aftenblad*.

Sandelson, S. G. (2018, 19 January). Forsking til å stola på? [Research we can trust?]. *Stavanger Aftenblad*.

Segerholm, C. (2012). The quality turn. *Education Inquiry, 3*(2), 115–122.

Sommer, D. (2012). *Barn i senmoderniteten. Barndomspsykologiske perspektiver* [Children in late modernity. Child psychological perspectives]. Bergen, Norway: Fagbokforlaget.

Statistic Norway (SSB). (2018). Kindergartens, 8 August. Retrieved from www.ssb.no/ en/utdanning/statistikker/barnehager/aar-endelige.

Stoltenberg, J. (2017). *Min historie* [My story]. Oslo, Norway: Gyldendal.

Størksen, I., & Rege, M. (2018a, 29 January). Mål: Et bedre læringsgrunnlag før skolestart [Aim: A better starting point for learning at school]. *Stavanger Aftenblad*.

Størksen, I., & Rege, M. (2018b, 8 February). Passer for både barnehage og førsteklasse [Fits for both the kindergartens and the schools]. *Stavanger Aftenblad*.

Størksen, I., Reikerås, E., & Rege, M. (2018, 24 January). Går ikke i barnehage for å bli flinke [Do not enter kindergartens to become clever]. *Stavanger Aftenblad*.

Studsrød, I., & Tuastad, S. E. (2017). *Barneomsorg på norsk. I samspill og spenning mellom hjem og stat* [Child care in Norwegian: interaction and tensions between home and state]. Oslo, Norway: Universitetsforlaget.

Thagaard, T. (2013). *Systematikk og innlevelse. En innføring i kvalitaiv metode* [Systematic and insight. An introduction to qualitative methods] (4th edn). Bergen, Norway: Fagbokforlaget.

The National Committee for Research Ethics in the Social Sciences and the Humanities (NESH). (n.d.). Ethical guidelines. Retrieved from www.etikkom.no.

Thoresen, I. T. (2018, 26 January). Kritikk av barnehageforsking nødvendig [Criticism against the research on kindergartens is necessary]. *Stavanger Aftenblad.*

Thorkildsen, I. M. (2013, 12 August). Moderne familier [Modern families]. *Dagbladet.* Retrieved from www.dagbladet.no/kultur/moderne-familier/60222907.

Tuastad, S. E. (2014). Førebygging og reparasjon. Gevisten av brei barnepoitikk [Prevention and repairment. The benefits of comprehensive policies for children]. In I. Ellingsen & R. Østerhaug (Eds.), *Barnevernets brennpunkt. Beslutningsdgrunnlag og beslutninge* [At the core of child protection. Decisions and the reasons for decisions] (pp. 17–41). Oslo, Norway: Universitetsforlaget.

Ulvund, S. E. (2017, 4 March). Barnehagen – leken må tas på alvor [The kindergarten – we must take play seriously]. *Dagbladet.*

Wiig, R. E., & Hobbestad, J. (2018, 6 March). Vi kjenner oss ikke igjen i kritikken [We do not recognize the criticism]. *Stavanger Aftenblad.*

14 Preschool quality research in Russia

Assessment for improving the quality

Igor Shiyan, Olga Shiyan, Aleksander Veraksa and Nikolay Veraksa

Introduction

The chapter is devoted to the results of an assessment of preschool education quality in Russia. The assessment was targeted at studying the existing weaknesses and deficiencies in the preschool education. As a toolbox, the Early Childhood Environment Rating Scale (ECERS-R) was used. The study was carried out on a random sample of kindergartens all over Russia. As a result of the study, data were gathered on most favourable aspects and most considerable deficiencies of the educational environment in kindergartens. Comparison of the study results with the Federal State Educational Standard on Preschool Education requirements helped discover that the following areas must be prioritised to further the development of preschool educational environment: individualisation of the learning process; supporting child initiative and autonomy; creating a more accessible and mobile environment; optimal conditions for the development of children's thinking capacity; imagination and creativity.

The challenge of contemporary early childhood education

The academic tradition of preschool education assumes acquisition of the models provided by an adult. Models can be regarded as ready-made schemes imposed on children's consciousness, which determine the content of their future products. In other words, the child's very thinking assumes a reproducible nature. The main criticism of this approach is based on the fear that children's creative abilities would be limited to, and oriented towards, the reproduction of academic standards (Miller & Almon, 2009). The need to support the child's personality, his/her emotional development, and the evolution of creativity and ethical consciousness is stressed (Wardekker, Boersma, Ten Dam, & Volman, 2012).

At the same time, a child who grows up in society must know basic rules of this society in order to be socialised. In fact, the cultural models are bearers of such rules. In this sense, the foundations of culture are situations of social interaction, which are normalised, standardised and stable. Properly speaking, culture cannot be built in any other way because social interaction presupposes certainty and stability. In this sense, cultural situations are situations that repeat many times – i.e. are reproducible. Moreover, when a child finds him or herself in a normal situation and obeys the accepted rules, the child becomes a social unit, without individuality. Once again, we emphasise that any social activity rests on stable forms of agreements, i.e. normalised situations, which characterise the interaction between participants in the process of social communication. The social functions of society give rise to the need for cultural norms.

A set of tasks and situations of a standard nature imposes age limitations on the child's acquisition of cultural forms. The greater number of cultural norms the child learns, the deeper he or she becomes 'rooted' into culture. Thus, preschool childhood is loaded with content that involves the maximum possible acquisition of cultural norms. The routine and reproducible nature of preschool institutions is emphasised in the work of Alasuutari and Markstrom:

> We use the concept of social order to refer to the rule system of the institution. The social order includes explicitly stated, and, hence, discursively formulated, rules, principles, and norms of preschool, and its routine-like habits. The latter is the sequel of everyday practices, i.e., recurrent events in the daily life of preschool and habitual discourses and premises.... The social order of an institution is always constructed. Preschool also presumes specific conduct, characteristics, and relationships among its actors–children, teachers, and parents.
>
> (Alasuutari & Markstrom, 2011, pp. 519–520)

The analysis of statements by teachers and parents in interviews that these authors conducted shows that reproducibility is a systemic characteristic of a preschool organisation. Obviously, the idea of the child's dependence on adults and the child's subordination to an adult predominates. The requirements for creating conditions for the manifestation of the child's autonomy and independence, which serve as preschool education goals, are 'governed by and allowed only within the limits of the institutional order' (Alasuutari & Markstrom, 2011, p. 530).

It remains an open question as to what makes it possible to develop a child's creative personality if reproducibility predominates. In her 2017 study, based on a survey of Chinese preschool teachers, Cheung showed that although the development of creativity was considered an absolute value, in practice, teachers did not have the wherewithal to implement it. In a situation of time shortage and a tight schedule for the children to fulfil various tasks, the teachers chose the strategy of getting the children to comply with the instructions of an adult, thus making it impossible for the children to show much initiative. Notwithstanding the educational reforms now underway, some teachers still consider that a successful lesson is the one carried out to the goal, which was set before; a lesson in which children talking a lot expressing themselves, is considered ineffective.

Currently many authors consider the child as the agent of the educational process and his life (Johansson, 2011), i.e. he/she influences the choice of the content to be mastered, and manages his/her own time (Komulainen, 2007). A rather popular answer to the question of how to implement this approach in practice is to let the child make his/her own choices. Indeed, the child is repeatedly given choices every day, for example, in US preschool educational practice. However, adults control the choices that are available to the child (Canella, 1997).

Some authors define their position based on the opportunities that are created in the preschool environment. The object–space environment acts in dual way, both as a set of standards and, in addition, allowing the child to act on it according to his own will without pressure from the adult, thus opening up new opportunities. This method allows children to follow a creative path. The position of some authors on an adult's proper position in relation to children's play is very typical in this respect. So, for example, Singer believes that an adult should abstain from interfering into children's play (Singer, 2015).

We believe that the subjective–spatial environment by itself does not guarantee that the child will take initiative and implement his/her intent successfully. He or she should get backing from adults. In this case, the adult acts as an intermediary between the child's initiative and its implementation. This idea finds expression in the concept of the 'voice of the child'. The understanding that the child has the right to a voice is largely based on the UN Convention on the Rights of the Child. 'The voice of the child' is directed orthogonally to the processes organised by the adult. However, many teachers see their task as making it comfortable for the child to incorporate his voice in the schemes already offered by adults and consistent with cultural norms and expectations. So, Alasuutari (2014) notes that a competent child today is understood as one who has the right to express his views and to be involved in discussing matters that concern him. However, as shown by the research and observation conducted, teachers often tend to disregard children's issues.

> Even though the principles of the Finnish ECEC are framed by the idea of the competent child, this study reveals that at the micro level the domestication of the idea is a complex process…. Therefore, the idea of the competent child is also partly 'lost in translation.' Even though it can be seen as a dominant discourse in education at the macro level, it is too simplistic to assume that it is self-evidently a dominant approach in the educational practices.
>
> (Alasuutari, 2014, p. 255)

In part, it seems to us, this trend is due to the fact that teachers often find the tasks of interaction with 'children's voices' difficult to understand. Similar data were obtained in another study. Sargeant and Gillett-Swan conducted a mass survey of primary school students, which showed that children were not only aware of the difficulties in the educational process, but also offered productive solutions for adults: 'Voice-inclusive practice is underpinned by an environment where the children feel free to participate at a level of their choosing. … Many teachers continue to select strategies that are reliant on the hierarchical maintenance of control and power' (Sargeant & Gillett-Swan, 2015, p. 188).

Thus, the key challenge of contemporary early childhood education is to combine the child's immersion in culture and to create the conditions for his or her self-expression and creative potential, to combine the opportunity for him or her to hear the adult and to be heard by adult.

Following the main trends, the Federal State Educational Standard on Preschool Education (2013) declared inherent value of childhood, child's emotional wellbeing, individualisation, spontaneity and autonomy of children, working in zone of proximal development as key values of Russian system of preschool education. So, the main challenge for the ECE professional community during last years were:

- providing the relevant tools of assessment of preschool education quality due to the values, stressed in the Standard;
- developing of the relevant educational methods and techniques to fulfil the educational goals and values of the Standard.

In turn, the Early Childhood Environment Rating Scale (2005) is a tool that evaluates the environment from two points of view at once – both the child's ability to obtain the culture (therefore, to get medium and good grades, the environment must be saturated, there should be many materials in music, mathematics, art and so on), and opportunities for creativity of the child (for high scores you need to create conditions for the self-expression of the child).

Articulation of issue and rationale for the relevance of the study for the development of preschool education in the Russian Federation

The idea of reviewing the Federal state educational standards is to a large extent motivated by both the global trends of updating and standardising education, and the current needs of the domestic teaching practices. Moving from strict regulation of the educational content complemented by setting requirements regarding conditions of teaching activity and learning outcomes is supported by a number of historical background factors.

These factors include:

1   Focusing education not on short-term and opportunistic results important for a secluded area of knowledge only, but rather on sustainable learning outcomes ensuring practical use of acquired knowledge (competencies) in various real-life situations.
2   Increasing impact of the environment, i.e. conditions in which the educational activity is undertaken, on learning outcomes. It is exactly due to these conditions that the students' influence on the content of their education either materialises or fails to materialise. The environment-driven

nature of education gave rise to a significant number of teaching practices in which precisely the nature of environment ensures development of students' skills to formulate and implement their own individual educational programmes; while teaching becomes focused on guiding and supporting students in implementing their individual educational programmes.

3   Moving from unified curricula and adoption of a regulation under which various educational institutions have their own curricula puts educational institutions in a position when they must learn to analyse their students' needs and adjust their educational activity accordingly. Such reflexive approach to work and reliance on results of monitoring surveys are becoming an integral quality of the modern-day educational activity. In connection with the above an increasingly significant role in preschool education is assigned to focusing the educational environment on individual development and performance (see Yudina, 2015). Autonomous development and timely adjustment of curricula implemented are becoming increasingly more important.

The Federal State Educational Standard on Preschool Education was adopted as far back as in 2013 and today it is extremely relevant to receive the feedback on its implementation. This situation gives rise to a need to analyse to what extent the kindergarten realities of today correspond to the benchmarks set in the Standard. To clarify the situation, an assessment of preschool education quality was carried out in Russia in 2016–2017, which was aimed at studying the existing strong points and deficiencies in the preschool education system of the capital city.

Prior to the assessment, the issue of selecting the measuring tool to be used had to be resolved. The Federal State Educational Standard on Preschool Education is a framework document, which is a huge advantage, since it allows for a broad variety of tentative curricula on the one hand and gives freedom to kindergartens to develop their own curriculum materials on the other. However, this also includes a known measure of risk: benchmarks are identified very generally and need to be made more specific to become instrumental. These conditions call for a quality assessment tool that would be reliable, i.e. operationally defining the Standard's general provisions, while at the same time allowing for variability of curricula.

Early Childhood Environment Rating Scales (ECERS-R) were selected as such assessment tool (Harms, Clifford, & Cryer, 2016). They are currently considered to be one of the most reliable and valid preschool education quality assessment tools in the world (Perlman, Zellman, & Vi-Nhuan, 2004; Shiyan, 2013). It is no coincidence that exactly ECERS scales are applied in the majority of cross-cultural assessments of preschool education quality (Tietze, Cryer, Bairrro, Palacios, & Wetzel, 1996; Vermeer, van Ijzendoorn, Carcamo, & Harrison, 2016; Zachopoulou et al., 2013;). ECERS was used in the famous British longitudinal survey EPPE (EPPSE) carried out from 1997 to 2014, which studied the impact of curricula on student achievement throughout primary and secondary schooling (Sylva, Melhuish, Sammons, Siraj-Blatchford, & Taggart, 2004). In addition, ECERS was proven to be a sufficiently flexible tool able to assess various educational environments (e.g. existing in Montessori teaching programmes, the Waldorf programme, the Swedish curriculum,[1] Step-by-Step, etc.) (Pramling , Sheridan, & Williams, 2006).

The 'Spirit of Scale' and the Federal State Educational Standard on Preschool Education requirements

In the course of piloting the scale in Russia in 2015 (Shiyan & Vorobyeva, 2015; Yudina, Shmis, Shiyan, & Shiyan, 2016), a comparison was made between requirements for preschool education stipulated in the Federal State Educational Standard for Preschool Education and those contained in the ECERS-R.

The following conclusions were drawn in the course of the analysis. First, the Federal State Educational Standard on Preschool Education (just like the Law 'On Education in the Russian Federation' (2012)) prohibits using child performance outcomes for preschool education quality assessment and requires that curriculum implementation conditions and its structure be used instead; while it is exactly the implementation conditions that are the subject of assessment for the Scales. Second, the key concepts of the standard, such as 'individualisation', 'inherent value of childhood', 'zone of proximal development', 'emotional well-being' and 'spontaneity and autonomy' are matched with environment characteristics such as 'accessibility of materials throughout the major part of the day', 'enhanced environment', etc. The scale corresponds to the abovementioned trends in the modern-day preschool education and key constructs of the Standard: its system of benchmarks may in short be characterised as 'an active and competent child'.

Third, in Russia ECERS-R was published under the heading 'Scales for Comprehensive Education Quality Assessment in Preschool Educational Institutions', because the creators of the tool use the concept 'educational environment' in its wide sense covering quality of the whole educational process. When referring to 'educational environment' the authors of ECERS-R mean arrangement of space (furniture, furnishings, equipment, etc. – i.e. characteristics that in the Standard are collectively referred to as 'objective-spatial environment'), time (daily schedule, balance of regulated and free activities, time for free play and movement, etc.) and interaction (nature of child–adult interaction, peer interaction and staff–child interaction). Therefore, indicators of ECERS-R cover the whole range of conditions that children are faced with when in kindergarten. Fourth, the Standard is of a framework nature while the Scales are detailed and descriptive (43 items containing at least ten indicators each) and are suitable for assessment of various and distinctly different programmes (see Yudina et al., 2016).

As a result of this comparison the experts concluded that ECERS-R correspond to the Federal State Educational Standard on Preschool Education ideology and that this tool may be viewed as a means of detailed implementation of the Standard in the spirit of child-focused pedagogy (Yudina et al., 2016). It's validity, reliability and consistency was tested and approved in Russia during previous stages of the study (Remorenko et al., 2017).

ECERS-R have been used many times as a tool in cross-cultural preschool education assessments. In particular, the assessments dealt with benchmarking the educational environment quality in the USA, Austria, Germany, Spain and Portugal, Sweden and South Korea, Finland, Denmark, Greece, Portugal, Cyprus and Romania, etc. (Vermeer et al., 2016).

Preschool education quality assessment design

The study was initiated by Federal Service for Supervision in Education and Science (the institution is responsible for monitoring of the education quality in all levels of education) and provided by the research team from Moscow City University.

The purpose of the Study is to identify trends in the development of the preschool educational practice in Russia and determine the level of its compliance with the Federal State Educational Standard on Preschool Education. The results obtained should be used to adjust the measures aimed at modernising preschool education in accordance with the requirements of the Standard.

Sample description and design of the assessment

The sample

The results presented in this work are based on the outcomes of applying ECERS-R scales in more than 1300 preschool groups. The sample was divided into two clusters: 'Best' (which were selected by local experts due to the results of different ratings and competitions) – 25 per cent and 'Random' – 75 per cent.

At the first stage of the Research (2016) 423 preschools (148 'Best' and 275 'Random') from 40 regions took part in the study. At the second stage of the Research (2017) 1301 preschools (323 'Best' and 978 'Random') from 74 regions (2.6 per cent of all preschools, 87 per cent of regions of Russia). Each preschool was represented by one random group; 367 groups took part in both stages of the study. The research was completed by the Laboratory of Child Development of the Institute of System projects of Moscow City University and 155 specially trained assessors.

Subject of expert observation

Preschool class educational environment components:

1   Objective–spatial environment.
2   Personal care conditions.
3   Conditions for the development of the child speaking and thinking skills.

4   Conditions for various types of child activity (cognitive, artistic and esthetic, etc.).
5   Staff–child interaction (all kindergarten staff who daily spend a significant part of the day with the children, i.e. no less than four hours of a 12-hour daily programme), and peer (staff–staff and child–child) interaction.
6   Daily programme structure.
7   Conditions for engaging parents into the learning process and conditions for meeting the staff personal and professional development needs.

A standardised assessment form was used for the observation. Additionally, an interview with the teacher based on the toolbox indicators was held.

Analysis of results

The results of the 2016 study show us that average score for the group of 'Best' kindergartens is 3.88 (on a 7-point scale), the average score for the group of 'Random' kindergartens is 3.37. This means that the score on the average in both cases is higher that the 'minimal quality' level.

Even the average score alone allows rendering an approximate assessment of the situation based on how the scale is designed. Although the tool is focused on assessing to what extent the environment helps ensure individualised teaching and learning through accessibility and saturation of the objective–spatial environment, the scale does not include separate indicators such as 'individualisation', 'accessibility' or 'saturation'. However, these characteristics are built in the majority of the scale's indicators: for the environment to score 5 points (good quality) it has to be saturated and accessible.

The low total score, in fact, reflects the established educational model in which the teacher is the main source of knowledge: the centre of gravity in teaching and learning activity lies in so-called 'lessons' at which children have minimal freedom of choosing materials or activities, teaching aids are distributed by the teacher and the children are encouraged to act according to a certain template. Mimetic response for preschoolers is a difficult and important objective, however, turning it into the central educational model gives rise to doubts and contravenes modern ECE and developmental psychology studies (Singer, 2015; Veraksa & Sheridan, 2018).

The following conclusions were drawn on the basis of the study:

1   The quality of education across the sample may be characterised as 'above minimal'.
2   Good results were obtained regarding items related to furniture although these high scores come together with much lower scores for space furnishing and its orientation towards children's needs. Virtually not a single institution had a bedroom designed to be used during the day. The study revealed that the learning environment is not sufficiently saturated and accessible to ensure children's free and spontaneous activity. In many

aspects, this reflects a long-standing tradition to focus curricula on frontal lessons where the initiative is fully in the hands of a teacher. There are practically no spaces for privacy or comfort in the classrooms. Children's works, outcomes of their recent activities or photographs are extremely seldom on display in classrooms. Therefore, one may conclude that the classrooms are furnished to accommodate children but are not oriented towards promoting their initiative and individuality.

3   Results of the study testify to the fact that technically the preschool departments have staff development conditions in place (they have methodological literature and offer opportunities for professional development, methodological support, etc.), however, these results are accompanied by significantly lower scores related with teaching activity of the teachers and degree of their focus on modern concepts of quality preschool education. It is obvious that the content of professional development courses and methodological support needs to be drastically reformed.

4   On the backdrop of quite high scores awarded to the sample for indicators related to care, supervision and child safety, the low scores for meal and sleep time stand out distinctly. In our view this is related to underestimation of routine processes by the kindergartens. Besides, attention should be paid to a large share of regulating and restricting teaching instructions in the course of teacher–child interaction.

Quite high scores were assigned to subscale 'Interaction' (hail/farewell, staff–staff interaction and child–child interaction). Even if one assumes that the presence of expert somehow impacted these indicators, the high scores undoubtedly confirm a good potential for interaction of both staff and kids. Significantly lower scores were assigned to the staff–child interaction indicator, and very low scores to the indicator 'Using speech to develop thinking capacity'. It is obvious that the latter two parameters are key to the child development from the point of view of both the theory of L.°S. Vygotsky and the new preschool education didactics (to a large extent based on the above theory) being designed today. Due to Vygotsky (1987) speech is the key means of thinking as higher psychical function. So, formulation of the thought in words is an important process for child's cognitive development. The role of adult as the one who presents the culture (and language as a part of it) for the child is extremely significant. This fact is stressed in ECERS-R (2005) by dedicating special subscale and some more items to the language and speech issue.

Thus, the issue of organising preschool teacher training and professional development to meet modern concepts of preschool education content and quality and to enable preschool teachers to fully implement the Federal State Educational Standard on Preschool Education is gaining utmost importance.

The assessment data also demonstrated:

•   lack of accessibility, saturation and mobility of the educational environment (low scores for all items related to the subscale 'Activities') means that there are not enough materials for children to choose the activity and the way of activity according to their own plan;

- low scoring on indicators that assess the opportunity for creativity (on items 'Art' and 'Music')

All of this leads to the conclusion that there are problems in fulfilling the following the Standard requirements:

1   educational process individualisation;
2   support of child initiative and autonomy.

Low scores on the item 'Speech use for the development of mental skills' are related to the fact that communication is more often used for instruction than for conversations; teachers are rarely included in children's play, develop children's ideas, ask open questions that encourage children to think. The situations of discussion in which an adult is interested in children's responses support different versions of the answers rather the exception than the rule.

It means that there is a problems in fulfilling the following the Standard requirement:

3   Creating conditions for the development of thinking capacity, imagination and children's creativity.

The second stage of the research was completed in 2017.

At first as in the previous study we discovered the difference between the 'Best' and the 'Random' parts of the sample (Figure 14.1).

Figure 14.1 presents the mean scores for each of 43 items, presented in ECERS-R numbered as they are in the Scale (maximum possible score is 7).

The data shows us the difference between the clusters. On one hand it proves that the criteria of selection of the 'Best' kindergartens by regional experts correspond to the ones in ECERS-R. On the other hand, the fact that the difference is not so big may be interpreted as an influence of federal and regional regulations (sanitary norms for example) and general stereotypes of teachers' and parents' common sense.

Second, the data shows us the tendency of the increasing level of early child education quality (Table 14.1).

Table 14.1 Comparison of the data from 2016 and 2017

Sample	The average score 2016	The average score 2017
Cluster 'Best'	3.88	4.05
Cluster 'Random'	3.37	3.74

Results of the study 2017

Comparison of 'Best' and 'Random' clusters

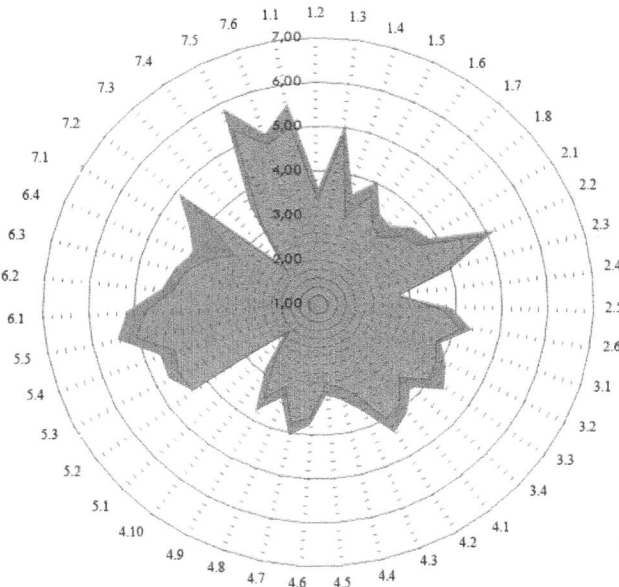

Average mean of scale score – 3,74 ('Random'); 4,05 ('Best')

Figure 14.1 Comparison of the best and random clusters 2017.

In both cases the differences between the results of 2016 and 2017 are statistically significant ($p \leq 0.01$)

The next question: do those results demonstrate the general increasing of the quality or they stress the effect of the research on the quality improvement? To investigate this question, we separated the group of the kindergartens who participated in the research twice from the general sample.

Table 14.2 Comparison of 'Best' and 'Random' preschools, participating for the first time: 2016–2017

Clusters	Results 2016	Results 2017 (first time)
'Best'	3.88	3.92
'Random'	3.37	3.69

Table 14.3 Comparison of preschools who participated in the research twice: 2016–2017

Clusters	The average score 2016	The average score 2017 (reparticipating)
'Best'	3.88	4.33
'Random'	3.37	3.88

The data shows us an increase in the scores in both parts of the sample. It proof that using ECERS-R as the assessment tool with clearly specified indicators to the professional community was helpful to increasing quality in early childhood education. Compared to the sample of newcomers (Table 14.2), the 367 kindergartens who participated in the research twice (Table 14.3) demonstrated more impressive dynamics of changes. We also find the significant differences in the means for subscales, comparing the results of 2016 and 2017 for the kindergartens who participated in the research twice. We consider that the feedback given by assessors after the first year of study made a critical influence on increasing the scores in those kindergartens.

Preschool environment and child's development

Preschool children develop complex psychological formations that allow talking about the great creative possibilities of children. Among them, we should pay attention to the development of the theory of mind, which is associated not only with the development of emotional intelligence, but also with the construction of complex communication interactions with peers and adults.

In the next step of our study we planned to answer the following question: which characteristics of the educational environment have the greatest impact on the social–emotional developing (theory of mind and emotion comprehension development) of preschool children? We used ECERS-R method (Harms, Clifford, & Cryer, 2005).

For the social–emotional development investigation Theory of Mind test (ToM), which is a NEPSY-II Developmental Neuropsychological Assessment subtest (Korkman, Kirk, & Kemp, 2007) was used. It aims to directly diagnose the development of various mental model components: the ability to understand other people's figures of speech, intentions, thoughts and feelings, the ability to distinguish between real and imaginary planes of reality as well as the understanding of false beliefs. This method is designed for children of up to 16 years and it includes 21 tasks. Also used was the 'Test of Emotion Comprehension' (TEC) (Pons & Harris, 2000) that is aimed at studying children's ability to understand the emotions of other people in different situations. This method was designed to diagnose preschool children and consists of 22 tasks, each of which is scored as either 0 or 1 point.

The study sample consisted of 706 children aged 5–6 years (Mean = 5.6 years) from 33 senior groups in Moscow kindergartens. The sample included 357

(50.6 per cent) boys and 349 (49.4 per cent) girls. This study was conducted in 2016–2018. All the psychological tasks were carried out individually, in a quiet room. One meeting lasting 15–20 minutes was organised for each child.

1 Kindergarten classes were divided into three groups based on their ECERS-R scores. As a result of the cluster analysis (the K-means clustering method), three levels of environmental quality were identified: low, medium and high. Having checked the score differences (first by using the Kruskel–Wallis criterion, then the t-criterion for independent samples in pairs), we found that the scores for all the ECERS-R scales differed significantly in all the clusters selected which allowed us to speak about qualitatively different types of educational environments. Almost half (48.7 per cent) of the children attend kindergartens with a low level of educational environment, slightly less than a quarter (24.0 per cent) go to kindergartens with the average one and slightly more than a quarter (27.3 per cent) go to those with the high one.

2 Using the Kruskal–Wallis criterion for several independent samples, it was established that the ToM measurements differ significantly in preschool children from educational environments of different types (K–W = 8.628, $p = 0.013$). Using the t-test for independent samples, we saw for ourselves that the ToM scores were significantly higher in preschool children from secondary-level educational environments than in all other children ($p < 0.005$).

3 Further, to obtain a more detailed analysis of the emotional development of children in different types of educational environment we checked the differences in the performance outcomes of individual tasks aimed at diagnosing the mental model and emotion comprehension (ToM and TEC) in preschoolers from educational environments at different levels (using the Chi-squared test).

4 The tasks aimed at determining the level of mental model development (ToM) produced the following outcomes: in 5 out of 21 tasks, the environmental level is associated with success, which means significantly different performance of tasks for preschoolers from groups with different environmental quality levels ($p < 0.005$). For example, in Task 1 of the procedure a child was shown a picture of a table with a box depicting cookies on it and told the story about a boy called Andrei:

> He opened the box and saw that Mom had put pasta in it. He was upset and put the box back in its place. Andrei's brother entered the room and saw the box with cookies depicted on it. What did Andrei's brother think was in the box?

Preschool children from kindergartens with a high environmental level cope with this task better (children, who told 'cookies' from high level – 83.2 per cent, medium – 76.8 per cent, low – 70.8 per cent; $\chi^2 = 10.176$,

$p=0.006$). In other tasks that proved to associate the quality of the educational environment with the performance of the task (i.e. the outcomes differed significantly in different environments), preschoolers from kindergartens with the average environmental level coped with the tasks better than the others did.

5   The analysis of tasks aimed at understanding emotions (TEC) showed that preschoolers who are brought up in kindergartens with different environments cope with five tasks out of 22 differently ($p<0.005$). Children from groups with a high or medium level of educational environment quality also successfully coped with the rest of the tasks aimed at emotion comprehension.

6   This study showed that the general level of environmental quality is indirectly related to the emotional and personal development of preschool children. It is important to note that the ECERS-R indicators tend to mingle the structural and procedural characteristics of the environment, i.e. the caregiver's material conditions and behaviour are taken into account simultaneously. To clarify the links obtained it would be interesting to analyse both the interactions between caregiver and children and the structural quality of the environment separately.

Conclusions

The ECERS-R is so designed that in order to obtain minimal quality the classroom must be adequately furnished; to be good the environment needs to be rich in development opportunities freely accessible for the child which in itself leads to changing the nature and ways of establishing norms in adult–child community (e.g. furnishing a space for privacy entails the need to establish rules of its use) supporting the adult–child interaction. High quality means full utilisation of all learning environment's opportunities in educational activity.

The comparison of 2016 and 2017 data shows us that ECERS assessment may be used as a basis for the efforts to improve preschool education quality. As a primary step, it would be advisable to use the available resources: rearrange the available space of classrooms, bedrooms and playgrounds, create comfort and privacy spaces indoors, improve conditions for staff, and introduce games and teaching aids related to multiculturalism. Improvement across these areas will quite promptly help to improve general scores. This means that the institution as itself and teacher's team has to be more into the process of making decisions about equipment and materials supplying. On the other hand, new architectural solutions for the kindergarten buildings have to be developed and extended.

A more serious effort is required in the mid-term: hard work is needed to bring the educational process in kindergartens in line with the Federal State Educational Standard on Preschool Education. The bulk of quality improvement potential lies in the process quality domain – i.e. in the area of teacher–child, child–child and child–environment interaction. In terms of policy-making it means that the system of preschool teacher preparation and in-service training have to be more oriented to the best practices. Teachers from advanced kindergartens have to be motivated to disseminate their teaching methods and experience. This process has already started in the most advanced universities and in-service teacher training institutions. Another focus is on better involvement of teacher's assistants into the educational process.

An important consequence of the study is that the self-organised networks of teachers and kindergartens interested in improvement of the early childhood education quality are appearing now. Members of the network are sharing their ideas, methods and practices, enriching each other.

The research completed in 2016–2017 will be prolonged as a longitude one. To build a more detailed picture of the ways to improve process quality, additional research, secondary to ECERS, will be needed (the effects of the pre-school quality on child development, the quality of organisational culture of the kindergartens, teacher's representations on education quality etc.). Such research would help better understand the context and specific deficiencies of the system and to find the best ways for its development. The results of the study may be used in different levels of the policy-making: federal, regional and at the level of the preschool institution.

Acknowledgements

The work was supported by Russian Scientific Fund 17-78-20198.

Note

1 Curriculum here means a national-level document establishing key requirements for preschool education. By their status, curricula correspond to state educational standards of the Russian Federation but are different from them as regards the range of parameters covered. In particular, a number of international curricula do not include requirements for logistics, etc.

References

Alasuutari, M. (2014). Voicing the child? A case study in Finnish early childhood education. *Childhood*, *21*(2), 242–259.

Alasuutari, M., & Markstrom, A.-M. (2011). The making of the ordinary child in preschool. *Scandinavian Journal of Educational Research*, *55*(5), 517–535.

Canella, G. S. (1997). *Deconstructing Early Childhood Education: Social Justice and Revolution*. New York: Peter Lang.

Cheung, P. R. H. (2017). Teacher-child-directed versus child-centered: the challenge of promoting creativity in Chinese preschool classrooms. *Pedagogy, Culture & Society*, *25*(1), 73–86.

Federal Law of the Russian Federation 'On Education'. (2012, 31 December). Retrieved from https://rg.ru/2012/12/30/obrazovanie-dok.html.

Federal State Educational Standard of Preschool Education. (2013, 25 November). Retrieved from https://rg.ru/2013/11/25/doshk-standart-dok.html.

Harms, T., Clifford, R. M., & Cryer, D. (2005). *Early Childhood Environment Rating Scale (ECERS-R) Revised Edition*. United States: Teachers College Press.

Harms, T., Clifford, R., & Cryer, D. (2016). *Scales for Comprehensive Assessment of the Quality of Education in Pre-school Educational Organizations (ECERS-R)*. Moscow: Natsionalnoye obrazovanie.

Johansson, E. (2011). Introduction: Giving words to children's voices in research. In E. Johansson & J. White, (Eds.), *Educational Research with Our Youngest: Voices of Infants and Toddlers* (pp.1–14). The Netherlands: Springer Science.

Komulainen, S. (2007). The ambiguity of the child's 'voice' in social research. *Childhood*, *14*(1), 11–28.

Korkman, M., Kirk, U., & Kemp, S. L. (2007). *NEPSY II. Administrative Manual*. San Antonio, TX: Psychological Corporation.

Miller, E., & Almon, J. (2009). *Crisis in the Kindergarten: Why Children Need to Play in School*. College Park: Alliance for Childhood.

Perlman, M., Zellman, G. L., & Vi-Nhuan, Le (2004). Examining the psychometric properties of the Early Childhood Environment Rating Scale Revised (ECERS-R). *Early Childhood Research Quarterly*, *19*(3), 398–412.

Pons, F., & Harris, P. L. (2000). *Test of Emotion Comprehension*. Oxford: Oxford University Press.

Pramling, S. I., Sheridan, S., & Williams, P. (2006). Five preschool curricula – comparative perspective. *International Journal of Early Childhood*, *38*(1), 11–15.

Remorenko, I. M., Shiyan, O. A., Shiyan, I. B., Shmis, T. G., Le-van, T. N., Kozmina Y. Y., & Sivak, E. V. (2017). Key problems of realization of FSES of preschool education on the results of the research with the help of 'Early Childhood Environment Rating Scale in preschool educational organisations (ECERS-R)': 'Moscow – 36'. *Sovremennoe Doshkolnoe Obrazovanie. Teoria i Praktika* [Preschool Education Today. Theory and Practice], *2*, 34–49.

Sargeant, J., & Gillett-Swan, J. (2015). Empowering the disempowered through voice-inclusive practice: Children's views on adult-centric educational provision. *European Educational Research Journal*, *14*(2), 177–191.

Shiyan, O. A. (2013). New ideas about the quality of early childhood education and its support mechanisms: The international context. *Preschool Education Today. Theory and Practice*, *5*, 68–78.

Shiyan, O. A., & Vorobyeva, E. V. (2015). New opportunities in the education quality assessment: ECERS-R scales tested in Russia. *Sovremennoe Doshkolnoe Obrazovanie. Teoria i Praktika*, *7*, 38–49.

Singer, E. (2015). Play and playfulness in early childhood education and care. *Psychology in Russia: State of the Art*, *8*(2), 27–35.

Sylva, K., Melhuish, E., Sammons, P., Siraj-Blatchford, I., & Taggart, B. (2004). *The Effective Provision of Pre-School Education (EPPE Project). Technical Paper 12*. London: Department for Education. Institute of Education, University of London.

Tietze, W., Cryer, D., Bairrro, J., Palacios, J., & Wetzel, G. (1996). Comparisons of observed process quality in early child care and education programs in five countries. *Early Childhood Research Quarterly*, *11*(4), 447–475.

Veraksa, N., & Sheridan, S. (Ed.). (2018). *Vygotsky's Theory in Early Childhood Education and Research: Russian and Western Values*. London: Routledge.

Vygotsky, L. (1987). Thinking and speech. In R. W. Rieber & A. S. Carton (Eds.), *The Collected Works of L. S. Vygotsky, Vol 1: Problems of General Psychology*. New York: Plenum.

Vermeer, F. J., van Ijzendoorn, M. H., Carcamo, R. A., & Harrison, L. J. (2016). Quality of child care using the environment rating scales: A metaanalysis of international studies. *International Journal of Early Childhood, 48*(1), 33–60.

Wardekker, W., Boersma, A., Ten Dam, G., & Volman, M. (2012). Motivation for school learning. In M. Hedegaard, A. Edwards, & M. Fleer (Eds.), *Motives, Emotions and Values in the Development of Children and Young People* (153–169). Cambridge: Cambridge University Press.

Yudina, E. G. (2015). ECERS scales as a method of assessing quality and development of the Russian preschool educational system. *Preschool Education Today. Theory and Practice, 7*, 22–27.

Yudina, E. G., Shmis, T. G., Shiyan, I. B., & Shiyan, O. A. (2016). Organizers' preface of ECERS-R scales Russian edition approbation. In T. Harms, R. Clifford, & D. Cryer. *Scales for Comprehensive Assessment of the Quality of Education in Pre-school Educational Organizations (ECERS-R)* (pp. 13–17). Moscow: Natsionalnoye obrazovanie.

Zachopoulou, E., Grammatikopoulos, V., Gregoriadis, A., Gamelas, A., Leal, T., Pessanha, M., Barros, S., Liukkonen, J., Loizou, E., Henriksen, C., Sanders, Olesen, L., & Ciolan, L. (2013). Comparing aspects of the process quality in six European early childhood educational settings. *6th International Conference of Education, Research and Innovation*. Conference abstracts, Seville, Spain.

15 Early childhood workforce in Serbia as a policy issue

Tijana Bogovac and Lidija Miškeljin

Introduction

Early childhood education and care (ECEC) in Serbia has a holistic orientation, and it is of direct public concern (The Government of the Republic of Serbia, 2019a). The ECEC system is long established, and it is an integral part of the education system as the first phase of formal education (Baucal et al., 2016). ECEC is carried on in preschool institutions that are founded on the municipality level and by status can be public or private (Baucal et al., 2016; The Government of the Republic of Serbia, 2019a). There is an integrated system of ECEC in Serbia with care, education and upbringing being intertwined. The multifunctional nature of preschool institutions implies that besides education as the main function, child nourishment, health, as well as social care and protection are provided (Baucal et al., 2016).

Along ECEC teachers, other professionals work in preschool institutions, such as pedagogues, psychologists, speech therapists, special education teachers – all contributing to the holistic approach to ECEC in Serbia. However, there are numerous challenges with ECEC in Serbia such as low coverage, inequality in access, lack of facilities and uneven geographical distribution being some (Baucal et al., 2016; Krnjaja & Pavlović Breneselović, 2013; UNICEF, 2012). These challenges are recognised within the Strategy document as well as relevant research and call for further development of ECEC in Serbia (Baucal et al., 2016; The Government of the Republic of Serbia, 2012; UNICEF, 2012).

Initial education, work conditions and work prospects of ECEC teachers are significant issues that influence the quality of ECEC in Serbia. Even though educational requirements for ECEC teachers in Serbia are high, the variety within initial education brings confusion in the conceptual and pedagogical trace of the profession. The challenges are present in the continual professional development too. In the chapter, the authors discuss ECEC teachers' initial and ongoing education, as well as gender issues and working conditions. Challenges within the context have been addressed as well as possible future developments. Finally, the need for extensive research as a foundation for future policy developments of ECEC teacher profession is highlighted.

ECEC teachers in Serbia

Early childhood professionals who are engaged with the education of children from six months to six years of age in Serbia are titled 'vaspitači', from the word 'vaspitanje', which means upbringing. The title of the early childhood professionals differs from the title of elementary school teachers and highlights the approach to children as holistic with care, education and upbringing being intertwined (Banković, 2014). The differences in the title portray the differences in the approach to children and early childhood education. The English term teacher in Serbia is closer to the title of professionals working in schools ('učitelji'), that derives from the verb to teach ('učiti') (Banković, 2014). The specific education for professionals that work with young children existed in Serbia from the very beginnings of the emergence of kindergartens in the 19th century (Banković, 2014; Gavrilović, 2003; Krnjaja & Pavlović Breneselović, 2013). As there is no direct translation of the title 'vaspitač', the term ECEC teacher will be used in the chapter to imply professionals that are engaged with the education of children in preschool institutions in Serbia.

ECEC teachers' title and obligations differ in accordance with the age group of children they work with. Nurse–teachers work with children from six months to three years, while ECEC (kindergarten) teachers work with children from three to six years of age (The Government of the Republic of Serbia, 2019a). While the emphasis of the work of nurse–teachers is more on care, the emphasis on the work of ECEC teachers is on upbringing and education of children from three to six years of age (The Government of the Republic of Serbia, 2019a; Ministry of Education, 2006). No matter whether an ECEC teacher works in a public or private kindergarten, he/she needs to possess the appropriate education (diploma) (The Government of the Republic of Serbia, 2019a).

ECEC teachers' initial education

There is complexity in the initial education of ECEC teachers in Serbia. Nurse–teachers need to possess at least the appropriate secondary-level education to be engaged in work with children in ECEC (The Government of the Republic of Serbia, 2019a). ECEC teachers that work with children from three to six years of age have two possibilities for initial education. They can opt for vocational high schools' or university degrees, Bachelor or Master degree (Baucal et al., 2016; The Government of the Republic of Serbia, 2017a). The dual educational path emerged with the Bologna process from 2005, when professional studies for ECEC teachers in Serbia have been transformed and raised to the tertiary level (Baucal et al., 2016; Miskeljin, 2018).

There are ten vocational high schools (post-secondary education designed to provide vocational education) and six faculties (providing education of academical orientation) educating ECEC teachers (Baucal et al., 2016; Krnjaja & Pavlović Breneselović, 2013). There are consequently different programmes of initial education for ECEC teachers in Serbia, some are vocational, while others are academic, and they last different periods of time, from 3 to 4 years (The Government of the Republic of Serbia, 2019a). Even though there are many options for the education of ECEC teachers in Serbia, the variety is said to bring difficulties such as conceptual differences within these programmes and confusion among different educational profiles and titles (Baucal et al., 2016; Krnjaja & Pavlović Breneselović, 2013).

Heterogeneous curricula and substantial differences in teaching methodology and training are also seen in ECEC teachers' initial education in Serbia (Miškeljin, 2018). Moreover, the content and pedagogy of the study programmes for the initial education of ECEC teachers are not aligned with the principles of the professional roles of teachers, nor with the concept of educational programme given in Strategy of Education in Serbia until 2020 and the National ECEC Curriculum Framework (Baucal et al., 2016; Miškeljin, 2018). The need to direct initial education towards the vision of ECEC teacher as the curriculum creator and reflective practitioner with the emphasis on the openness to the local community and families, as well as diversified programmes and forms of ECEC is underlined (Miškeljin, 2018; The Government of the Republic of Serbia, 2012). Alignment of the ECEC teachers' study programmes to the European education area and novelties in teaching methodology and practical learning is also emphasised (Miškeljin, 2018).

Therefore, research shows that there are many challenges with the initial education of ECEC teachers in Serbia. It can be concluded that currently there is no clear vision of the role of ECEC teachers in initial education programmes. This becomes especially interesting in the actual moment of the implementation of the new National Curriculum Framework of ECEC in Serbia (Ministry of Education, 2018a) and urges for harmonising the conceptual and pedagogical basis of the job with the curriculum framework. These are all future developmental challenges within the policy projections in Serbia.

ECEC teachers' ongoing education

Once formally qualified, when they start working, ECEC teachers go through a year-long mentoring programme, the period in which they are supported by a mentor, a professional that possesses the license. After this period, they take the national exam in order to obtain the professional licence (Ministry of Education, 2018b). During this period, all the segments of the professional role are practised and evaluated with the mentor, which is documented.

During the induction period and after acquiring the licence, ECEC teachers continue the process of continuous professional development (Ministry of Education, 2018b). The concept of professional development consists of in-service training and career advancement by acquiring professional titles: pedagogical counsellor, independent pedagogical counsellor, senior pedagogical counsellor and high pedagogical counsellor (Miškeljin, 2018). Continuing professional development in Serbia, like in the great majority of European countries, is a professional requirement for teachers (Eurydice, 2015). It is obligatory, part of career advancement and personal development, and teachers have the autonomy to plan their professional development (Miskeljin, 2018).

The professional development reflects the concept of lifelong learning (Miskeljin, 2018). It is one of the indicators of quality standards in work of preschool institutions in Serbia (Ministry of Education, 2018c). However, continual professional development in Serbia is often criticised for not supporting reflective professionalism within kindergartens as learning communities, that could contribute to the continuous transformation of ECEC system but puts emphasis on 'individual professionalism' (Baucal et al., 2016; Krnjaja & Pavlović Breneselović, 2013; Miskeljin, 2018). The dominant model of professional development of employees in Serbia is still based on the mechanistic model (Krnjaja, 2010) or autonomous professionalism (Hargreaves, 2000). Such professionalism emphasises the isolation and separation of educators from other colleagues while professional development has the function of supporting changes, compatible with the existing education system (Pavlović Breneselović & Krnjaja, 2012). The focus is on its extension, efficiency and effectiveness. On the other hand, contemporary research shows that professionalism in ECEC is strongly linked to the ability for critical reflection on pedagogical practice and to the competence of being able to change practice (Pavlović Breneselović, 2014; Urban, Vandenbroeck, Van Laere, Lazzari, & Peeters, 2012). This approach requires the provision of opportunities for the early childhood workforce to engage in collaborative learning and critical reflection. Moreover, the team's competence within the process of learning and reflexive questioning of one's own practice, cooperation with other institutions, experts and children's families inside and outside the system, networking with researchers and institutions of the initial education and coherent system of support is needed (Pavlović Breneselović, 2014; Miskeljin, 2015; Urban et al., 2012). Nevertheless, this is not recognised in the concept of continuous professional development in Serbia. The concept of continuous professional development based on 'individual professionalism' (Hargreaves, 2000) sets professional development apart from the development of practice in the ECEC centre and apart from changes in the system shaped up by educational policies. Therefore, ongoing ECEC teachers' education and professional development are areas that also need to be harmonised with overall vision on ECEC onwards.

Other professionals within preschool institutions

The holistic orientation of ECEC in Serbia (Gavrilović, 2006) implies that different professionals work in preschool institutions in addition to nursery and ECEC teachers. These are associates (social workers, nutritionists, nurses for preventative health care, special educators) and expert associates (pedagogue, psychologist, speech therapist, pedagogue for visual/music arts and physical education and associates) (Baucal et al., 2016; The Government of the Republic of Serbia, 2019a, 2019b). There are also pedagogical assistants that provide assistance and additional support to children concerning their needs, and cooperate with teachers and professional staff, parents or legal guardians (The Government of the Republic of Serbia, 2019a).

The associates have supporting roles in the activities regarding food, nurture, health and social care (The Government of the Republic of Serbia, 2017a). Expert associates have advisory roles and support quality development of ECEC in curriculum development, quality of children–adult relations, building relations with family and local community in order to introduce new approaches to learning, play and creativity etc. (Krnjaja & Pavlović Breneselović, 2013; The Government of the Republic of Serbia, 2019a).

The existence of the team of various professionals in preschool institutions is often highlighted as a quality advantage in ECEC in Serbia (Banković, 2014; Baucal et al., 2016; Gavrilović, 2006; Krnjaja & Pavlović Breneselović, 2013). The team provides for the holistic approach to ECEC in Serbia, as nutrition, health and social care and educational function are comprised. The researchers also perceive the multiprofessional teams in ECEC in Serbia as an asset, as the interactive process between early childhood professionals could promote and supports peer learning and collaboration through co-construction of knowledge with teams that function as learning communities (Pavlović Breneselović & Krnjaja, 2013; Urban et al., 2012).

However, there are challenges in utilising the potential of the professional variety. Research shows that the existing norms with large number of groups, spatial 'dispersion' of settings of a single preschool institution, challenges with initial education for expert associates and 'imprecise, inconsistent, too ambitious definitions of jobs and tasks of expert associates impede quality realisation of the roles of expert associates' (Baucal et al., 2016, p. 38). The official data shows that there are only 2 per cent of expert associates of all employees in the ECEC sector in Serbia (Miskeljin, 2018; Statistical Office of the Republic of Serbia, 2017). This section shows that even though there is a huge resource with ECEC workforce in Serbia brought about by its holistic direction and existence of various professionals in the field, there are challenges in utilising the richness of this potential that is linked with initial education, work conditions, professional development and quality of ECEC.

Gender disparity

There is gender inequality with regards to the ECEC workforce in Serbia, which is traditionally present in Serbia (Krnjaja & Pavlović Breneselović, 2013). Even though at its very beginnings, in the 19th century, ECEC teachers' jobs were appointed to men, soon after it had become a female profession that was in line with the maternal perception of the job (Gavrilović, 2003). In 2019, there were 29,106 of professionals working in the sector in Serbia, 27,655 of which are women, that is 95.05 per cent of the working population, while men accounted for only 4.95 per cent. The data for ECEC teachers shows that 98.11 per cent of ECEC teachers are female, while there are only 1.89 per cent of male ECEC teachers in Serbia (Statistical Office of the Republic of Serbia,

2019). The result is in line with previous research results that showed that male teachers account for less than 2 per cent of employed teachers (Baucal et al., 2016), which shows that the traditional view of ECEC teachers' profession as predominantly female still persevere (Banković, 2014). At the moment, there are no policy measures to stimulate greater representation of men in the profession.

Work conditions

Salaries of teachers in public institutions in Serbia are regulated at the central level. It is prescribed that the base for salaries in preschool institutions cannot be lower than the base for salaries in schools. On the other hand, it can be increased from the funds of the institution or local self-government units (The Government of the Republic of Serbia, 2019a). In private preschool institutions, salaries of ECEC teachers are established autonomously, and there is no official data on the methods or amounts (Eurydice, 2015). Due to budgetary deficits and the fiscal savings plan, Serbia was the only country in Europe with a decrease in teachers' salary in 2014 when it was reduced by 10 per cent (Eurydice, 2015).

With regards to working hours, ECEC teachers have a 40-hours working week (The Government of the Republic of Serbia, 2019a). Thirty hours weekly are allocated for direct work with children, while ten hours are assigned for planning, programming and evaluation of work, preparation and organisation of their work as well as collaboration with parents and other participants of ECEC processes and professional development (Miskeljin, 2018).

Even though legally equal, traditionally and according to the public perception, the social status of the ECEC teachers' profession is ranked lower than elementary or secondary school teachers (Miskeljin, 2018). The profession is often perceived as child minding (UNICEF, 2012). In the Strategy of Education Development in Serbia 2020, poor social standing and the low economic status of ECEC teachers' profession are pointed out as some of the key issues that produced additional ramifications on the quality of candidates interested in the profession (The Government of the Republic of Serbia, 2012; Miskeljin, 2018). Consequently, law status can be considered as one of the core issues of ECEC preschool workforce in Serbia.

The findings from a qualitative study on Serbian ECEC teachers' understanding of their professional identity (Bogovac, 2016) show the challenges teachers state belong to all the systems of their ecological environment: number of children per group, lack of resources, extensive documentation, problems in communication with parents or colleagues. Unfavourable ratio children–adults are often characterised as a factor that negatively influences ECEC teachers' job satisfaction (Krnjaja & Pavlović Breneselović, 2013; Nišević & Colić, 2010). Banković (2014) discusses the need for improvements in working conditions and salaries, more favourable employment prospects, union organisation and more supportive infrastructure for a quality early childhood sector.

On the other hand, ECEC teachers are organised under a dedicated association of ECEC teachers, with the developed code of ethics, which organises seminars and conferences and is advocating for professionalisation (Banković, 2014). There are several unions of professionals working in the field of ECEC in Serbia: Association of ECEC teachers of Serbia, Association of Nursery ECEC teachers of Serbia, Association of Preschool Expert Associates and Associates, Pedagogical Society of Serbia, Association of Psychologists of Serbia etc. There are other modes of networking, made either around specific programmes (such as Montessori), projects, specific training programmes, or informally such as Facebook groups etc. (Krnjaja & Pavlović Breneselović, 2013). The participants in the research on ECEC teachers' understanding of their professional identity showed strong professional integrity based on reflection, self-development, supported by professional exchange and professional development (Bogovac, 2016).

In conclusion, there are favourable as well as unfavourable aspects of work conditions of ECEC teachers in Serbia. While it is important to tackle the ones that negatively influence ECEC teachers' work satisfaction, it is of great importance to keep the positive aspects that are of contribution.

Challenges with regards to ECEC workforce in Serbia for the policy

The chapter has shown various challenges for the policy projections with regards to the ECEC workforce in Serbia. The research demonstrates that there is confusion among different educational profiles and titles, heterogeneous curricula, substantial differences in teaching methodology and conceptual differences within programmes of initial education of ECEC teachers in Serbia (Baucal et al., 2016; Krnjaja & Pavlović Breneselović, 2013; Miskeljin, 2018). Moreover, there is no alignment with the principles of the professional roles of teachers, neither with the Strategy of Education in Serbia until 2020 nor with the National ECEC Curriculum Framework (Miskeljin, 2018). The emphasis on continual professional development in Serbia is on individual professionalism or autonomous professionalism and mechanistic model of professional development (Baucal et al., 2016; Hargreaves, 2000; Krnjaja, 2010; Krnjaja & Pavlović Breneselović, 2013; Miskeljin, 2018). It sets professional development apart from the development of practice in ECEC centres as well as apart from changes in the system shaped up by educational policies.

The chapter has also shown that even though there is a huge resource within ECEC workforce in Serbia with various professionals engaged in preschool institutions, there are many challenges such as work conditions, initial education of expert associates and complex job tasks (Baucal et al., 2016) that hinder capacity of the richness of the resource in ECEC. Moreover, while there is gender inequality among ECEC workforce, there is a lack of policy measures to stimulate greater equality of men in the profession. Additionally, the status of the ECEC teachers' profession is ranked low, and the profession is often perceived as child minding (UNICEF, 2012). These produce ramifications on the quality of candidates interested in the profession (Miskeljin, 2018; The Government of the Republic of Serbia, 2012). Consequently, law status can be considered as one of the core issues of ECEC preschool workforce in Serbia. Finally, there are many challenges with regards to work conditions such as the unfavourable child–adult ratio.

Conclusion and recommendations

The question of initial ECEC teachers' education is one of the core questions for future ECEC quality development in Serbia. The level of education of the early childhood teachers, as well as the corpus of professional knowledge, does not in itself lead to the quality of the process of early childhood education and care. Many authors point out that professionalism in the field of early childhood education and care is closely related to the ability to critically reflect on pedagogical practice and the ability to change the practice. Research on what competencies are needed in early childhood education and care suggests that the quality of professional staff requires the competence of an individual, but also of the educational system itself (Urban, Vandenbroeck, Van Laere, Lazzari, & Peeters, 2011). Competence in the context of early childhood education and care should be seen as a characteristic of the entire system (Pavlović Breneselović, 2014).

The need to reform the system and curriculum for the initial education of ECEC teachers is highlighted in recent consulting reports (Baucal et al., 2016). The necessity of the mutual alignment of study programmes and competencies that the students need to acquire to become professional teachers are stressed. Moreover, the core competencies required for ECEC teachers' profession are defined by the National Qualifications framework on the system level, which also requires changes in the initial education of preschool teachers as the role is portrayed as more complex, based on professional knowledge, skills and values that are perceived as developing (Ministry of Education, 2018d). On the curriculum level, changes in content and pedagogical approach in initial education of teachers should be aligned with contemporary postulates on key competencies of professionals in education for the 21st century (e.g. training for reflexive practice), as well to contemporary understanding of childhood, child and learning (Baucal et al., 2016). In order to achieve this, it is necessary to work on the development of a system of professional development with the focus on deconstructing the meaning of quality educational practice, understanding professional development/learning as a process of reviewing and building a common meaning, and understanding the importance and role of social exchange in learning and developing the capacity for reflection. All the above is closely related to the ability to critically reflect on pedagogical practice and the ability to change the practice. Therefore, it is necessary to initiate a change in the concept of professional development by supporting forms of professional development/learning that involve researching their practice, professional networking, project development and collaborative action.

To sum up, the chapter implies that future policy conception of the ECEC workforce in Serbia should be based on the vision of the ECEC teacher as the creator and researcher of the curriculum with the emphasis on the openness to the local community and families and diversified programmes and forms of ECEC (Baucal et al., 2016; Miskeljin, 2018). Moreover, continual professional development should support reflective professionalism within kindergarten as a learning community that could contribute to the continuous transformation of ECEC system (Pavlović Breneselović, 2014; Urban et al., 2012). Such an approach requires the provision of opportunities for the whole early childhood workforce to engage in collaborative learning and critical reflection, cooperation with other institutions, experts and children's families inside and outside the system, networking with researchers and institutions of the initial education and coherent system of support (Miskeljin, 2015; Pavlović Breneselović, 2014; Urban et al., 2012). In the light of the conception of initial and professional education, the existence of multiprofessional teams in Serbia remains a valuable source. Work conditions and the law status of ECEC preschool workforce in Serbia is also a challenge that needs to be addressed within policy onwards. Finally, there is a need for further research on the issue of ECEC teachers' education, work conditions and job prospects in order to inform future policy developments on ECEC and ECEC teachers' profession in Serbia.

References

Banković, I. (2014). Early childhood professionalism in Serbia: Current issues and developments. *International Journal of Early Years Education, 22(3)*, 251–262.

Baucal, A., Pavlović Breneselović, D., Miškeljin, L., Koruga, D., Stanić, K., Avramović, M. (2016). *Early Childhood Education and Care (ECEC) in the Republic of Serbia: Situational Analysis and Recommendations.* Consulting report for World Bank.

Bogovac, T. (2016). *Serbian Preschool Teachers' Understanding of Their Professional Identity.* Master of Science thesis, University of Gothenburg. Retrieved from www.hioa.no/eng/About-HiOA/Faculty-of-Education-and-International-Studies/Department-of-Early-Childhood-Education/IMEC/Student-s-master-theses/Tijana.

Eurydice. (2015). Teachers' and school heads' salaries and allowances in Europe 2014/15. Retrieved from http://eacea.ec.europa.eu/education/eurydice/documents/facts_and_figures/188EN.pdf.

Gavrilović, A. (2003). *Nastanak i razvoj predskolskih ustanova u Srbiji* [The emergence and development of preschool institutions in Serbia]. Beograd: Službeni glasnik, 305–329.

Gavrilović, A. (2006). Multifunkcionalna delatnost predškolskih ustanova [Multifunctional work of preschool institutions]. *Nastava i vaspitanje, 55*, 57–69.

Hargreaves, A., (2000). Four Ages of Professionalism and Professional Learning, Teachers and Teaching: *History and Practice, Vol. 6*, No. 2.

Krnjaja, Ž. (2010). Profesionalni razvoj iz ekološke paradigme [Professional Development in the Perspective of Ecological Paradigm]. *Andragoške studije, 2(2)*, 121–140.

Krnjaja, Ž., & Pavlović Breneselović, D. (2013). *Gde stanuje kvalitet–Politika uspostavljanja kvaliteta u predškolskom vaspitanju Knjiga 1* [Where does the quality live. Policies of building early childhood education quality]. Belgrade: Institute for Pedagogy and Andragogy, Faculty of Philosophy, University of Belgrade.

Ministry of Education (2018a). *Osnove programa predškolskog vaspitanja i obrazovanja – Godine uzleta* Curriculum Framework for Preschool Education – Years of Ascent]. Serbia: Official gazette.

Ministry of Education (2018b). *Pravilnik o stalnom stručnom usavršavanju i napredovanju u zvanja nastavnika, vaspitača i stručnih saradnika* [Rulebook on continual professional development and career advancement of teachers, preschool teachers and expert associates]. Serbia: Official Gazette.

Ministry of Education (2018c). *Quality standards in work of institutions in Serbia.* Serbia: Official gazette.

Ministry of Education (2018d). *Rulebook on preschool teacher competences and professional development.* Serbia: Official gazette.

Miskeljin, L. (2015). From the autonomy of the profession to collaborative professionalism. In *The Fourth International Interdisciplinary Scientific Conference Methodical Days 2015, Competences of Preschool Teachers for the Knowledge Society, Proceeding Book* (pp. 39–47). Kikinda: Preschool Teachers Training College in Kikinda.

Miskeljin, L. (2018). Serbia ECEC workforce profile. In J. Peeters & L. Miskeljin (Eds.), *Towards a New Initial Training for ECEC Teachers in Serbia.* Consulting report for UNICEF Serbia (not published).

Nišević, S., & Colić, V. (2010). Profesionalni status, zadovoljstvo poslom i stručni profil vaspitača i učitelja [Professional status, job satisfaction and professional profile of preschool teachers and teachers]. *Nastava i vaspitanje, 59*(2), 314–325.

Pavlović Breneselović, D. (2014). Kompetencije ili kompetentnost: različiti diskursi profesionalizma vaspitača [Competencies or being competent: Different discourses to preschool teachers professionalism]. *Vaspitanje i obrazovanje, 34*(2), 57–68.

Pavlović Breneselović, D., & Krnjaja, Ž. (2012). Perspektiva vaspitača o profesionalnom usavršavanju sa stanovišta sistemske koncepcije profesionalnog razvoja [Teachers perspective about professional development from the systemic standpoint]. *Andragoške studije, 1*(2), 145–162.

Statistical Office of the Republic of Serbia (2019). *Pre-primary Education in the Republic of Serbia, 2018/2019 School Year.* Belgrade: Cigoja.

The Government of the Republic of Serbia (2012). *Strategy for Education Development in Serbia 2020.* Belgrade: Cigoja.

The Government of the Republic of Serbia. (2019a). *Law on Preschool Education.* Belgrade: Official Gazette.

The Government of the Republic of Serbia. (2019b). *Law on the Foundations of the Education System.* Belgrade: Official Gazette.

UNICEF (2012). Investing in early childhood education in Serbia. Retrieved from: www.unicef.org/serbia/WP_Preschool_education.pdf.

Urban, M., Vandenbroeck, M., Van Laere, K., Lazzari, A., & Peeters, J. (2011). *Competence Requirements in Early Childhood Education and Care. Final report.* London and Brussels, European Commission. Directorate General for Education and Culture.

Urban, M., Vandenbroeck, M., Van Laere, K., Lazzari, A., & Peeters, J. (2012). Towards competent systems in Early Childhood Education and Care. Implications for policy and practice. *European Journal of Education, 47*(4), 508–526.

16 In-service early childhood teachers' perceptions of professionalism and professionalisation in Singapore

Shifting sands in a political and policy landscape

Hilary Monk and Sivanes Phillipson

Introduction

The professional status of early childhood teachers is in a constant state of re-evaluation worldwide, as various educational reforms are instigated by local and national government authorities (c.f., Arimoto, 2013; Harwood, Klopper, Osanyin, & Vanderlee, 2012; Lim, 2017). Gupta (2018, p. 12) argues that 'waves of neoliberal globalisation have influenced changes in educational and economic policies' internationally including Asian countries such as India, Singapore, China, Sri Lanka and the Maldives. Gupta goes on to contend, among others, how the rise of consumerism has led to increased enrolment in preschools and quality teacher shortages. Along a similar vein, Lim (2018) clearly situates early childhood care and education in the Singaporean context as being at an 'ideological and political crossroad' where 'policies need to urgently shift in ways to pay close attention to the widening social and achievement gap' between the advantaged and the disadvantaged (p. 660). Her argument is connected to the need for 'improved accessibility, affordability, and quality of services' (p. 649) as well as issues around policy development, curriculum and pedagogy, teacher preparation and research.

It is within this political and ideological landscape of 'shifting sands' that the teachers in our study considered the concept of professionalism and professionalisation. What does it mean to be an early childhood professional? Are early childhood educators professionals? Will higher standards and accountabilities lead to the professionalisation of the early childhood sector? It is with these questions in mind that we move to discuss the concepts of profession, professional and professionalisation in this chapter.

Profession, professional and professionalisation

There are many and varied interpretations of the concept of 'professional'. The literature seems to indicate that the term is contested and questioned (Chalke,

2013; Moss, 2010; Osgood, 2006; Rauschenbach & Riedel, 2016). Historically, the term 'profession' was associated initially with those in religious orders being committed to something understood as being worthwhile, moral and ethical (Feeney, 2012). Medicine, law and theology were grouped as 'classical professions' or elite groups of people who gained knowledge and qualifications through a university education. Professionals were separated from traders and artisans who acquired practical skills through apprenticeships (Crook, 2008). These elitist categories remained unquestioned for centuries, however today the terms profession and professional are more widely used and commonly linked to people that have studied for and gained formal qualifications before entering their chosen vocation.

The parameters by which a professional is identified, for example specific and exclusive skills and knowledge, membership of a specific group and registration or accreditation to practice, suggest that membership of a profession is limited to a specific group of 'qualified' people (Chalke, 2013). This becomes problematic for early childhood educators who may gain their qualifications as pre-service teachers but who often develop their skills, knowledge and expertise while engaging in practice, post qualifications (Chalke, 2013; Osgood, 2006). Crook (2008) explains this plurality of views and understandings as a move from 'social trust professionalism to expert professionalism' (p. 24). Yet where does this place the early childhood educator in terms of their professional status? How do they 'measure up' in terms of being socially trusted and expert professionals like doctors or lawyers? Is knowledge valued over skills when it comes to professionalism? Working with young children requires physical acts of caring such as nappy changing, emotional engagement to tune in to the needs of young children and their families, as well as educational endeavours such as intentional teaching, planning, evaluation and reflection, so does that limit them from being considered as professionals?

Interestingly over a decade ago Hargreaves (2000, p. 152) found that teachers spoke about '*being professional*' before they spoke about being '*a professional*' [emphasis in the original]. As authors, we wonder if this is any different today with early childhood teachers being concerned about their conduct, the standards they adhere to and the quality of their work – being professional, before their standing or status in the eyes of the community or their remuneration – being a professional. A flow on from this is the contention, does stronger professionalisation of the early childhood field lead to greater professionalism? Does more recognition in the eyes of the community and higher pay actually improve the quality of the education children receive? This is a major concern when considering the rapid and constant changes early childhood teachers presently experience as new policies and reforms are introduced by regulatory authorities and governments. Johnston (2014) found that teacher autonomy and agency linked to professionalism and professionalisation was reduced as teachers found themselves overwhelmed by reforms and accountability. Constant change can lead to a sense of instability or metaphorically 'standing on shifting sand'.

How early childhood educators approach their identity as professionals can impact their profile and credibility within the education sector as well as the wider community including government authorities. This is in line with Rodd's (2013) suggestion that early childhood educators should accept 'personal and professional responsibility to raise the profile, value, credibility and status of young children, families and early childhood in the eyes of the general community' (p. 209). In the same vein, Martin, Keast and Anders (2017) discuss the concept of 'the agentic professional' (p. 68) linked to the ways in which teachers' position themselves taking personal or collective responsibility within professional dialogue. Although Martin et al. focus on pre-service teachers' pedagogical reasoning, the concept of professional agency is relevant to our study. Similarly, Edwards (2015, p. 780) explains 'to be agentic we need to be able to make responsible strong judgements about the worth of our intensions when we take actions'. However, Moss (2010) questions a focus on professionalism and professionalisation, asking if 'reconceptualising the concept of professionalism so much as to accommodate what is important such as the idea of multiple knowledges and democratic practice [could] render the concept meaningless?' (p. 8). Yet he also argues 'the need to properly value the work of all educators, and especially those in the early childhood field who are currently treated as second-class workers' (p. 17).

From the literature, we can see that the challenges and dilemmas facing early childhood educators and their quest as professionals range in size and scope. Meeting the daily demands of children and families, valuing the ethic of care, alongside commitment and passion for high-quality education collides with the demands of assessment, documentation, standards, regulations and reforms. It is within this context that we asked the question 'what do early childhood educators understand and believe about professionalism and their own status as professionals in the Singaporean context today?'

Study design

Participants

Our study spanned four years and took place in two phases. Participants were in-service early childhood educators enrolled in a Bachelor degree programme delivered in Singapore by an Australian University. The unit 'Professional Engagement', was taught as a four-day block intensive with ongoing web-based teaching across a 12-week term. There were 78 students involved in phase one. Phase two occurred two years later with a further group of 71 students, bringing the total to 149 participants.

Data generation

Data resulted from an in-class non-graded activity spanning 45 minutes. Student teachers were asked to work in groups of five to eight persons to visually create and explain a metaphor of professionalism. Ethical clearance was obtained from the University Human Ethics Committee and before the face-to-face sessions in Singapore, student teachers were provided with information regarding the in-class activity, research procedures and ethics before the intensive session as well as before the activity began during the session. In addition, student teachers were made aware that the activity would not be graded and were asked to not disclose their names on their visual metaphors. Although all student teachers were asked to participate in the learning activity as part of the unit, they were given the opportunity to opt in to the research project by completing consent forms. These forms were handed in with their visual metaphors and not accessed by the researchers until after the completion of all assessments for the unit. There were no consequences for groups of students who decided not to participate in the research project.

Student teachers from both phases were asked to respond to the same stimulus statement 'Professionalism in the early childhood sector in Singapore is like … because …' Groups discussed their response and decided on a metaphor that represented their ideas. They portrayed the metaphor in a visual drawing on a poster and wrote an accompanying statement. Each group explained their visual metaphor to the full class. Field notes were developed by the authors during and following the class presentations.

Metaphors as data-generation tools. Visual metaphors were chosen as data-generation tools because they provide opportunities for in-depth investigation of personal opinions, beliefs and values while aiding reflection, group consensus and creative interpretation. Lakoff and Johnson (1980), seminal researchers in the field, explain 'our ordinary conceptual system, in terms of which we both think and act, is fundamentally metaphorical in nature' (p. 3). They go on to explain that people commonly use metaphor as a way of understanding and giving meaning to ideas and experiences.

Both Tannehill and MacPhail (2012) and Thomas and Beauchamp (2011) found that examining the metaphors used by student teachers was useful in recognising and identifying their beliefs about teaching and learning especially when exploring abstract concepts. Landau, Robinson and Meier (2014) clarify that

> metaphor is not – as convention wisdom would have it – simply a matter of words; rather, it is a cognitive tool that people routinely use to understand abstract concepts (e.g. *morality*) in terms of superficially dissimilar concepts that are relatively easier to comprehend (e.g. *cleanliness*) (p. 4).… The concept that one tries to understand is the *target*, whereas the concept used for this purpose is the *source*. Targets are generally abstract, complex, and difficult to comprehend, whereas sources represent more concrete, perceptual and embodied experiences [emphasis in the original].

(p. 5)

Accordingly, the creation of visual metaphors by groups of student teachers allows for the sharing and unpacking of ideas that are both personal and complex using a reflexive approach (Hadar & Brody, 2013). Such an activity can aid connection and relationship with educational contexts such as early childhood teacher professionalism.

Data analysis

We draw on two levels of analysis to help us to explore and understand particip-ants' perspectives of professionalism. First, we used polytextual thematic analysis (Gleeson, 2011), and second, we used Rogoff's (1995, 2003) three planes of analysis. Gleeson offers an approach whereby the visual is analysed in its own right whereas Rogoff provides an opportunity to explore the personal, interper-sonal and institutional planes within the visual components of the themes derived from Gleeson's approach along with the verbal and written words of the participants. Together these analytical tools allow us to triangulate the written, spoken and visual texts recognising that within this study, the meanings and articulations from each of layer of data overlap and are based on each other (Silver, 2013).

We began by categorising repetitive features or themes allowing patterns to be seen. Gleeson (2011) encourages the use of descriptive titles and defi-nitions linked to the visual images. This allows the images to be clustered in meaningful ways. Rogoff's planes of analysis draw on foregrounding per-sonal, interpersonal and institutional perspectives, recognising that these per-spectives are interrelated aspects of participant's participation in social rela-tionships. Moving from clustering the images to exploring the clusters using the three planes of analysis leads to rich and deep analysis of both sets of text, the visual text and the written/spoken text. The sorting, comparing and clustering were completed as an iterative process by each author separately before coming together to compare and refine the categories and themes. Table 16.1 lists the visual images that student teachers produced as data for this study.

Table 16.1 List of visual metaphors

Phase One (10 images)		Phase Two (12 images)	
1	Octopus	11	Rainbow
2	Juggler	12	Rojak
3	Batik	13	Artist
4	Bamboo	14	Seedling
5	Treasure chest	15	Fireworks
6	Ugly duckling	16	Ants underground
7	Seedling	17	Burger
8	Rose	18	Opening and closing door
9	Tunnel	19	Starbucks
10	Tower	20	Candle
		21	Circus
		22	Master key

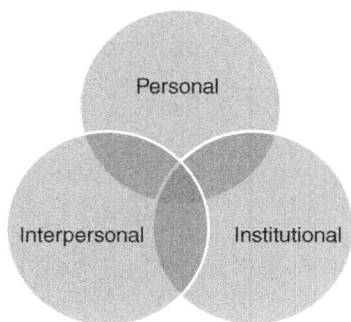

Figure 16.1 Rogoff's (1995; 2003) three inter-related planes of analysis.

This chapter highlights three interrelated clusters of images exemplified by six images, three from each phase as seen in Figure 16.1. The Tunnel and the Ants Underground contain the most common features related to the personal plane (individual worker, cleaner, babysitter, multitasking, unseen and underground). The Seedling and the Rojak represent the common features related to the interpersonal plane (people and cultures linked together, supporting one another, giving, sharing, respecting each other, combining together). Whereas the Ugly Duckling and the Master Key represent the common features related to the institutional plane (professionalism representing a future hope, change, growth, development and a key to unlock dreams). Each set of images portray professionalism as a multilayered, shifting and changing phenomenon. These six visual metaphors form the focus of the findings and discussion in this chapter.

Findings and discussion

The broad themes that emerged from the data exemplified different dimensions and perceptions of professionalism and professionalisation of the early childhood field in Singapore. On a personal plane, professionalism linked to what student teachers understood to be seen and unseen especially in relation to their personal roles and responsibilities. On an interpersonal plane, professionalism was understood by participants as relationships with one another in an early childhood centre room, service or across the nation. On an institutional plane, professionalism was strongly linked to unlocking ways in acknowledging professionalisation of the early childhood sector. Each of the layers are discussed next.

Layers of personal professionalism – seen and unseen

Student teachers in this study used the images of a teacher in an underground tunnel and ants working underground (Figure 16.2) to illustrate the work that they do as individuals that was seen by them but often unseen and unrecognised by the 'outside world'. The group that drew the teacher in the tunnel explained that

> professionalism in early childhood education in Singapore is like a tunnel hidden in the mountain because being an educator comes along with the perspectives of what others think of and see you as. Teaching is a lonely job. Teachers are seen as nannies, helpers, babysitters and cleaners.

They spoke of the layers of personal professionalism of doing a good job, multi-tasking and being responsible. These ideas link to what Hargreaves (2000, p. 152) explains as 'being professional'. He defined being professional as a personal sense of taking responsibility for the care and education of young children and at the same time being resilient as an educator. We link this complex personal condition of a teacher with the feeling of 'being in the tunnel' or 'ant working underground'.

The student teachers that created the image of ants working underground also spoke of 'working hard behind the scenes' being 'support pillars to society, nurturing the future business people and the future accountants and the future leaders of Singapore'. Again, their sense of professionalism was embodied by working hard, never giving up, being resilient, strong and flexible. This image clearly demonstrates the notion of what is seen by the student teachers themselves and what is unseen by others. The student teachers see their work as hugely important for their children's development as well as for Singapore's future success. Their work, however, goes largely unnoticed and unappreciated as pointed out by Moss (2010).

Both metaphors articulate the relationship that teachers have with the work they do, not only in meeting their own needs for value and importance but also in putting aside personal feelings in order to meet the expectations of others. This means they have to show commitment and resilience in spite of the working conditions, status and expectations placed on them by others. Their success in meeting this expectation can be seen as a measure of their own professionalism as suggested by Reindl, Kaiser and Stolz (2011). Reindl et al. claim that 'professionals are usually highly committed to their tasks and to the solution of complex problems so that their work itself [is] rewarding' (p. 5). However, this level of commitment can be problematic, leading to accumulative teachers' work, where there is always something more that needs to be done leading to long hours and lack of personal time. Sometimes, this kind of accumulative work is worsened by greater expectations from parents, and those in leadership and authority (Phillipson, 2017).

In order to further understand the personal view point that the student teachers presented, we need to see the interpersonal aspect of how these student teachers deal with the 'others' in their working and personal environment. The interpersonal lens provides a deeper understanding of the professionalism that the student teachers work towards in realising their goals towards professionalisation.

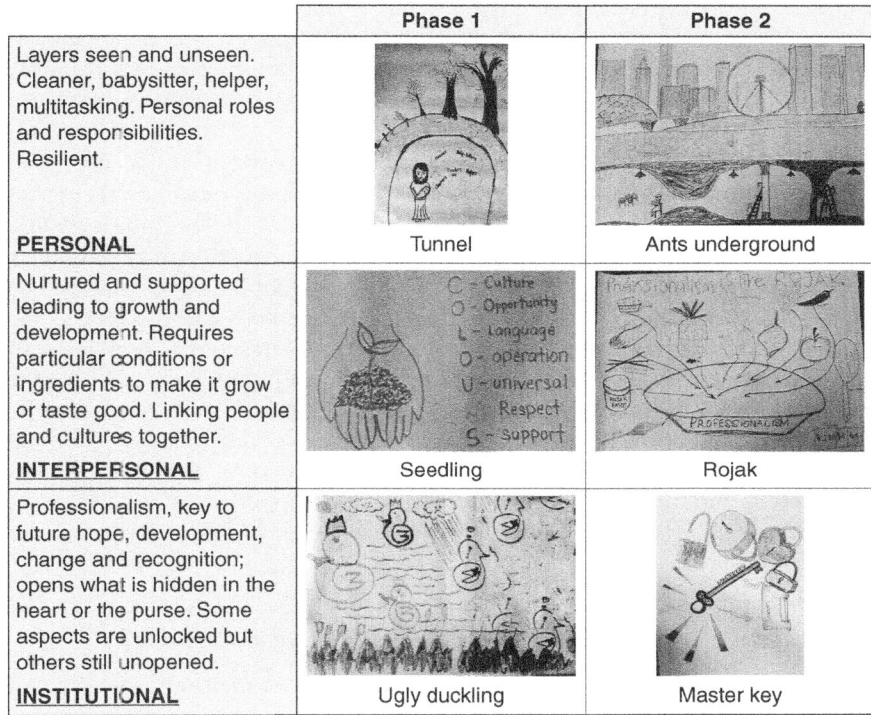

	Phase 1	Phase 2
Layers seen and unseen. Cleaner, babysitter, helper, multitasking. Personal roles and responsibilities. Resilient. **PERSONAL**	Tunnel	Ants underground
Nurtured and supported leading to growth and development. Requires particular conditions or ingredients to make it grow or taste good. Linking people and cultures together. **INTERPERSONAL**	Seedling	Rojak
Professionalism, key to future hope, development, change and recognition; opens what is hidden in the heart or the purse. Some aspects are unlocked but others still unopened. **INSTITUTIONAL**	Ugly duckling	Master key

Figure 16.2 The three sets of images highlighted in this chapter.

Links of interpersonal professionalism – supported and unsupported

The participants in this study created metaphors of a seedling and a meal of Rojak (see Figure 16.2) to portray the interpersonal and relational nature of professionalism. The seedling depicted professionals being nurtured in a context of multiculturalism and colour provided by others (children, families and staff), while a meal of Rojak symbolised the drawing together of many different ingredients (and relationships) that complement and support one another to create a unique and pleasing dish.

The group that drew the seedling being nurtured within caring hands spoke of professionalism as recognising the support and respect of those around them. That the seedling could not grow unless the conditions for growth were maintained. This group of student teachers named these conditions for the growth of professionalism as the acronym COLOUR – Culture, Opportunity, Language, Operation, Universal, Respect and Support with a specific focus on the nurturing of multiculturalism. Here interpersonal professionalism can be understood as staff being supported and supporting one another through being respected, being given and taking opportunities to develop interpersonal cultures within centres as well as within the early childhood sector as a whole. Embracing the cultures and languages of the teachers, children, families and communities. This sense of interpersonal professionalism is full of complexities and relational challenges, yet with support and respect a strong and beautiful plant will grow. However, a lack of respect and support is likely to lead to the plant wilting and dying.

Similarly, the student teachers who drew the bowl of Rojak portrayed culture, relationship, working together and the creation of something that tastes good and brings life and energy to those who partake of it. This dish is created locally and enjoyed by local people and may not be valued or understood by those outside of the 'group' (the centre or early childhood organisation). The ingredients are all different, bringing diverse tastes, smells and textures to the meal signifying the different skills, knowledge and abilities of the teaching staff and management that create a sense of interpersonal professionalism. Like the metaphor of the seedling, the Rojak dish also portrays the complexity of relationships between groups of people who are diverse yet joined in purpose, vision and commitment to their roles as early childhood professionals. It takes time and commitment to develop respectful and supportive relationships yet they are essential for teamwork where struggle, growth and transformation take place can take place.

Landscapes of institutional professionalisation – locked and unlocked

The third theme that emerged from the data was that of the landscapes of institutional professionalisation drawing on the idea of professionalism being a 'backdrop' for the growth and development of the early childhood education profession. The two metaphors that expressed these ideas illustrated visions of future and hope. Students represented these ideas through the use of a common child's fairy tale, the Ugly Duckling, and a set of padlocks with a key to unlock them (see Figure 16.2). The student teachers re-conceptualised the story of the Ugly Duckling mixing it with the story of Cinderella. Aspects of change and transformation are strongly portrayed in both stories as the ugly duckling becomes a swan and Cinderella a princess. Both stories speak of future hope that somehow seems impossible and yet emerges over time. This time element is challenging yet at the same time develops strength and perseverance in both story characters. This move from a deficit or hidden view to a strengths or open view of the early childhood field and professionalism can also be seen in the metaphor of the padlocks.

The student teachers who drew the padlocks portrayed one open and three yet to be opened. The padlocks themselves portrayed a range of institutional aspects – colleagues, parents, children, government, law and policy. However, it was also interesting to note the different shapes of the padlocks with one being shaped as a heart and another a purse. Professionalism is portrayed as a master key and, to open the locks, this master key needs to be the right fit to unlock the potential and possibility locked up in the early childhood sector. The opening of locks reveals a sense of more, something that is presently hidden and suppressed behind a façade or lock and only the privileged few understand and can see inside. The key of professionalism opens the way to greater influence, recognition and status. Yet questions need to be asked – does greater professionalism come at a cost? Is that cost the professionalisation of the field and what does that entail? Does professionalisation including associated rules, regulations and accountability actually limit the very aspects of professionalism such as autonomy and ethics that early childhood educators are trying to attain? For professionalisation to take its shape in the way epitomised in this metaphor, we acknowledge that there are 'shifting sands' in the political and policy landscape of professionalisation.

The shifting sands of the political and global landscape

Consumerism, individual choice, polities, regulations and the global struggle for self-control have been identified by a number of authors addressing the subject of professionalism in early years contexts (see Chalke, 2013; Moss, 2010; Rauschenbach & Riedel, 2016; Warren, 2014). Moss (2010) strongly argues that professionalism may actually 'be a distraction that risks diverting us from the real task in hand – an education and educators able to respond to the huge challenges facing us' (p. 17). Moss is not negating early childhood educators' need for pay parity and status with other educators in the primary and secondary sectors. However, he questions if reconceptualising professionalism from a hierarchical and traditional concept is the way to compensate the challenges faced by early childhood educators. The professional identity of early childhood educators is often described in terms of the relationships they have with children, parents, families and colleagues – relationships that are warm, trusting, nurturing and caring (Simpson, 2010; Warren, 2014). It is these relationships that are valued within the context of early childhood professionalism, yet where do they 'fit' within traditional views of professionalism and new understandings of professionalisation?

Rauschenbach and Riedel in their 2016 article discuss professionalisation of the early childhood workforce in regards to what they term 'academisation of educators' (p. 68). They discuss the traditional view of early childhood educators as linked to females, motherliness and personal fulfilment being the main qualifications needed for early childhood educators. These authors go on to explain the rise of academisation including the requirements for degree-qualified staff impacting professional hierarchy in day care centres with new graduates from university degree courses being largely unprepared for day-to-day practice in centres. They wonder about the differentiation of job profiles, as well as the status of educators qualified at different levels and the development of 'second-class' educators and what challenges these issues might bring to the field. Rauschenbach and Riedel raise these issues in relation to the German Early Childhood workforce but these issues are prevalent globally as governments and authorities introduce policies for greater accountability and higher-quality educators. While such policies may bring gains in the recognition and status of early childhood educators, questions are asked regarding the restructuring of educational settings and pedagogical practices.

In the Singaporean context, early childhood education can be understood as a private and commercial sector with government policy objectives and initiatives linked to improved access, affordability and quality education (Lim, 2018). A range of options are available for families to choose from including centre-based care and home-based care such as nannies, grandparents and live-in foreign domestic helpers. Lim provides an overview of key government initiatives over the last decade, as well as discussion regarding the implementation and uptake of these initiatives. Of concern are the policy reforms that may or may not lead to quality services for all young children and families in Singapore, particularly those living in the lower income levels. She calls for rigorous research that creates 'a comprehensive picture of existing curricular approaches and pedagogies … child diversity, teacher learning, [and] leadership practices' (pp. 659–660). Lim and other authors (e.g. Choo, 2010) articulate the historical development of early childhood education in Singapore, particularly the separation of kindergarten (available initially to those able to afford it) and child care with a more welfare-based orientation. When considering early childhood educators as professionals and the professionalisation of the sector it is clear to see the impact of these ideological 'roots' – kindergarten teachers educate and child care workers care for children. These ideological roots are challenged when kindergarten classes are part of full-day care services and not morning or afternoon sessions that last just a few hours.

More recently, government policy developments have focused on the creation of Ministry of Education-run kindergartens that provide 'seamless preferential' access to highly sort after local schools (Ministry of Education, 2017). Such policies lead to further 'shifting sands' related to the professional status of these kindergartens and their teachers, in the eyes of families and the early childhood workforce. Does this bring a new shift downwards in relation to the status of early childhood educators working in the child care sector with infants, toddlers and young children? This is a question for much needed research in the ECE 21st century context in Singapore.

Conclusion

The educators in our study shared their ideas and perceptions of being a professional in the context of Singapore. They identified what we have termed the shifting sands of professionalism and professionalisation that they were experiencing. Their visual metaphors highlighted personal, interpersonal and institutional aspects of professionalism alongside the professionalisation of the early childhood sector. They acknowledged the unseen and unrecognised work they did and at the same time their metaphors portrayed layers of hope for the future. A future that in some ways seemed out of reach such as Cinderella becoming a princess yet as real and possible as the ugly duckling becoming what he was in reality from the beginning, a beautiful swan. For this future hope to be realised, it will be important to keep a careful check on the continued commercialisation and privatisation of early childhood education where business models and franchises at local and global levels emphasise particular kinds of teacher performance and professionalism, and where professionalisation comes at the cost of in-house curricula that emphasis particular tasks to be completed alongside specific teacher professional development (Gupta, 2018; Lim, 2017). This brings us back to the concerns that Moss (2010) highlights of the educator being reduced to 'technical status' (p. 17), which seems to be in opposition to the autonomous and socially trusted expert early childhood professional that the teachers in our study understood as their hope for the future.

References

Arimoto, A. (2013). *The academic profession in international and comparative perspectives: Trends in Asia and the world.* Paper presented at the International Conference on the Changing Academic Profession Project 2013, Hiroshima University, Japan.

Chalke, J. (2013). Will the early years professional please stand up? Professionalism in the early childhood workforce in England. *Contemporary Issues in Early Childhood*, *14*(3) 212–222.

Choo, K. K. (2010). The shaping of childcare and preschool education in Singapore: From separatism to collaboration. *International Journal of Child Care and Education Policy*, *4*(1). 23–34.

Crook, D. (2008). Some historical perspectives on professionalism. In B. Cunningham (Ed.), *Exploring Professionalism* (pp. 10–27). London: Bedford Way Papers.

Edwards, S. (2015). Recognising and realising teachers' professional agency. *Teachers and Teaching*, *21*(6), 779–784. doi:10,1080/1354062.2015.1044333.

Feeney, S. (2012). *Professionalism in Early Childhood Education: Doing Our Best for Young Children.* Boston, MA: Pearson.

Gleeson, K. (2011). Polytextual thematic analysis for visual data: Pinning down the analytic. In P. Reavey (Ed.), *Visual Methods in Psychology: Using and Interpreting Images in Qualitative Research.* (pp. 314–329). Hove: Psychology Press.

Gupta, A. (2018). How neoliberal globalisation is shaping early childhood education policies in India, China, Singapore, Sri Lanka and the Maldives. *Policy Futures in Education*, *16*(1), 11–28. doi:10.1177/1478210317715796.

Hadar, L. L., & Brody, D. L. (2013). The interaction between group processes and personal professional trajectories in a professional development community for teacher educators. *Journal of Teacher Education*, *64*(2), 145–161.

Hargreaves, A. (2000). Four ages of professionalism and professional learning. *Teachers and Teaching: History and Practice*, *6*(2). 151–182.

Harwood, D., Klopper, A., Osanyin, A., & Vanderlee, M.-L. (2013). 'It's more than care': Early childhood educators' concepts of professionalism. *Early Years: An International Research Journal*, *33*(1), 4–17. doi:10.1080/09575146.2012.667394.

Johnston, J. (2014). Issues of professionalism and teachers: Critical observations from research and the literature. *The Australian Education Researcher*, *42*(3), 299–317. doi:10.1007/s13384-014-0159-7.

Lakoff, G., & Johnson, M. (1980). *Metaphors We Live By*. Chicago, IL: The University of Chicago Press.

Landau, M. J., Robinson, M. D., & Meier, B. P. (2014). Introduction. In M. J. Landau, M. D. Robinson & B. P. Meier (Eds.), *The Power of Metaphor: Examining its Influence on Social Life* (pp. 3–16). Washington, DC: American Psychological Association.

Lim, S. (2017). Marketization and corporation of early childhood care and education in Singapore. In M. Li, J. L. Fox, & S. Grieshaber (Eds.), *Contemporary Issues and Challenge in Early Childhood Education in the Asia-Pacific Region*. Singapore: Springer Science+Business Media.

Lim, S. (2018). Early childhood education and development in Singapore. In M. Fleer & B. van Oers (Eds.), *International Handbook of Early Childhood Education*. Singapore: Springer Science+Business Media.

Martin, J. Keast, S., & Anders, L. (2017). Becoming professionally agentic: Researching pedagogical reasoning in initial teacher education. In J. Nuttall, A. Kostogriz, M. Jones, & J. Martin (Eds.), *Teacher Education Policy and Practice: Evidence of Impact, Impact of Evidence*. Singapore: Springer Science+Business Media.

Ministry of Education. (2017). A smoother transition from MOE kindergarten to primary school [Press release]. Retrieved from www.moe.gov.sg/news/press-releases/a-smoother-transition-from-moe-kindergarten-to-primary-school.

Moss, P. (2010). We cannot continue as we are: The educator in an education for survival. *Contemporary Issues in Early Childhood, 11*(1). 8–18.

Osgood, J. (2006). Deconstructing professionalism in early childhood education: Resisting the regulatory gaze. *Contemporary Issues in Early Childhood, 7*(1). 5–14.

Osgood, J. (2010). Reconstructing professionalism in ECEC: The case for the 'critically reflective emotional professional'. *Early Years: An International Research Journal, 30*(2), 119–133. doi:10.1080/095751462010.490905.

Phillipson, S. (2017). Partnering with families. In S. Garvis & D. Pendergast (Eds.), *Health and Wellbeing in Early Childhood* (2nd edn) (pp. 223–237). Cambridge: Cambridge University Press.

Rauschenbach, T., & Riedel, B. (2016). Germany's ECEC workforce: A difficult path to professionalization. *Early Childhood Development and Care, 186*(1), 61–77. doi:10.108 0/03004430.2015.1014811.

Reindl, C. U., Kaiser, S., & Stolz, M. L. (2011). Integrating professional work and life: Conditions, outcomes and resources. In S. Kaiser, M. Ringlstetter, D. Eikhot, & M. Cunha (Eds.), *Creating Balance? International Perspectives on the Work-life Integration of Professionals* (pp. 3–26). Heidelberg: Springer.

Rodd, J. (2013). *Leadership in Early Childhood: The Pathway to Professionalism* (4th edn). Sydney: Allen & Unwin.

Rogoff, B. (1995). Observing sociocultural activity on three planes: Participatory appropriation, guided participation, and apprenticeship. In J. V. Wertsch, P. del Rio, & A. Alvarez (Eds.), *Sociocultural Studies of Mind* (pp. 139–164). Cambridge: Cambridge University Press.

Rogoff, B. (2003). *The Cultural Nature of Human Development*. New York: Oxford University Press.

Silver, J. (2013). Visual methods. In C. Willig (Ed.), *Introducing Qualitative Research in Psychology*. (3rd edn). New York: Open University Press.

Simpson, D. (2010). Being professional? Conceptualising early years professionalism in England. *European Early Childhood Education Research Journal, 18*(1), 5–14.

Tannehill, D., & MacPhail, A. (2012). What examining teaching metaphors tells us about pre-service teachers' developing beliefs about teaching and learning. *Physical Education and Sport Pedagogy, 19*(2), 149–163.

Thomas, L., & Beauchamp, C. (2011). Understanding new teachers' professional identities through metaphor. *Teaching and Teacher Education, 27*(4), 762–769.

Warren, A. (2014). 'Relationships for me are the key for everything': Early childhood teachers' subjectivities as relational professionals. *Contemporary Issues in Early Childhood, 15*(3). 262–271.

17 Critical aspects for the preschool quality in Sweden

Sonja Sheridan, Susanne Garvis, Pia Williams and Elisabeth Mellgren

Introduction

Governments around the world are interested in how quality can be improved within early childhood settings to allow all children to have the best start in life (Bertram et al., 2016; OECD, 2017; Urban, 2015). The importance of high-quality preschool for children's health, wellbeing, lifelong learning and development is indisputable (Sheridan, Pramling Samuelsson, & Johansson, 2009; Sylva et al., 2006; Sylva, Melhuish, Sammons, Siraj-Blatchford, & Taggart, 2010). Several longitudinal research projects in the United States, Australia and the United Kingdom show that high-quality preschools support all children's social, emotional and cognitive development, promote growth experiences (including nurturing and attachment), and facilitate positive interaction and communication among preschool teachers and children (Sylva et al., 2010). On the contrary, low-quality preschools seem to reproduce socioeconomic structures, which leads to poor social, emotional, educational, health, economic and behavioural outcomes for children at risk (Hansen & Nordahl, 2016; Manning, Homel, & Smith, 2010; Sylva et al., 2010). In that way, low-quality preschools reproduce social inequality and equity that leads to societal deprivation for children and their families as well as society. Early intervention through high-quality preschool is therefore important to make the necessary changes in children's lives to allow positive life trajectories (Heckman, 2000; Sylva et al., 2010).

High-quality preschool programmes within other countries have been shown to produce tangible and intangible societal benefits. This means there are not only short-term benefits for the child's development, there are also long-term benefits for the child as well as society. These include increased taxes due to higher earnings of programme participants, reduced victimisations and their associated personal and criminal justice costs, and improvement in quality of life (Heckman, 2000). This idea is highly congruent with Vitaro, Barker, Brendgen and Tremblay's (2011) emphasis on the 'school-related pathway' (involving school readiness and engagement) as a child developmental pathway that serves as the theoretical foundation for the development of early childhood education policy.

Research on links between children's health, wellbeing and learning are also emerging in the Nordic region. In Norway, 200 preschools are currently being studied around quality and learning (Bjørnestad, 2017). In Denmark, relationships between the preschool quality and the differences in children's perceptions of their own mental and social wellbeing has recently been conducted (Hansen & Nordahl, 2016). In another study of the preschool quality in 104 Danish preschools, an important contribution was the incorporation of children's perspectives of their own learning and social wellbeing (Næsby, 2016). In Sweden, Persson (2015) has shown how increased educational awareness of a competent and well-educated staff in preschool has effects on children's wellbeing and learning in the long term.

Research on preschool teacher competence highlight that teacher competence is one of the main aspects for the preschool quality (National Association for the Education of Young Children (NAEYC), 2006) and where pedagogical awareness, content/subject knowledge, didactical approaches, learning orientation and attitudes are all crucial (Pramling & Pramling Samuelsson, 2011; Sheridan, 2016; Sylva et al., 2010; Williams & Sheridan, 2019). In a meta-analysis of preschool quality, the education level of the teachers or caregivers was positively correlated to overall early childhood education and care (ECEC) qualities measured by the Environment Rating Scale (Manning, Garvis, Flemming, & Wong, 2017). Vital is the competence to create a negotiated and challenging play and learning-oriented environment, in which, preschool teachers are physically, emotionally and cognitively present in the 'here and now' (Jonsson, 2013; Sheridan, Williams, Sandberg, & Vuorinen, 2011). This type of 'here and now' competence is also emphasised by Stern (2003), who identify attention and awareness as vital competences for teachers in being able to be present in children's interactions and activities at particular moments in time. Further, high quality in teacher–child interplay is regarded as being characterised by communication, reciprocity, a sharing of interests, attention and learning objects (Siraj-Blatchford, 2007, 2010). It can be concluded that today's preschool teachers need a scientific approach and knowledge in order to be able to relate everyday situations to educational theories, the preschool curriculum and research findings (Sheridan & Williams, 2018; Sylva et al., 2010).

The research review highlights that high quality in preschool is vital for children's school success, academic achievement and lifelong learning. The aim of this chapter is to investigate critical aspects for the quality of Swedish preschool. Research focusing on critical aspects for the quality shows how they influence children's conditions for learning and wellbeing in preschool, which in turn affect conditions for an equal start in life and future school success (Sylva et al., 2010). By understanding the concept of quality within Swedish preschools, we can identify critical aspects (e.g. level and content of preschool teacher training, preschool teachers' communication and interaction, subject knowledge, didactics, young children's play and learning) that contributes to improved learning outcomes for children. Areas of improvement can be communicated back with preschools to allow enhanced practice to support child outcomes and to the university for enhanced education for students.

The chapter is based on findings from three different studies of the Swedish preschool quality using the Early Childhood Environment Rating Scale (ECERS) (Harms & Clifford, 1980; Harms, Clifford, & Cryer, 2015). The first study was conducted in 2001 (Sheridan 2001), the second in 2009 (Sheridan, Pramling Samuelsson, & Johansson, 2009) and the third in 2017 (Sheridan & Williams, 2017; Sheridan, Williams, Mellgren, & Garvis, 2018). These studies describe variations in the quality of the participating preschools over time. The results contribute to an international understanding about quality in early childhood education and provide the opportunity for Swedish research on preschool quality to develop. The chapter concludes with consequences about the differences in quality in Swedish preschools.

The Swedish preschool context

In Sweden, preschool teachers have a 3.5-year academic education that is based on scientific evidence and proven experience and results in a Bachelor's degree. The current preschool teacher education was introduced in 2011 and is governed by national policy, curricula and guidelines (Svensk författningssamling (SFS), 2010: 541). It embraces both theoretical and practical education, conducted as courses at the university and preschool practical training. Through the educational programme, preschool teacher students are to develop a professional identity as a preschool teacher. After completing the programme, the preschool teacher students should have knowledge and abilities that are necessary to independently take responsibility for pedagogical activities in preschool, and provide for children's right to care, development and learning. One key goal is for the preschool teacher students to learn how to create high-quality conditions for children's learning and development in preschool.

In the Education Act (SFS, 2010: 800), it is stipulated that preschool is a separate school form, within the Swedish school system. Swedish preschool is also governed by a national curriculum (The National Agency for Education, 1998/2018). The curriculum was first introduced in 1998 and has since then been revised in 2006, 2010, 2015 and in 2018. The aim of the revisions is to raise the pedagogical ambition of preschool, working in line with preschool teaching and didactics, integrating values, learning, play and care. During the revision processes, goals related to literacy, mathematics, science and technology were developed and strengthened and a new area of evaluation and development of the quality of preschool was introduced. Children's right to participate and influence ongoing activities in preschool, as well as the overall learning environment have also been strengthened, both in the curriculum (The National Agency for Education, 1998/2018) and in the Education Act (SFS 2010: 800).

The term teaching has until now been an uncommon concept in the Swedish preschool context. However, in the revised curriculum 2018, the concept of teaching is accentuated, defined as goal-oriented processes, aiming for development and learning. Teaching situations need to take a child perspective and create experiences that are interesting and meaningful to the children. Thus, teaching in preschool can be defined as communicative, interactive and relational and needs to be understood in a societal context (Jonsson, Williams, & Pramling Samuelsson, 2017; Sheridan & Williams, 2018). Teaching the youngest children is part of a preschool in change, which involves protecting the preschool tradition and distinctiveness, while simultaneously introducing innovation and development.

Most Swedish children (84 per cent) are in preschool from an early age and preschool is usually open from 6.30 a.m. to 6.00 p.m. Often, the children are organised into toddler groups (1–3 years old), sibling groups (1–5 years old), and older groups (3–5 years old). The size of these groups can vary as well as the constitution of the working teams (Williams, Sheridan, & Pramling Samuelsson, 2018). On a national level 40 per cent are preschool teachers, with a university degree, and the others are mainly nursery nurses with a certificate gained after two years at upper secondary/senior high school. However, the percentage of uneducated staff is continually rising due to retirements and that too few preschool teachers are educated.

> When children turn 6 years of age they attend preschool class/preparatory class. In July 2018, preschool class became mandatory, meaning the school starting age in Sweden changed from seven years to six years.
> (Regeringens proposition, 2017/18:9)

In recent years, the Organisation for Economic Co-operation and Development (OECD) (2015) has reported that the quality of Swedish preschools has declined, moving from first place within the OECD countries to now number three. Studies also report on increasing group sizes within preschools, stress among preschool teachers, increasing child stress, as well as other issues, which affects the quality of preschool (Sheridan, Williams, & Pramling Samuelsson, 2014; The National Agency for Education, 2016; Williams et al., 2018).

Theoretical framework

This chapter builds on research from studies that are based on interactionist perspectives. The learning environment in preschool is seen as a complex and multidimensional phenomenon constituted of the interaction between societal and educational goals for preschool, the content of the preschool teacher education, preschool teachers' competence and didactical approaches, children's learning and preschool practices. Over the past decades, the ecological systems model by Bronfenbrenner (1979, 1986) has provided a useful theoretical framework for understanding the process and interactions of change within preschool institutions (Sheridan et al., 2009; Sylva et al., 2010). The model underscores the extent to which children's outcomes depends on a dynamic interplay between the individual, family, education setting, community and the broader socioeconomic and cultural context.

This theory has been developed and extended by Garbarino (1992) and Miller, Dalli and Urban (2011), who imply a critical ecology of the early childhood profession. The ecological perspective contributes to the understanding of social policy issues affecting preschool, the profession of preschool teaching, and educational factors such as content and activities in both the theoretical and practical parts of the preschool teacher education and how this in turn shapes policy, preschool teacher education and preschool practice over time. Through the ecological system approach, preschool, preschool teacher education and society are examined from different interrelated systems: macro-, exo-, meso-, micro- and chrono.

While the microsystem is usually based on human development (the individual) it can also be extended to organisational development (the preschool and the preschool teacher education). Mesosytems are constituted through networks and interactions between preschools and the preschool teacher education. The exosystem consists of local policy, research and the profession. Social policy operates through the macrosystem by reflecting societal intentions and ideologies relating to views of the child, education and competence. In a specific society, understanding the macrosystem provides knowledge of the overall goals for preschool and preschool teacher education suggesting how these goals ought to be implemented through practice as values, content and activities. Using the terminology of Garbarino and Scott (1992), the macro system serves as a 'master blueprint' for preschool and the preschool teacher education as it is and as it ought to be. The chronosystem in this study will serve as change over time.

An intersubjective perspective of quality

The research that this chapter reports from is also based on an intersubjective perspective on quality, which is constituted of four interacting dimensions of pedagogical quality. These are (1) society, (2) teachers, (3) children and (4) learning contexts (Sheridan, 2009). The four quality dimensions are derived from a meta-analytical process of deconstruction and reconstruction of research on quality in preschool. Each dimension is constituted by qualities that are unique to that dimension and that can be related to structures, processes, contents and results (Donabedian, 1980; Sheridan, 2009). Depending on how the dimensions interact with one another, learning environments of different quality are created. Thus, from an intersubjective perspective of quality, the learning environment in preschool can be seen as a complex system of interplay between policy, people, material resources and pedagogical processes. The four dimensions of quality will be used as analytical lenses for interpretation to show the interactive and relational nature of preschool quality.

Together these theoretical perspectives contribute to the understanding of preschool quality and how it affects the conditions for children's and preschool teacher students' learning in preschool.

Aspects of preschool quality in Sweden over time

In three studies, the quality of the participating preschools was analysed from an intersubjective perspective on quality and the ecological system theories, in the light of research on preschool quality and related to the goals and intentions of the Swedish curriculum for preschool. Together the results from these studies describe and highlight critical aspects for the quality that are of interest in a policy perspective, for the profession and for the field of early childhood research.

The studies were conducted between 2001 and 2017. During this period, vital changes took place concerning preschool. The number of children aged 1–5 years increased in preschool by about 20 per cent as well as the preschool availability, which also increased by approximately 20 per cent. In 1999, 65 per cent of children aged 1–5 years were in preschool compared to 84 per cent in 2017 (The National Agency for Education, 2017). The number of employees has increased by more than 50 per cent in the last decade and the shortage of trained staff, especially in metropolitan areas, is concerning. During this period, there has also been an increasing segregation and an extensive migration to the metropolitan regions in Sweden (Persson, 2015). Taken together, these societal changes affect preschool and its quality in different ways.

In the first study, which was conducted in 2001, an adapted version (Kärrby, 1989) of the first developed version of the ECERS (Harms & Clifford, 1980) was used (Sheridan, 2001). The mean quality of 20 preschools was 4.50. Although it is a small number of preschools, the quality is comparable to the quality of other Swedish preschools, evaluated with the ECERS (Andersson, 1999; Bjurek, Gustafsson, Kjulin, & Kärrby, 1992; Kärrby, 1997; Kärrby & Giota, 1994, 1995). In a 2001 study (Sheridan, 2001), both external and self-evaluations of quality with ECERS was used and this provided an opportunity to compare these evaluations with one another. In general, the teachers evaluate their own preschool class's total average quality higher (4.76) than the external evaluator (4.50). There is a tendency for teachers in preschool classes, externally evaluated as having low quality, to overrate their own quality, while teachers in preschool units of high quality seem to evaluate their quality lower. There was a wide range of mean scores between the external evaluator and the teachers and between the teachers' evaluations within each working team, creating a meeting of perspectives and possibilities for fruitful dialogues of how the quality can be improved. Interesting to note was that there was a higher agreement among working teams in preschools that had been evaluated as being of high quality by the external evaluator.

Three preschools evaluated to be of low quality and three of good quality were selected for in-depth studies. Thirty-nine five-year-old children were interviewed about their conceptions of decision making and how they experienced their possibilities for exercising influence in their own preschool. The results show that children's opportunities to participate and influence what goes on in preschool are limited, except in their own activities and play. It is through play that children negotiate, participate on equal terms, influence, take turns, and learn the value of reciprocity and equality. Through play, they also learn that taking turns is one aspect of democracy, while taking the initiative leads to power over the content/theme. Seemingly, these children practiced democracy in preschool, but mainly among friends and in their own play. Even if the overall experience of participation was limited, there was a clear tendency. The children from high-quality preschools experienced that they were able to participate and to exercise influence to a larger extent than the children from low-quality preschools. In the latter, children more often expressed that they were not seen and listened to, and that they could hardly ever influence what went on in preschool (Sheridan & Pramling Samuelsson, 2001). The results show that there is a gap between the perspective of the child and the preschool teacher (Sheridan, 2001).

The results were used to plan a targeted development programme based on a model for action research. Significant to the Model of Competence Development is that the content and form are depending on each other continuously interacting and influencing one another. The participating working teams enhanced their preschool quality from an average of 4.50 to 4.98 on the ECERS. The improvement of quality can be explained by the massive and directed development input, which throughout the development work continuously changed and evolved through the influence of the teachers themselves. Another important aspect is that the competence development programme took place over a long time, embracing the whole working team, and was directed both towards the individual pedagogue as well as the whole working team. Particularly rewarding to the teacher was the illumination of their strengths. This confirmation challenged them to improve their weaknesses as well. The results from this study highlight that children's participation and influence, preschool teacher's competence, pedagogical awareness and the ability to approach the perspective of the child are critical aspects for the preschool quality as well as continuous staff education and training.

The second study was conducted in 2009 (Sheridan, Pramling Samuelsson, & Johansson, 2009) using a revised version of the adapted ECERS (Harms & Clifford, 1980; Kärrby, 1989). The quality of the 38 participating preschools had a mean value of 4.44. The quality of these preschools can be compared to findings made by The National Agency for Inspection (2011). For example, in their study, preschool teachers express that they lack knowledge of how to document individual children's learning processes or how to use the knowledge gained from documentation as a base for evaluation and means of enhancing the preschool quality. Children's learning was also taken for granted.

In the study of 2009, the variation in quality between the 38 participating preschools was notable. Ten preschools were evaluated as being of an excellent quality, 19 of a good quality, and nine were of low quality, with a range of 2.90–6.24. Again, both external and self-evaluations of quality with ECERS was used and compared, confirming the results of 2001. In focus for the second study was the relationship between the preschool quality and children's wellbeing, learning and development. The result highlighted three qualitatively different learning environments, namely: Separating and Limiting environments, Child-Centred Negotiating environments and Challenging Learning environments. The variety of learning environments of low, good and high quality created unequal conditions for children's wellbeing, learning and development. The results also highlighted tendencies towards a link between high quality in pre-school and children's learning of mathematics and communication, showing that even children under three years of age, participating in the nine preschools of high quality, were more successful in communication and language and early mathematics tasks, compared to the children in the low and medium-quality preschools. The variety of learning environments of low, good and high quality indicates that children have unequal opportunities for learning in preschool.

In the first study, four teacher educational orientations or teaching approaches were identified. In this study, the four teaching approaches became more crystalised and the characteristics of the teacher's educational orientations sharper. The teaching approaches of *abdication and dominance* are related to low-quality preschools. Low quality in teacher–child interaction was character-ised by teachers who used teaching approaches in which rules, norms and obe-dience were emphasised or where there was no control at all. In preschool units with strict control, structured teacher-directed activities occurred. They seemed to be planned from an adult perspective and focused on activities for the whole group. Throughout the day learning situations had the characteristics of narrow patterns of interaction (Bae, 1997). That means that the teacher had an unfocused attention, was emotionally remote or distant, did not confirm the child's experiences, and only reacted to the content of what was being said and not to the way it was said. In preschools evaluated as having no control, planned activities seldom occurred and the initiative came mainly from the children.

In preschools evaluated as being of good quality, the teachers used a teaching approach that can be characterised as *negotiating*. The teachers had a focused attention, made room for the child's contribution, confirmed the child's experi-ence, responded sensitively, listened intently and let the child pursue his or her own line of reasoning. Time in those preschools was characterised by both teacher and child-initiated activities. The focus of the teacher was, however, more on the activity itself than on what was happening to the child, that is, what the child had learned and understood in relation to the activity, except when it came to the development of children's social competence. The focus of learning was mainly on the child's emotional and social development. Social learning opportunities were created, but the activities were seldom based on the child's previous knowledge and interests.

In high-quality preschools teachers mainly used a *learning-oriented teaching approach*. Their focus was on children's learning of specific objects and they created conditions for the child to learn about the object intended. They created a learning environment that was rich in learning opportunities and were engaged in children's experiences and knowledge formation. Children participated in activities together with the teacher and communicated about issues in the past, present and future.

One main difference between the *learning-oriented teaching approach* and the approaches of *abdication, dominance and negotiating*, is preschool teachers' understanding of how children learn and make meaning about different contents, situations and phenomena. The preschool teachers who had a *learning-oriented teaching approach* focused on children's learning of specific objects, and they created conditions for children to learn about the object intended. In low and good-quality preschools, the teachers seemed to assume that children learned what was intended by participating in different activities.

The knowledge generated by this study provides additional evidence that conditions for children's learning largely depend on the quality of the learning environment and on preschool teacher's competence to teach, their didactical approaches and ways to communicate and interact with the children (Pramling & Pramling Samuelsson, 2011; Sheridan et al., 2009; Sheridan & Williams, 2018; Williams & Sheridan, 2019).

The third study was conducted in 2016 and 2017 (Sheridan & Williams, 2017; Sheridan, Williams, Mellgren, & Garvis, 2018; Sheridan, Shiyan, & Shiyan, 2018; Williams & Sheridan, 2019). The overall aims were to improve the quality of preschool, the preschool teacher education and preschool teacher students' practical training in preschool. In this study, the Early Childhood Environment Rating Scale (ECERS-3) (Harms, Clifford, & Cryer, 2015) was used to evaluate the quality of preschool. The study embraced 153 preschools with a mean value of 3.97 ranging from 2.38 to 6.11. The preschools were from 12 municipalities, representing a variation of geographic areas, living conditions, ethnical and socioeconomic backgrounds.

The results highlight stable and distinct patterns of variation in quality related to different items and subscales. The results show that preschool teachers are highly competent to interact and communicate socially with children, give good care and to organise whole group activities in a functional and for children, in an interesting way. Low quality is related to all kinds of learning activities. Low quality is for example to be found in items related to science, mathematics, written numbers and literacy, which can be explained by the novelty of these subject areas in the Swedish preschool curriculum. Preschool and preschool teacher education is not yet in the process of educating preschool teachers in these areas and didactical approaches of how to work with them in a thematic, play and learning-oriented way (Sheridan & Williams, 2018). More surprising is that low quality is also found in relation to areas such as book reading, dramatic play, arts etc. These are areas that are traditionally regarded as the core of early childhood pedagogy. Thus, the results highlight a need for preschool teachers to develop teaching, didactical and subject knowledge in a broad range of areas.

The knowledge gained by these studies provides additional evidence that some aspects are more critical than others to the preschool quality and for policy decisions.

Conclusion

The chapter explored critical aspects for the preschool quality over time, deepening the knowledge about quality and allowing policy makers and other administrators to make informed decisions about Swedish preschool at a structural level. As more parents choose preschool for their children, the demands and expectations of high-quality preschool becomes a shared interest for parents, policy makers and professionals.

Research conducted over the past two decades on Swedish preschool quality and conditions created for children's wellbeing, learning and development reveals an unchanging and significant variation in preschool quality, highlighting children's unequal conditions for learning (Sheridan, 2001; Sheridan et al., 2009; Sheridan, Williams, Mellgren, & Garvis, 2018; Williams & Sheridan, 2019). An analysis through the four quality dimensions (Sheridan, 2009) in relation to Bronfenbrenner's ecological system theory (1979, 1986) highlights a gap between children and teachers' perspectives and between policy intentions and the preschool practice. The results indicate a decrease in quality in certain areas and an enhancement in others. The task of preschool teachers is to create conditions for children to encounter all the learning experiences they have the right to do in preschool (The National Agency for Education, 1998/2018). The knowledge of the importance of interaction and communication with children has entered preschool practice and teachers have become more skilled in communicating socially with the children. However, the ECERS evaluations in relation to higher demands in the revised Swedish preschool curricula have shown problems around learning activities, including the development of preschool teachers' didactical knowledge and how to teach young children in preschool.

In this perspective, it is also important to underscore that different versions of ECERS were used in the three studies and that the demands on learning activities had a stronger focus in ECERS-3, highlighting the lack of competence in this area.

To achieve higher quality, according to ECERS, teachers require strong knowledge to plan suitable learning experiences and activities for children. Interpreted from a Swedish curriculum perspective, learning orientation includes the development of overall competences such as social competence, cooperation, mathematical understanding, becoming aware of and practicing reading and writing as a way to communicate with others, participation in nature activities, science, technology, etc. Learning orientation also includes situations in which children can develop so-called everyday life skills, such as being responsible, active, creative, communicative, flexible, reflective, solving problems, taking initiative, thinking critically and learning how to learn (European Union, 1996, 2007).

The consequence of this is that activities in preschool cannot be based purely on the child's initiative. Children have to be taught and challenged by teachers, who go beyond their previous knowledge and extend it (Sheridan, Shiyan &

Shiyan, 2018; Veraksa & Sheridan, 2018). Taking the child's previous experience as the point of departure, the teachers have to get involved and engage the children's interest in the unknown and create situations in which the child can negotiate, cooperate, reflect and develop standpoints and critical thinking.

Thus, in order to educate skilled and professional preschool teachers, the quality of the preschool teacher education as well as the quality of preschool, in which the preschool teacher students do their practical training, becomes vital. The competence of preschool teachers also plays an important role as they act as models for students during their practical training in preschools.

Critical aspects for the preschool quality need to be in focus for preschool teachers' education and competence development. They need to develop their pedagogical awareness, teaching, didactical and subject knowledge, competence to relate to children in dialogue, creating a sustainable shared thinking, developing child-focused strategies, clarifying and communicating an object of knowledge, challenging children's thinking while uniting play, care and education. It is primarily in interaction and communication, which are characterised by high sensitivity, responsiveness and dialogue about different contents, that is predicting the development of children's language, cognitive and social abilities in the long term. These aspects are also identified in other research (see Persson, 2015; Pramling and Pramling Samuelsson, 2011; Sheridan, 2016; Sheridan et al., 2009; Sheridan & Williams, 2018; Williams et al., 2018).

If we want preschool to become more teaching and learning-oriented in the direction of the overall goals, and at the same time avoid falling into the trap of formal and teacher-directed activities, new approaches to research, education and evaluations are also needed. The knowledge of what is highly valued, and how the world looks from the perspective of the child, is crucial for teachers when they create conditions for the children to learn and develop. It is vital that preschool teachers develop a scientific approach and knowledge in order to relate everyday situations to educational theories, the preschool curriculum and research findings (Sheridan & Williams, 2018; Sylva et al., 2010).

Preschool needs to become an important place for early intervention to allow all children an equal start in life. Especially as low-quality preschools seem to lead to societal deprivation for children and their families as well as society (Hansen & Nordahl, 2016; Manning et al., 2010; Sylva et al., 2010). Early intervention, through high-quality preschool, is therefore important to make the necessary changes in children's lives to allow positive life trajectories (Heckman, 2000; Sylva et al., 2010). The Swedish studies can provide a platform for future discussion across countries about policies and practices to improve the quality of learning and wellbeing in preschools, especially across the Nordic region.

References

Andersson, M. (1999). *The Early Childhood Environment Rating Scale (ECERS) as a tool in evaluating and improving quality in preschools*. Studies in Educational Sciences, 19. Stockholm: Institute of Education Press.

Bae, B. (1997). *The adult-child relationship: spacious and narrow patterns.* Paper presented at the ENSAC-Conference, Trondheim, Norway, 31 August–3 September.

Bertram, T., Pascal, C., Cummins, A., Delaney, S., Ludlow, C., Lyndon, H., Hencke, J., Kostek, M., Knoll, S., & Stancel-Piatak, A. (2016). *Early Childhood Policies and Systems in Eight Countries: Findings from IEA's Early Childhood Education Study.* International Association for the Evaluation of Educational Achievement (IEA), Hamburg, Germany. Retrieved from www.iea.nl/fileadmin/user_upload/Publications/Electronic_versions/ECES-policies_and_systems-report.pdf.

Bjørnestad, E. (2017). Better provision for Norway's children in ECEC. Retrieved from www.hioa.no/eng/Research-and-Development/Our-research/Research-and-Development-at-the-Faculty-of-Education-and-International-Studies/R-D-Projects-at-the-Faculty-of-Education-and-International-Studies/Better-Provision-for-Norway-s-children-in-ECEC.

Bjurek, H., Gustafsson, B., Kjulin, U., & Kärrby, G. (1992). *Effektivitet och kvalitet i barnomsorgen, En studie av daghem i Göteborgs kommun* [Efficiency and quality in preschool, a study of preschool settings in Gothenburg]. Report no. 1992:7. Gothenburg: University of Gothenburg, Department of Education.

Bronfenbrenner, U. (1979). *The Ecology of Human Development: Experiments by Nature and Design.* Cambridge, MA: Harvard University Press.

Bronfenbrenner, U. (1986). Ecology of the family as a context for human development: Research perspectives. *Developmental Psychology, 22,* 723–742. doi:10.1037/0012-1649.22.6.723.

Donabedian, A. (1980). The definition of quality and approaches to its assessment. In A. Arbor (Ed.), *Explorations in Quality Assessment and Monitoring, Vol. 1.* Michigan, MI: Health Administration Press.

European Union (1996). *Council for Cultural Cooperation.* Strasbourg: Education committee.

European Union (2007). Nyckelkompetenser för livslångt lärande: En europeisk referensram [Key competences for lifelong learning: A European reference]. Retrieved from https://center.hj.se/download/18.364f88fa12fd35278838000423/1520583354688/keycomp_sv.pdf.

Garbarino, J. (1992). *Towards a Sustainable Society: An Economic, Social and Environmental Agenda for our Children's Future.* Chicago, IL: The Noble Press.

Garbarino, J., & Scott, F. M. (1992). *What Children Can Tell Us.* San Francisco, CA: Jossey-Bass.

Hansen, O. H., & Nordahl, T. (2016). *Learning in Preschool – a Report.* Aalborg: Aalborg University.

Harms, T., & Clifford, R. (1980). *The Early Childhood Environment Rating Scale.* New York: Teachers College Press.

Harms, T., Clifford, R., & Cryer, D. (2015). *The Early Childhood Environment Rating Scale* (ECERS-3). The third revision. New York: Teachers College Press, Columbia University.

Heckman, J. J. (2000). Policies to foster human capital. *Research in Economics 54*(1), 3–56.

Jonsson, A. (2013). *Att skapa läroplan för de yngsta barnen i förskolan: Barns perspektiv och nuets didaktik* [Creating curriculum for the youngest children in preschool: Children's perspectives and didactics of the present moment]. Göteborg: Acta Universitatis Gothoburgensis.

Jonsson, A., Williams, P., & Pramling Samuelsson, I. (2017). Undervisningsbegreppet och dess innebörder uttrycka av förskolans lärare [The concept of teaching and its meanings expressed by preschool teachers]. *Forskning om undervisning och lärande, 1*(5), 90–109.

Kärrby, G. (1989). *A Swedish Research Version of the Early Childhood Environment Rating Scale* (ECERS). Göteborg: Gothenburg University: Department of Education.

Kärrby, G. (1997). Bedömning av pedagogisk kvalitet – Förskolan i fokus [Evaluation of pedagogical Quality – Focus on the preschool]. *Pedagogisk forskning i Sverige, 2*(1).

Kärrby, G., & Giota, J. (1994). Dimensions of quality in Swedish day care centers – an analysis of Early Childhood Environment Rating Scale. *Early Child Development and Care, 104*, 1–22. doi:10.1080/0300443941040101.

Kärrby, G., & Giota, J. (1995). Parental conceptions of quality in daycare centers in relation to quality measured by the ECERS. *Early Child Development and Care, 110*, 1–18.

Manning, M., Garvis, S., Flemming, C., & Wong, G. (2017). *The relationship between teacher qualification and the quality of the early childhood care and learning environment.* Campbell Systematic Reviews. 2017, 1. doi:10.4073/csr.2017.1.

Manning. M., Homel, R., & Smith, C. (2010). The effects of early developmental prevention programs in at-risk populations on non-health outcomes in adolescence. *Children and Youth Services Review, 32*(4), 506–519.

Miller, L., Dalli, C., & Urban, M. (2011). Early childhood grows up: Towards a critical ecology of the profession. In L. Miller, C. Dalli and M. Urban (Eds.), *Early Childhood Grows Up: Towards a Critical Ecology of the Profession.* Anthology. Dordrecht, The Netherlands: Springer.

Næsby, T. (2016). *Litteraturstudie af forskning om Environment Rating Scales. Projektevaluering af kvalitet i dagtilbud* [Literature study of research on Environment Rating Scales. Project evaluation of quality in daycare]. Aalborg: University College of Northern Denmark.

National Association for the Education of Young Children (NAEYC) (2006). *New NAEYC: Early Childhood Program Standards and Accreditation Criteria.* Washington DC: National Association for the Education of Young Children.

Organisation for Economic Co-operation and Development (OECD). (2015). Family data base. Retrieved from www.oecd.org/els/family/database.htm.

Organisation for Economic Co-operation and Development (OECD). (2017). *Starting Strong 2017: Key OECD Indicators on Early Childhood Education and Care.* Paris: OECD Publishing. Retrieved from www.oecd-ilibrary.org/education/starting-strong-2017_9789264276116.

Persson, S. (2015). *En likvärdig förskola för alla barn. Innebörder och indikatorer* [An equal preschool for all children. Implications and indicators]. Vetenskapsrådets rapportserie. Stockholm: Vetenskapsrådet.

Pramling, N., & Pramling Samuelsson, I. (Eds.). (2011). *Educational Encounters: Nordic Studies in Early Childhood Didactics.* Dortrecht, Holland: Springer.

Regeringens Proposition. (2017/18:9). Skolstart vid sex års ålder [Schoolstart at six years of age]. Stockholm: Regeringen. Retrieved from www.riksdagen.se/sv/dokument.../proposition/skolstart-vid-sex-ars-alder_H503.

Sheridan, S. (2001). *Pedagogical Quality in Preschool. An Issue of Perspectives.* Akademisk avhandling. Göteborg: Acta Universitatis Gothoburgensis. Retrieved from http://hdl.handle.net/2077/10307.

Sheridan, S. (2009). Discerning pedagogical quality in preschool. *Scandinavian Journal of Educational Research, 53*(3), 245–261. doi:10.1080/00313830902917295.

Sheridan, S. (2016). Preschool teachers' pedagogical awareness – a key competence. *Journal of Korean Council for Children & Rights, 20*(4), 523–542.

Sheridan, S., & Pramling Samuelsson, I. (2001). Children's conceptions of participation and influence in preschool: A perspective on pedagogical quality. *Contemporary Issues in Early Childhood, 2*(2), 169–194. Retrieved from www.triangle.co.uk/ciec/.

Sheridan, S., Pramling Samuelsson, I., & Johansson, E. (Eds.). (2009). *Barns tidiga lärande. En tvärsnittsstudie om förskolan som miljö för barns lärande* [Children's early learning. A current study of preschool as an environment for children's learning; in Swedish]. Antologi. Göteborg: Acta Universitatis Gothoburgensis. Retrieved from http://hdl.handle.net/2077/20404.

Sheridan, S., Shiyan, O., & Shiyan, I. (2018). Preschool quality and conditions for children's learning in preschool in Russia and Sweden. In N. Veraksa & S. Sheridan (Eds.), *Vygotsky's Theory in Early Childhood Education and Research. Russian and Western Values* (pp. 193–205). London: Routledge.

Sheridan, S., & Williams, P. (2017). *The Swedish preschool quality.* Paper presentation in VI Research-to-Practice Conference Early Childhood Care and Education. 10–13 May, 2017, Lomonosov Moscow State University, Russia.

Sheridan, S., & Williams, P. (2018). *Undervisning i förskolan. En kunskapsöversikt* [Teaching in preschool. A research review]. Stockholm: Skolverket.

Sheridan, S., Williams, P., Mellgren, E., & Garvis, S. (2018). *Quality evaluations with ECERS-3 in Swedish preschools – results from an ongoing project.* Paper presented at the 20th International ECERS Conference, Aalborg, Denmark 23–25 May, 2018.

Sheridan, S., Williams, P., & Pramling Samuelsson, I. (2014). Group size and organisational conditions for children's learning in preschool: A teacher perspective. *Educational Research*, 56(4), s. 379–397. Nr. 205796.

Sheridan, S., Williams, P., Sandberg, A., & Vuorinen, T. (2011). Preschool teaching in Sweden – a profession in change. *Educational Research*, 53(4), 415–437. Nr. 148365.

Siraj-Blatchford, I. (2007). Creativity, communication and collaboration: The identification of pedagogic progression in sustained shared thinking. *Asia-Pacific Journal of Research in Early Childhood Education*, 1(2), 3–23.

Siraj-Blatchford, I. (2010). A focus on pedagogy: Case studies of effective practice. In K. Sylva, E. Melhuish, P. Sammons, I. Siraj-Blatchford and B. Taggart (Eds.), *Early Childhood Matters: Evidence from the Effective Pre-school and Primary Education Project* (pp. 149–165). London: Routledge.

Stern, D. (2003). *Ögonblickets psykologi* [The psychology of the present moment]. Stockholm: Natur och Kultur.

Svensk författningssamling (SFS). (2010:541). *Förordning om ändring i högskoleförordningen (1993:100)* [Regulation amending in higher education degree]. Stockholm: The Ministry of Education and Science in Sweden.

Svensk författningssamling (SFS). (2010:800). *The Education Act.* Stockholm: The Ministry of Education and Science in Sweden.

Sylva, K., Melhuish, E., Sammons, P., Siraj-Blatchford, I., & Taggart, B. (2010). *Early childhood matters. Evidence from the Effective Pre-school and Primary Education project.* London: Routledge.

Sylva, K., Siraj-Blatchford, I., Taggart, B., Sammons, P., Melhuish, E., Elliot, K., & Totsika, V. (2006). Capturing quality in early childhood through environmental rating scales. *Early Child Research Quarterly*, 21(1), 76–92. doi:10.1016/j.ecresq.2006.01.003.

The National Agency for Education. (2016). *Barngruppens storlek i förskolan. En kartläggning av aktuell pedagogisk, utvecklingspsykologisk och socialpsykologisk forskning* [Group size in preschool. A survey of current pedagogical, developmental psychological and social psychological research]. (Skolverkets rapport nr 433). Stockholm: Skolverket.

The National Agency for Education (2017). *Skolverkets jämförelsetal 2016* [Comparative numbers for 2016]. Retrieved from www.skolverket.se/skolutveckling/statistik.

The National Agency for Education. (1998/2018). *Curriculum for Preschool Lpfö 98. Revised 2018.* Stockholm: The National Agency for Education.

The National Agency for Inspection. (2011). Förskolans pedagogiska uppdrag [The pedagogical assignment of preschool]. *Kvalitetsgranskning, Skolinspektionens rapport 2011:10.* Diarienummer 40-2010:314. Stockholm.

Urban, M. (2015). From 'closing the gap' to an ethics of affirmation. Reconceptualising The Role of Early Childhood Services in Times of Uncertainty. *European Journal of Education, 50,* 3, 293–306. Retrieved from https://doi.org/10.1111/ejed.12131.

Veraksa, N., & Sheridan, S. (2018). (Eds.). *Vygotsky's Theory in Early Childhood and Research. Russian and Western Values* (pp. 3–8, 206–213). London: Routledge.

Vitaro, F., Barker, E. D., Brendgen, M., & Tremblay, R. E. (2011). Pathways explaining the reduction of adult criminal behaviour by a randomized preventive intervention for disruptive kindergarten children. *Journal of Child Psychology and Psychiatry, 53*(7), 748–756. doi:10.1111/j.1469-7610.2011.02517.

Vygotskij, L. (1986). *Thought and Language* (Revised Edition). Cambridge, MA: MIT Press.

Williams, P., & Sheridan, S. (2019). Förskollärarkompetens – skärningspunkt i undervisningens kvalitet [Preschool teacher competence – the point of intersection of quality in teaching]. *Barn, 36*(3–4), 127–146.

Williams, P., Sheridan, S., & Pramling Samuelsson, I. (2018). A perspective of group size on children's conditions for wellbeing, learning and development in preschool. *Scandinavian Journal of Educational Research.* Retrieved from https://doi.org/10.1080/00 313831.2018.1434823.

18 Turning the tide

Publicisation of early childhood education and care in Taiwan

Yi-Hui Lin and Yvonne Yu-Feng Liu

Introduction

The government has a key role to play in developing a high-quality environment for early childhood education and care in Taiwan. Over the last decade, fundamental legislation of early childhood education and care, national core-curriculum and teacher education in early childhood education have been accomplished and announced to welcome a new era for children in Taiwan; however, research has predicted that 'Thirty years from now, it will be rare to see children walking along the streets of Taiwan' (Cheng, 1995). Low fertility rates have brought great challenges to even the most developed countries, and Taiwan is no exception. Taiwan's ex-President Ma even stated that the low birthrate is a serious national security threat. The number of babies being born in Taiwan has declined steadily in recent years. Additionally, the birthrate of Taiwan currently sits in the bottom three or four in the global rankings. Therefore, the Taiwan government has recently placed the focus of early childhood policy on making the citizen 'happy to marry, willing to give birth, and able to rear'.

The reasons for this declining birth rate are very much open for discussion; moreover, these can be a result of internal individual's factors and external social factors. The internal individual's factors lie in growing individualism, attitude towards marriage, value of children, and so on; however, those individual-level mechanism factors are hard and seldom discussed (Chen, 2012; Freeman, Xiaohong, Ping, Wenshan, & Gietel-Basten, 2018; Hoffman & Hoffman, 1973). For external social factors, the unfriendly workplace environment, the escalating cost of raising a child, the lack of qualified and valued day care services and some social concerns such as increasing environmental pollution, dissatisfaction with the highly competitive education system and worsening social order are some of the main factors that encourage people not to have children in Taiwan. More specifically, maternity leave allowances in Taiwan are set at just eight weeks on full pay, while husbands' paternity leave is even lower at just three days. While there is a legal allowance of up to two years unpaid parental leave, most families cannot afford basic living costs on a single-salary and most employers will not countenance any arrangement that impedes an organisation's operation.

In order to solve the internal individual's factors and external social factors described above, national parenting policies have always been created around these. The Taiwan government offers various baby bonuses to address the plummeting birth rate, including financial incentives, support to parents to help them combine work and family, and broad social change supportive of children and parenting. Those planning policies can be divided into two stages: 0 to two years old, and two to five years old. In the 0 to two-years-old part, the Four-year Forward-looking Infrastructure Development Program (FIDP) has *Spatial Construction of Friendly Child Rearing in the Trend of Fewer Children*, which promotes community public child care services, building child care resource centres, provides baby boxes, improves family (social) welfare service centres, constructs social welfare centres to achieve public child care. For two to six year olds, in addition to an increasing number of public kindergartens and the promotion of non-profit kindergartens, private kindergartens will be invited to join the public policy plan.

Plans under the FIDP, a comprehensive initiative aimed at addressing Taiwan's key infrastructure needs over the next 30 years, seek to accelerate the establishment of community-based public day care for children aged 0–2 years as well as construction of new kindergartens for those 3–6 years. These two initiatives are being implemented by the Ministry of Health and Welfare (MOHW) and Ministry of Education (MOE), respectively. These efforts are designed to alleviate the economic burden on parents, remove barriers to women's employment and reverse the declining birthrate.

The two political parties in Taiwan, Kuomintang (KMT) and Democratic Progressive Party (DPP), are classified wing on the political spectrum. In order to win in the frequent election and to please voters, the parties put forward social welfare policies that are beneficial and therefore inevitable. Although the Taiwan government has realised that more needs to be done in order to construct a friendly childrearing environment and encourage fertility, exactly what should be done remains elusive.

To present what the Taiwan government has done in childrearing and early childhood education and the possible effects that come with these policies are the aims of the current study. This study focuses on: (1) What research exists in relation to the crisis of low fertility in Taiwan? (2) What are the current government policies put in place to address the low fertility challenges? (3) What are the ongoing government strategies for a better future in early childhood education and care (ECEC)? Research reports and public documents from the Taiwanese government were gathered and analysed for the purposes of this study.

Research and reports

Research about child care policies and strategies from other countries is available. In Japan, the government's strategies on education system, economy and womens' social participation all relate to early childhood and care. In order to solve the problem of low birth rate in Japan, the government set a new direction to create a better future for raising children (Wong, 2013). Reports from the National Academy of Educational Research also presented that in Japan, South Korea, Singapore, German and Finland, the public child care system from the government steers the development of ECEC. Free education or a free care system in the early years are also trends in those countries (Lin, 2013).

Supporting the development of higher quality in ECEC requires effort from different areas such as family-friendly working conditions, low-cost child care centres and a continuous child care allowance to relieve the financial burden on parents. Those supportive elements are essential for bringing up children but it is not possible that these can be achieved by individual families. Therefore, the government has to take more responsibility for children care.

In fact, studies and reports from the Taiwanese government have mentioned the possibility of public early childhood education and care for a long time. Multiple dimensions, such as legislation, national financial budget and total early childhood education and care service system improvement have to be taken into consideration (Hsu, 2008). It is also a huge change to involve several central departments and their strategies in order to form a new ECEC network (Lin & Hsieh, 2005). After many years, however, public early childhood education and care policy is still partially implemented but not comprehensive. In forming the implantation of policy, the top-down methods demonstrated in many foreign policy and strategies researches were adopted but empirical studies presenting the bottom-up need in the Taiwanese context were missing.

According to Chen, Liao and Chang (2008), 85 per cent of parents are aware of the low birth rate's negative influence on Taiwan's future development. Limited empirical research points to the two main reasons behind the low birth rate. One important reason is the cost of child care. From the parents' point of view, they must cover the expense of infant care, day care institutions, choice of preschool and the cost of maternity leave from the very beginning (Huang, 2017). Another reason is the shortage of systematic support for child care. Chen, Tu and Lee (2014) stressed the importance of better provision of infant care, low-cost public child care, supportive parenting courses and the assessment of child care institutions. A recent survey shown on Taiwanese major media also pointed out the bigger contextual influence. Besides the expense of care and education, costly housing and long working hours also have an influence on young couples' willingness to have children (Qiou, 2018).

One crucial drawback of current surveys is that they are either small-scale studies with a limited population or have not been through a rigorous research process. It is difficult for policy makers to see the reality as a whole and to systematically consider the influential elements. Furthermore, those studies were not empirical enough to present the reality and need from the field. Parent voice from the real world is the key element that needs to be studied in order to solve the low birth rate challenge. If the friendliness of the child care environment is critical to the birth rate in Taiwan, studies and researches from parents' empirical data, users' feedback about current educare systems and longitudinal connection among child care institutions needs to be examined.

Policies and strategies

Both the Organisation for Economic Co-operation and Development (OECD) and the United Nations Educational, Scientific and Cultural Organisation (UNESCO) have reviewed and published the early childhood education and care policy implementation experiences of selected countries. These reports have suggested that appropriate public investment by governments into early childhood education, child care services, and into a women, family or child friendly environment could be one of the most effective ways to maintain women's labour force participation rates and to raise birth rates (Bos, Phillips-Fain, Rein, Weinberg, & Chavez, 2016; Taguma, Litjens, Kim, & Makowiecki, 2012).

Despite the documentation of decline in traditional gender roles in Taiwan for both men and women, men are still more traditional compared to women (Chuang and Lee, 2003). Surprisingly, even though women's attitudes are more liberal than men's, women still consider the family as their primary task, and their jobs secondary. Therefore, the highest Taiwan administrative executive department, Executive Yuan, have realised the need for married women (the current national child care system) to be relieved of their family burden in order to participate in the workforce (An & Peng, 2016; Lee, 2009). The Population Policy White Paper, 'Fewer Children, Population Aging, and Immigration' (Yuan of the Republic of China, 2013) pitched children as the country's citizens-to-be. Therefore, in a related early childhood education and care of the Population Policy White Paper, the policy is to construct a complete children's education and care service system, and implement comprehensive nursery and preschool education as well as after-class services for children of school age (Executive Office of the Executive Yuan, 2013).

In the conclusion of the current Population Policy White Paper, the specific measures of ECEC are divided into four segments: nannies' system, free tuition, ECEC professional workers and diversified ECEC institutions.

Community child attendant care system

The Taiwan government established a national system of nannies management in 2000. The Ministry of Interior passed the Childcare Provider Supervising and Childcare Subsidies Scheme, and it began to place childminder services under public governance and the social welfare principal and based it on the idea of universal social services. This scheme was designed to support working parents as well as socially and economically disadvantaged families by providing child care resources and government-initiated subsidies for child care services in order to relieve family pressure on child care and finance. Over the past 20 years, the duty of child care by parents dropped from 72 per cent to 51.82 per cent, and on the contrary, and the duty of child care by nannies increased from 6 per cent to 9.07 per cent (Executive Office of the Executive Yuan, 2013). This means that infant day care centres and qualified child care providers in family child care service centres are needed for the dual-income parents and nuclear families. Child care costs occupy a large proportion of household expenses and cause a heavy financial burden for many families with young children (Lin & Kamo, 2015; Tsai, 2014). Therefore, developing a public care system is crucial in helping citizens to balance their family care and job responsibilities, as well as to avoid commodification of children care.

In 2017, the Executive Yuan further implemented the nationwide child care subsidy programme in which parents who qualify will receive a monthly subsidy of NT$6,000 (US$196) for each child up to the age of two years who attends a semi-public–private kindergarten or who is looked after by babysitters who have signed a contract with the government. However, the policy has attracted criticism from parents, government-contracted kindergartens and babysitters. Without a social basis in social democracy, the reform policy was a result of the efforts made by state feminists, who not only advocated for the notion of a public child care system, but also cooperated with state bureaucrats to design and plan the entire programme. This programme should not be considered merely as a cash subsidy or a management measure for childminder services; it is a vital infrastructure with the ideal of developing a public child care system in Taiwan. Nevertheless, this study also revealed that this reform did not proceed smoothly. The controversy that arose during the planning process and the backlash after the implementation of the programme showed that this reform had faced severe challenges.

Free tuition

Preschool or kindergarten education in Taiwan, which serves children from the age of four years to six years, is not compulsory, but its systematic development has been greatly aided by the passing of the 1981 Early Childhood Education Law. Therefore, in recent years, the federal government has implemented three initiatives to address preschool education concerns: creating an early childhood education voucher programme, providing free education for five year olds, and supporting young children from families in need. The initial step is the early childhood education voucher system, in which children who attend approved private kindergartens in Taiwan become eligible for annual vouchers of US$322. By subsidising private preschool tuition, vouchers were intended to narrow the growing inequalities in education choices between wealthier and poorer families. After that, in 2008, President Ma promised continued efforts to make preschool education free for all five year olds, instead of relying on vouchers to subsidise the costs of schooling. Free admission for five year olds was one of the political promises in President Ma's 2008 election campaign, and it was then changed into the Free Tuition Education Project for five-year-old Children by the Ministry of Education and was launched in 2011. Children who are at least five full years of age, attending a public kindergarten or child care centre, or enrolled in a 'Private Cooperation (Partnership) Program' are beneficiaries of the policy. Following the trend of early childhood education and child care public governance, the Taiwan government may continue to provide nation-wide free preschool tuition for five-year-old children.

The implementation of the free tuition policy in Taiwan has its concern, which is the rapidly falling birthrate. In 1995, the fertility rate was 1.8 total fertility rate (TFR), but in 2010 it dropped to 0.9 TFR, the lowest birthrate in the world that year (Sui, 2011). Although the fertility rate has risen since, concerns over the costs of raising a child in Taiwan have persisted. Increasing funding for early childhood education and care, then, was viewed as an incentive for young couples to marry earlier and to have more children. While the Ministry of Education worked to increase funding for education of five year olds, it also worked to expand kindergarten options for families. Specifically, the government began promoting the creation of government–utility, privately operated kindergartens.

Early childhood education and care educators

In 2012, the Early Childhood Education and Care Act was implemented, which was a revolutionary move in the Taiwan preschool system. Since then, nurseries and kindergartens have been integrated into 'preschools', in which toddlers from the age of two years onwards are given complete and thorough education and care in the preschool until they enter elementary school. This Bill consolidated the education and care of toddlers under a single administrative system, putting into practice a toddler-centred strategy that focuses on the toddler's best interests. Taiwan is also the first country in Asia to consolidate the two systems (Ministry of Education, 2015). However, there are teachers and educare givers (in Taiwan, an educare giver is someone who has graduated from the Department of Early Childhood Education but hasn't trained in teacher education) in preschools after kindergartens and nurseries integrated in 2012 (Kao & Chen, 2017). Both teachers and educare givers can carry out teaching and nursing duties for children between the ages of two and six years, but a teacher is required in senior class (for children between the ages of five to six years).

Moreover, many educare givers attend the 'Preschool Staff Members Attend Preschool Teacher Pre-vocational Education Program' to achieve the right to teach in preschools. The Ministry of Education also grants professional development activities and formulates the core-curriculum, guidelines for professional standards of teachers and teacher's professional literacy for preschool teachers and educare givers. From August 2013, there are 32 credits for standardised core courses for preschool educators. Every educator in preschool will be certified as an educare giver or a preschool teacher. In 2018, the professional competence of preschool educators and teachers began the phase of public hearings and more clear standards will be set for departments of early childhood education and teacher education.

Diversified ECEC institutions

In Taiwan, the education system is currently a 6–3–3–4 structure that offers compulsory education. Although preschool education is not part of the compulsory education and educational system, there are currently public preschools (i.e. pre-schools affiliated with public elementary schools), private preschools and private non-profit preschools. Public preschools (i.e. preschools affiliated with public elementary schools) in Taiwan have more outdoor space, qualified teachers, thematic curricula and funds to support this; therefore, it always attracts parental selection. Nevertheless, public preschools' service hours do not meet the needs of dual-income families.

In, 2012, the Ministry of Education proposed another type of school, private non-profit preschool, to parents. Non-profit preschools are government–utility, privately operated preschools and are a joint venture between the government and private individuals (or organisations), with government providing the hardware (e.g. physical space) and private individuals providing software (e.g. teaching staff and curriculum). The creation and maintenance of private non-profit preschools (including teachers' salaries) are carefully monitored by local education departments as well as by professional early childhood education personnel teams.

Also, the government has increased the number of public preschools in disadvantaged regions and islands, with priority given to areas where the supply of preschool services is insufficient; has raised the proportion of elementary schools in indigenous areas with attached preschools to 83 per cent; increased the number of non-profit preschools; and encouraged public–private partnerships to set up day care centres and child care resource centres.

In 2018, in order to accelerate the expansion of high-quality and affordable early childhood education and care services, private preschools that meet the requirements signed a cooperation contract with the government, which is called 'quasi-public preschool'. The cooperation requirements are tuition criterion, preschool educators' salary, preschool evaluation, environment security inspection, education and care quality. In quasi-public preschool, the tuition that the parents pay is no more than US$150 per month for each child. For example, child A attends the private preschool and the parents usually pay an average of US$330 per month. After the preschool becomes a quasi-public one, the parents only need to pay US$150 per month, and the extra cost US$180 will be paid by the government to the preschool directly. For the family that has three or more children, the monthly contribution of each child shall not exceed US$115. Moreover, for low-income families, the fee can be waived totally.

Processing projects for a better future

In order to raise the sustained downturn in fertility rates, the Taiwan government has implemented the Forward-looking Infrastructure Development Program in order to create child care spaces. Moreover, this plan is designed to meet Taiwan's development needs for the next generation. The Forward-looking Infrastructure Development Program will be funded by a special budget to be divided into three terms over a four-year period (2017–2021). In the ECEC part, the policies can be divided into two subprojects: Community-based public nurseries (for age two years and under) and Friendly child care spaces (for ages 3–6 years) (Executive Office of the Executive Yuan, 2013).

Subproject 1: community-based public nurseries (for age two years and under)

The plan will combine national and community resources to help ease the burden of parenting and support families raising children. There are six goals under this subproject.

First, promote community-based public nurseries: local governments will receive subsidies to create affordable, safe, small-community, home-style care nurseries that combine the advantages of nursery centres and home child care services (e.g. nanny programmes). These nurseries will offer quality services at reasonable prices. The plan will also inject resources into indigenous and rural nurseries, customising services to accommodate local culture and at locations close to families.

Second, establish nursery resource centres: unused space or buildings will be converted or renovated into child day care centres and equipped with proper facilities. These centres will form community-centred networks that provide localised, high-quality integrated nursery resources and services close to home, including nursery and care consultation and educational activities for the whole family. In resource-deprived areas, mobile outreach services will be deployed to provide children's toys and books for loan, sending resources into the community to improve accessibility.

Third, set up or improve regional family (social) welfare service centres: as part of efforts to strengthen the social safety net, the plan will provide local governments with subsidies to set up one regional family (social) welfare service centre for every 150,000 people, or according to police precinct jurisdictions. These centres will offer comprehensive family welfare services to support child raising and create tight networks of community-based welfare services so that families in the community can receive quality care.

Fourth, set up multifunctional social welfare buildings: local governments will receive subsidies to renovate, repair and equip social welfare buildings to meet the needs of the whole family and individual members, including to renovate family-friendly rooms, nursing rooms and barrier-free facilities as part of a range of nursery and welfare services close to home. The buildings will also integrate the welfare needs of family members, providing a localised, quality service network close to home that promotes cross-generational interaction and strengthens core family functions.

Fifth, provide childrearing information packets: provide complete information on childrearing knowledge and service resources to help expecting families get ready for life with a newborn. These information and resources will help parents save time in finding resources and ease the stress of child care, narrow the information gap between rural and urban areas, and convey the government's care and support for families with newborns.

Sixth, infrastructure objectives: the plan aims to establish 120 community-based public nurseries, set up 170 nursery resource centres, provide 630,000 childrearing information packets, set up or improve 94 regional family (social) welfare service centres and 40 multifunctional welfare buildings, improve service capacities, and make welfare services more widespread and closer to the people that need them.

Subproject 2: friendly child care spaces (for ages 3–6 years)

Using a one-time subsidy strategy for the construction of new preschools, the plan will help local governments resolve problems of insufficient space for public preschools, and ease parenting burdens by providing quality and sustainable educational and care services.

First, increase the supply of public education and care services: local governments will receive subsidies to construct new public preschools on extra school grounds or on unused sites where old schools have been torn down.

Second, build dedicated spaces for young children: local governments and applicant schools may select their own architects to incorporate special characteristics from the school and surrounding community into the construction process, creating a safe and secure education and care environment that reflects the culture of the people and the characteristics of the land. This will be a special space for young children to freely explore and learn, and will serve as an example for other local governments when building safe education and care service environments.

Third, infrastructure objectives: by the 2020 academic year, the plan expects to subsidise the establishment of 200 classes at 50 public preschools, providing opportunities for 5800 children to attend public preschools, and offer work opportunities to 600 preschool educators.

Conclusion

At present, the most controversial issue in Taiwan is the policy of quasi-public preschools. Most OECD countries also adopt public policies to ensure the rights of early childhood education and care. However, the quasi-public preschool creates chaos. Can the policy solve the problem of low fertility pain and promote the quality of early childhood education and care for all children in Taiwan? The number of public preschools that meet the needs of parents has always been limited. As a result, the ratio of public and private is 3:7. Private preschools are the main force of early childhood education and care and the 'profit-seeking demand' has long dominated early childhood education and care services. Private preschools have stated that much of the tuition reported to the Ministry of Education was 'understated', and the parents actually had to pay for additional services and courses and related materials.

On the other hand, preschools with high tuition fees (e.g. whole English preschool, English–Chinese bilingual preschool or other specific preschools) are not willing to cooperate with the government, which will result in the 'M-form' early childhood education and care environment, which is in opposition to the spirit of publicisation. It is an anti-publicisation practice for government-subsidised parents to send children to private preschool. Education is humanity's best hope and most effective means in the quest to achieve sustainable development. What does a high-quality preschool look like? Early childhood education and care has a role to play in constructing a sustainable society; however, the function of M-form early childhood education and care may be questioned.

Another issue is about educators' income. The average salary for private preschool educators was US$910 every month and is not satisfactory (Cheng & Chen, 2011). The salary issue is that at the press conference in May of 2018, the Executive Yuan claimed that the policy of quasi-publicisation could improve the salaries of preschool educators. This statement provoked great opposition from numerous private preschools because of the urban and rural differences in preschool educators' salary. They also pointed out that the system design is out of line with the reality of Taiwan. The tuition that parents pay is usually relatively low in the south. How could one ask for the preschool educators' salary to be like the north? This controversy made the government soften its position and it declared that the preschool educators' salary has to be related and adapt to the local conditions. Lee (2003) pointed out that the salary could influence job satisfaction; the higher the financial reward the higher the job satisfaction. The statement that quasi-publicisation can reverse the private preschool educators' job conditions and further create qualified early childhood education and care has been called into question by public opinion.

In conclusion, the publicisation polices of early childhood education and care should not be considered merely as a cash subsidy or a management measure; it is a vital infrastructure with the ideal of developing a public early childhood education and care system in Taiwan. Nevertheless, the resulting disputes also revealed that this reform did not proceed smoothly. The controversy that arose during the planning process and the backlash after the implementation of the programme showed that this reform had faced severe challenges from top to bottom. To look forward for a better future of ECEC in Taiwan, it is crucial that government steers its development. There are two major steps that need to be implemented in order to achieve better ECEC in Taiwan. First, the quantity and quality of ECEC institutions. There should be enough affordable child care institutions that offer an appropriate curriculum with qualified educators to form the solid core of ECEC. Furthermore, the ECEC supporting systems and outer related systems have to be well connected and co-function to underpin the development in the inner ECEC system. The public sectors will be the gatekeepers to watch and guide the better future of ECEC in Taiwan.

References

An, M. Y., & Peng, I. (2016). Diverging paths? A comparative look at childcare policies in Japan, South Korea and Taiwan. *Social Policy & Administration*, 50(5), 540–558.

Bos, J. M., Phillips-Fain, G., Rein, E., Weinberg, E., & Chavez, S. (2016). Connecting all children to high-quality Early Care and Education. Retrieved from: www.air.org/system/files/downloads/report/High-Quality-Early-Care-and-Education-International-October-2016.pdf.

Chen, J. L., Tu, M. J., & Lee, L. C. (2014). Parental satisfaction for early childcare in New Taipei City. *Journal of Human Development and Family Studies*, 16, 79–102.

Chen, S. M., Liao, Y. K., & Chang, C. C. (2008). A survey on the baby bust trend and education reforms in Taiwan. *Education Policy Forum*, 11(3), 1–31.

Chen, Y. H. (2012). Trends in low fertility and policy responses in Taiwan. *The Japanese Journal of Population*, 10(1), 78–88.

Cheng, J. (1995). More senior citizens, fewer kids. *Free China Review*, 45(12), 42–46.

Cheng, J. N., & Chen, Y. (2011). The empirical study of the kindergarten teachers' job satisfaction in Taiwan: Exploring the effect of the intrinsic demand, external reward, and organizational treatment. *The Journal of Human Resource and Adult Learning*, 7(2), 127.

Chuang, H.-L., & Hsih-Yin, L. (2003). The return on women's human capital and the role of male attitudes toward working wives. *American Journal of Economics and Sociology*, 62(2): 435–459.

Executive Office of the Executive Yuan. (2013). The Survey of Marriage and Employment of Women in 2013.

Freeman, E., Xiaohong, M., Ping, Y., Wenshan, Y., & Gietel-Basten, S. (2018). 'I couldn't hold the whole thing': The role of gender, individualisation and risk in shaping fertility preferences in Taiwan. *Asian Population Studies*, 14(1), 61–76.

Hoffman, L. W., & Hoffman, M. L. (1973). The value of children to parents. In J. T. Fawcett (Ed.), *Psychological Perspectives on Population* (pp. 19–76). New York: Basic Books.

Hsu, Y. D. (2008). A legal analysis of the policy of the preschool education in Taiwan (NSC97-2410-H006-016-MY02). Retrieved from www.grb.gov.tw/search/planDetail?id=1682735&docId=0.

Huang, S. T. (2017). The financial support for childcare in Taiwan. *Reports of Manpower Planning and Development*, 17, 33–62.

Kao, Y. S., & Chen, Y. L. (2017). Am I a teacher? How educare givers in Taiwan construct their professional identity during socialisation into public preschools. *Asia-Pacific Journal of Teacher Education*, 45(1), 53–70.

Lee, M. (2009). Transition to below replacement fertility and policy response in Taiwan. *The Japanese Journal of Population*, 7(1), 71–86.

Lin, T. Y., & Hsieh, H. L. (2005). Grade K education policy idea: An analysis of policy formulation feasibility. *Educational Resources and Research*, 63, 67–83.

Lin, W. S. (2013). The comparison of education policies in low birth rate era. Retrieved from www.naer.edu.tw/files/16-1000-5330.php?Lang=zh-tw.

Lin, Y. F., & Kamo, Y. (2015). A comparative analysis of determinants of birth rates in East Asian and Western countries. *Population Review*, 54(1).

Qiou, B. S. (2018, 2 April). The reasons of low birth rate in Taiwan. Retrieved from www.cna.com.tw/news/afe/201804020033-1.aspx.

Sui, C. (2011, 15 August). Taiwanese birth rate plummets despite measures. *BBC News*. Retrieved from www.bbc.com/news/world-asia-pacific-14525525.

Taguma, M., Litjens, I., Kim, J. H., & Makowiecki, K. (2012). Quality matters in early childhood education and care. *Japan: OECD*. Retrieved from http://search.oecd.org/korea/50219964.pdf.

Tsai, P. Y. (2014). *Difficulties in Work-family Reconciliation in Taiwan. Contemporary Social Issues in East Asian Societies: Examining the Spectrum of Public and Private Spheres* (pp. 164–177). Hershey, PA: Information Science Reference.

Wong, L. F. (2013). Early childhood education and care reform in Japan – debate on integration or separation of YOCHIEN and HOIKUSHO and the cultivation of high qualified citizens. *Educational Resources and Research, 111*, 55–98.

Yuan of the Republic of China. (2013). Population Policy White Paper, Fewer Children, Population Aging and Immigration. Retrieved from www.ris.gov.tw/c/document_library/get_file?uuid=2aeaecfd-9b4d-49a4-b46a-f08123aeee34&groupId=11159.

19 Early childhood education in the Netherlands

Parental engagement as a policy view

Elisabeth Duursma

Importance of parent engagement in early childhood

A child's home environment and the early childhood education programme they attend are the two most influential environments for young children (Halgunseth, 2009). Bronfenbrenner's ecological systems theory provides a good model to examine children's development within the context of a system of relationships that form the child's environment. When studying a child's development, it is important to not only consider the child's immediate environment but also focus on the interaction of the larger environment: the child's direct family and the early childhood programme and the interaction between the two. Bronfenbrenner's model emphasises the importance of a two-generation approach in early child care programmes (Bronfenbrenner, 2005; Hallam, Han, Vu, & Hustedt, 2016): A child's family is the primary context for early development and when parents and early childhood programmes form strong connections, this can positively promote children's development and learning (Shonkoff & Philips, 2000).

Parental engagement, involvement and participation are terms that are frequently intermingled. Parental engagement usually refers to parents engaging with their children's education, care, both at home and at the early childhood education and care (ECEC) centre (Smit, Driessen, & de Wit, 2009). Parental participation refers to a specific form of parental engagement where parents participate in the activity of an ECEC, such as a clean-up day (Smit et al., 2009).

Parental involvement is evident when parents show behaviour of shared responsibility for the development and education of their child (De Vries, 2017). There is a large research base showing strong evidence for the effectiveness of early parental engagement for improving child outcomes (e.g. Cabrera, Shannon, & Tamis-LeMonda, 2007; Lang et al., 2014; McWayne, Hampton, Fantuzzo, Cohen, & Sekino, 2004). When parents and educators establish positive partnerships to support children's development and learning, this benefits child outcomes (Loughran, 2008; National Council for Curriculum and Assessment, 2009). One of the key findings on effective parental engagement is the fact that one-off or isolated events are ineffective and insufficient (Australian Research Alliance for Children and Youth (ARACY), 2015). Some robust longitudinal studies and meta-analyses have shown a strong relationship between parental engagement attitudes and behaviours and improved academic child outcomes (Jeynes, 2012). For example, parents engaging in shared reading with their children benefits children's language development directly (e.g. Bus, van IJzendoorn, & Pellegrini, 1995; Mol & Bus, 2011). However, at times the research is inconsistent due to different conceptualisations and measurements of parent engagement, as well as limitations to study design (ARACY, 2015). ARACY (2015) argues in their review of the research literature on parent engagement and child outcomes that co-design or co-creation with families is key to success and in order for family engagement to be effective, it requires a systemic, integrated and sustained approach. Both parents and educators are responsible for a successful home–ECEC collaboration and effective communication between the two parties is key to enhance children's development and learning (Christenson & Sheridan, 2000; Edwards, Sheridan, & Knoche, 2008).

Recent changes in Dutch ECEC policies on parent engagement and educator requirements and its implications

In 2014, the organisation responsible for inspecting the quality among early childhood education and care in the Netherlands increased the number of requirements regarding parents and parental engagement. Despite the increased focus on parents and their engagement, many Dutch ECECs showed a decrease in quality in this area. Most of the deficits centred around the following aspects: (1) absence of parental committee, (2) procedure for complaints is not written down, (3) procedure for complaints is not made known to parents and (4) possibility of putting disputes in front of a dispute committee (Inspectorate of Education, 2017). Many of these deficits are due to the fact that the Law has changed to strengthen the position of parents in early childhood care and education.

A report by the Dutch Working Group on Early Childhood Education and Care (Working Group ECEC) (2014) provided key principles for a quality framework within ECEC that includes parent engagement. As families are characterised by social, socioeconomic, cultural and religious diversity, this diversity should be respected as a fundamental element of European societies (Working Group ECEC, 2014). Families should be fully involved in each aspect of their child's care and education. Therefore, Dutch ECECs should be designed in partnership with families and based on mutual respect and trust (Working Group ECEC, 2014). This includes providing support for parents and educators where needed in terms of child care and development, as well as family needs (Working Group ECEC, 2014).

Recently the quality requirements in the Dutch law on child care have changed. Most of these changes are related to the number of children per educator. For example, where currently one educator would care for four infants, this number will be reduced to one educator for three infants. Another change affects the language level of the educator. Starting in 2019, all educators, even casuals, need to be able to have the language level of someone who has finished high school and a vocational training (level 3 out of 4). Educators who currently score below this level will be provided with additional training. In each ECEC one educator will become the policy educator who provides coaching for other educators in their daily practices (Rijksoverheid, 2018). A review of the literature by Henrichs, Slot and Leseman (2016) on the impact of in-service training at ECECs in Western countries reported that there is very little research on the effectiveness of in-service training of Dutch educators to improve the quality of care. A recent Dutch randomised control trial in 33 ECECs, though, provided a consultancy programme for programme directors to improve quality of care (Helmerhorst, Fukking, Riksen-Walraven, Gevers Deynoot-Schaub, & Tavecchio, 2017). The researchers trained the programme director in assessing and improving the quality of educator–child conversations. The programme was successful in improving quality in those areas specifically targeted. This study offers opportunities to evaluate and improve quality of care through in-service training or consultancy.

At this point it is unclear if the extra professional development required of educators includes a focus on parent engagement, as this is the key to a healthy development of each child enrolled in an ECEC. Preservice training and professional development for educators should put more emphasis on how to engage and maintain parental engagement with the primary focus on the child's well-being and development. Although educators have known for years that it is important to engage parents, one of the primary barriers identified to effective home–ECEC partnerships is the preparation of educators with concrete knowledge, skills, as well as positive attitudes about parental involvement (Broussard, 2000). Preservice educators often come to their training with preconceived notions, not only about teaching but also about working with parents. Preservice educators often think about interactions with parents in terms of parent–educator conferences, having parent volunteers, or communicating with parents through letters or email (Kim & Taylor, 2016). Baum and McMurray-Schwarz (2004) found that many pre-service educators had the perception that conflict and criticism would be a characteristic of their relationships with parents. Preservice educators also tended to have fairly stereotypical notions of power of gender and social class with parents who did not speak English as a primary language and those living in poverty being less involved (Graue & Brown, 2003). Although very little research exists in this area in the Netherlands, the same perceptions as reported by Graue and Brown (2003) could possibly be attributed to Dutch (pre-service) educators as well, as the public debate and social policies have been dominated for years about concerns regarding non-Western immigrants in the Netherlands. The immigrants were, and still are, often perceived as not being employed, depending on the state for benefits and as being from a cultural background that is incompatible with Dutch norms and values (Schinkel, 2007, 2010). The segregation of ethnic groups and classes, as well as the policies to prevent integration, add to potential preconceived notions of (pre-service) educators (Veldboer, Duyvendak, & Bouw, 2007; Veldboer, Kleinhans, & Duyvendak, 2002). It is not easy to address these issues but the proposed changes could have the potential to increase educators' skills in engaging parents of different socioeconomic, linguistic and cultural backgrounds, as the shared goal of educators and parents is the development and wellbeing of the child.

Different ways of family engagement with ECECs

There are many ways families can engage with their child's early childhood programme, for example through targeted initiatives that focus on particular areas such as literacy (Maureen, Miller, Richardson, & Sacks, 2015) or maths (Klein, Starkey, Clements, Sarama, & Iyer, 2008). It is important for families to participate in their children's education as this can promote cognitive and emotional resilience, in particular in stressful circumstances such as poverty or growing up in a neighbourhood with few resources (Halgunseth, Peterson, Stark, & Moodle, 2008; Waanders, Mendez, & Downer, 2007). Other ways of connecting with families can be through parent education to develop specific parenting strategies (Hallam et al., 2016; McIntyre & Phaneuf, 2008).

Home visits are another option for early childhood programmes to connect with families and actively work together around the child's development. Home visits can either be stand-alone programmes or an additional component of an existing centre-based programme. Home visits offer a unique opportunity for early childhood programmes to build relationships with parents and their young children as they can be tailored towards individual family needs. This can be particularly helpful for vulnerable families whose children might be at risk for developmental or educational delays (Hallam et al., 2016). Home visits are often overlooked within the field of education but have shown promising results for both children and families within public health and early childhood mental health (e.g. Biluka et al., 2005; Filene, Kaminski, Valle, & Cachat, 2013). Home visits offer a unique way for parents and early childhood educators to interact.

Home visits can be an additional part of an existing centre-based programme or function as a stand-alone programme. The benefits of home visits include the unique opportunity to build relationships and deliver services at an individual level. This might be particularly helpful for high-risk parents or caregivers. Research has suggested that the overall structure of home-visiting programmes may increase family engagement due to the features that make accessing the services easier for higher-risk parents (Ammerman et al., 2005; Hallam et al., 2016). The general structure of a home-visiting programme makes accessing services or connecting with early childhood programmes easier. This applies in particular to higher-risk parents, as they do not need to travel or have to make arrangements for care of siblings. Parents might feel more comfortable at home and a home visit offers a great opportunity for early childhood teachers to get a better sense of the child's family and their environment (Hallam et al., 2016). Home visits should be considered a strategy for creating a personalised setting for building relationships and offering services. Home visits could also create a unique opportunity for educators to learn about different families, their values and beliefs. However, Gomby (2005) warned that home visits should not be used as a complete intervention in itself. Conducting just home visits does not automatically equate to having an early childhood programme's goals met (Hallam et al., 2016). There have been mixed results on the effectiveness of home-visiting programmes (e.g. Filene et al., 2013; Goyal, Teeters, & Ammerman, 2013). Researchers including Daro (2006), Hallam et al. (2016) and Segal, Opie, & Salziel (2012) argued that most home-visiting programmes do in fact contribute to better engagement and improved outcomes, but there are often issues around research design and methodology, as well as differing expectations regarding what 'meaningful change' looks like.

Home visits are not common for families with a child enrolled in a Dutch ECEC.

Some intervention programmes for disadvantaged families include a home-based programme that sometimes includes a home visit. However, these programmes are targeted at disadvantaged families who are less likely to use any type of child care in the Netherlands due to a variety of factors. Child care subsidies, for example, are primarily for families where both parents work. Disadvantaged families are more likely to use playgroups and preschools as they tend to be cheaper and often fit better with parents' childrearing beliefs and values as they will have a free non-authoritarian pedagogical climate (Leseman & De Winter, 2013). However, Dutch ECECs could consider making home visits a part of ECECs, in particular when families are less likely to engage with educators due to linguistic or cultural barriers.

Opportunities for parental engagement

Engaging parents offers the opportunity for educators to communicate with them about their views on education and child development and connect the home environment with the ECEC (Ligtermoet & Zwetsloot, 2000). This is very important for children as it gives them a feeling of safety, forming the basis for their development. Engaging parents and communicating with them offers far more in children's interest such as promoting child friendships, confidence, social interaction and support for parents. It also assists educators in providing practical support and information as well enhances quality for the ECEC (Ligtermoet & Zwetsloot, 2000).

Individual and informal exchange of information about practical issues between parents and educators is often unproblematic. This frequently occurs when parents drop off or pick up their children or when they have parent meetings. Formal contact with parents as a group is often organised in parental committees in the Netherlands, which either function or not (Ligtermoet & Zwetsloot, 2000). However, there are numerous missed opportunities to connect the child's home environment with the ECEC and to discuss parents' views on their child's development and education and talk about norms and values (Ligtermoet & Zwetsloot, 2000). Ligtermoet & Zwetsloot (2000) argued that what is important in the first place are the opportunities to connect and educationally adjust the individual contact between parents and educators. In the second place, it is about the contact between educators and parents as a group as an ECEC can be considered a small community (Ligtermoet & Zwetsloot, 2000) When considering the ECEC as a small community, there is more interaction and a broader pedagogical adjustment if more parents are engaged. This benefits the community of the ECEC.

It is possible to encourage educators to create opportunities for connections, pedagogical adjustment and other issues important for children's development and wellbeing (Van Dijke & Terpstra, 1998). Educators show more self-confidence, respect, openness and equality towards parents and engage with one another about pedagogical issues. This benefits open communication with parents and their colleagues. Van Dijke & Terpstra (1998) found in their pilot study of providing Dutch educators training in engaging parents that educators enjoyed communicating with parents, even when it was sometimes challenging. This offered more opportunities for pedagogical adjustments between parents and educators (Van Dijke & Terpstra, 1998). It is essential to have an alignment between the home environment and the ECEC to provide children with a sense of safety and help promote their development (Ligtermoet & Zwetsloot, 2000). For example, when educators respond entirely differently to a child than his/her parent, the child will be less likely to attach itself to the educator and can develop a sense of insecure attachment. When parents and educators communicate and discuss children's education and the adjustment between home and ECEC, this sense of insecure attachment of the child to the educator can be prevented.

Many Dutch parents do not realise how large the impact of (high quality) ECECs is on child development and education. Allewijn (2009) reported that most Dutch parents find it important for their child to have a 'good day' at the ECEC and do not view an ECEC as a place for education or where children need to learn something. Dutch parents think children mostly learn social skills at ECECs and because the ECEC does not have a clear role in children's education, parents and educators usually only discuss educational issues when a problem arises (Allewijn, 2009). Possible explanations are the fact that parents often do not know what to expect as ECECs are relatively new in the Netherlands and most parents did not attend an ECEC themselves. Many educators tend to have low levels of education and often find it challenging to engage parents in discussion about child's education. This might make it more difficult to reach the alignment between home and ECEC. Most Dutch ECECs have an educational policy plan that offer good starting points for discussion between parents and educators.

Father engagement in early childhood

Engagement of fathers in children's early development and care has received increased interest from both researchers and practitioners (e.g. Lamb & Tamis-LeMonda, 2004). We know that when fathers are engaged with their young children, their children tend to have better language, cognitive and social skills (e.g. Pleck, 2010; Sarkadi, Kristiansson, Oberklaid, & Bremberg, 2008) Father engagement is as good a predictor for child development as mother's (e.g. Rohner & Veneziano, 2001). When children have the opportunity to develop secure attachments to multiple people, this benefits their development. More engagement, by mother and father, benefits children's development (Donkers & Hoogeveen, 2017). Men, women and children benefit when more men are engaged with children's development and education. Men also benefit when they spend more time with their children and women have more opportunities for employment when fathers and mothers share caring tasks more equally (Allen & Daly, 2007).

Mothers still spend considerably more time with their children than fathers. Different from most other Western countries, 61 per cent of all Dutch women in paid employment only work part-time (OECD, 2013). One reason for this in the Netherlands is the high percentage of women who work part time. Although the government has rolled out numerous schemes to increase the working female population, 75 per cent of employed women in the Netherlands work part time or less than 36 hours a week. For employed men, this percentage is only 14 per cent (Portegijs, Cloïn, Roodsaz, & Olsthoorn, 2016). Although men are more engaged with their children than before, a recent study by Donkers & Hoogeveen (2017) among 111 Dutch fathers reported that health care and education professionals do not engage men with their child's development and education. Although men were least positive about engagement by health professionals during pregnancy, only 60 per cent of fathers reported that early childhood educators found fathering important (Donkers & Hoogeveen, 2017). The authors recommend that ECECs specifically include fathers by, for example, changing the language they use: instead of using parents, they specifically mention fathers or male caregivers. They also suggest to ask fathers about their specific wishes and needs and ask fathers to come up with their own ideas for activities as they will be more likely to engage (Donkers & Hoogeveen, 2017).

Enhancing parental engagement at Dutch ECECs

The Dutch organisation for parents with children enrolled in ECECs, Belangen Vereniging van Ouders in de Kinderopvang (BOINK), provides advice on how ECEC parent committees can improve parental engagement (BOINK, 2011). When parents and educators in the Netherlands frequently exchanged information, it had a positive effect on their communication, and it improved children's wellbeing at the ECEC (Riksen-Walraven, 2000). It could be expected that when parents and educators engage at a deeper level on the development of children, this would benefit children as both parents and educators can promote children's education and development in more specific ways, which might be particularly useful for Dutch ECECs as they tend to focus on social skills (BOINK, 2011). Riksen-Walraven (2004) identified four components of pedagogical quality within (Dutch) ECECs: (1) Maintain physical and emotional safety, (2) contribute to child's personal competency, (3) contribute to child's social competency and (4) transmit norms and values. These four components frame the pedagogical principles for the Dutch law on ECECs (BOINK, 2011). ECECs in the Netherlands decide themselves how they translate these principles into practice and in their own pedagogical plan. This plan can be converted into a pedagogical policy that explains and illustrates how these four aforementioned goals can be achieved (BOINK, 2011; Riksen-Walraven, 2004). The pedagogical policy will frequently be adapted to specific ECECs in case they have multiple locations into an ECEC-specific working plan. This plan includes topics such as daily schedule, policy on outdoor play or how to deal with difficult child behaviours. Everything described in this pedagogical policy- and workplan can be traced back to Riksen-Walraven's four components of quality (BOINK, 2011).

It is important for children's development and wellbeing that educators show warmth, are engaged and provide individual attention (e.g. Burchinal, 2017). These are skills related to social interaction. Many parents in the Netherlands find this is a difficult skill to evaluate as it requires pedagogical knowledge (BOINK, 2011). Most parents lack this knowledge, although they usually have an intuition about whether an educator can provide adequate comfort when a child is upset. However, to gauge these social interaction skills and to discuss for example, a lack of these skills with the educator can be challenging. However, there are external means available in the Netherlands to observe interactions and to train educators, for example, video feedback (BOINK, 2011). A Dutch ECEC parent committee can review the pedagogical work plan of the ECEC to see if there is enough practical information but also look at whether the primary pedagogical goals of Riksen-Walraven (2004) can be found in the document. Parents can then discuss if there are things missing or can be improved and put this down in an action plan.

Standards for parental engagement in the Netherlands

Parental engagement in the Netherlands can take different levels according to de Vries (2017): At the first level, ECECs send primarily information to parents and educators decide on the content, the form and the moment. At the second level, ECECs send information and parents can send information back. However, there is no real collaboration between parents and educators. At the third level, ECECs and parents share and look for new information together with the goal of promoting child development. At this level it is not just about informing one another but collaborating (de Vries, 2017). This third level of parental engagement is based on self-determination theory (Deci & Ryan, 1985). Self-determination theory argues that people become motivated and empowered when the following three basic needs are met:

1   autonomy or being able to make choices;
2   relationship or attachment;
3   competency.

These basic needs are valid for both educators and parents. Educators want to be good professionals, competent in their work. They value their autonomy and want to make their own professional choices. Finally, they are social oriented and value attachment. Dutch parents want to be autonomous in their child's education and have the feeling that they can educate without too much external support and make the right choices in terms of distribution of work and care. They also want their child to do well as a result of being competent educators. Finally, they want to experience the attachment with the ECEC of their child (de Vries, 2017).

The American Parent Teacher Organisation, which brings together parents and teachers, maintains six standards. The six standards are, in collaboration with the Parent Teacher Association, translated and adapted for the Dutch situation into ten standards (de Vries, 2016). The standards are based for a large part on the work of Epstein (2001), which has demonstrated that parental engagement benefits children's achievement (e.g. Van Voorhis, Maier, Epstein, & Lloyd, 2013). These criteria offer ECECs the foundation to develop a healthy collaboration with parents. The ten criteria of effective parental engagement in ECECs are as follows (de Vries, 2017):

1   The ECEC has developed a clear view on collaboration, together with parents. The information which ECECs provide to parents shows that the ECEC finds it important to collaborate with parents. The importance of parental engagement is also visible in educators' behaviour. For example, at the ECEC it is clear from the start how parents can communicate with educators when something is not right.

2   The ECEC shows that educators and parents are both actively engaged with the policy of the ECEC. For example, by having panel discussions with parents or brainstorming between educators and parents about certain themes. Educators and parents know what will happen with their input. When there is an important change, the ECEC staff will ask several parents to think along with them.

3   It is obvious at the ECEC that educators, children and their parents are always welcome. For example, educators know parents' names.

4   Parents and educators continuously collaborate to establish a healthy development of the child by using play, at home and at the ECEC. Educators always check with parents about their child's development, as they basically co-parent with the parents.

5   Conversations between educators and parents are based on equality as each can actively contribute to the conversation. The locations of where the conversations take place are comfortable and equal for everyone and there is ample of time for all participants. For example, the ECEC has a special space for discussions with parents and educators.

6   Educators and parents feel responsible for each other and their children and they can address this when needed. They speak respectfully about one another within and outside the ECEC. It can be important for parents to

know each other as well and ECECs might organise meetings for parents. ECECs demonstrate in this way that they are more than an organisation that looks after children but that they are a community where children come together and parents are part of this.

7   The child's file is accessible for educators and parents. Parents are invited to contribute information to the file. For example, when children access special services outside the ECEC, parents can provide this information to the ECEC.

8   The ECEC is open to improvements and their way of dealing with complaints is transparent. Everyone can see what the official complaints are and what happens with these complaints, taking privacy rules into consideration. ECECs are open to parental suggestions and will inform you of what they do with it, even when they decide not to act upon it.

9   Parents are present at the starting conversations and at other agreed contact moments. It is clear at these moments for both educators and parents when they are expected to be present and why. For example, parents agree with the educators how they keep in touch with one another for the rest of the year.

10 Laws and rules are made clearly and actively by the ECEC and abided by everyone.

For example, it is important that adults provide a good example for parents. When parents take their children to the ECEC, they do not use their phone while driving.

These criteria can be used as a checklist for Dutch ECECs to evaluate whether the collaboration with parents is sufficient or can be improved. It is recommended to fill out the checklist with a number of parents in order to address the needs and requirements of both sides.

Conclusion

Parental engagement is an essential component when children participate in ECECs. Parent engagement can take different forms but is most successful when both educators and parents take an active approach towards informing and supporting one another in order to promote the child's development. More systematic research is needed on the current state of parent engagement in Dutch ECECs as little research has been done in this area. We also need more information on pre-service and professional development training around parent engagement and best practices. When the ECEC is viewed as a community where children bring educators and parents together, it is easier to engage parents around their children, but also around other parents. This benefits the entire community of families and educators. The government needs to play an active role in assuring that quality in ECECs also includes parent engagement and the association to child outcomes.

Future directions

Recent child care policy changes in the Netherlands are aimed at increasing the quality of care in the country. As child care in its current form is a relatively new phenomenon for Dutch parents, it is important to educate parents about the benefits of high-quality child care on child development. This will require a shift in thinking on both parents' and educators' parts from ECECs being basically childminding facilities to communities of high-quality care benefiting child development. The recent policy changes require ECECs to engage parents more directly and offer opportunities for parents and educators to work more closely in creating these communities of care. It will be important to evaluate the effectiveness of the policy changes and whether there is an increase in parental engagement benefiting children's development.

The new language requirements for educators are aimed at increasing the quality of care as well. Hopefully this requirement will encourage the debate on the relationship between educators' level of education and quality of care and will ask policy makers, researchers, educators and others whether changes are needed in terms of educator training requirements. The language requirement could also positively benefit parental engagement as educators might be better equipped to directly involve parents in the shared care of their child. If the government invests in providing additional training for educators, as well as evaluating the effectiveness of the policy changes, we will be able to examine if the quality of care improves, as well as the engagement with parents increases as well.

References

Allen, S. M., & Daly, K. J. (2007). The Effects of Father Involvement: An Updated Research Summary of the Evidence. Centre for Families, Work & Well-being, University of Guelph.

Allewijn, E (2009). *Gedeelde opvoeding op het kinderdagverblijf? Een onderzoek naar de samenwerking en afstemming tussen ouders en pedagogisch medewerkers* [Shared educating at the early childhood and education centre? An examination of the collaboration and alignment between parents and early childhood educators]. Leuven: Katholieke Universiteit Leuven (proefschrift).

Ammerman, R. T., Putnam, F. W., Stevens, J., Holleb, L. J., Novak, A. L., & Van Ginkel, J. B. (2005). In-home cognitive behaviour therapy for depression: An adapted treatment for first-time mothers in home visitation. *Best Practices in Mental Health, 1,* 1–14. doi:10.1177/1534650106286533.

Australian Research Alliance for Children and Youth (ARACY). (2015). Progressing parental engagement in the ACT: Our evidence base measuring parental engagement. Retrieved from www.det.act.gov.au/__data/assets/pdf_file/0006/811878/150900_EATD-Technical-Report_text_rev2-2.pdf.

Baum, A., & McMurray-Schwarz, P. (2004). Preservice teachers' beliefs about family involvement: Implications for teacher education. *Early Childhood Education Journal, 32*(1), 57–61.

Biluka, O., Hahn, R. A., Crosby, A., Fullilove, M. T., Liberman, A., Moscicki, E., & Task Force on Community Preventive Services (2005). The effectiveness of early childhood home visitation in preventing violence: A systematic review. *American Journal of Preventative Medicine, 28*, 11–39.

Belangen Vereniging van Ouders in de Kinderopvang (BOINK). (2011). *Opvoeden op het kinderdagverblijf voor oudercommissies* [Organisation for interests of parents in early childhood education]. Retrieved from www.boink.info/cms/streambin.aspx?documentid=67.

Bronfenbrenner, U. (2005). *Making Human Beings Human: Bioecological Perspectives on Human Development.* Thousand Oaks, CA: Sage.

Broussard, C. (2000). Preparing teachers to work with families: A national survey of teacher education programs. *Equity & Excellence in Education, 33*(2), 41–49. doi:10.1080/1066568000330207.

Burchinal, M. (2017). Measuring early care and education quality. *Child Development Perspectives, 12*(1), 3–9. doi:10.1111/cdep.12260.

Bus, A. G., Van IJzendoorn, M. H., & Pellegrini, A. D. (1995). Joint book reading makes for success in learning to read: A meta-analysis on intergenerational transmission of literacy. *Review of Educational Research, 65*(1), 1–21.

Cabrera, N., Shannon, J., & Tamis-LeMonda, C. (2007). Fathers' influence on their children's cognitive and emotional development: From toddlers to pre-K. *Applied Developmental Science, 11*(4), 208–213. doi:10.1080/10888690701762100.

Christenson, S. L., & Sheridan, S. M. (2001). *School and Families: Creating Essential Connections for Learning.* New York: Guilford Press.

Daro, D. (2006). *Home Visitation: Assessing Progress, Managing Expectations.* Chicago, IL: Ounce of Prevention Fund and Chapin Hall Center for Children. Retrieved from www.theounce.org/pubs/HomeVisitation.pdf.

Deci, E. L., & Ryan, R. M. (1985). *Intrinsic Motivation and Self-determination in Human Behavior.* Berlin: Springer.

de Vries, P. (2017). *Samenwerking tussen kinderopvang en ouders. Kennisdossier kinderopvang BKK* [Collaboration between early childhood education centres and parents. Knowledge File]. Bureau Kwaliteit Kinderopvang. Retrieved from www.stichtingbkk. nl/images/Kennisdossier_BKK_201703_LR.pdf.

Donkers, E., & Hoogeveen, K. (2017). Wat wil de man? Ervaringen van mannen met vaderbetrokkenheid [What does the man want?)]. *De stem van ouders voor succesvolle samenwerking, 22*, 13–17.

Edwards, C. P., Sheridan, S. M., & Knoche, L. (2008). Parent engagement and school readiness: Parent-child relationships in early learning. Faculty Publications, Department of Child, Youth, and Family Studies, 60. Retrieved from http://digitalcommons.unl. edu/famconfacpub/60.

Epstein, J. (2001). *School, Family, and Community Partnership: Preparing Educators and Improving Schools.* Boulder, CO: Westview.

Filene, J. H., Kaminski, J. W., Valle, L. A., & Cachat, P. (2013). Components associated with home visiting program outcomes: A meta-analysis. *Pediatrics, 132*(Suppl 2), 100–109. doi:10.1542/peds.2013-1021H.

Gomby, D. (2005). *Home Visitation in 2005: Outcomes for Children and Parents.* Washington, DC: Committee for Economic Development: Invest in Kids Working Group.

Goyal, N. K., Teeters, A., & Ammerman, R. T. (2013). Home visiting and outcomes of preterm infants: A systematic review. *Pediatrics, 132*, 502–516. doi:10.1542/ peds.2013-0077.

Graue, E., & Brown, C. (2003). Preservice teachers' notions of families and schooling. *Teaching and Teacher Education, 19*(7), 719–735. doi:10.1016/j.tate.2003.06.002.

Halgunseth, L. (2009). Family engagement, diverse families, and early childhood education programs: An integrated review of the literature. *Young Children, 64*(5), 56–58.

Halgunseth, L., Peterson, A., Stark, D. R., & Moodle, S. (2008). *Family Engagement, Diverse Families, and Early Childhood Education Programs: An Integrated Review of the Literature.* Washington, DC: NAEYC and Pre-K Now. Retrieved from www.naeyc.org/files/naeyc/file/ecprofessional/EDF_Literature%20Review.pdf.

Hallam, R. A., Han, M., Vu, J., & Hustedt, J. T. (2016). Meaningful family engagement in early care and education programs: The role of home visits in promoting positive parent-child interactions. In J. A. Sutterby (Ed.), *Family Involvement in Early Education and Child Care* (Advances in Early Education and Day Care, Vol, 20) (pp. 51–66). Bingley: Emerald Group Publishing.

Helmerhorst, K. O. W., Fukking, R. G., Riksen-Walraven, M. A., Gevers Deynoot-Schaub, M. J. J. M., & Tavecchio, L. W. C. (2017). Improving quality of the child care environment through a consultancy programme for centre directors. *International Journal of Early Years Education, 25*(4), 361–378.

Henrichs, L. F., Slot, & Leseman, P. P. M. (2016). *Professionale ontwikkeling in voorschoolse voorzieningen. Een literatuurstudie naar doeltreffende professionaliserings-vormen- en activiteiten* [Professional development in preschool services. A literature review of effective professionalism practices and activities]. Universiteit Utrecht, the Netherlands. Retrieved from https://dspace.library.uu.nl/handle/1874/342310.

Inspectorate of Education. (2017). Toezicht en handhaving kinderopvang. Landelijke rapportage 2016 [Supervision and enforcement of early child care and education. Nationwide report 2016]. Utrecht, The Netherlands. Retrieved from www.onderwijsinspectie.nl/documenten/rapporten/2018/04/06/toezicht-en-handhaving-kinderopvang-landelijke-rapportage-2016.

Jeynes, W. (2012). A meta-analysis of the efficacy of different types of parental involvement programs for urban students. *Urban Education, 47*(4), 706–742. doi:10.1177/0042085912445643.

Kim, K. J., & Taylor, L. K. (2016). Preservice teachers' self-efficacy in working with families: can an immersive course make a difference? In J. A. Sutterby (Ed.), *Family Involvement in Early Education and Care* (Advances in Early Education and Day Care, vol. 20) (pp. 1–22). Bingley: Emerald Group Publishing.

Klein, A., Starkey, P., Clements, D., Sarama, J., & Iyer, R. (2008). Effects of a pre-kindergarten mathematics intervention: A randomized experiment. *Journal of Research on Educational Effectiveness, 1*(3), 155–178.

Lang, S. N., Schoppe-Sullivan, S. J., Kotila, L. E., Feng, X., Dush, C. M., & Johnson, S. C. (2014). Relations between fathers' and mothers' infant engagement patterns in dual-earner families and toddler competence. *Journal of Family Issues, 35*(8), 1107–1127. doi: 10.1177/0192513X14522243.

Lamb, M. E., & Tamis-LeMonda, C. S. (2004). The role of the father: An introduction. In M. Lamb (Ed.), *The Role of the Father in Child Development* (4th edn) (pp. 1–31). New York: Wiley.

Leseman, P. P. M., & De Winter, M. (2013). Early childhood services and family support in the Netherlands. In V. Barnekow, B. B. Jensen, C. Currie, A. Dyson, N. Eisenstadt & E. Melhuish (Eds.), *Improving the Lives of Children and Young People: Case Studies from Europe* (Volume 1: Early Childhood) (pp. 15–31). Copenhagen, Denmark: World Health Organisation.

Ligtermoet, I., & Zwetsloot, L. (2000). *Ouders betrekken bij kindercentra. Het kan!* [Engaging parents in early childhood education. It is possible!]. Nederlands Instituut voor Zorg en Welzijn/NIZW. Utrecht: The Netherlands.

Loughran, S. B. (2008). The importance of teacher/parent partnerships: Preparing pre-service and in-service teachers. *Journal of College Teaching & Learning, 5*(8), 35–38. http://dx.doi.org/10.14221/ajte.2016v41n11.4.

Maureen, M. V., Miller, M. B., Richardson, J. A., & Sacks, M. K. (2015). Literacy bags to encourage family involvement. *Reading Improvement*, 52(3), 131–136.

McIntyre, L. L., & Phaneuf, L. K. (2008). A three-tier model of parent education in early childhood. *Topics in Early Childhood Special Education*, 27(4), 214–222. https://doi-org.ezproxy.uow.edu.au/10.1177/0271121407311239.

McWayne, C., Hampton, V., Fantuzzo, J., Cohen, H. L., & Sekino, Y. (2004). A multivariate examination of parent involvement and the social and academic competencies of urban kindergarten children. *Psychology in the Schools*, 41, 363–377. doi:10.1002/pits.10163.

Mol, S. E., & Bus, A. G. (2011). To read or not to read: A meta-analysis of print exposure from infancy to early adulthood. *Psychological Bulletin*, 137(2), 267–96. doi:10.1037/a0021890.

National Council for Curriculum and Assessment. (2009). Building partnerships between parents and practitioners. Retrieved from www.ncca.biz/Aistear/pdfs/Guidelines_ENG/Practitioners_ENG.pdf.

OECD (2013). OECD employment outlook 2013. Retrieved from https://doi-org. ezproxy.uow.edu.au/10.1787/empl_outlook_2013_en.

Pleck, J. H. (2010). Paternal involvement: Revised conceptualization and theoretical linkages with child outcomes. In M. E. Lamb (Ed.), *The Role of the Father in Child Development* (5th edn) (pp. 67–107). New York: Wiley.

Portegijs, W., Cloïn, M., Roodsaz, R., & Olsthoorn, M. (2016). *Lekker vrij!? Vrije tijd, tijdsdruk en de relatie met de arbeidsduur van vrouwen* [Time off? Leisure time, time pressure and the association with women's working time]. The Hague: Sociaal en cultureel planbureau/Atria, Kenniscentrum voor emancipatie en vrouwengeschiedenis.

Rijksoverheid (2018). Overzicht maatregelen IKK 2019 en 2023. Retrieved from www. veranderingenkinderopvang.nl/documenten/publicaties/2018/05/15/overzicht-maatregelen-ikk-2019-en-2023.

Riksen-Walraven, M. (2000). *Tijd voor kwaliteit in de kinderopvang* [Time for quality in early childhood education and care]. Amsterdam: Vossiuspers AUP (Oratie).

Riksen-Walraven, M. (2004). Pedagogische kwaliteit in de kinderopvang: doelstelingen en kwaliteitscriteria [Educational quality in early childhood centres: targets and criteria of quality]. In R. van IJzendoorn, L. Tavecchio, & M. Riksen-Walraven (Eds.), *De kwaliteit van de Nederlandse kinderopvang* [The quality of Dutch early childhood education] (pp. 100–123). Amsterdam: Boom.

Rohner, R. P., & Veneziano, R. A. (2001). The importance of father love: History and contemporary evidence. *Review of General Psychology*, 5(4), 382–405. 10.1037/1089-2680.5.4.382.

Sarkadi, A., Kristiansson, R., Oberklaid, F., & Bremberg, S. (2008). Fathers' involvement and children's developmental outcomes: A systematic review of longitudinal studies. *Acta Pædiatrica*, 97(2),153–158.

Schinkel, W. (2007). *Denken in een tijd van sociale hypochondrie. Aanzet tot een theorie voorbij de maatschappij* [Reflecting in times of social hypochondria: Approach to a theory past society]. Kampen, The Netherlands: Klement.

Schinkel, W. (2010). The virtualiziation of citizenship. *Critical Sociology*, 36(2), 265–283. doi:10.1177/0896920509357506.

Schulting, A. B., Malone, P. S., & Dodge, K. A. (2005). The effect of school-based kindergarten transition policies and practices on child academic outcomes. *Developmental Psychology*, 41(6), 860–871. doi:10.1037/0012-1649.41.6.860.

Segal, L., Opie, R. S., & Salziel, K. (2012). Theory! The missing link in understanding the performance of neonate/infant home-visiting programs to prevent child maltreatment:

A systematic review. *The Millbank Quarterly, 90*(1), 47–106. doi:10.1111/j.1468-0009.2011.00655.x.

Shonkoff, J. P., & Philips, D. A. (2000). *From Neurons to Neighborhoods: The Science of Early Child Development*. Washington, DC: National Academy Press.

Smit, F., Driessen, G., & de Wit, C. (2009). *Stappenplan optimalisering ouderbetrokkenheid in de Voor- en Vroegschoolse Educatie* [Roadmap to optimise parental engagement in early childhood education]. ITS, Radboud University Nijmegen.

Van Dijke, A., & Terpstra, L. (1998). *Pedagogische vernieuwen. Een kader voor pedagogische vernieuwing voor groepsopvang in kindercentra* [Educational revival. A framework for educational revival for centre-based care in early childhood education centres]. Utrecht: NIZW.

Van Voorhis, F. L., Maier, M., Epstein, J. L., & Lloyd, C. M. (2013). *The Impact of Family Involvement on the Education of Children Ages 3 to 8: A Focus on Literacy and Math Achievement Outcomes and Social-emotional Skills*. New York: MDRC.

Veldboer, L., Duyvendak, J. W., & Bouw, C. (Eds.). (2007). *The Mixfactor. Integratie of segregatie in Nederland* [The mixfactor. Integration or segregation in the Netherlands]. Amsterdam: Boom.

Veldboer, L., Kleinhans, R., & Duyvendak, J. W. (2002). The diversified neighbourhood in Western Europe and the United States: How do countries deal with the spatial distribution of economic and cultural differences? *Journal of International Migration and Integration, 3*(1): 41–64. doi:10.1007/s12134-002-1002-y.

Waanders, C., Mendez, J., & Downer, J. (2007). Parent characteristics, economic stress, and neighbourhood context as predictors of parent involvement in preschool children's education. *Journal of School Psychology, 45*(6), 619–636.

Working Group on Early Childhood Education and Care under the Auspices of the European Commission (Working Group ECEC). (2014). Proposal for key principles of a quality framework for early childhood education and care. Retrieved from http://ec.europa.eu/assets/eac/education/experts-groups/2011-2013/ecec/ecec-quality-framework_en.pdf.

20 A critical review of early childhood education and social policies in Turkey

Şenil Ünlü Çetin

Introduction

In Turkey, the early childhood education system serves for four major aims: (1) supporting children's physical, mental and emotional development and helping them to have good habits; (2) preparing children for primary education; (3) providing equality for children coming from disadvantaged environments and families; (4) helping children to speak Turkish appropriately (Milli Eğitim Bakanlığı (MEB), 2015). In other words, in the Turkish education system, early childhood education (ECE) primarily aims to meet children's developmental and educational needs. To reach these aims, ECE falls under the responsibility of the MEB and the Ministry of Family and Social Policies (ASPB) in Turkey. According to the MEB Directive for Early Childhood and Primary Education Centers (MEB, 2014), ECE consists of education services provided to children between the ages of 36 and 66 months. This refers to the fact that in Turkey ECE services are provided when the children reach their 36th month of age. Before this age, services provided for children are governed by the ASPB, and the centres that belong to this ministry are known as crèches or day care centres. In other words, the services provided to children under the age of 36 months are known as care giving services instead of education services. This is one of the most important problems in Turkey's early childhood care and education system and will be discussed later in this chapter. Those centres that belong to the MEB are classified as preschools, kindergarten classes and practice classes. Preschools provide services to children between the ages of 36 and 66 months in independent buildings, while kindergarten classes provide services to children between the ages of 48 and 66 months on primary school premises. Practice classes are for children between the ages of 36 and 66 months, and they are a unit of the department of child development in vocational high schools. Crèches are for children between the ages of 0 and 36 months, and day care centres are for children between the ages of 0 and 66 months. All these early childhood care and education centres have to use the national ECE programmes. There are two education programmes: one for children aged 0–36 months, and one for children aged 36–66 months. The MEB's ECE centres operate a dual education system. ECE is free in public (state-run) preschools. To work as a teacher in

ECE centres belonging to the MEB, one should have at least a four-year university degree. This is not the case for early childhood education and care (ECEC) centres belonging to the ASPB. In these centres, the teachers are required to have at least a vocational high-school diploma, while the administrative staff are required to have a four-year university degree.

Reports used for reference

The ECEC system in Turkey is developing, but still there are some important problematic issues. These are: (1) lack of ECEC services for children under the age of 36 months of age; (2) low schooling ratio for children between the ages of 36 and 66 months; (3) unequal opportunities for access to ECEC services; and (4) lack of information regarding quality and monitoring issues. I identified these problematic issues based on research conducted by important and well-known organisations and provide detailed information about all dimensions of the Turkish ECEC system. For this part, I used recently published governmental documents and reports. The first report used was 'The Supply and Demand Situation of Child Care Services in Turkey: A Mixed method Study'. This was a study conducted by the World Bank in 2015. The data for the research was collected from five different cities in Turkey: Denizli, Istanbul, Gaziantep, Eskişehir and Samsun. These cities were purposefully selected because they met two criteria: child care services and the level of women's participation in the labour force. Data for the study was gathered from 603 separate early ECEC services including preschools, kindergarten classes, preschools affiliated with the MEB but opened in a state organisation, private preschools, kindergarten classes in private schools etc. The supply part provided information on the characteristics of offered ECEC services such as the programme, registration, costs and fees, human resources, daily routines, parent involvement, regulations and standards, and characteristics of the programme's building, all of which were obtained through interviews with administrators and observations made by the researchers. The demand part obtained information from a total of 570 parents from the same five cities. Some of them filled in charts (371 parents, all mothers); the rest participated in focus group interviews (199 parents: 146 mothers and 73 fathers). This report clearly indicated the most problematic issues from the perspectives of both service providers and service users, i.e. parents.

The second report used was 'Dissemination and development of early childhood education in Turkey', a report prepared by the World Bank in 2013. This report investigated the situation of ECEC in Turkey and suggested solutions for the problems identified in the report. Another report used, 'Equal chance to each child: Situation and suggestion for Early Childhood Education in Turkey' was prepared collaboratively with the ERG (Education Reform Initiative) and the AÇEV (Mother and Child Education Foundation) in 2016. In this report, ECE in Turkey was critically evaluated in terms of availability and quality. Some calculations regarding the benefits of enrolment in ECE were presented, and social policy suggestions were given with the aim of highlighting the importance of each child participating in at least one year of quality ECE before commencing formal education, and bringing these issues to the surface. 'Participating in early childhood education and care in Turkey' was another report used. This report was prepared by the ERG and AÇEV in 2017 using the data from the Turkish Population and Health Survey 2013 (TPHS), carried out in order to examine the effects of socioeconomic variables on involvement in ECE. TPHS 2013 included 3220 mothers of children aged 0–5 years old, and 4363 children aged 0–5 years old. This research indicated how age and family characteristics influence children's enrolment in ECE and highlighted problematic issues suggesting certain social policies. The last report used was 'Situation of 0-6 years old children in Turkey: Information note'. This report was presented by AÇEV (2017) and, through a holistic approach, investigated the population, family characteristics, health and education services provided to children aged 0–6 years old as identified by the National Population Statistics published by the Turkish Statistics Agency in 2013 and MEB Educational Statistics (MEB, 2017).

MEB Educational Statistics will be used in addition to these reports. The statistics provided below are useful for understanding the current situation of ECEC and for evaluating the effectiveness of the social policies that will be presented in the next part. Recent statistics available are for the 2016–2017 academic year. These statistics are published by the MEB, so it can be said that they accurately depict the ECEC in the national education system.

Contents of the reports

The abovementioned reports and examination of national statistics indicated some major problematic issues concerning the current ECEC system in Turkey. These are: (1) the lack of ECEC services for children under the age of three years; (2) the low schooling ratio for children aged 36–66 months; (3) the lack of equal opportunities for access to ECEC services; (4) the lack of information about quality and monitoring issues. This part will provide detailed information on each issue. After each issue is presented it will be followed by a section called 'Related social policies applied in Turkey'. This part will provide information on how social policies affect that particular problematic issue.

Lack of ECEC services for children under the age of three years

Early childhood and education services provided for children aged 0–3 years old in Turkey fall under the responsibility of ASPB. Although there is not any clear information regarding the number of crèches and day care centres that provide services for children under the age of three years, in the report by the World Bank (2015) it was revealed that only 6 per cent of the capacity of existing services was assigned for children under the age of three years and that only

53.2 per cent of this capacity was used by parents. Similarly, the report by the ERG and AÇEV (2017) indicated that the percentage of ECEC services for children up to the age of three years that are actually used is less than 1 per cent in 2013 (there is no current information about enrolment in ECEC services by children aged 0–2 years old). When compared with the Organisation for Economic Co-operation and Development (OECD) average of 39 per cent for the schooling ratio of children at the age of two years, the situation in Turkey is a dire one. One of the main reasons for this problem is the lack of legislation obligating the state to provide education services for children under the age of three years. Another reason concerns demand. According to the report by the World Bank (2015), which investigated the supply and demand situation, the majority of participating parents said they preferred home-based care for children under the age of three years. In other words, almost all fathers and the majority of mothers reported that children under the age of three years should be cared for and taught by their mothers. This preference only changes when participants were asked 'What age is acceptable for enrolment in centre-based care if the mother is working and alternative care is not available (relative, caregiver or grandmother)?' The age mentioned by participating mothers dropped to one or two years. This means that parents only prefer centre-based care for children under the age of three years if the mother is working and there is no other option for child care (if available, most of the parents preferred grandmother care). The main reason for this low demand is the lack of quality ECEC services for this age group. All participants (working mothers, non-working mothers, fathers and mothers from villages) used more negative statements about ECEC services, i.e. the parent believed that centre-based services were not able to meet younger children's healthy social and emotional development and safety needs. Unfortunately, this trend also continues at the age of three years. Although mothers mostly accept three years as the beginning age (World Bank, 2015), the net schooling ratio for children aged three years is only 9 per cent, which is way below the OECD average of 78 per cent. Although it seems that there is equilibrium between supply and demand for early ECEC services, we know today that the period between the ages of 0 and three years is really important for all the child's developmental domains. Rich environments provided during this period really support healthy development. Participation in quality ECE as early as possible will result in better school readiness and greater academic achievement in the future (ERG & AÇEV, 2016). Also, it is widely known that there is a positive correlation between demand for ECEC services for younger children and mother enrolment in the labour force. In other words, having greater access to ECEC services for young children will improve the employment opportunities for women, which means a higher income and better life conditions for the whole family. According to TPHS (2013) data, 42.5 per cent of unemployed women who participated in the study stated that the main reason for their being unemployed was having a young child (ERG & AÇEV, 2017). Moreover, only 13 per cent of working mothers send their children to ECEC services, while the majority of working mothers (34.5 per cent) leave the children with their grandmothers. There are two main reasons for this issue: (1) centre-based child education and care opportunities are both limited and not affordable for parents and (2) existing available centres that provide services for children aged 0–36 are not preferred because of safety issues.

Related social policies applied in Turkey

Currently, there are no social policies that would increase the schooling ratio for children aged 0–36 months old. One possible reason for this situation can be widely observed societal perception, which gives priority to mother-care for the first three years. This reduces the demand for infant toddler education. Another possible reason might be the lack of physical and economical infrastructure. When providing infant and toddler education opportunities, for both young children and their families, there should be a strong economical investment which will lead to a better physical infrastructure. Unfortunately, a low budget is provided for education in general and for ECE in particular. Therefore, many social policies related to care of children aged 0–36 months focus on home-based and motherly care.

The first social policy applied is *Maternity leave*. This is provided only for mothers, and is one of the most commonly applied social policies. Mothers are entitled to a total of 16 weeks (eight weeks before and eight weeks after the birth) paid parental leave. To encourage breast-feeding, mothers who give birth have a right to receive 132 TL (€26.4) after the birth. This money is paid just once.

The second social policy is *Breast-feeding permission for the working mother*. In 2016, breast-feeding leave became an opportunity that was provided to working mothers. For civil servant mothers, nursing leave is three hours a day for the first six months following the end of maternity leave. For the second six months, time provided for mothers decreases to just half an hour a day. For mothers who are working in the private sector, nursing leave is half an hour a day during the first year after the birth. The mother is free to choose when she uses these hours. The third social policy applied is *Half-day working*. After the birth of a child, civil servant mothers have the right to work half a day. For the first child mothers can work half a day for two months; for the second child this period increases to four months and for subsequent births it becomes six months. Mothers who use this right cannot use nursing leave at the same time. This practice was carried out in 2016, as well. Another policy, *Salary for grandmother caring*, was applied in 2017. Grandmothers, paternal or maternal, who care for their 0–3-year-old grandchild are paid 425 TL (approximately €85) a month for a period of one year. This practice was carried out in ten pilot cities. Following the end of maternity leave, in order to help mothers return to work, the ASPB and the Social Security Agency (SGK) provide this money to grandmothers who provide for their grandchildren aged three years or under. This payment is not given to all grandmothers who provide care for their children since it is tied to certain conditions such as being a Turkish Republic citizen, not having health problems etc. Furthermore, parents whose monthly income is more than 4,212.18 TL (approximately €795.14) a month and who have a care giver for the child or who have a child older than three years of age cannot receive this help for the grandmother. This practice was launched in pilot cities in 2017. So far, there is not any information as to whether this payment will continue in following years or be expanded to other cities.

When we considered the benefits for the child, the mother and the whole family of engaging in quality ECEC services earlier, it has to be said that there ought to be social policies that tackle this problematic issue, and that those social policies should aim for the following: to provide more high-quality and affordable ECEC services for children aged between 0 and three years; to change social norms that prioritise home-based or maternal care for this age group; to increase awareness of the importance of the period between the ages of 0 and three years, and the benefits of quality ECEC services for this age group. In the report by the ERG and AÇEV (2017), it was suggested that there is a need for more advocacy activities and education for mothers in order to change the minds of parents who prefer maternal care up to the age of four years. Unfortunately, when we examined the abovementioned existing social policies we saw the exact opposite. In other words, the existing policies encourage home-based care, particularly maternal care, and no effort is being made to increase the schooling ratio of younger children by providing quality, centre-based services.

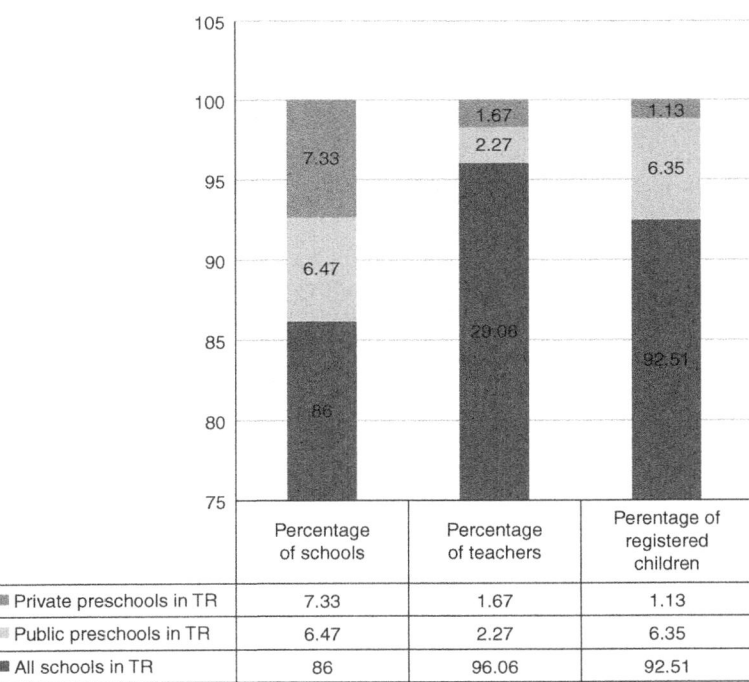

	Percentage of schools	Percentage of teachers	Perentage of registered children
■ Private preschools in TR	7.33	1.67	1.13
▨ Public preschools in TR	6.47	2.27	6.35
■ All schools in TR	86	96.06	92.51

Figure 20.1 Statistics of national education system vs national ECEC system.

Low schooling ratio for children aged 36–66 months old

In Turkey, the fundamental educational budget comes to 3.5 per cent of gross domestic product (GDP), which is lower than the rate in OECD countries (6 per cent), and lower than the Education Action Plan for 2030 (4.5 per cent, ERG & AÇEV, 2017). When budget distribution is examined, it is seen that ECE has the lowest budget. In Figure 20.1 it can be seen that in all domains (number of schools, classroom, teachers and registered children) the ECEC system makes up no more than 7.5 per cent of the whole education system. The majority of the ECEC services (83.8 per cent) are provided by state institutions and organisations (World Bank, 2015). The majority of state service providers

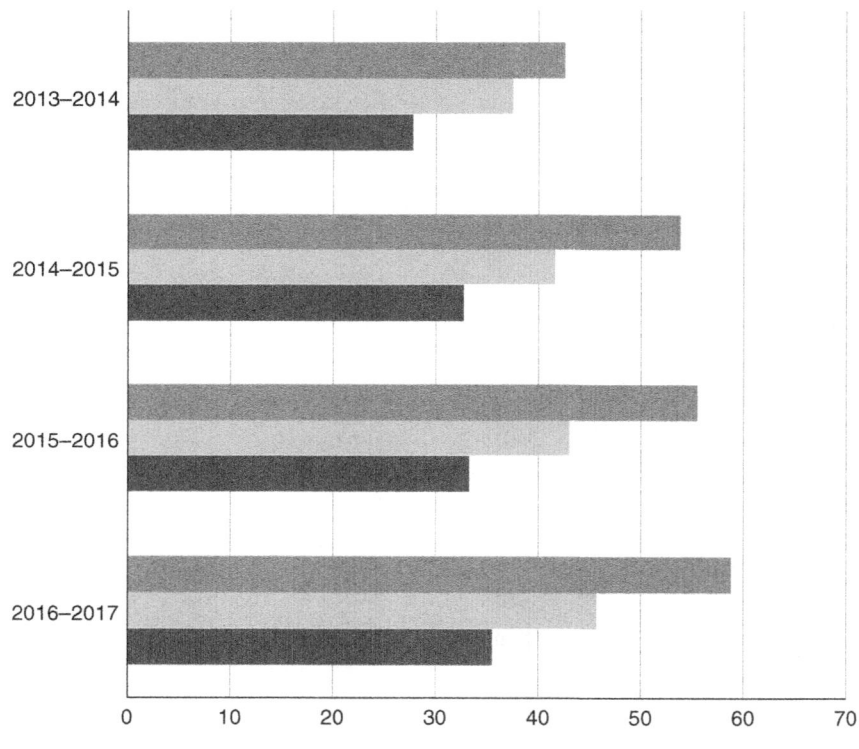

	2016–2017	2015–2016	2014–2015	2013–2014
Age 5	58.79	55.48	53.78	42.54
Age 4–5	45.7	42.96	41.57	37.46
Age 3–5	35.52	33.26	32.68	27.71

Figure 20.2 Schooling ratio by educational year and level of education.

are kindergarten classes, which provide services in primary school buildings. This means that enrolment rates for ECEC services in Turkey are higher for children aged four and five years.

Figure 20.2 shows the net schooling ratio for different age groups. As can be seen in the table, the net schooling ratio, which is calculated by comparing the number of registered children to the number of the total population for the same age group, shows that age of enrolment into the ECEC system is 36 months, and the highest registration in the ECEC system is seen at the age of five years, which is one year before formal school age. In other words, participation in ECEC services in Turkey begins at the age of 36 months and increases up to the age of 60 months. After the age of 60 months, ECEC enrolment begins to decrease and enrolment in formal education increases (ERG & AÇEV, 2017). Although Figure 20.2 indicates an increase in the net schooling ratio in the last five years, these rates are still way below than the average rates for OECD countries.

According to Education at a Glance report of the OECD (2016), the average schooling ratio for three years is 71 per cent; it is 86 per cent for four years and 95.19 per cent for five years. However, in Turkey these rates are 35.52 per cent, 45.7 per cent and 58.79 per cent, respectively. Similarly, according to the level of income per capita, the school ratio for ECEC should be higher than 60 per cent but it is only 35.52 per cent for children aged 3–5 years. According to World Bank (2015) research, the majority of available services in Turkey are for children aged five years old. According to TPHS-2013, 60 per cent of children between the ages of 36 and 71 months never used ECEC services; 25 per cent were enrolled in ECEC services and 15 per cent were registered at primary school (as cited in ERG & AÇEV, 2017).

The main reasons influencing the schooling ratio for children aged 36–66 are: expensive preschool fees, lack of preschool facilities in and around the neighbourhood (ERG & AÇEV, 2016), location of preschool facilities (ERG & AÇEV, 2016; World Bank, 2015), families' socioeconomic status (ERG & AÇEV, 2016, 2017; World Bank, 2015), mothers' educational level and working conditions (ERG & AÇEV, 2016, 2017; World Bank, 2015).

Related social policies applied in Turkey

ECE is one area that has been given priority over the past ten years. Over the period 2009–2010, the MEB prepared two main goals for the beginning of the 2014–2015 academic year: (1) 100 per cent schooling ratio for children aged 60–72 months and (2) reaching 50 per cent schooling ratio for children aged 36–72 months (World Bank, 2013). In order to achieve these goals, a scheme to provide 100 per cent access for children aged 60–72 months was launched in 32 pilot cities at the end of the 2008–2009 academic year. The number of cities involved in this pilot scheme was increased first to 57 and then to 71 in the following two academic periods (2010–2011 and 2011–2012). With this project ECEC services for the target group children were made totally free. Additionally, in 2010 MEB began its 'Strengthening of Early Childhood Education' project, which was funded by the European Union and United Nations International Children's Emergency Fund (UNICEF) in order to provide quality ECEC services for disadvantaged children and their families by developing community-based service models and partnerships in collaboration with state institutions, municipalities and non-governmental organisations (ERG & AÇEV, 2016).

As a result of these policies, the schooling ratio for five year olds increased to 65.7 per cent in the 2011–2012 academic year. This rate is the highest schooling ratio seen in the past ten years. Even today, after seven years, the net schooling ratio for this age group is 58.79 per cent. The main reason for this issue is the 4 + 4 + 4 educational system, which lowered the start age for compulsory formal education to 60 months. Due to the negative consequences this system has for children, parents and teachers, the start age for compulsory formal education can be 66 months with the decision of the family. Despite this regulation, since it is free, the majority of families continue to send their children to formal education (ERG & AÇEV, 2016). Today, all governmental strategic plans show that improving the schooling ratio for ECE has been included into the government's objectives. According to the MEB's Strategic Plan for 2015–2019, the goal is for 92 per cent of those children entering formal education to have had at least one year of ECE beforehand. Similarly, a 70 per cent net schooling ratio is the goal for children aged 4–5 years old. The strategies that the MEB plans to use in order to achieve these goals are: (1) diversifying the models of ECEC services and disseminating ECEC services for disadvantaged families and districts and (2) making regulations to decrease the cost of ECEC services for families. Similarly, making ECE obligatory is seen to be one of the objectives of the Ministry of Development's Medium-Term Program (2017–2019).

Unequal opportunities for access to ECEC services

Access to ECEC services is not equal for all children in Turkey. All the reports indicated a huge variation in the enrolment rates of children in ECEC services depending on their Socio-Economic Status (SES) and their residential area. In Turkey, cities are in a better position with respect to the provision of ECEC services. As can be seen in Figure 20.3, there is a huge discrepancy between cities and the villages in terms of the number of ECEC centres, teachers and registered children. This discrepancy is also observed between cities.

For instance, the net schooling ratio for children aged four years old is highest in Erzincan (58.29 per cent), Giresun (55 per cent) and Tokat (52.20 per cent), and lowest in Osmaniye (24.20 per cent), Gümüşhane (26,87 per cent) and Gaziantep (27.76 per cent). Similarly, the net schooling ratio for children aged five years old is highest in Kilis (100 per cent), Hatay (88.53 per cent) and Erzincan (87.46 per cent) and lowest in Gümüşhane (47.70 per cent), Bayburt (57.12 per cent) and Istanbul (58.89 per cent). This means that there is a 34.09 per cent difference between the highest and lowest

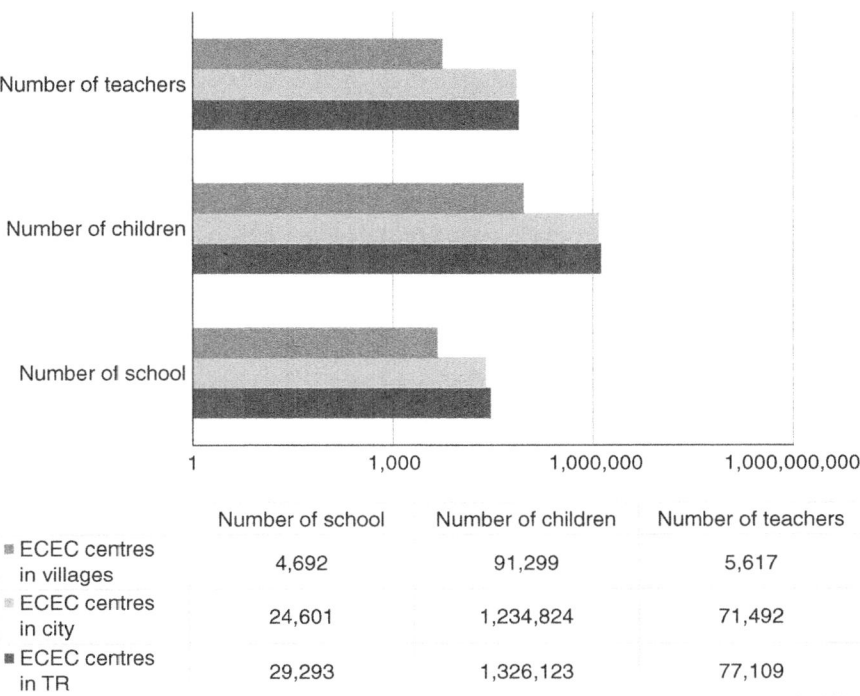

	Number of school	Number of children	Number of teachers
▪ ECEC centres in villages	4,692	91,299	5,617
▪ ECEC centres in city	24,601	1,234,824	71,492
▪ ECEC centres in TR	29,293	1,326,123	77,109

Figure 20.3 ECEC statistics based on residential area.

schooling ratio for children aged four years old, and this discrepancy increases to 52.3 per cent for children aged five years old.

A similar discrepancy is reported between high-SES families and low SES families. According to the World Bank (2015) report, the average fee is 100 TL for public preschools and 249 TL for private preschools for half-day programmes, and 509 TL for whole-day programmes. Of the public preschool administrators who participated, 18 per cent revealed that 80 per cent of registered children came from wealthy families; this percentage increases to 55.3 per cent for private preschool administrators. Data gathered from 1500 parents of preschool-aged children also indicated that high preschool prices was the most commonly cited reason for not sending the children to ECEC services (ERG & AÇEV, 2016). The report published by the World Bank (2013) also revealed that on average mostly disadvantaged families have four more children than high-SES families, while high-SES families are 60 times more likely to have a child enrolled in an ECEC centre than mostly disadvantaged families. This means that the possibility of being registered in a preschool is 60 times higher for children of wealthy families.

Based on the data provided by the Turkish Statistics Agency, the report by AÇEV and ERG (2017) revealed that only 18 per cent of children aged

3–5 years from families in the poorest 20 per cent bracket are registered in pre-school, kindergarten classes or crèches; this figure increases to 55.1 per cent for children belonging to families in the richest 20 per cent bracket. One of the main reasons for this huge gap between high and low SES children's enrolment in ECEC services is the fees that families must pay. The report by AÇEV and ERG (2016) revealed that although the ECEC services provided by the MEB are free, families have to pay a fee of between 50 TL and 200 TL to the pre-school for meals, educational materials etc. According to Article 67 of the Law on Early Childhood Education, preschools fees are decided by the Provincial Governor's Office. In Izmir, for example, these fees were 'at least 350 TL and at most 450 TL' for the 2017–2018 educational year (Tarlığ, 2017). For the 2019–2020 educational year, in Ankara, the capital city of Turkey, the Provincial Governor's Office decided fees between of 30 TL and 160 TL based on the district of the preschool in the city (MEB, 2019). Today, this situation is totally different for private preschools since there is not any lower or upper limit for prices of private schools identified by government Therefore private preschools have an opportunity to designate their own prices based on the neighbourhood they are located in, programme they applied and their target group. As the result, annual prices at private preschools range between 8000 TL and 53,000 TL (1 euro = 5.25 TL; Eğitim Caddesi, 2016). According to the Özdemir (2018), the fees for private preschools change between 13.500 TL and 47.000 TL.

Related social policies applied in Turkey

The abovementioned statistics obviously indicate that children in Turkey do not have an equal chance of accessing ECEC services. Reports used in this chapter suggested that all governmental resources should be directed at increasing the number of ECEC services provided to disadvantaged districts and families (ERG & AÇEV, 2016, 2017; World Bank, 2013). These reports were published by leading influential and important institutions but unfortunately their suggestions were not reflected in social policies. In other words, there are, in fact, no working social policies to address the issue of unequal availability of ECEC services. As mentioned before, free ECE began to be applied in 32 pilot cities. Unfortunately, these cities were chosen from among the ones that already had higher schooling ratios. The reason for this was that a new budget would not be required to develop the infrastructure of the cities involved.

Lack of information regarding quality and monitoring issues

The last issue addressed in this chapter concerns the quality and monitoring issues for provided ECEC services. There are a lot of regulations for ECEC services affiliated with the MEB and ASPB. According to the World Bank (2015) report, of the MEB's requirements for the opening of private ECEC services affiliated with the MEB, 24 involve infrastructure and only ten requirements are related to curriculum, human resources and quality of teaching. Similarly, for regulations for ECEC services affiliated with the ASPB, only seven requirements are related to the quality of care service, while 21 items are related to infrastructure. In this case, infrastructure refers to the physical conditions of the centre. Moreover, research has indicated that the quality standards in Turkey only meet four out of the ten indicators used by the OECD to compare ECEC quality and participation (Aran et al., 2009, as cited in World Bank, 2013). These are: 80 per cent of the care staff should be well educated, 50 per cent of the early childhood teachers should be well educated, there should be a 1 : 15 child to adult ratio and all the children should be provided with basic child health services.

Another quality issue concerns the early childhood teacher education process. Although there is a national programme for the teacher education course that is applied in all universities with slight variations, there is no information as to whether or not all universities fill in the content of courses with the same opportunities for candidate early childhood teachers. For instance, as mentioned above, the larger cities have more private and public kindergartens, meaning that academic staff can collaborate more easily with them, and student teachers are able to see many different kinds of preschools before they graduate. Unfortunately, it is totally different for the universities in small cities. In most cases, there are very few preschools for the university students to carry out their practicum. Thus, this issue means that students in universities in small cities do not have any chance to see different kinds of preschools or even different teachers. Students carry out their practicum in the same school and even with the same teacher in at least two of the three practicum courses. This situation is not limited to practicum courses, either. In the larger cities there are more opportunities for academic staff to work collaboratively with community institutions such as museums, libraries, NGOs etc. The quantity and quality of academic staff is yet another issue. The universities in larger cities have more academic staff than in small city universities, which have at most four or five academic staff in the Early Childhood Teacher Education Departments. This means that academic staff in the larger cities give fewer courses in their areas of expertise, while academic staff in small cities give many courses, some of which are outside their area of expertise. In addition to this, small city universities may lack the technological apparatus or physical conditions that would increase the quality of courses such as technological tools, laboratories, practice kindergartens etc. All these issues have a bearing on the quality of teachers graduating from these universities.

Lastly, the system for monitoring the quality of ECEC services is another important issue for achieving standardised quality levels. Unfortunately, the MEB and ASPB inspectors are not ECEC experts. This situation mostly limits them to checking quality issues with respect to regulations, which mainly govern the structural components of buildings rather than educational matters.

Related social policies applied in Turkey

Quality of provided ECEC services is one of the main areas that is reflected in social policies. Within the scope of the EU's Strengthening of Early Childhood Education project, several quality standards were developed in cooperation with AÇEV, UNICEF and MEB in 2010. These quality standards applied to the teaching process, daily routines, the objectives and indicators used in the curriculum, and types of activity. This is a very important step for ECEC in Turkey. During this project, the national ECE curriculum was fully overhauled resulting in a child-centred, flexible, holistic and play-based form (for more details look at Volume I, p. 226). Unfortunately, today there are no available resources showing how these efforts have changed or influenced quality in practice.

Teacher education is also seen as an important part of increasing quality in ECEC services. In order to increase the quality of the teacher education aspect, the curriculum was overhauled in 2006 (World Bank, 2013). A very recent renewal was explained by the Yüksek Öğretim Kurumu (CoHE) on 17 May 2018. With this change, YOK aimed to improve teacher quality by reducing the number of compulsory course credits so as to provide opportunities for student teachers to engage in social activities, more teaching practice etc. Through these renewals and the efforts made by the MEB, priority was given to the Teaching Practices course; an attempt was made to decrease the ratio of student teachers to academic; finally, a web platform was introduced on which student teachers are evaluated by the practicum teacher and the academic staff at the same time. However, the abovementioned gaps between universities still exist, and no effort has been made to rectify this using social policies.

Conclusion

Throughout this chapter, I have tried to focus on large-scale research into ECEC services in Turkey, conducted and published by leading organisations such as the World Bank, AÇEV, the ERG and the MEB, and then follow this up with a review of the social policies implemented in the country.

After examining the aforementioned report, five major problematic issues regarding the current ECEC system stood out: (1) the lack of services provided for children under the age of three years; (2) the low schooling ratio for children aged 36–66 months; (3) the unequal availability of ECEC services for disadvantaged groups; and (4) the lack of available information regarding the quality and monitoring of ECEC services. During the chapter an attempt was made to provide detailed and statistical information and then review the current social policies regarding each issue.

In conclusion, it can be said that ECEC services in Turkey are improving, but it is obvious that the current situation for ECEC is way below expectations and desired levels. Even though the government tries to intervene in the abovementioned problematic issues through social policies that are mainly decided with the collaboration of the related organisations, this intervention is insufficient with no clear follow-up. Meaning, there is no information about how social policies are working. Furthermore, there is a problem concerning the sustainability of these social policies. Namely, the majority of social policies function as short-term and interlocutory interventions. It is clear that in Turkey there is a serious need for social policies that:

- Will help increase the number of ECEC services provided for children under the age of three. Initially, ECEC services for children aged 0–36 months will be provided by the MEB. This would achieve two important things: (1) it would change social norms that accept the age of four years as the start age for ECEC services and the belief that child care is the priority for children under the age of three years with education having secondary importance, and (2) it would increase the employment ratio for women, which in turn would increase children's enrolment rates in ECEC services.
- Will increase public's knowledge and understanding about the importance of positive educational and developmental consequences of infant toddler education. This way, teachers who work with infant and toddlers will be respected more as professional staff rather than being seen as a caregiver. This would result in more candidate early childhood educators who wish to work with younger children when they enter their professional lives.
- Will revise the teacher education programme for ECE. Actually, in Turkey, there is a common curriculum used by whole universities that provide early childhood teacher education programmes. This curriculum includes courses that comprise information from age 0 to six years. However, no there are specific courses about younger children. With a new change in 2018, only one course, which is 'Education in İnfancy and Toddlerhood', was added to this curriculum. Unfortunately, one course is not enough to increase teacher candidates' qualifications to work with younger children. More courses can be added to the curriculum that are specific to the infancy and toddlerhood period. More practicum opportunities can be provided to candidate early childhood educators, or in order to train in-service teachers or candidate early childhood educators to work with younger children undergraduate certificate programmes can be provided.
- Will help to increase the schooling ratio for children aged between 36 and 66 months. The new educational system that began in 2012, known as 4 + 4 + 4, lowered the start age for formal schooling, resulting in a drop in the ECEC schooling ratio for children aged five years old. When this system began, children aged five years old were obligated to begin formal education. However, after experiencing the negative consequence of this obligation, the decision as to whether or not the child should start formal education at the age of five years was left to the families. Some families – particularly families with high SES (ERG & AÇEV, 2017) – send their children to ECEC services while families with low SES send their children to free primary education. Today, this difference still exists, and the gap between children who entered ECEC services and those who begin formal

schooling directly continues to grow. Therefore, the government should include ECE in the compulsory formal education process.

- Will help increase the availability of ECEC services to disadvantaged groups – families with low SES and residing in rural areas – through providing totally free ECEC services and increasing the number of schools. To increase the number of children who benefit from ECEC services, public preschools introduced the dual education system. Unfortunately, since this system does not meet working parents' demands, families tend to send their children to private preschools. However, since quality ECEC service prices are higher than families can afford, some parents necessarily opt for home care and/or cheaper, poor-quality ECEC services. Therefore, there is a strong need to increase the number of schools that provide free whole-day education. Furthermore, some regulations could be made to standardise school prices.
- Will encourage efforts to gather information about quality issues. Data could be collected regularly allowing for the consequences of implementations to be seen clearly, for problems to be eliminated and for new social policies to be put forward.

Overall in Turkey, the ECEC system is given importance and is improving gradually. However, it has some major problems, such as lack of services for younger children, unequal opportunities for access to ECEC services, low schooling ratio and lack of or a low-quality monitoring system. Although some of those issues were taken into account by applied social policies there is not any data about how those social policies are influential to deal with the problems. Hopefully, ECEC will be considered seriously and new and strong social policies that depend on research results will be applied and the system will be strengthened in the coming years.

References

Education Reform Initiative & Mother and Child Education Foundation (ERG & AÇEV). (2016). Her çocuğa eşit fırsat: Türkiye'de erken çocukluk eğitiminin durumu ve öneriler [Equal chance to each child: Situation and suggestion for early childhood education in Turkey]. Retrieved from www.egitimreformugirisimi.org/wpcontent/uploads/2017/03/ERG_HERKES-İCİN-ESIT-FIRSATTURKIYEDE-ERKEN-COCUKLUKEGITIMININ-DURUMU-VE-ONERILER.web_.pdf.

Education Reform Initiative & Mother and Child Education Foundation (ERG & AÇEV). (2017). Türkiye'de Erken Çocukluk Eğitimi ve Bakımına Katılım: Bilgi Notu [Paticipating to early childhood education and care in Turkey: Information note]. Retrieved from www.egitimreformugirisimi.org/yayin/turkiyede-erken-cocukluk-bakimi-ve-okul-oncesi-egitimekatilim/.

Eğitim Caddesi (2016). Çocuğunuzu 53 bin TL'ye anaokuluna yollar mısınız?, Retrieved from www.egitimcaddesi.com/2016-anaokulu-ogrenim-ucretleri/.

Milli Eğitim Bakanlığı (MEB). (2014). Regulation of Ministry of Education early child-hood and primary school education. Retrieved from http://mevzuat.meb.gov.tr/dosyalar/1703.pdf.

Milli Eğitim Bakanlığı (MEB). (2015). Ministry of Education strategic plan 2015–2019. Retrieved from http://sgb.meb.gov.tr/www/millegitim-bakanligi-2015-2019-strate-jik-planiyayinlanmistir/icerik/181.

Milli Eğitim Bakanlığı (MEB). (2017). National education statistics formal education 2016/17. Retrieved from http://sgb.meb.gov.tr/meb_iys_dosyalar/2017_09/08151328_meb_istatistikleri_orgun_egim_2016_2017.pdf.

Milli Eğitim Bakanlığı (2019). Public preschool fees for 2019/2020 educational year. Retrieved from https://ankara.meb.gov.tr/www/2019-2020-egitim-ogretim-yili-resmi-okul-oncesi-egitim-kurumlari-ucretleri-duyurusu/icerik/1400.

Mother and Child Education Foundation (AÇEV). (2017). Türkiye'de 0–6 yaş çocuğunun durumu: Bilgi Notu [Situation of 0–6 years old children in Turkey: Information note]. Retrieved from www.acev.org/wpcontent/uploads/2018/01/Tu%CC%88rkiyede-0-6-Yas%CC%A7C%CC%A7ocug%CC%86unDurumu.24.10.17.pdf.

Organisation for Economic Co-operation and Development (OECD). (2016). *Education at Glance 2016: OECD Indicators.* Paris: OECD Publishing. Retrieved from http://download.ei-ie.org/Docs/WebDepot/EaG2016_EN.pdf.

Özdemir, M. (2018). Kolejler el yakıyor, *Milliyet.* Retrieved from www.milliyet.com.tr/gundem/kolejler-el-yakiyor-2674419.

Tarlığ, T. (2017). Okul öncesi eğitimde ücret karmaşası, *Hürriyet.* Retrieved from www.hurriyet.com.tr/okul-oncesi-egitimde-ucret-karmasasi-40544590.

World Bank (2013). *Türkiye'de erken çocukluk eğitiminin yaygınlaştırılması ve geliştirilmesi* [Development and dissemination of early childhood education in Turkey]. Washington, DC: World Bank. Retrieved from https://abdigm.meb.gov.tr/projeler/ois/egitim/009.pdf.

World Bank. (2015). *Türkiye'de çocuk bakım hizmetlerinde arz ve talep durumu: Bir karma yöntem çalışması* [Supply and demand situation of early childhood education and care in Turkey: A mixed method study]. Washington, DC: World Bank. Retrieved from www.worldbank.org/tr/country/turkey/publication/supply-and-demand-child-careservices-turkey-a-mixed-methods-study.

Yüksek Öğretim Kurumu (CoHE). (2018). Teacher education undergraduate programs, Retrieved from www.yok.gov.tr/tr/web/guest/ogretmenlik_lisans_yeni_duzenleme.

21 Policy and childhood
Making sense of systems

Sivanes Phillipson and Susanne Garvis

Introduction

This book focuses on research highlights on current practices that reflect policies of 19 countries from around the world. For these 19 countries, the authors purposefully problematise the key components of teacher education and family practices that influence how young children's development and learning is assisted and enhanced. Most importantly, the authors discuss the changing directions in early childhood education in their own countries and the importance of continuous research in informing these changes.

In this conclusion chapter, we explore what we know today about early childhood education especially in regards to quality of education, and the role of teacher education and families in relation to children's outcomes. We complete this exploration through an analysis of the 19 chapters in this book using a verbatim analysis to outline the main themes cutting across the book. This chapter then concludes by outlining recent research and challenges within the field of early childhood education, which are reflected in the discussion of the 19 countries in this volume as well as the past two volumes in this Early Childhood Education in the 21st Century series.

What do we know from the 19 countries?

The main aim of the three books in this series is to have a shared understanding of the key values and practices that impact early childhood education and care across the globe. The premise is that

> if one country is able to find possible solutions to providing effective teacher education and professional learning activities or able to provide positive and intimate ways of working in partnership with parents, strategies and ideas can be shared to provide ways forward.
>
> (Garvis & Phillipson, 2019, p. 271)

It is then vital in this conclusion chapter that we review and synthesise the main themes that arise from the 19 countries' sharing of the policy dependent rules and exercises that cut across teacher practices, training and family involvement in children's learning and care.

In order to find out the main themes of the 19 chapters in this book, a verbatim analysis is completed with all 19 chapter contents. Leximancer v 4.5. is used for the analysis. Leximancer is a software that replicates the manual coding procedures used in content analysis to identify the underlying core themes and relationships between themes that form the basis of any conceptual framework (Smith & Humphreys, 2006). Being automated, Leximancer generates a logarithmic analysis that is free of bias during the coding process, thereby removing issues such as coder reliability and subjectivity. In other words, the algorithms within Leximancer identify and rank the themes by the relationships that verbatims have with each other using the summed co-occurrence with all other themes.

Basically, the themes in this book are populated through a sorting process. The algorithm begins at the top of the ranking and creates a theme group that is centred on it. It then goes to the next ranked theme, and either joins the nearest theme and adjusts the centroid of that theme but only if the next theme is near enough to any other theme group centroid on the map, or it starts a new theme group. Leximancer generates a thematic summary that includes a connectivity score to indicate the relative importance of the themes, with the most important theme at 100 per cent being found at the top. The subsequent grouping of themes enables the mapping of any relationships between the concepts. Finally, Leximancer produces a visualisation of the thematic grouping and their associations with each other (Smith & Humphreys, 2006). The themes that are presented in this visual map for this book are Policy, Education, Teachers, Learning and Children (see Figure 21.1).

Children: education and care for them

The biggest concept with the largest number of verbatim count is the concept of *Children* at 769 counts with visible subconcepts of care and support including families' services, social care and day care institutions in their system. Interestingly, this finding highlights the long-standing debate over who should care for and educate young children early in their developmental stages. This debate is more dominant in some countries than others. For example, the growth of the Danish day care system is based on the idea that a child below age three should be cared for at home and that older children should attend kindergarten (Chapter 5). However, it is noted that the government funding and initiative have been well established for Danish children to be cared for while their parents are at work. Parents in Denmark have to pay service fees while most day care institutions are publically funded. The same debate exists in Korea as well, and it is acknowledged that the Korean government has reformed their policies to extend financial help in the form of resources and facilities in day care centres and kindergartens. This assistance to parents of young children is given with the view that every child should have an equal beginning regardless of the family background and income status.

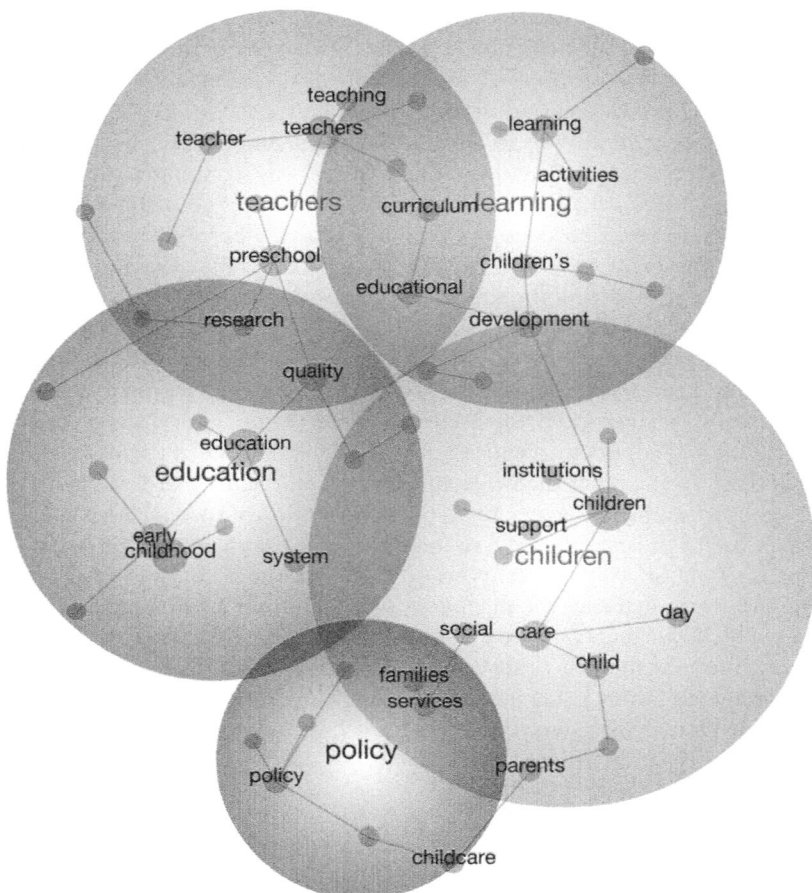

Figure 21.1 Concept map of themes connected to policification of childhood.

Considering how important the welfare of children is to all the countries in this book, it is ironic that one of the main challenges that all these countries face is a continuity of care and support for such care for young children. Accordingly, one of the subconcepts that appears in the concept map is the care and support for children. Incidentally, while many governments want children to attend early childhood services, there is a growing recognition that early childhood staff have higher sick rates, stress and anxiety compared to other professions (Sosinsky et al., 2016). This can lead to early childhood staff having more sick days or leaving the profession all together. As such, the continuity of care becomes an issue for young children, especially the youngest in care. Children may have different staff looking after them, increasing their own stress and anxiety.

The continuity of care model is an intentional grouping of staff and children to enhance the consistency in caregiving (Sosinsky et al., 2016). Ideally, infants and toddlers remain with the same caregiver across multiple years (Cryer, Hurwitz, & Wolery, 2000). The premise is that the child and the caregiver stay together for extended periods of time, with strong trust between the child, family and caregiver developed (Sosinsky et al., 2016; Theilheimer, 2006). In some countries, the continuity of care consists of multiage classrooms where children will stay in the same group until they start formal schooling.

Limited empirical studies have examined the effects of continuity of care on children (Sosinsky et al., 2016), with a call for future research to more fully understand associations with child outcomes as well as the potential impacts of continuity of care on teachers, families and peers (Horm et al., 2018). Horm et al. have shown that continuity of care is associated with higher teacher ratings of child self-control, initiative and attachment when in infant–toddler rooms, with teachers also reporting less behavioural concerns from the young children. As noted by Sosinsky et al. (2016), the continuity of care model, however, requires unique skills from teachers who work across a variety of developmental needs of young children and who have to adapt to changes over time as the child groupings change. This area is largely unexplored in the research literature and needs further research.

Education: quality as a rule

The next concept with the second largest number of verbatim count is the concept of *Education* at 722 counts with visible subconcepts of early childhood system, quality and research. The subconcepts quality and research are also found as subconcepts with the third biggest concept of *Teachers* with a verbatim count of 632. This finding reveals that teacher quality and research on teacher education and quality is a dominant part of the early childhood system to be effective across the 19 countries.

For instance, the Swedish authors bring to our attention the gap between children's and teachers' perspectives and between policy intentions and pre-school practices. They conclude that their analysis of this gap has shown problems around teaching and learning especially preschool teachers' didactical knowledge and how they teach young children in preschool (Chapter 17). Equally, it is found in the Greek education context that lack of attention to regulation initiatives in light of funding cuts is a glaring problem for early childhood education and care (ECEC) in Greece. The Greece situation is made worse by the mixed messages that the education system espouses – quality is important yet there are limited national regulations to ensure and mandate quality in the best possible manner (Chapter 9). Hence, it is imperative that we look closely at the nature of quality and the meaning it brings to the context of early years learning and development.

Many studies over the years have shown the effects of high-quality early childhood education and care on children's social–emotional and cognitive development (e.g. Burchinal, Vandergrift, Pianta, & Mashburn, 2010; Curby et al., 2009; Howes et al., 2008; Mashburn et al., 2008). When exploring the definition of high quality, two types of quality are identified that are thought to be important for child development (Sylva et al., 2006) – structural and process. Structural quality refers to characteristics that control the structure of the learning environment such as group size, children-to-teacher ratio and teacher qualifications (Howes et al., 2008). Process quality refers to children's day-to-day experiences in the early childhood setting and encompasses interactions with others, activities and their overall experience (Thomason & La Paro, 2009). Structural quality is considered the precursor to process quality (Cryer, Tietze, Burchinal, Leal, & Palacios, 1999). Structural quality is also the objective of many regulatory bodies in countries that implement quality regulations and national curricular. The intention is that through macroeconomic funding of ECEC, benefits towards process quality will also be made by supporting structural quality (Vandell et al., 2010). This understanding has led to increased spending for early childhood across many countries to improve and control overall quality. In particular – till today – many countries have focused on what is referred to as the 'iron-triangle' of structural quality of children-to-teacher ratio, group size and teacher formal qualifications (c.f. Phillipsen, Burchinal, Howes, & Cryer, 1997).

Research studies, however, have shown that while national monitoring and regulation may be strong around structural quality, countries may still exhibit considerable variation in process quality (i.e. children's everyday experience) such as in the Netherlands (Helmerhorst, Riksen-Walraven, Vermeer, Fukkink, & Tavecchio, 2014; Leseman & Slot, 2013). Some studies have found that there is only weak or no correlations between child-to-teacher ratio and process quality (Pessanha, Aguiar, & Bairrao, 2007; Pianta, Mashburn, Downer, Hamre, & Justice, 2008) and group size and quality (Pessanha et al., 2007). Furthermore, a few Dutch studies have also indicated that group size and child-to-teacher ratios are not related to emotional and educational process quality (Slot, Leseman, Verhagen, & Mulder, 2015). These findings suggest though there is plenty being done in terms of structural quality, there seems to be a disconnection between structural and process quality. This conclusion demands for more research into the relationship between structural and process quality as well as the influence of adults on children's individual experiences, so that further improvement can be made to close the gap between structural and process. Of course, a greater understanding of the context is also needed, given that variation seems to occur within and across countries (Garvis & Phillipson, 2018).

Teachers: curriculum, educational and in-service learning

The education levels of early childhood teachers are fundamentally crucial to enhancing quality. The Leximancer concept map (see Figure 21.1) shows that the fourth concept of *Learning* with a verbatim count of 524. This concept shares two main subconcepts with the concept of *Teachers*, i.e. curriculum and educational, highlighting two crucial factors in the development of effective ECEC. Accordingly, Manning, Garvis, Flemming and Wong (2017) found that higher teacher qualifications are significantly correlated with higher-quality ECEC. In the 2017 meta-analysis examining research since the 1980s, the authors found positive correlations between children's language and reasoning and programme structure. The results suggested that the statistically significant association is not dependent on culture or context given that the evidence was from several countries.

It is obvious then that teacher education needs to focus on attainment of high-quality structural knowledge of curriculum so that they can produce high-quality process content that provides children with the appropriate learning contents. Such learning, as advocated by the Finnish chapter in this book, can happen with playful activities and free play that can develop children's self-regulation skills. Well-qualified teachers with high content knowledge and skills will know how to provide such children play with learning activities that create independent initiatives and choice making. These activities allow for creativity within a learning context that has participatory teaching approach of teachers. The Finnish authors, Kangas et al., in this book clearly set out that the play activities are actually secondary in relation to teacher-initiated and routine activities (Chapter 7). This finding highlights that teachers need to pay more attention to reflective practices on existing pedagogical supports to play-based activities, capitalising on children routines and play.

Results such as found in Finland are in line with research, which shows that in addition to formal qualifications of the preschool teacher, in-service training and continuous professional development that involves reflective praxis is needed to contribute to process quality (Zaslow et al., 2010). This professional development can consist of on the job training, coaching and other strategies that focus on working with young children. For example, a meta-analysis (Fukkink & Lont, 2007) on caregivers' interactions competence after specialised training focusing on teacher–child interactions showed medium-sized effects, indicating the importance of having teacher participatory approach in play-based activities in ECEC. Likewise, there is evidence of the importance of teachers attending in-service training (Hamre et al., 2012; LoCasale-Crouch et al., 2011), and activities such as mentoring, coaching and consultation (Domitrovich et al., 2009; Pianta et al., 2008). Many of the countries in this book recognise the need for early childhood teachers to have more support, especially in relation to preparing children for independent learning and seamless transition into primary schooling. The Estonian authors, for example, stress that both 'teachers and principals need more support to enhance their competence in addressing pedagogical leadership and human resource management issues' (Chapter 6). This proposition is echoed throughout this book, with further emphasis on the professional development for the workforce to incorporate a diverse coverage of communication and leadership skills. While this area remains understudied, the growing evidence does suggest that regulatory bodies need to focus on professional learning and in-service activities to improve process quality around teacher–child interactions, especially in better learning processes in play-based activities. The cost of implementing such activities however is expensive and time consuming, hence, increasing the overall cost of early childhood education and care. The question is then – how committed governments and organisations are to the overall quality improvement in early childhood? Perhaps a sideway glance to what families can contribute to this improvement can explain some of the systems movements in ECEC.

Policy: families' services and parents

Increasing research from across the globe highlights the importance of families in children's early learning. Families, in particular parents, are recognised as the 'first educators' of their children who are instrumental in providing foundational learning experiences (Phillipson, Sullivan, & Gervasoni, 2017). Parents' beliefs and values play a role in how involved they are, with those with aspirations determined to see their children get the best education possible. In preparing their children for schooling, parents' perception of their child's readiness motivates their input as the first educators. These perceptions and involvement that parents display vary according to family background and cultural beliefs (Phillipson, Phillipson, & Kewalramani, 2018).

Interestingly, the final concept in the Leximancer concept map (see Figure 21.1) shows how *Policy* with a verbatim count of 402 has the main subconcept of policy in child care with overlapping subconcepts of families' services and parents as major players in the system. It seems obvious then that the policy for child care is dictated by the needs of families and parents' perceptions of what is important for their children's learning and development from an early age. Though this obvious finding is evident across the 19 countries in the book, the Canadian authors lament how

> historically and currently, the federal Canadian government has made and continues to make promises to address the lack of access to quality child care services for Canada's families and youngest citizens. Yet in 2018, few of these policy promises have come to fruition, typically sidelined, reduced or abandoned for political, rather than rational, empirically informed reasons
>
> (Chapter 3)

What this situation highlights is the need for governments to recognise the value in public policy for leadership and funding in ECEC to build early care and education that nurtures wellbeing of children.

The importance of the role that families play is further accentuated by early childhood educators' growing understanding of the need to establish positive partnerships with parents. In early childhood contexts, where children tend to participate on a part-time basis and perhaps for a year or two only, establishing genuine partnerships with families can be challenging (Phillipson, 2017).

Additionally, strong parent and educator collaboration increases the positive enhances parent–educator–child interactions to develop children's overall growth and learning (Pfiffner, Villodas, Kaiser, Rooney, & McBurnett, 2013; Plath, Crofts, & Stuart, 2016). However, the role of both families and educators in children's development has become more complex and challenging with the need to assess, formalise and politicise children's learning from an early age. It is thus paramount that effective ways are found to connect parents with early childhood educators because young children experiencing consistent adult–child interactions both at home and in early childhood settings assist children's learning and development. There is a rise in provisions in policy statements for partnerships between homes and schools. Nevertheless, there is a lack of clear actionable support for parents to engage confidently with early childhood educators and school teachers (Phillipson et al., 2017; 2018).

Recent challenges to ECEC

Baby PISA

In 2012, the Organisation for Economic Cooperation and Development (OECD) proposed an assessment for early learning outcomes known as the International Early Learning and Child-wellbeing Study (IELS). The assessment, dubbed 'baby PISA' aims at exploring the learning and wellbeing of five year olds.

The IELS collects, similar to PISA, assessment information from different domains as well as information about the early childhood education context and homes. According to OECD (2019) the IELS study is an international survey that assesses children at age five years across three countries, identifying key factors that drive or hinder the development of early learning. The purpose of the study is to provide countries with a common language and framework, encompassing a collection of robust empirical information and in-depth insights on children's learning development at a critical age. With this information, countries will be able to share best practices, working towards the ultimate goal of improving children's early learning outcomes and overall wellbeing. The International Early Learning and Child Well-being Study (OECD, 2019) will:

- Provide robust empirical data on children's early learning through a broad scope of domains that comprise cognitive and social and emotional development.
- Identify factors that foster and hinder children's early learning, both at home and in early childhood education programmes.
- Provide findings that will allow parents and caregivers to learn about interactions and learning activities that are most conducive to child development.
- Inform early childhood education centres and schools about skill levels of children at this age as well as contextual factors related to them that they

could use to make more informed decisions about curricula and pedagogical methods.

- Provide researchers and educators in the field of early education with valid and comparable information on children's early learning, and characteristics obtained from a range of sources and accompanied by a broad scope of contextual variables.

As yet few details about the study have been released. It is known that the three countries taking part in a pilot study are England, the United States and Estonia. The four early learning domains that are being measured:

1   Emerging literacy skills: oral language and listening comprehension; vocabulary; phonological awareness.
2   Emerging numeracy skills: working with numbers; numbers and counting; shape and space; measurement; pattern.
3   Self-regulation: working memory; mental flexibility/adaptability; self-control.
4   Social and emotional skills: trust; empathy; prosocial behaviours.

The early childhood education community waits to see the reports about the pilot study and how the OECD intends to implement the study to other OECD countries. There is a fear that 'Baby PISA' will change curriculum and the structure of early childhood education in a bid to be considered the 'winners' in the OECD, at the expense of children's outcomes. Some countries have already chosen not to participate, based on lobbying from key stakeholder groups within each country. These countries include Belgium, Canada, Denmark, Germany, Norway and Sweden.

The fading effect of pre-kindergarten learning

Recent studies have reported that positive impacts created for children in pre-kindergarten programmes fades or decreases to 0 as children progress through formal schooling (e.g. Clements, Sarama, Wolfe, and Spitler, 2013). 'The negative outcomes, although not without precedent, are surprising to many' (Whitehurst, 2018, p. 183). In a study of the Tennessee Voluntary Pre-kindergarten programme, Lipsey, Farran and Durkin (2018) found that children who participated during pre-kindergarten had sizable gains in academic skills and dispositions, however, these benefits faded or turned negative by the end of grade three. Other studies have shown negative long-term impacts on children and families because of the expansion of free public centre-based child care (Baker, Gruber, & Milligan, 2015), where care rather than education and learning is the focus for the children. Furthermore, children who stay at home quickly catch up to children who attended kindergarten upon entering school (Bailey, Duncan, Odgers, & Yu, 2017). The influence of parents who can provide excellent at-home care and education for children appears to provide substitution for early childhood programmes (Baker et al., 2015).

These recent studies highlight that it is high time for the field of early child-hood research to reflect on the relationship between policy and practice for enhancement of childhood. Questions that emerge out of this reflection can be: (1) Has policy taken into consideration research findings effectively? (2) Does the cost of policy implementation in structural change result in high-quality process? (3) Many studies focus on academic success and school readi-ness of children. Should we be focusing on other benefits of early childhood education that may not be as well researched but important for young chil-dren? (4) If families can provide quality learning experiences for children, that appear just as good as formal kindergarten, how can we still assure policy makers to invest in preschools and continuity of care? These reflection ques-tions are important now more than ever in making sense of education and care systems across the globe, given that many countries have invested heavily in early childhood education and care.

References

Bailey, D., Duncan, G., Odgers, C., & Yu, W. (2017). Persistence and fadeout in the impacts of child and adolescent interventions. *Journal of Research on Educational Effec-tiveness, 10*(1), 7–39.

Baker, M., Gruber, J., & Milligan, K. (2015). Non-cognitive deficits and young adult outcomes: The long-run impacts of a universal child care program. Retrieved from http://dx.doi.org/10.3386/w21571.

Burchinal, M. R., Vandergrift, N., Pianta, R., & Mashburn, A. (2010). Threshold ana-lysis of association between child care quality and child outcomes for low-income chil-dren in pre-kindergarten programs. *Early Childhood Research Quarterly, 25*(2), 166–176.

Clements, D., Sarama, D., Wolfe, C., & Spitler, M. (2013). Longitudinal evaluation of a scale-up model for teaching mathematics with trajectories and technologies: Persis-tence of effects in the third year. *American Educational Research Journal, 50*(4), 812–850.

Cryer, D., Hurwitz, S., & Wolery, M. (2000). Continuity of caregiver for infants and toddlers in centre-based child care: Report on a survey of center practices. *Early Child-hood Research Quarterly, 15*(4), 497–514.

Cryer, D., Tietze, W., Burchinal, M., Leal, T., & Palacios, J. (1999). Predicting process quality from structural quality in preschool programs: A cross-country comparison. *Early Childhood Research Quarterly, 14*(3), 339–361.

Curby, T. W., LoCasale-Crouch, J., Konold, T. R., Pianta, R. C., Howes, C., Burchinal, M., Bryant, D., Clifford, R., Early, D., & Barnarin, O. (2009). The relations of observed pre-k classroom quality profiles to children's achievement and social compet-ence. *Early Education and Development, 20*(2), 346–372.

Domitrovich, C. E., Gest, S. D., Gill, S., Bierman, K. L., Welsh, J. A., & Jones, D. (2009). Fostering high-quality teaching with an enriched curriculum and professional development support: The Head Start REDI Program. *American Educational Research Journal, 46*(2), 567–597.

Fukkink, R. G., & Lont, A. (2007). Does training matter? A meta-analysis and review of caregiver training studies. Early Childhood Research Quarterly, 22(3), 294–311.

Garvis, S., & Phillipson, S. (2018). Teachers' and families' perspectives in early childhood education and care: A reflection of 19 countries. In S. Phillipson & S. Garvis (Eds.),

Teachers' and Families' Perspectives in Early Childhood Education and Care: Early Childhood Education in the 21st Century Vol III (pp. 265–271). London/New York: Routledge.

Hamre, B. K., Pianta, R. C., Burchinal, M., Field, S. T., LoCasale-Crouch, J., Downer, J., Howes, C., LaParo, K., & Scott-Little, C. (2012). A course on effective teacher-child interactions: Effects on teacher beliefs, knowledge and observed practice. *American Educational Research Journal, 49,* 88–123.

Helmerhorst, K. O. W., Riksen-Walraven, M. J., Vermeer, H. J., Fukkink, R. G., & Tavecchio, L. W. C. (2014). Measuring the interactive skills of caregivers in child care centers: Development and validation of the caregiver interaction profile scales. *Early Education and Development, 25*(5), 770–790.

Horm, D. M., File, N., Bryant, D., Burchinal, M., Raikes, H., Forestieri, N., Encinger, A., & Cobo-Lewis, A. (2018). Associations between continuity of care in infant-toddler classrooms and child outcomes. *Early Childhood Research Quarterly, 42*(1), 105–118.

Howes, C., Burchinal, M., Pianta, R., Bryant, D., Early, D., Clifford., Burchinal, M., Pianta, R., Brynat, D., Early, D., Clifford, R., & Barbarin, O. (2008). Ready to learn? Children's pre-academic achievement in pre-kindergarten programs. *Early Childhood Research Quarterly, 23*(1), 27–50.

Leseman, P. P. M., & Slot, P. L. (2013). *Kwaliteit en curriculum van voorschoolse opvang en educatie in Nederland* [Quality and curriculum of early childhood education and care in the Netherlands]. Utrecht: The Netherlands: Utrecht University Department of Special Education.

Lipsey, M., Farran, D., & Durkin, K. (2018). Effects of the Tennessee Prekindergarten Program on children's achievement and behavior through third grade. *Early Childhood Research Quarterly, 45*(4), 155–176.

LoCasale-Crouch, J., Kraft-Sayre, M., Pianta, R. C., Hamre, B. K., Downer, J. T., Leach, A., Burchinal, M., Howes, C., La Paro, K., & Scott-Little, C. ((2011). Implementing an early childhood professional development course across 10 sites and 15 sections: Lessons learned. *NHSA, 14,* 275–292.

Manning, M., Garvis, S., Flemming, C., & Wong, G. T. W. (2017). The relationship between teacher qualification and the quality of early childhood care and learning environment. *Campbell Collaboration.* Retrieved from https://campbellcollaboration. org/library/teacher-qualification-and-quality-of-early-childhood-care-and-learning. html.

Mashburn, A. J., Pianta, R. C., Hamre, B. K., Downer, J. T., Barbarin, O. A., Bryant, D., Bur. chinal, M., Early, D. M., & Howes, C. (2008). Measures of classroom quality in prekindergarten and children's development of academic language, and social skills. *Child Development, 79*(3), 732–749.

Organisation for Economic Co-operation and Development (OECD). (2019). The international early learning and child well-being study – the study. Retrieved from www. oecd.org/education/school/the-international-early-learning-and-child-well-being-study-the-study.htm.

Pessanha, M., Aguiar, C., & Bairrao, J. (2007). Influence of structural features on Portugese toddler child care quality. *Early Childhood Research Quarterly, 22*(2), 204–214.

Pfiffner, L. J., Villodas, M., Kaiser, N., Rooney, M., & McBurnett, K. (2013). Educational outcomes of a collaborative school-home behavioral intervention for ADHD. *School Psychology Quarterly, 28*(1), 25.

Phillipson, S. (2017). Partnering with families. In S. Garvis & D. Pendergast (Eds.), *Health and Wellbeing in Early Childhood* (2nd edn) (pp. 223–237). Cambridge, UK: Cambridge University Press.

Phillipsen, L. C., Burchinal, M. R., Howes, C., & Cryer, D. (1997). The prediction of process quality from structural features of child care. *Early Childhood Research Quarterly, 12*(3), 281–303.

Phillipson, S., Phillipson, S. N., & Kewalramani, S. (2018). Cultural variability in the educational and learning capitals of Australian families and its relationship with children's numeracy outcomes. *Journal for the Education of the Gifted, 41*(4), 348–368. doi:10.1177/0162353218799484.

Phillipson, S., Sullivan, P. A., & Gervasoni, A. (2017). Engaging families as the first mathematics educator of children. In S. Phillipson, A. Gervasoni, & P. A. Sullivan (Eds.), *Engaging Families as Children's First Mathematics Educators: International Perspectives* (pp. 3–14). Singapore: Springer.

Pianta, R., Mashburn, A., Downer, J., Hamre, B., & Justice, L. (2008). Effects of web-mediated professional development resources on teacher-child interactions in pre-kindergarten classrooms. *Early Childhood Research Quarterly, 23*(4), 431–451.

Plath, D., Crofts, P., & Stuart, G. (2016). Engaging families in early intervention for child conduct concerns. *Children Australia, 41*(1), 49–58. doi:10.1017/cha.2015.5.

Slot, P. L., Leseman, P. P. M., Verhagen, J., & Mulder, H. (2015). Associations between structural quality aspects and process quality in Dutch early childhood education and care settings. *Early Childhood Research Quarterly, 33*(4), 64–76.

Smith, A. E., & Humphreys, M. S. (2006). Evaluation of unsupervised semantic mapping of natural language with Leximancer concept mapping. *Behavior Research Methods, 38*(2), 262–279.

Sosinsky, L., Ruprecht, K., Horm, D., Kriener-Althen, K., Vogel, C., & Halle, T. (2016). Including relationship-based care practices in infant-toddler care: Implications for practice and policy. Brief prepared for the Office of Planning, Research and Evaluation, Administration for Children and Families, US Department of Health and Human Services.

Sylva, K., Siraj-Blatchford, I., Taggart, B., Sammons, P., Melhuish, E., Elliot, K., & Totsika, V. (2006). Capturing quality in early childhood through environmental scales. *Early Childhood Research Quarterly, 21*(1), 76–92.

Theilheimer, R. (2006). Molding to the children: Primary caregiving and continuity of care. *Zero to Three, 26*(3), 50–54.

Thomason, A. C., & La Paro, K. M. (2009). Measuring the quality of teacher-child interactions in toddler child care. *Early Education and Development, 20*(2), 285–304.

Vandell, D. L., Belsky, J., Burchinal, M., Steinberg, L., Vandergrift, N., & NICHD ECCRN. (2010). Do effects of early child care extend to age 15 years? Results from the NICHD study of early childhood care and youth development. *Child Development, 81*(3), 737–756.

Whitehurst, G. J. (2018). The positive impacts of public pre-K fade quickly and sometimes reverse: What does this portend for future research policy? *Early Childhood Research Quarterly, 45*(4), 183–187. https://doi.org/10.1016/j.ecresq.2018.02.016.

Zaslow, M., Anderson, R., Redd, Z., Wessel, J., Tarullo, L., & Burchinal, M. (2010). Quality, dosage, thresholds, and features in early childhood settings: A review of the literature (OPRE2011-5). Retrieved from https://www.acf.hhs.gov/sites/default/files/opre/quality_tables_0.pdf.

Index